No man is worthy of liberty himself, who seeing his brother enslaved, does not use his every effort...to set him free.

A Free Born Briton, Newcastle upon Tyne, 1826

In no place in the United Kingdom has the American Slave warmer friends than in Newcastle.
William Wells Brown, Boston, 1855

There are three urgent and indeed great problems that we face not only in the United States of America but all over the world today. That is the problem of racism, the problem of poverty and the problem of war.
Martin Luther King, Newcastle upon Tyne, 1967

This is the first time in a European country that I have ever had so much fanfare and people admiring me and loving me and coming out to meet me and greet me like this.
Muhammad Ali, Newcastle upon Tyne, 1977

CONTENTS

Acknowledgements   9

Introduction: 'An Inextricable Network of Mutuality'   13

Part One: The Visit

Chapter One: 'Happy and Honored to Accept': Bringing   23
Martin Luther King to Newcastle

Chapter Two: 'Barbs and Arrows': Explaining Martin Luther   39
King's Decision to Come

Chapter Three: 'What Your Movement is Doing is Right':   51
Reactions to Martin Luther King and the Early Civil
Rights Movement on Tyneside

Chapter Four: 'We Do Not Have a Copy':   63
Martin Luther King's Lost Newcastle Speech

Part Two: Local Contexts, Global Connections

Chapter Five: Deep Roots: Slavery, Race and Radicalism   77
in the North East to 1833

Chapter Six: 'Brethren in the Cause of Universal   95
Freedom in America': Peace, Politics and Abolitionism
in the North East before the US Civil War

Chapter Seven: 'God Bless the Policy of Emancipation!':   117
The North East and the African American Freedom
Struggle from the Civil War to the Rise of Jim Crow

Chapter Eight: The Challenges of Diversity: Cultures of   131
Welcome, Cultures of Hate

CONTENTS (Continued)

Part Three: Take a Look at America

Chapter Nine: 'The Developing Darkness': Martin Luther   161
King and the Intersection of North East, British and US
Race Relations in the 1960s

Chapter Ten: From Righteous Streams to Rivers of Blood: 187
Martin Luther King, Enoch Powell and Race Relations on
Tyneside, 1968

Part Four: Legacies and Lessons

Chapter Eleven: Tending the Cords of Memory: 207
The Road to Freedom City 2017

Chapter Twelve: Echoes and Arcs: Martin Luther King,   233
Race, Religion and Politics on Tyneside in the 21st Century

Guide to abbreviations used in Notes   247

Notes   249

Index   298

ACKNOWLEDGEMENTS

I would like to thank the many organisations and individuals who have helped to make this book possible. I am particularly indebted to Northumbria University for granting me a semester-long sabbatical to do the bulk of the research and writing for this book. Thanks to Charlotte Alston, Tanja Bueltmann and David Gleeson, the University also provided financial support for the publication of a book that is three times longer than originally planned and far more handsomely illustrated than would have been possible without this aid. I am also grateful to my colleagues in Northumbria's Humanities Department, notably Joe Hardwick, James McConnel, Peter O'Connor and others associated with the British and Irish Worlds Research Group who helped me to shape this project. I would also like to express my appreciation to Bill Purdue and Keith Shaw, also at Northumbria, who shared their knowledge of North East history and politics; to Anya Hockey, Megan Hunt and Adam Sharp, American Studies students at Northumbria, who helped with elements of the research; and, especially, to David Brown of Manchester University and Hannah-Rose Murray of Nottingham University whose combined expertise in the history of racial thought, slavery, abolitionism and politics in the 19th century Atlantic World was invaluable.

At Newcastle University, Andrea Henderson, Umbereen Rafiq and Melanie Reed helped to track down files, photos and folks associated with King and his time on campus, as did Geraldine Hunwick and Mick Sharp with whom I collaborated to translate some of this research into a public exhibition at the Robinson Library as part of Freedom City 2017. My thanks also to Adam and Patrick Collerton, Nick Megoran and Chi Onwurah, all of whom I got to know as fellow members of the Freedom City 2017 Steering Committee, for their encouragement, insights and information. It was hugely gratifying—and not a little humbling—to see my research used as the foundation and occasionally inspiration for some of Freedom City 2017, a multifaceted commemoration of the 50th anniversary of King's visit that sought to create a living legacy of education, social engagement and progressive politics around the message he brought to Newcastle. My friend and fellow civil rights historian, Ben Houston of Newcastle University, Murphy Cobbing of BBC Radio Newcastle, with whom I worked on various documentaries based on the story of King's visit, and Carrie Supple, founder of Journey to Justice, were also very supportive. So, too, were Paul

Barry, Peter Kane, Peter O'Donnell and Randall Stephens, who generously supplied several images used in the book from their personal collections. David Hepworth at Tyne Bridge Publishing, a division of Newcastle City Council, immediately recognised the social as well as historical significance of the book and was a friendly, patient and highly resourceful editor and publisher.

Half a lifetime ago, my preliminary research into this topic appeared, in much different form, as 'A King in Newcastle: Martin Luther King, Jr. and British Race Relations, 1967-1968' in *Georgia Historical Review*, LXXIX, 3, (Fall 1995), pp.599-632. I am grateful to that journal for publishing my first brief foray into this subject—and apologise for not knowing nearly as much then as I do now about the circumstances of King's visit to Newcastle, or of its place in the racial history of the North East, or of its connections to several centuries of links between the region and the African American freedom struggle.

My biggest debt is to my family. Chris and Dave Walker did more granddaughter-sitting than usual while I worked on the book. After seeing me write nearly 100,000 words on the subject, my daughter Katie is now almost convinced that I really did once discover long-lost footage of Martin Luther King making a speech in Newcastle. But she knows for sure that her generation would do well to think about and learn from King's message as they confront the challenges of a 21st century where the problems of racism, poverty and war that preoccupied King remain all-too-pressing concerns.

Above all, this book was made possible by my wife, Jenny. As ever, Jen shouldered a disproportionate share of domestic burdens while I worked on it. Like Katie, she even did a stint as a research assistant, helping to chase down newspaper articles and information on diversity in local schools. Moreover, as a prematurely retired scholar of the US civil rights movement and sometime proof-reader, she offered valuable advice on style, structure and substance. Jen was heavily involved in both the Martin Luther King Memorial Conferences that took place in Newcastle in the 1990s—and was rewarded with the unsurpassable joy of preparing the indexes to two books derived from those events. No doubt, she will have helped to index this book, too. In the circumstances, it seems only fitting that the book is dedicated to her, with much love and gratitude.

Brian Ward,
Newcastle upon Tyne, July 2017

INTRODUCTION

'An Inextricable Network of Mutuality'

He wasn't even supposed to speak; his office in Atlanta had made that very clear. Yet there he was, in the heart of Newcastle upon Tyne: Martin Luther King, Jr., the foremost figure in the US civil rights movement, making an impromptu speech in which he linked the African American freedom struggle to developments in British race relations and issued a call for people of goodwill to meet the global challenges of war, poverty and racism. Underneath scarlet academic robes, King was dressed smartly in a dark morning suit, although conspicuously missing the handkerchief he had planned to wear in his breast pocket. The date was November 13, 1967. The occasion was the award to King of an Honorary Doctorate in Civil Law by the University of Newcastle upon Tyne. The place was the elegant, wood-panelled King's Hall in the University's Armstrong Building, where more than 400 students and staff gathered with a range of civic dignitaries, eager to see and hoping to hear one of the most iconic figures of modern history.

This book tells the inside story of King's visit. It explains why he was invited, unpicks the tortuous, sometimes star-crossed and occasionally farcical preparations for his visit, and describes the events of the day itself. It explains why King bothered to come to Newcastle at all, flying the Atlantic to spend less than eleven hours in a city in the North East of England that he knew little about in the midst of a brutal work schedule and at a time of enormous professional strain and personal doubt. And it explains what happened to that handkerchief.

Brief though King's visit was, it had a profound impact on those who met with him or heard him speak so eloquently about the triple evils of racism, poverty and war in words both timely and timeless. And yet, a decade or so later, the city and the University that had welcomed him so warmly in November 1967, and mourned him so deeply after his assassination in April 1968, had all but forgotten that King had ever been in the North East.[1]

During these years of neglect, even the spellbinding speech that King gave in Newcastle was lost to history. This book describes how in 1992, a junior lecturer in American history, who modesty prohibits me from mentioning by name (clue: his name can be found on the cover of this book) discovered a substantial portion of that speech on film. That archival discovery stimulated a revival of interest in King's visit during the 1990s. Interest waned again during the early 21st century, only to be rekindled in the second decade of the new millennium, reaching unprecedented heights during the Freedom City 2017 celebrations that marked the 50th anniversary of King's trip. This book explores why King's visit periodically slipped from public and institutional memory on Tyneside in ways that reveal the mix of chance, serendipity, utilitarianism and individual and group action that dictates why some historical events are forgotten while others are remembered and cherished. In this regard, the book extends a flourishing literature on race and the construction of social memory in the US that, for all its rich insights, has paid relatively little attention to international efforts to commemorate the long African American freedom struggle.[2]

King's visit to Newcastle reminds us that the US civil rights movement of the 1950s and 1960s was always an international phenomenon. It was fundamentally shaped by global political developments, notably the Cold War and the emergence from colonial rule of many independent African, Asian and Middle-Eastern nations.[3] In America, white segregationists were forever claiming that campaigns for black rights were really inspired or maybe even funded by communists and that King himself was a puppet or dupe of the Soviet Union. Conversely, African Americans and their allies pointed out that it was impossible for the US to claim leadership of the free world and pose as the champion of democracy against communist totalitarianism—and therefore court those newly independent 'Third World' nations—while it routinely denied civil and voting rights to vast numbers of its own non-white citizens. African American leaders such as Martin Luther King and Malcolm X regularly sought international support for their cause and linked it to world-wide struggles for freedom, justice and equality. King's visit to Newcastle was in this tradition, revealing much about his evolving sense of international leadership and responsibility, but also about how expressions of approval and encouragement from overseas strengthened his resolve to continue the struggle in the US, especially at times of acute political and personal crisis.

The book also sets the story of King's trip to Newcastle within the context of another largely forgotten story, one that connects the North East of England to the long African American freedom struggle. This connection is itself part of a similarly underappreciated history of racial, ethnic and religious diversity in the region that stretches back centuries, even predating the 18th and early 19th centuries when the region's economic growth was inextricably linked to the odious workings of the transatlantic slave trade as well as to the mining, shipbuilding, railway and engineering industries for which it became best known. Paradoxically, during the same period, the North East also became a stronghold of anti-slavery activity. This was part of a deep seam of elite and popular political radicalism that included a strong commitment to peace activism. These pacifist traditions endured in various guises into the 20th and 21st centuries. In 1934, for example, Arthur Henderson, Member of Parliament for Newcastle and, as Home Secretary, the first Labour Party cabinet minister to hail from the region, was awarded the Nobel Peace Prize for his work towards international disarmament.[4] Thirty years later Martin Luther King received the same honour and on his 1967 visit to England he spoke passionately against nuclear arms and the Vietnam War, as well as for economic and racial justice.

Without presuming to offer anything resembling a comprehensive history of radical politics, peace activism or race relations in Newcastle, or on Tyneside, or across the North East, the book shows how King's visit fits into and illuminates those complex and entangled histories. Although conventionally thought of as a 'white' region, there were people of African descent living in the North East during Roman times when Moors helped to garrison Hadrian's Wall, the eastern terminus of which was, appropriately enough, at Wallsend on the River Tyne. There were Arabs and Asians in the region from the late 19th century, not to mention significant migrant communities from Ireland and continental Europe. It is important to recover this diversity, particularly in the face of contemporary appeals to a reactionary kind of white racial, ethnic and religious chauvinism that celebrates a mythical, idealised, racially pure and uniformly Christian British past, while blaming a variety of 'foreigners' for its disappearance. And while professional historians and sociologists have long investigated the experiences of non-whites in Britain and noted their enormous contribution to the nation's history, their efforts have had only limited impact on mainstream popular consciousness—a problem exacerbated by the increasingly narrow and insular focus of much history teaching in British schools. As the historian-broadcaster David Olusoga puts it, 'with black history and black people largely expunged from the mainstream narrative of British history, we have been left with a distorted and diminished vision of our national past…Black British history is everyone's history and is all the stronger for it.'[5]

David Olusoga's personal story is fascinating and speaks to some of the key themes in this book. Olusoga is of mixed-race: a 'Geordie Nigerian,' he avers with some pride. His Nigerian father and white British mother met at Newcastle University in the 1960s. Although he was born in Lagos, when his parents separated he was raised by his mother on a Newcastle council estate in the 1970s and 1980s. There, he suffered racial taunts in the street and his house was attacked so often by racist thugs that he eventually had to move. This was an era of burgeoning support for the neo-Nazi National Front with its white supremacist ideology, vile racist rhetoric, violence and calls for the repatriation of non-white immigrants. Olusoga felt, as he puts it with epic understatement, 'profoundly unwelcome in Britain. My right, not just to regard myself as a British citizen, but even to be in Britain seemed contested.'[6] Neither in his monumental book, *Black and British*, nor in the articles he wrote, nor in the interviews he gave as a major BBC television series aired to accompany it, was there any indication that Olusoga was aware while growing up that Martin Luther King had visited Newcastle just a few years earlier, quite possibly while his parents were studying at the University. Private, public and scholarly memories of King's time in Newcastle and its significance had simply been allowed to fade.

While silent on King, David Olusoga does note that Frederick Douglass, the most important African American abolitionist of the mid-19th century, spent a good deal of time in Newcastle.[7] This book shows that Douglass was part of a steady stream of fugitive slaves and black abolitionists from the US who found the North East a place of refuge and especially warm welcome. Although geographically located on Britain's North Sea, rather than its Atlantic coast, these African American visitors and the region's multiple linkages to slavery and abolitionism mean that the North East occupies a fascinating, if rather unconventional place within the history of the Black Atlantic. Theorised and deployed by an eclectic range of scholars, perhaps most influentially by Paul Gilroy, the Black Atlantic draws attention to how the transatlantic slave trade generated an African diaspora and created intricate connections among the nations and empires clustered round the Atlantic Ocean, with profound consequences for all those places and all their inhabitants that have endured to the present day.[8] Martin Luther King, like Olaudah Equiano and Douglass before him, and like Jimi Hendrix, Muhammad Ali and Harry Belafonte after him, was in a rich tradition of Black Atlantic sojourners who found their way to Newcastle.

With corners in West Africa, Western Europe and the Americas, the Black Atlantic was itself a distinctive part of an elaborate Atlantic World system of commerce and migration—involuntary in the case of slaves, of course—that connected people, capital and goods, along with their cultures and ideas.[9] Counterintuitive though it may seem from simply looking at a map, this book suggests that important aspects of the histories of Tyneside and the North East of England, like that of Britain as a whole, are best understood as part of the entwined histories of the Black Atlantic and the Atlantic World.

Yet, even the vast Atlantic World is ultimately insufficient as a geographic and historical backdrop to the larger story of race and race relations in the North East, some of which connects the region to South Asia, the Middle-East and Eastern Europe, all important sources of immigration during the 20th and 21st centuries. Perhaps the crucial underlying point here is that even the most local of local history is always shaped by broader regional, national, and international trends and forces; conversely, even the most local of local events can offer insights into much wider and deeper historical issues. In some ways, then, this study takes inspiration from the Romantic poet-artist-mystic and abolitionist William Blake, who wrote in 1803 of what it might be like 'To see a world in a grain of sand.' While the claims of this book are a little more modest, they nonetheless rest on the belief that there is virtue in taking a granular approach to a fascinating piece of local history such as King's visit to Newcastle to see how just how much it might reveal of far bigger historical and geographical worlds.[10]

Partly because of its strong anti-slavery tradition and the cavalcade of African American fugitive slaves and abolitionists visiting the North East in the mid-19th century, the region quickly developed a reputation for unusual levels of tolerance and progressive racial politics. However, that reputation was occasionally punctured by ugly eruptions of hate and violence against racial and other minorities that exposed undercurrents of prejudice and discrimination churning beneath the generally calm surface of North East race relations. This complex story of tolerance and vilification, of inclusion and exclusion, of open-mindedness and pinched parochialism, continues to play out in the 21st century amid major changes in the region's demographic profile. The local meanings, wider implications and enduring relevance of King's 1967 visit are best understood in terms of this historic ebb and flow.

As post-World War Two Britain tried to deal with the demise of its Empire and the new dynamics of a Commonwealth, King's career and developments in American race relations were watched with great interest, whether as a cautionary tale or as a guide to how best to deal with Britain's changing racial landscape. Indeed, the significance of King's visit in 1967 was inextricably linked to the rising levels of immigration into Britain from what was then euphemistically known as the 'New'—as in non-white—

Commonwealth. Although the number of West Indian, Asian and African immigrants to the North East remained low, both in absolute and proportionate terms, that did not prevent heated discussions and popular protests over the relative merits of immigration restriction, repatriation, and greater legal protection for minority rights. King's appearance in Newcastle—and news of his murder just five months later—intensified local and national debates over Britain's racial future.

Half a century later, in a post-Brexit world, those debates retain a remarkably contemporary feel. In the 1960s, fear, ignorance and craven political opportunism combined with genuine concerns over jobs, housing, education, social services and healthcare in an ailing increasingly post-industrial economy to fuel the search for scapegoats to blame for the loss of power, status and opportunity felt by many people. As David Olusoga's experience suggests, the second decade of the 21st century is certainly not the first period in the history of Newcastle, Tyneside and the North East that citizens of colour, along with other kinds of refugees, asylum-seekers and migrants seeking a better life—sometimes simply seeking to hang on to life itself as they flee war, terror, persecution, and poverty in their homelands—have proved easy targets for demonisation, verbal abuse and physical assault.[11]

In the North East, strong traditions of tolerance and democratic accountability had initially flourished in the midst of slavery and aristocratic political rule; they laid the foundations for the 'cultures of welcome' that endure in the city's 21st century status as a City of Sanctuary and in the work of many volunteer organisations dedicated to alleviating the material and mental distress of migrants, asylum-seekers and refugees.[12] Yet a noxious mix of anti-migrant sentiment and Islamophobia still threatens the region's social cohesion. It is against this backdrop that King's words in Newcastle about the need for stringent, firmly enforced legislation to protect minority rights against the effects of bigotry, hate crimes and discrimination seem especially pertinent. Similarly, few would disagree that racism, war and poverty are still among the most grievous threats to the peace, security and well-being of the entire world, even if they might want to add sexism, homophobia, religious intolerance, terrorism, and environmental neglect to the list of global toxins. Above all, however, it is King's insistence in Newcastle that the fate of the peoples of the world are ultimately 'tied together in an inextricable network of mutuality' that seems to retain what, on another occasion, he described as 'the fierce urgency of now.'[13]

This, then, is the story of King's visit to Newcastle, set in the quadruple intersecting and transnational contexts of King's political activism and developments in the US civil rights and black power movements of the 1960s; the North East's and Britain's changing race relations; a largely forgotten history of local links to the long African American freedom struggle; and the story of efforts to find appropriate ways to commemorate King's visit. It is written in the hope that it may play a small part in the process whereby King's words and the example of his own fight for peace and social justice finally secure a permanent place in popular memory—and that they will inspire others to take up the challenge that he issued in Newcastle in 1967: the challenge to make the planet that we all have to share a better, more compassionate, peaceful, and just place.

Part One:

The Visit

CHAPTER ONE

'Happy and Honored to Accept':
Bringing Martin Luther King to Newcastle

On March 8, 1967, the University of Newcastle upon Tyne issued a rather low-key press release announcing several forthcoming events. Alongside news of a symposium on 'Liquid – Liquid Extraction' organised by the Department of Chemical Engineering and word that Mr. Brian Hackett, Reader in Landscape Architecture, had agreed to deliver a centennial lecture at the University of Illinois, was the simple announcement that 'An Honorary Degree will be conferred on the following at a special Congregation to be held in November in the King's Hall of the University: D.C.L. Martin Luther King, Jr.'[1]

Martin Luther King, Jr., since the Montgomery Bus Boycott of 1955-56, the pre-eminent leader of the campaign for African American civil and voting rights and a globally recognised champion of freedom and justice, had accepted the University's invitation to come to Newcastle to receive an Honorary Doctorate in Civil Law. It was a major coup for the University, which became the first and only institution in the United Kingdom to honour King in this way. Securing King's agreement to come to Newcastle had not, however, been an entirely trouble-free process—and there would be a few more heart-stopping moments before the civil rights leader, accompanied by Rev. Andrew Young, his friend and lieutenant in the Southern Christian Leadership Conference (SCLC), arrived safely in Newcastle on November 13, 1967 for a brief but historic visit.[2]

More than a year earlier, on October 22, 1966, Lord [William] Wynne-Jones, then Professor of Chemistry and Pro-Vice-Chancellor at the University, had set in motion the formal train of events that led to King's visit by formally nominating the civil rights leader for an honorary degree. On November 3, the proposal was discussed for the first time at meeting of the University's Honorary Degrees Committee.[3] Wynne-Jones's personal motivations in nominating King are unclear, but the local Labour party activist, who had been made a life peer in 1964, certainly had a keen interest in matters American. In 1967, for example, Wynne-Jones, Maurice Goldsmith of the London-based Science of Science Foundation, and former

Newcastle City Council leader and Chair of the North East Economic Planning Council T. Dan Smith visited the US to examine the 'Research Triangle' created in North Carolina by Governor Luther Hodges, hoping to emulate it in the North East through a Regional Science Committee.[4] At the next meeting of the Honorary Degrees Committee, on November 28, 1966 it was confirmed that King would be invited to accept an honorary DCL at a congregation scheduled for May 17, 1967.[5]

Beyond Wynne-Jones's personal involvement, several other factors help to explain why the University chose to honour King at this time and in this way. Indeed, Wynne-Jones may simply have put his name forward because protocol required that somebody had to be named as *the* nominee; the invitation to King was probably a genuinely collective decision, with the University's first Vice-Chancellor, Charles Bosanquet, a decisive influence. Some context here is useful. The University of Newcastle upon Tyne had only become an independent institution in 1963, when Armstrong College and the former King's College of Durham University merged and a new University charter was granted. This put Newcastle in the curious position of being technically a 'new' university, while still being widely thought of as an 'old' university thanks to its links to Durham, founded in 1832 and, after Oxford and Cambridge, the third oldest of all English universities.

Vice-Chancellor Bosanquet was certainly eager to demonstrate that Newcastle was a dynamic modern civic university, actively engaged with the major social issues of the day. Writing to senior University officials in late 1965, Bosanquet outlined his plan to use honorary degrees to raise the institution's profile by aligning itself with individuals who had made outstanding contributions to the economic, political, social and cultural life of the city, region, or broader national and international communities. Honorary degrees, Bosanquet explained, would help the University to publicise its mission and values to the general public: '...The objectives [of honorary degrees] would be two; the first is to give to the influential people of this region a better understanding of what this University does, in addition to the teaching of students; the second would be to give to the interested public at large a correct impression of the freshness and vigour of this University.'[6]

This last point was very important in the 1960s when British universities, particularly some of the newer institutions, were often hot-beds of progressive ideas and social activism. This was not really the case at Newcastle, where the student body, dominated by the products of grammar and public schools, was rather conservative. While there were conspicuous exceptions, Newcastle students tended to eschew political protest. C.B. 'Nick' Nicholson, President of the Students' Representative Council in 1967, told Francis Glover that 'Newcastle was not an especially radical campus, especially compared to LSE [London School of Economics].'[7] Historian Sylvia Ellis came to a similar conclusion in her study of British student activism against the Vietnam War. Newcastle students were usually a half-step behind their peers around the country in mobilising around the great social causes of the day.[8]

Counterintuitively, in an era when most university administrations were desperate to keep a lid on escalating student protests against a wide range of societal and campus ills, Bosanquet may have been trying to stimulate a greater sense of political engagement and social activism among Newcastle students that would match his vision for the newly independent institution. As Nick Nicholson recalled, Bosanquet was quite open and 'happy to attend forums' to address student problems and broader issues of concern.[9]

In sum, awarding honorary degrees to major public figures such as King allowed Newcastle to establish a distinctive sense of identity, demonstrate a commitment to progressive social ideas and, always a concern for university administrations, compete with other institutions for students, funds, and publicity. As Bosanquet put it, 'In the last three years so much publicity has been obtained by new universities (such as Sussex) that the public are in danger of thinking that we, and the other, older universities are "stuck in the mud" and that we have less to offer that is relevant to the needs of the second half of the twentieth century.'[10] From the University's perspective, a visit from a renowned international figure such as King would simultaneously raise its public profile and reflect its desire to fulfil what Bosanquet called its 'corporate responsibility' to demonstrate its relevance beyond the walls of the academy.[11] Bosanquet's personal sense of urgency on this matter may have been heightened by the fact that he was nearing retirement, eventually standing down on September 30, 1968.[12]

Another figure who probably exerted a crucial influence behind the scenes was Bosanquet's wife, Barbara, an American from a family of Christian philanthropists. According to the Bosanquets' daughter Kathleen Potter, her mother's family had helped to raise funds for the Hampton and Tuskegee Institutes, two of the oldest historically black colleges in the US. It is not too much of a stretch to surmise that, even if the idea to honour King did not emanate from Barbara Bosanquet, she was fully supportive of it. Potter believed that her mother and father shared 'a keen interest in social justice and the civil rights movement.'[13]

Whatever the precise circumstances of the nomination, the University Senate unanimously accepted the Honorary Degrees Committee's recommendation to award King a DCL. On December 14, 1966, the University Registrar, E.M. [Ernest] Bettenson wrote to inform King of the honour and invite him to attend the University's May congregation.[14] This, however, is where plans began to unravel.

Bettenson addressed his initial letter to King at 454, Dexter Avenue, Montgomery, Alabama. This was the site of the Dexter Avenue Baptist Church where King had arrived, still working to complete his Doctorate in Theology from Boston University, in 1953. But King had left Montgomery in January 1960 to join his father as co-pastor of the Ebenezer Baptist Church in his hometown of Atlanta. It was the first sign that, while the University's leadership was undoubtedly sincere in its desire to honour King's accomplishments, it sometimes struggled with the details and logistics. Fortunately, Bettenson's mis-addressed letter was forwarded to the SCLC's headquarters in Atlanta; unfortunately, it arrived in mid-December 1966, while King was in the Caribbean working on his book *Where Do We Go From Here: Chaos or Community?* Dora McDonald, King's secretary at the SCLC and destined to become the main link between King and the University, wrote back to acknowledge receipt of the invitation and promising to show it to King on his return to Atlanta.[15]

There followed a long and, at the Newcastle end, nervous silence that was finally broken on January 7, 1967 when Bettenson wrote to Dora McDonald once more requesting 'an early reply about whether Dr. King will be able to accept the degree.' Suspecting that King himself might still be unaware of the University's invitation, Bettenson asked McDonald, 'is it at all possible for you to forward my letter or in some other way communicate with him?'[16] More silence. On January 17, as the University's deadline for announcing its honorary degree recipients for May approached, an increasingly anxious Bettenson splurged £2.19.6 on a telegram to McDonald in Atlanta: 'Grateful reply possibility Dr. King able to accept honorary degree. University being pressed to make announcement.'[17] Still more silence.

Bizarrely, although Bettenson was now in direct contact with McDonald at King's organisational base in Atlanta, he continued to send a succession of missives to King at a Montgomery address the civil rights leader had not occupied for seven years—and then wondered why King seemed slow to respond. On February 23, for example, the Registrar wrote again to King in Montgomery and asked innocently, 'We wonder whether there has been some failure of communication so that either you have not received my letters or we have not received yours since the letter which Miss McDonald wrote on the 23rd December. We have to announce that honorary degrees are going to be conferred on the others invited for the 17th May. This announcement makes no difference to our hope that you might be able to come on 17th May or some other day in 1967.'[18]

By coincidence, on the same day that Bettenson sent this letter to King at the wrong address, King had personally cabled the Registrar to inform him that he 'Would be happy and honored to accept honorary degree in November when I will be in England. Regret that it is not possible to be there in May. Please advise if November is satisfactory for special convocation.'[19] This was the first personal communication from King and Bettenson was both delighted and relieved. Although King's inability to travel to Newcastle in May meant that the University would have to arrange a special ceremony, Bettenson immediately wrote back to King, that it was 'a real pleasure to know that we can see you in November.' He asked for further details of how long King would be able to stay in Newcastle and expressed the University's hope 'that you will be accompanied by Mrs. King.'[20] He then proceeded to send this critical confirmation letter to the redundant address in Montgomery.

By this time, the occupants of 454, Dexter Avenue in Montgomery were apparently getting rather fed up with the steady stream of letters from Newcastle. Bettenson's confirmation was sent back across the Atlantic via the local US Mail office with the words 'Moved not forwardable' scrawled on the envelope. When Bettenson found his own unopened letter to King among his post on March 23, he admitted he was 'horrified to receive it back.'[21] His anxiety was exacerbated becuase the University had already issued its March 8 Press Release publicly announcing King's forthcoming visit. Closer scrutiny of that Release reveals that Bettenson was not the only one at Newcastle uncertain about King's whereabouts and affiliations. In the Release, King is gnomically described as a 'pastor, Baptist Church, Alabama, U.S.A. since 1954,' which not only missed the fact that King had been at Ebenezer Baptist Church in Atlanta, Georgia since 1960 but also implied that there was only one Baptist Church in the whole of Alabama— and that Alabama was a city or town, rather than a state. In what was clearly a bad day in the press office, the Release also misnamed the SCLC, substituting Council for Conference.[22]

Ever dutiful, Bettenson hurriedly wrote to King again, incorporating a copy of his original boomeranging letter in the new text. 'Misfortune seems to dog our correspondence,' he commented ruefully. But at least he had discovered the magic formula, adding at the end of his latest missive, 'I am sending this letter to the Atlanta address with sincere regrets for any inconvenience which the delay has caused.'[23]

Thereafter, preparations went relatively smoothly for a while. On September 2, Dora McDonald telegrammed to confirm that 'Dr. King finds it possible to be with you Monday November 13 1967 to receive honorary degree. Please let us know if this date is satisfactory.' Bettenson, taking no chances, replied by both telegram and letter, expressing the University's delight that King was coming and once again requesting details of King's other engagements and preferences regarding the timing of the degree ceremony.[24] At this point, the plan was for King to arrive in Newcastle from London by train on either Saturday, November 11 or Sunday, November 12. Bosanquet wrote personally to King, advising him against trying to fly north in November 'as there is more risk of fog.' On behalf of himself and his wife, the Vice-Chancellor offered their home at 15, Adderstone Crescent, near the picturesque Jesmond Dene, as a place to stay while King was in Newcastle. He also repeated his hopes that Mrs. King would be able to accompany him on the trip and told King that he hoped to be able to host 'a dinner party in your honour on the evening of Monday, November 13,' after the degree ceremony. The following day, the schedule was for King to leave Newcastle, either heading back to London or taking a trip up to Edinburgh in Scotland.[25]

King had long been interested in Edinburgh. The prospect of a visit may even have been a factor in his decision to accept the invitation to Newcastle. In November 1950, while still a student at Crozer Theological Seminary in Chester, Pennsylvania, King wrote to Professor Hugh Watt at Edinburgh University expressing a desire to study for a PhD there. King requested 'an application form, a catalogue of the Divinity School, and any information that would be valuable to me at this point.' Six weeks later, King was accepted by Edinburgh University, but chose instead to go to Boston University for his doctoral studies.[26]

Fifteen years later, in May 1965, shortly after the campaign for Voting Rights in Selma, Alabama, where the terrible official and unofficial violence that greeted peaceful protestors made headlines around the globe, King had received a letter from a precocious Edinburgh University postgraduate, Lord James Douglas-Hamilton. The President of Debates at the University and subsequently a Tory Member of Parliament and Baron Selkirk of Douglas, Douglas-Hamilton invited King to the University to participate in a debate on the motion 'That legislation cannot bring about integration.' King was to be pitted against someone Douglas-Hamilton intriguingly described as 'a prominent and effective British reactionary.' Douglas-Hamilton made a strong pitch. He noted that Edinburgh was 'a cosmopolitan city' and that the University could boast 'many international students'—neither of which Newcastle or its University could confidently claim in the 1960s. Moreover, Douglas-Hamilton explained to King that while President of the Oxford Union as an undergraduate he had helped to organise a series of televised debates, several on apartheid and race relations, that included the black nationalist Malcolm X and the esteemed African American author and activist James Baldwin among its participants.[27]

King received hundreds of similar invitations from around the globe and turned most of them down, as he did the invitation from Douglas-Hamilton. This begs the question of why King would accept the invitation from Newcastle, when he rejected so many other similar and potentially even more attractive propositions—a question to which we will return in Chapter Two. When he did arrive in Newcastle in November 1967, the motion that Douglas-Hamilton had wanted him to debate, about the role of law in helping to create a more equitable and harmonious society, had become even more urgent due to developments in British race relations. It was a theme King would discuss extensively during his Newcastle visit.

Arrangements for King's trip continued to go relatively smoothly in the early Autumn of 1967. On October 30, however, preparations were suddenly thrown into chaos when King was jailed in Bessemer, Alabama, convicted on a contempt of court charge that dated back to the Birmingham civil rights campaign of 1963. On Good Friday, April 12, 1963, King had defied a temporary court injunction that prohibited civil rights demonstrations in Birmingham. He spent Easter weekend in jail, where he composed his celebrated 'Letter from Birmingham City Jail,' perhaps the most powerful expression of his commitment to nonviolent direct action protest tactics and a philosophical defence of his willingness to disobey what he deemed to be unjust and immoral racist laws. When he stood trial, King and ten of his co-defendants were found guilty of criminal contempt, sentenced to five days imprisonment and fined $50, although the sentences were to be held in abeyance while appeals were heard. It was not until October 9, 1967, when the Supreme Court issued a final order denying King and his co-defendants a rehearing on their convictions, that King finally exhausted all legal options. On October 30, King, accompanied by fellow SCLC leaders Wyatt Walker and Ralph Abernathy, went to jail in Bessemer.[28]

King had been jailed many times during his civil rights activities. Never before, however, had news of his incarceration generated such an instantaneous expression of concern at the University of Newcastle upon Tyne. On November 1, a telegram was sent in the Vice-Chancellor's name asking for confirmation that King would still be able to make the trip: 'Regretfully understand Dr. King now imprisoned and plans possibly upset. Essential we know whether he will be in Newcastle November 13th. Grateful reply soonest.'[29] Later that day, Dora McDonald responded reassuringly that 'Dr. King will arrive Newcastle by train morning of November 13th as planned. Departing same afternoon at 4pm. Regret inability to spend more time at university.' The message was that King would still come, but for a severely truncated visit.[30]

Despite Miss McDonald's assurances and press reports that the prison sentence would only last for five days, there was still understandable concern that King might not be able to come. On November 3, Bettenson wrote to the secretary of the Lord Mayor of Newcastle, outlining the arrangements for the special congregation to which members of the City Council had been invited, but confiding, 'Quite unofficially, everything is a little extraordinary because I cannot avoid a slight doubt in my mind as to whether the honorary graduand will actually turn up!'[31] Bettenson expressed similar caution in a letter the following day to the Duke of Northumberland, Chancellor of the University, who had agreed to preside over the degree ceremony. 'Personally,' Bettenson admitted, 'I am still keeping my fingers crossed and am promising all concerned that I will let them know if we have a last minute cancellation.' From his ancestral home in Alnwick Castle, the Duke replied that he would 'attend the Lunch as well as the Congregation on Monday 13th – that is assuming that Dr. King has been released from gaol!'[32]

Persistent doubts as to whether King would make the trip did not prevent the University continuing with essential preparations. Two first-class reservations were made for a 1am train out of London's King's Cross Station on the morning of Monday, November 13. King and Andrew Young, who Dora McDonald had explained would accompany King, were to spend Sunday afternoon and evening at the Hilton Hotel in London, before catching the overnight 'Tynesider' to Newcastle. The two men were also booked onto the 16:08 return train from Newcastle to London. Vice-Chancellor Bosanquet, who played an increasingly active role in arrangements as the date of the visit approached, authorised the University Cashier to provide £21.12.0 in cash so that the tickets could be bought in advance and mailed to the Hilton for King and Young to collect.[33]

Elsewhere in the University, an unlikely hero emerged in the person of George R. Howe, the Chief Clerk. In late September, before King's imprisonment, Howe had diligently ensured that all the necessary rooms were booked: the King's Hall in the Armstrong Building, where the ceremony would take place; the Gallery in the Percy Building, where a reception would be held; the Refectory, where lunch was scheduled.[34] Howe joined Bettenson who, notwithstanding nagging doubts about whether King would show up, had a huge personal investment in making the event a success, to sort out the nitty-gritty details of what would happen on campus. Close examination of those arrangements reveals much about the social and political dynamics of the University and the broader Tyneside community in the late 1960s.

On November 3, Bettenson had un-crossed his fingers sufficiently to write to the entire staff of the University, plus external members of the University's Court, Council and Senate, inviting them to attend a 'Special Honorary Degree Congregation' for Martin Luther King, Jr. scheduled for 2.30pm on November 13. Those wishing to attend were asked to return a form, indicating if they also wished to walk in the academic procession before the ceremony, 'not later than first post on Saturday, 11th November 1967.' Bettenson was not sure how many people would be interested, but he reassured staff that 'If there are clear signs that the King's Hall will not hold all who wish to come it may be possible, given early warning, to arrange for the Ceremony to be relayed by closed circuit television to a lecture room.' He added that, 'It is not proposed to issue tickets though seats will be reserved for a limited number of University guests.'[35]

The same day, Bettenson sent a separate letter to members of the University Senate inviting them and their wives to a reception in the Gallery of the Percy Building at 12.15pm. The Senators were asked to complete a form that was a classic of bureaucratic overkill. For some reason, there were separate questions for '(a) I hope to attend' and '(b) I shall not attend.' Even more striking was the fact that the Senate was obviously exclusively male. The reply form invited Senators to indicate '(c) I shall be accompanied by my wife' or '(d) I shall not be accompanied by my wife.' The implication was not only that this was an all-male preserve, but that everyone on the Senate in 1967 was heterosexual—at least publicly just a few months after homosexual acts between consenting adults had been decriminalised—with a wife available to bring or not bring. The University may have taken a bold step to align itself with the cause of racial equality by honouring King, but like most universities of the day it was still a long way off the pace when it came to matters of gender equality and sexual orientation.[36]

Vice-Chancellor Bosanquet took personal responsibility for contacting student leaders. He asked Nick Nicholson and Paul Brooks, President of the Union Society, to gather 'some of our students,' for 'an informal meeting over coffee' with King at 11am. The young men were urged to try to include 'students from overseas,' by which he doubtless meant students of colour.[37] As things transpired, Paul Barry, the photographic editor on *The Courier* student newspaper, speculated that he may have been the only person of colour among the thirty students who gathered for an unforgettable audience with King in Committee Room A of the Union Building.[38] Nick Nicholson was also asked if he would carry the ceremonial mace and lead the academic procession into the King's Hall, which he gladly agreed to do, having first checked with Bettenson about the dress code. 'Dark lounge suit and gown, and in your case, hood,' was the correct attire, the Registrar told him.[39]

Once the necessary invitations had been sent, George Howe moved impressively into top gear. He wrote to Mr. Rickerby of Messrs Gray and Sons in Durham to order academic dress for King, asking Rickerby to come to the ceremony early at 2pm 'to assist in robing various Members of the Academic Procession.'[40] He wrote to his colleague Miss Sanderson in the Bursar's Office to make sure Room 214, upstairs in the Armstrong Building, was set aside for robing purposes. And he began to make provisional plans in case the King's Hall could not accommodate all those who wished to attend the event. 'In the event of closed circuit television being used to relay the Ceremony will you please advise which lecture theatres are suitable and available for this purpose,' he asked Miss Sanderson.[41]

In all universities, the pomp and circumstance surrounding degree ceremonies have their own strict set of rules. At Newcastle, one of the rules was that the University Bedel led the academic procession and carried the ceremonial mace, apparently receiving an honorarium for discharging these duties. Howe's diplomatic skills were tested by the Vice-Chancellor's decision to invite Nick Nicholson to have that honour. Again, Bosanquet's motivations are not entirely clear. However, given the personal efforts he made to set up a meeting between King and student representatives, it reflected his belief that exposure to King and what he stood for would be of special interest and benefit to Newcastle students. Happy though he was to reap the publicity that King's visit guaranteed, Bosanquet wanted to use King's visit to inspire and empower a younger generation. In any event, on November 6, George Howe delivered the bad news to the Bedel, Mr. J. Stapylton, that he would not be leading the procession. Howe sweetened the pill by reassuring Stapylton, 'I hasten to add that this is without prejudice to your fee.' Stapylton was asked to ensure that the mace and the supports upon which it rested during the ceremony were ready. He was also and instructed to make appropriate signage available around the campus and especially in the Armstrong Building: 'Academic Procession; Silence Ceremony in Progress; Arrows; No Smoking, etc.'[42]

As the big day approached, Howe was fastidious in his attention to detail. He wrote to T. Spence, a calligrapher in Whitley Bay, apologising for the short notice, but asking him to prepare a parchment to be given to King at the ceremony, stipulating that he should have it in hand 'by not later than Saturday 11th November.' Determined to head off any possible disruption to the smooth running of the day or King's enjoyment of the event, he contacted Professor Petch of the Department of Metallurgy asking him to 'arrange for the Foundry and Fume Extractor Plant not to be in operation during the hours 2.00p.m. to 4.00p.m. on Monday, 13th November,' lest the noise interrupt the ceremony.[43] In a similar attempt to control external noise, Howe wrote to the University's Estates Manager to make sure that construction work in the inner quadrangle outside the Armstrong Building was suspended for the duration of the ceremony and to ask that all the University's flags should be 'flown at full mast from 9.0 a.m. to 5.0 p.m.'[44]

Howe was eager to ensure that campus, especially the King's Hall, was looking its best on November 13. He wrote to the Clerk of Works, asking him to help lay fresh carpet and to 'install the ceremonial dais in the King's Hall,' while suggesting that the dais could do with some repairs. 'Will you please ensure that the dais is retouched in the parts which have been damaged since the last ceremony,' he wrote. On the Friday before the Monday event, Howe was still not happy with the way things looked in the Hall. Noting that 'the inspection cover in the panelling behind the dais is again hanging by one hinge,' he asked the Clerk of Works, 'Will you please as a matter of urgency repair this inspection cover in time for the Ceremony on Monday afternoon.'[45]

Howe's concern for the comfort of the University's distinguished guests knew no limits. The Head Porter in the Armstrong Building, Mr. McLaren, was asked to 'ensure that the forecourt is swept, toilets cleaned...that all screens are removed from the entrance and placed over the usuall (sic) eye-sores,' as well as setting up 356 seats in the King's Hall, with another fifty placed in reserve for use in the gallery.[46] He even wrote to the University's chief heating engineer, not only asking Mr. Blair to 'ensure that the temperature in King's Hall is at a comfortable level at 2.0 p.m. on Monday 13th November,' but also advising him on precisely how this might be done: 'I would suggest that you turn off the radiator behind the Registrar's table (at the left of the dais looking at the dais).'[47] Such precautions were only sensible given the vagaries of the Newcastle weather. Although, after some light early morning showers, November 13 turned out to be chilly but fine, Howe was taking no chances. Not only were there to be 'hat and coat stands at the top of the Philosophy corridor in the Armstrong Building,' Howe also secured 'a supply of umbrellas' in case of rain.[48]

In the final days before the visit, Howe drafted a series of briefing notes for the University staff who were to act as marshals and ushers at the ceremony. Remarkably, given King's stature, Howe indicated that 'The Ceremony will not be relayed by closed circuit television,' as there was insufficient interest in the occasion among the wider University community to warrant it. Nevertheless, he was compelled to cram 80, not 50, extra chairs into the gallery, in addition to the 356 seats on the floor of the King's Hall.[49]

The same briefing also contained what would subsequently become an important clue in the search for contents of the the impromptu speech King gave that day. Twenty seats in the gallery overlooking the main body of the Hall were reserved for members of the press, while Howe warned that Assistant Registrar Mr. G. Ashley, who served as Senior Marshal for the day, 'may be called to attend to the members of the Press and T.V. Engineers.'[50] Although for the next quarter of a century, the University lamented that King's remarks had gone unrecorded, in the days leading up to the Congregation, George Howe was busy making arrangements to accommodate television cameras. A handwritten check-list shows that Howe arranged for engineers from 'TTT'—Tyne Tees Television, the North East service of the commercial Independent Television Network—to come into the King's Hall at 10am to check lighting and microphones and set up their cameras in the gallery.[51]

Perhaps the most surprising aspect of the preparations was the security operation. It was, to say the least, low-profile. Several staff members were detailed to mill around the door at the north end of the King's Hall, in the impressive lofty marble lobby just inside the main entrance to the Armstrong Building from the Queen Victoria Road. From there they directed members of the Academic Procession up the staircase to the Robing Room in the Department of Naval Architecture, while other guests were ushered towards the West Door. Once the ceremony was underway, a solitary porter was assigned to guard the North Door.

Elsewhere, a member of the administrative staff, Miss Christie, was charged with supervising the seating of guests who entered the King's Hall via the West Door. During the ceremony itself, Christie was dispatched to guard that door. Another administrator, Mr. Read, patrolled the South Door, but at least he had a porter to assist him. This door was the point of entry for the Academic Procession: the two men were responsible for closing the door after the Procession had entered the Hall and opening it again after the ceremony was concluded so that the Procession could leave. The South Door porter was also instructed that he 'must not leave his post on any account,' and that he was 'responsible for maintaining silence during the ceremony.'[52] As things turned out, the only unscheduled voice heard during the ceremony belonged to Martin Luther King. Inside the Hall itself, there was no additional security, although marshals were obviously expected to be vigilant. In one of his briefing documents, George Howe explained that Mrs. Kell would be on duty in the Gallery, from where she could 'keep an eye open for the undesirable characters with toilet rolls and/or soft fruit.'[53]

As should be clear by now, George Howe was a 'belts and braces' sort of man who left nothing to chance. The deployment of Mrs. Kell as his main security force suggests that he thought the threat to King's well-being while on campus was minimal; but it was clearly not entirely out of the question that some elements in Newcastle might wish to protest against his presence. Howe certainly felt concerned enough to arrange for police assistance, although the fact that he only asked for two officers reflects his assessment of the risk level. One policeman was on duty outside the Percy Building while King was at the reception with staff. The officer then accompanied the luncheon party on its short walk to the University Refectory, where he loitered until they transferred again to the nearby King's Hall. A second officer was stationed outside the Armstrong Building from 1.45pm until the ceremony was over.[54]

That was it. Security was essentially left to two policemen, two porters, and three marshals whose real jobs were in university administration—including the redoubtable Mrs. Kell, with her keen eye for fruit and paper weaponry. Intriguingly, several people who met King on campus or who witnessed the degree ceremony later recalled seeing some kind of black bod-yguard, maybe guards, accompanying him.[55] It is just about possible that King picked up a security detail in London, maybe courtesy of the US Em-bassy. Yet, the documentary record from the Newcastle end, which is remarkably complete, makes no mention of any additional security; nor does the less voluminous, yet still plentiful correspondence from Atlanta. Neither the photographs nor the film shot that day shows any evidence of this extra security.

What there is, however, is plenty of evidence that some people in New-castle struggled to work out exactly who Andrew Young was—he certainly was not Mrs. King—or why he was there. In his letter inviting the Duke of Northumberland to preside over the Honorary Degree Ceremony, Vice-Chancellor Bosanquet had erroneously referred to King's travelling com-panion as '(I think) his son, the Reverend Andrew King.'[56] Dorothy Booth, wife of Norleigh Booth, a partner in the firm of Watson and Burton, the University's solicitors, was present at the lunch in the Refectory and at the Ceremony. She remembered King being accompanied by 'a young man, his secretary I think,' adding that he 'was a devoted admirer of the Doctor.'[57] Clearly, there was confusion regarding Young's status and it is conceivable that some people thought he was a personal bodyguard.

In fact, Young was a major civil rights leader in his own right in 1967. Just three years younger than his friend and colleague King, Young would go on to become a Georgia Congressman and later still the Mayor of At-lanta. In between, he served as the US Ambassador to the United Nations during the presidency of another notable Georgian with a connection to Newcastle, Jimmy Carter. In May 1977, Carter won the hearts of local Geordies when he stood outside the Civic Centre and began a speech with the rallying cry of fans of Newcastle United Football Club, 'Ha'way-tha-Lads!'[58]

Although Martin Luther King was one of Carter's heroes, the President made no reference to King's visit to the city less than a decade earlier. The chances that Carter knew anything about it are negligible. What is perhaps more surprising is that nobody from the City Council appears to have made the link to King's visit either. By 1977, King's visit had been all but forgot-ten in Newcastle, just as memories had withered in the University that honoured him and where he had given his last public speech outside North America.

But all that was still to come. In November 1967, there was no mis-taking the excitement that took hold in the University as the day of King's visit finally dawned. And while, given the multiple snags that had plagued the preparations, it might make for a better story to be able to report that chaos and confusion reigned on Monday, November 13, 1967, the truth of the matter is that Bosanquet's enthusiasm, Bettenson's dogged courtship of King and Howe's meticulous planning paid off handsomely. Everything went precisely according to plan. King and Young arrived at Newcastle Central Station shortly before 6am. As was agreed, they stayed in their sleeper compartment until 8am when they were greeted by the Vice-Chancellor and taken to his home on Adderstone Crescent. There they met with Barbara Bosanquet, breakfasted and freshened up. Before leaving for the University, they also chatted with the family of Laurence Kane, who had worked as Steward at the Vice-Chancellor's residence since June 1962. The Kane family lived upstairs in the capacious lodge and, before leaving for campus, King signed an autograph for Mrs. Edna Kane and for Barbara Bosanquet. Edna Kane was also the recipient of a very special gift. King gave her the dress handkerchief from the pocket of his suit jacket. It was a peculiarly intimate gesture of thanks for the warm welcome he had received, in keeping with the graciousness that, according to those who met with him in Newcastle, King displayed throughout his visit. Although only a young teenager at the time, the Kanes' son Peter was well-aware that his parents were thrilled to encounter this great man in their home.[59]

Once on campus, the tightly packed schedule—the coffee with students, the sherry reception with staff and University Senators, a seated buffet lunch, where King was placed between the Duke of Northumberland and Lord Wynne-Jones, a snatched conversation with the local press, and finally, at 2.30pm the ceremony itself—also went off without a hitch. Mrs. Kells was not called into action. Shortly after the ceremony, King and Young were whisked away to Central Station and, less than eleven hours after they had pulled into Newcastle on the Tynesider, the two men were safely aboard their train down to London. The following day, they flew back to the US.

Back in Newcastle, it was business as usual for George Howe. The day after King's visit he wrote to the Bursar's Office to communicate a complaint that the Congregation had made it impossible for the porters to discharge their regular duties without incurring overtime. 'There was a general complaint yesterday that the porters in the Armstrong Building were not given sufficient time to clear up after the Congregation and reset the King's Hall for the choir practice today,' Howe wrote. 'Will you please as a matter of policy in future allow the day after the Congregation to give the staff a chance to remove chairs, etc., and to rearrange for other functions, as on this occasion I understand a considerable amount of overtime will be involved.' It may have been a unique moment in the life of the University and the city, but it had brought with it all-too-familiar work-a-day-problems for Howe and his staff.[60]

CHAPTER TWO

'Barbs and Arrows': Explaining Martin Luther King's Decision to Come

The two most remarkable aspects of Martin Luther King's visit to Newcastle were that he initially accepted the invitation and then bothered to actually make the trip given all that was going on in his life in November 1967. He was hardly short of similar invitations and, although he accepted at least eighteen honorary doctorates during his lifetime, he could not hope to keep up with all the requests to accept awards, make appearances, or give speeches and interviews that came flooding in from all around the world, including Britain.

In early October 1966, for example, King had been courted by David Bilk on behalf of the British National Union of Students. Bilk, the brother of popular trad-jazz clarinettist Acker Bilk and co-director of a London-based talent agency, proposed a tour of ten 'larger British Universities' for February or March 1967 when King could explain 'the past, present and future of your own movement in the US and how you see this in context of world race relations.' In addition to covering travel and accommodation, Bilk offered King a 'cash guarantee (either for each lecture or for a period of ten to fourteen days) plus an appreciable percentage of revenue taken, this to be disposed of by yourself in any way you think fit.' Bilk suggested that the BBC might be interested in covering some of the tour and that this was another 'potential source of financial revenue.' Since King routinely channelled his speaking fees into Movement coffers, there was little for him to gain personally from this tour in financial terms. Still, the revenue may have been tempting for the perennially cash-strapped SCLC.[1]

King took a while to respond to Bilk's letter, mostly because, like the first letters sent to him from Newcastle, it arrived while he was in Jamaica working on *Where Do We Go From Here?* It probably did not help expedite matters that Bilk had also written to not one but two incorrect addresses, sending copies to both the headquarters of the National Association for the Advancement of Colored People (NAACP) in New York and the Dexter Avenue Baptist Church in Montgomery. Eventually, on February 7, at precisely the same time as he was weighing up whether to accept Newcastle University's invitation, King replied to Bilk, politely declining to sign up to his ambitious plan. 'My schedule for the next academic year,' he noted, 'is so heavy that it will be impossible for me to come to Britain for such a tour.' However, he did express the hope that 'my schedule will soon ease up so that I can accept more of the invitations that come across my desk.'[2]

King's hopes of a lighter work load during the final year of his life proved fanciful. Nevertheless, it may be that Bilk's invitation, with its promise of large enthusiastic British audiences—'It goes without saying that practically everyone in this country is deeply interested in your work,' Bilk had gushed—inclined King to try to fit in a shorter trip, capped by the Newcastle Honorary Doctorate, if at all possible.[3] Of course, when he formally accepted the Newcastle invitation, King had also intended to visit Edinburgh. When that plan was scrapped his trip became much more compressed. King's revised schedule required him to fly overnight from Chicago to London on Saturday November 11 into Sunday November 12, make his way from Heathrow Airport to the Hilton Hotel at Park Lane in central London, and from there to King's Cross Station for the 274-mile train journey on a sleeper train to Newcastle, returning to London immediately after a hectic day on campus that culminated in the Honorary Degree ceremony, and then flying back to the US the following day. In all, King and Andrew Young spent less than forty-eight hours in England and barely more than eight waking hours in Newcastle. This was an amazing gesture just to pick up the latest in a succession of honorary doctorates, this one from a provincial British university whose precise whereabouts initially eluded King and his staff. Dora McDonald's letter to the University on September 27, 1967 had asked innocently if Newcastle was a plane ride away from London or whether King and Young could just get a taxi.[4]

That King should have come at all was even more startling given the specifics of what he had on his mind and on his calendar at the time. He had just been in prison and was still not particularly well when he was released on November 4. He had been transferred from a jail in Bessemer to another in Birmingham during his internment so that he could receive better treatment for a virus.[5] Once free, King had no opportunity to recuperate. On November 5, he was back in Atlanta to present his regular Sunday sermon at Ebenezer Baptist Church. From Atlanta, he travelled north to Cleveland, where he campaigned for Carl Stokes in his bid to become that Ohio city's first black mayor. On election day, November 7, King was out in the streets, bars, and shopping malls frequented by black Clevelanders, rallying support. When Stokes triumphed, King felt snubbed because he received no call to express gratitude for his efforts and was not invited to join the victorious candidate on the rostrum at the celebration party. This sense of grievance may partly explain King's rather unenthusiastic response to a question posed at the coffee morning with Newcastle students. The Students' Union treasurer, Tony Sorenson, asked King to comment on the significance of the election of black mayors in both Cleveland and Gary, Indiana, where Richard Hatcher had also recently won. 'I think it would be foolish to make too much out of these results,' King explained, 'because both these men were Democrats in Democratic strongholds and their majorities were not very high.'[6]

On the day after the Cleveland election, King met with reporters to discuss the SCLC's plans for a Poor People's Campaign, which King hoped would unite the dispossessed of all races in acts of massive civil disobedience focused on Washington, but which would also incorporate a nationwide series of paralysing demonstrations. During the week before his departure for England he was busy planning this campaign with his aides. On Saturday, November 11, he flew to Chicago to address an anti-Vietnam rally hosted by the National Labor Leadership Assembly for Peace. In preparing his remarks, there is evidence that King's imminent trip to England was on his mind. His speech focused on the domestic impact of the Vietnam War. In particular, King lamented the toll it was taking on President Lyndon Johnson's Great Society programmes to alleviate poverty, expand opportunity, and create a more equitable America. Thus, King yoked together the triple themes of war, poverty and racism that would be the centrepiece of his remarks in Newcastle. In his notes, he drew attention to a recent resolution by the British Labour Party calling upon the Labour government to 'Disassociate itself completely from U.S. Policy in Viet Nam,' and to lobby the US government to end the bombing of North Vietnam immediately and unconditionally.[7] He finished his Chicago speech in mid-afternoon and flew overnight to London. Barely two days later, he was back home, arriving in Atlanta to record some speeches for the Canadian Broadcasting Company. Small wonder that in Newcastle, Andrew Young had confessed to Dorothy Booth 'that he was rather exhausted on this trip as Martin Luther King was indefatigable and never stopped working.'[8]

Why, then, did King bother to honour such an inconvenient and relatively inconsequential engagement at a time of poor health and in the midst of so many other pressing commitments? In the circumstances, few people would have been surprised if King had cancelled or postponed his visit. The simplest answer is that King had made an undertaking to attend and was merely honouring it in the same way that he honoured most of his other appointments. There is doubtless some truth in this, but there was also something rather more revealing and significant in King's willingness to make the gruelling journey to Newcastle. This is apparent if one considers, not just the sheer volume of his workload, but the precise nature of his intellectual, social and tactical preoccupations in late 1967 and, just as crucially, his psychological condition and general morale during the last months of his life.

The Martin Luther King of 1967 and 1968 was not the confident and generally optimistic King of the early civil rights movement when the main objective had been to end the flagrant civil and voting rights abuses rife in the segregated South. The successes of that movement, as measured by the Civil Rights Acts of 1957, 1960 and, most crucially, 1964, and by the Voting Rights Act of 1965, had effectively outlawed statutory discrimination. The legislation had, however, left in place obstinate institutional and informal, systemic and practical, barriers to black advancement across America, while at the same time raising black awareness of, and determination to destroy, those barriers. In August 1965, just days after President Lyndon Baines Johnson signed the Voting Rights Act, rioting broke out in the Watts district of Los Angeles, eventually claiming thirty-four lives and causing damage estimated at $40 million. The riots offered a bloody wake-up call to those who thought that African American grievances had been addressed simply by the passage of legislation outlawing the kind of formal segregation and disenfranchisement that had characterised the Jim Crow South.[9]

Throughout the entire US, there was ample evidence that racial prejudice, discrimination and economic disadvantage continued to restrict black opportunities. As frustrations with the rate and extent of real progress grew, elements within the African American freedom struggle became far more radical. In June 1966, civil rights leaders, King among them, continued a 'March Against Fear' started in Mississippi by James Meredith—an iconoclastic black activist who had come to public attention in 1962 when he had desegregated the University of Mississippi and precipitated a white riot that was only quelled by federal troops—after he had been shot and wounded. As the march reached Greenwood, the cry of 'black power' competed with and sometimes drowned out more familiar chants of 'Freedom Now.' Militant new organisations emerged, prominent among them the Black Panther Party which was founded in Oakland, California, but which quickly established chapters in many cities. Often these new groups embraced the right of armed self-defence, offering a brand of black nationalism and sometimes black separatism that looked and sounded very different from the nonviolent tactics and integrationist agendas of the early civil rights movement.[10]

As black power gathered momentum, King and other advocates of nonviolent direct action were left groping for a viable strategy by which to challenge persistent prejudice and continued discrimination throughout the US. In particular, King was chastened by his experiences in Chicago in 1966, when he struggled to organise the sort of massive nonviolent protests that had been so successful in the South. Exposure to the full force and violent fury of white racism in Chicago, had given King and his allies clear notice that new tactics were needed to promote an effective campaign against nationwide patterns of racism and discrimination.[11]

King's response to this challenge was to interpret the African American predicament, less in terms of an exclusively black problem and more as part of an intersecting, mutually reinforcing matrix of racial and class-based inequality. Although he consistently resisted the specific terminology of Marxism and roundly rejected the atheism that often accompanied it, King moved towards an analysis of the African American freedom struggle that saw it as part of a global struggle of the oppressed against the triple evils of poverty, racism and imperialism, the last a force that manifested itself most conspicuously in war. This view had much in common with Marxist theory in its emphasis on the divisive, violent and oppressive consequences of un-moderated capitalism.[12] As he explained to the 11th annual conference of the SCLC, just three months before he repeated the same sentiments in Newcastle, what was needed was a fundamental re-evaluation of the values of western society. He insisted that 'the problem of racism, the problem of economic exploitation, and the problem of war are all tied together. These are the triple evils that are interrelated.'[13]

Exorcising these evils, King believed, required some form of peaceful social democratic revolution that would redirect governmental action in more enlightened and progressive directions. He wanted to build an inter-racial alliance of all the working men and women of America, all the marginalised and disadvantaged, in order, as he had put it in an address to the SCLC's 1960 annual conference, to 'Redeem the soul of America.'[14] By 1967, King was convinced that the vehicle for this crusade for racial and economic justice should be a Poor People's Campaign, not a Poor *Black* People's Campaign. This, he explained, was an ambitious effort to 'bring the social change movements through from their early and now inadequate protest phase to a stage of massive, active, nonviolent resistance to the evils of the modern system...Let us not therefore think of our movement as one that seeks to integrate the Negro into all the existing values of American society.' Rather King wanted to recalibrate those values. 'The Movement must address itself to the restructuring of the whole of American Society,' King told SCLC staff at a retreat in Frogmore, South Carolina on November 14, 1966.[15]

This was not quite the radical departure in King's thinking that some at the time assumed, or that many subsequent commentators have claimed. Many years previously, while a doctoral student at Boston University, King had written in 1951 that he believed 'Capitalism has seen its best days.' By 1967 he was openly stating his belief that 'The evils of capitalism are as real as the evils of militarism and evils of racism.'[16]

This public radicalism made him a new collection of enemies to add to those who had always opposed and often threatened him. It alienated some of the white liberals who felt that the civil rights struggle had effectively ended in victory with the passage of the Voting Rights Act in 1965 and the establishment of de jure equality; such people viewed King's continued agitation for de facto equality of opportunity as, at best, wanton troublemaking and, at worst, as dangerously subversive. After April 4, 1967, when King used a speech at the Riverside Church in New York, to make public his longstanding private opposition to America's military involvement in Vietnam, King's anti-war stance had similarly angered many former allies, including President Johnson. Partly as a consequence of his increasingly sour relations with King, Johnson frequently cut King out of White House discussions on racial matters, preferring to deal with Roy Wilkins, chairman of the NAACP. Johnson also allowed the FBI a free hand to extend efforts to spy on, harass, and generally discredit King that had begun under the administration of John F. Kennedy.[17]

Influential sections of the mainstream US media also turned against King, branding him unpatriotic on Vietnam and hinting that only communist ties or sympathies could explain his new preoccupations with capitalism, imperialism and democratic socialism. Even some black commentators and activists, among them Carl T. Rowan and King's long-time friend and key advisor Bayard Rustin, vocally disapproved of King's public opposition to Vietnam: the former as part of a steady stream of attacks on what was characterised as King's new radicalism; the latter because he genuinely felt that it was a mistake to divert energies from the black American struggle into the realm of foreign affairs, particularly if it risked losing the support of those white liberals with whom Rustin thought King should be seeking to forge progressive political alliances.[18]

At the same time, as the FBI tried to undermine the African American freedom struggle and make political capital from King's extramarital dalliances, King himself was engaged in an intense bout of self-scrutiny and doubt. As he struggled to understand the psychological coordinates of his own personality, he guiltily confronted what he referred to as the 'schizophrenia ... within all of us.' On several occasions he made public testimony of his all-too-human failings and brooded on his own sense of unworthiness and failure. 'I make mistakes tactically. I make mistakes morally and get down on my knees and confess it and ask God to forgive me,' he told his Ebenezer congregation in October 1967.[19]

King was under enormous political and personal strain in 1967. He suffered from periodic, but intense, crises of confidence and poor self-esteem during which he struggled to retain his clarity of vision and sense of purpose. Occasionally, he felt so thoroughly overwhelmed by the sheer intractability of the problems he confronted in America that he lurched between an ever more radical vision and simple despair. 'The whole thing will have to be done away with,' he told his friend Rev. D. E. King the day before he flew to England. 'I have found out that all that I have been doing in trying to correct this system in America is in vain.'[20] He was especially frustrated by his inability to harness the energies of young northern blacks, energies which he saw dissipated in the urban violence of the long hot summers of 1966 and 1967. Perhaps most crucially he was increasingly sceptical about his own ability to offer further leadership to the Movement. 'I'm tired now,' he told local ministers in Atlanta, when they called on him to head new demonstrations against continued racial injustice in that city. 'I've been in this thing for thirteen years now and I'm really tired.' People still expected him to have answers but, he confided to his wife Coretta Scott King, he no longer felt that he had any.[21]

In short, King in late 1967 was strategically, emotionally and physically exhausted by his years at the forefront of the freedom struggle. 'It was,' suggested Andrew Young, 'really gettin' him down.'[22] Although the initial plans for the Poor People's Campaign had temporarily rekindled his optimism about the possibilities of effecting significant change, he remained rather depressed by the state of the movement for civil rights and social justice in America and was thoroughly disillusioned by the constant criticism and lack of support for his new social and economic initiatives. White folksinger Joan Baez, a veteran of countless benefit concerts for King and the Movement, overheard him confess in October 1967 'that he just wanted to be a preacher, and he was sick and tired of it all.'[23]

It was in this context of frustration, anxiety and creeping despair at home that recognition of his efforts from abroad assumed a special significance and therapeutic value for King. This had certainly been the case when he was awarded the Nobel Peace Prize in 1964. The announcement of that award had come at another time of personal trial. He was in the St. Joseph Infirmary in Atlanta at the time and, according to Coretta Scott King, 'completely exhausted, tired and empty.' The Prize provided a tremendous lift to King after a disappointing civil rights campaign in St. Augustine, Florida and his loss of face at the 1964 Democratic Convention in Atlantic City, when he was widely criticised for supporting a compromise proposal to seat just two token members of the integrated delegation from the Mississippi Freedom Democratic Party rather than pushing to oust the entire whites-only delegation of Mississippi Democratic Party regulars.[24] King had described the Nobel Prize as 'the foremost of earthly honors' and interpreted it as, in the words of historian David Garrow, 'not simply a personal award, but the most significant endorsement possible of the civil rights struggle.' Moreover, the prize had restored King's appetite for the struggle and reassured him of the importance of his own contribution to it.[25]

The Nobel Peace Prize also encouraged King to take more seriously his role as an international leader engaged in a global fight for human freedom, racial justice and peace. Biographer David Lewis suggests that King's acceptance speech in Oslo featured 'some of the first public words on the subject of world peace, and ... clearly portended further pronouncements on international peace.'[26] King had actually signalled this shift—in truth, the amplification of themes that he had spoken of often—in England, en route to Norway to collect the Prize in December 1964. King had stopped off in London where he spoke before 1,300 people at St. Paul's Cathedral. His international perspective was clear as he spoke of how, 'God is not interested in the freedom of white, black, and yellow men, but in the freedom of the whole human race.' Responding to questions about apartheid in South Africa, King told them, 'More and more I have come to realize that racism is a world problem.'[27]

While in London, Bayard Rustin and local Caribbean Quaker community organiser-activist Marion Glean had arranged for King to meet with representatives of several British immigrant groups. On December 7, many of those representatives heard him give another globally-inflected address at the Westminster City Temple Hall at a meeting sponsored by Christian Action where, in addition to talking extensively about US race relations, he called for a boycott of South African goods to force an end to apartheid. He denounced the 'madness of militarism,' explaining how, 'in a day when Sputniks and explorers are dashing through outer space and guided ballistic missiles are carving highways of death through the stratosphere, no nation can win a war. It is no longer the choice between violence and nonviolence; it is either nonviolence or non-existence.'[28]

At Temple Hall, King also took the opportunity to speak at greater length on the changing face of British race relations at a time of rising immigration by non-white Commonwealth citizens. Foreshadowing some of what he would say in Newcastle less than three years later, King insisted that 'the problem of racial injustice is not limited to any one nation. We know now that this is a problem spreading all over the globe,' before homing in on the British situation and casting America as a cautionary tale:

> And right here in London and right here in England, you know so well that thousands and thousands of colored people are migrating here from many, many lands—from the West Indies, from Pakistan, from India, from Africa. And they have the just right to come to this great land, and they have the just right to expect justice and democracy in this land. And England must be eternally vigilant. For if not, the same kind of ghettos will develop that we have in the Harlems of the United States. The same problems of injustice, the same problems of inequality in jobs will develop. And so I say to you that the challenge before every citizen of goodwill of this nation is to go all out to make democracy a reality for everybody, so that everybody in this land will be able to live together and that all men will be able to live together as brothers.[29]

As he spoke, King got a rude confirmation of just how hard that might be to achieve in an increasingly diverse Britain. Members of the white supremacist League of Empire Loyalists heckled King and shouted 'Keep Britain White' before being evicted by ushers.[30]

Shortly after meeting with King in London, Marion Glean was among those who formed the Campaign Against Racial Discrimination (CARD). A bi-racial umbrella association made up of many organisations, CARD was chaired by West Indian David Pitt, who in 1959 had been the first black British parliamentary candidate when he failed to win a seat for the Hampstead constituency. Pitt subsequently became leader of the Greater London Council and eventually, as Baron Pitt of Hampstead, a Labour Party peer. The Pakistani writer Hamza Alavi served as Vice-Chair. CARD modelled itself closely on American civil rights precedents, although perhaps with more debts to the NAACP's legal and propaganda campaigns for equal rights than to the direct action protests of the SCLC and the Student Non-violent Coordinating Committee (SNCC). Initially focusing on efforts to repeal the 1962 Commonwealth Immigrants Act, which Pitts complained 'makes racialism respectable in Britain. Its inspiration and application is racialist. It makes immigrants second-class citizens,' CARD, like King and the early US civil rights movement that inspired it, also sought to expose and outlaw 'discrimination in housing, employment, advertising, insurance, public places, education, credit facilities, clubs offering public facilities, Government departments and bodies receiving Government grants, subsidies and licences.'[31] Nationally, CARD was notable, in the words of sociologist Kalbir Shukra, as 'the first substantial postwar attempt of black and white activists to intervene in national British politics on the "race question".'[32] It was also responsible for nurturing one of Newcastle's most charismatic and dedicated black activists of the late 1960s and early 1970s, Chris Mullard.

King's appreciation of the global dimensions of the struggles for peace, economic justice and racial equality in which he was engaged intensified over the next few years. 'A Christian movement in an age of revolution cannot allow itself to be limited by geographic boundaries,' he explained in a speech prepared on the eve of a 1965 trip to Europe. 'We must be as concerned about the poor in India as we are about the poor of Indiana,' he urged.[33]

Perhaps King's extraordinary willingness to keep his appointment in Newcastle is best explained in terms of his own burgeoning sense of international responsibility and solidarity as well as a means to bolster his self-esteem and restore some measure of confidence that his efforts were appreciated and valuable at a time of grave personal doubt. Certainly, these twin impulses were apparent in the speech he gave after accepting his degree. As he had done on receipt of the Nobel Peace Prize, King accepted his award from Newcastle as the representative of a much larger social movement. 'In honoring me today,' he explained to those gathered in the King's Hall, 'you not only honor me but you honor the hundreds and thousands of people with whom I have worked and with whom I have been associated in the struggle for racial justice. And so I say thanks, not only for myself but I also thank you for them and I can assure you that this day will remain dear to me as long as the cords of memory shall lengthen.'[34]

King also revealed the personal inspiration and resolve he drew from this international recognition. Again, the sentiments and even the phrasing echoed how he had greeted news of his Nobel accolade in 1964 by declaring that, 'it will give me new courage and determination to carry on in this fight to overcome the evils and injustices in this society.'[35] In Newcastle, he assured his hosts that their honour was of 'inestimable value for the continuance of my humble efforts. And although I cannot in any way say that I am worthy of such a great honor, I can also assure you that you give me renewed courage and vigor to carry on in the struggle to make peace and justice a reality for all men and women all over the world.'[36] Andrew Young felt that this kind of international respect was important, not just to King as an individual, but to the Movement in which he was the most renowned figure. 'He didn't need to fly all the way over there to get recognised by Newcastle, and yet he did,' Young reflected later. 'I think it gave an extra prestige to our movement to have the international support that we had.'[37]

Back in Atlanta, faced by a resumption of hostilities from his many opponents, in January 1968 King finally found time to write, with unusual poignancy, a personal letter of thanks to Vice-Chancellor Bosanquet:

> This is a belated note to say that one is always humbled on the occasion of receiving an honorary degree from such an outstanding University as Newcastle upon Tyne, and, yet, in the course of constant criticism and malignment of one's best efforts, the recognition by an institution of higher learning of the historic significance of one's work in the ministry is a tremendous encouragement, far overshadowing the barbs and arrows from the daily press.[38]

King was slightly mistaken to think that the degree had much to do with his work in the ministry or as a theologian where, in formal terms, his original intellectual contribution, as opposed to his genius for the practical application of a socially engaged theology, was modest.[39] According to Ralph Holland, a member of the Honorary Degrees Committee which had recommended King, a Doctorate of Civil Law, rather than a Doctorate of Divinity or Theology, 'was deemed appropriate as he was certainly regarded as a political rather than a religious leader.'[40]

In formally presenting King for the degree, the University's Public Orator, J. H. Burnett, referred to both aspects of King's career, describing how King had been 'nurtured not only in the tradition of the "Bible Belt" but in the home of a distinguished pastor, a deeply Christian environment where high thinking, eloquent expression and a social conscience were his daily inspiration.' In a smart summary of King's protest methods, Burnett described his 'unique weapon' for social change as 'an amalgam of Christian precepts, the solid rock of the Negro religious traditions, the social and philosophical ideas of [Walter] Rauschenbusch and [Georg] Hegel and the Gandhian technique of non-violence.' He concluded his introduction by asking the Chancellor, 'both as a symbolic gesture and as the highest mark of distinction this University can afford, to confer upon Martin Luther King, Christian pastor and social revolutionary, the degree of Doctor of Civil Law, *honoris causa*.'[41] Ultimately, while nodding respectfully towards the faith that underpinned King's activism, the University was principally acknowledging the international significance of King's social and political achievements. At a time when few in his homeland were doing the same, King had gratefully accepted the invitation to come to Newcastle, a city where his efforts had already attracted a good deal of press and public attention.

CHAPTER THREE

'What Your Movement is Doing is Right':
Reactions to Martin Luther King and the Early Civil Rights Movement on Tyneside

By November 1967, Martin Luther King was well known to the British public. He had already visited Britain, or more precisely London, five times, always attracting extensive media attention. On March 24 1957, when he spent four days in the capital en route to Ghana's independence celebrations, King spent the afternoon with the great Trinidadian Marxist historian-novelist-activist C.L.R James, the West Indian author George Lamming, and David Pitts, destined to become the first Chairman of CARD.[1] He passed through again briefly in early 1959 on his way to India and was back in late October 1961, when he was interviewed by Jonathan Freeman about his upbringing, faith, and civil rights activism on the BBC's prestigious *Face to Face* TV programme. He next visited London on September 22, 1964, in transit to receive an Honorary Doctorate from the Theological School of the Protestant Church in Berlin. In Germany, he once again felt buoyed at a difficult time by the international appreciation of his efforts. 'Your expression of support and confidence is both heartwarming and comforting,' he wrote to his host, Dr. Martin Fischer, 'it gives me new courage and vigor to carry on.' And, of course, he was back in London again in early December 1964, on his way to Oslo to receive the Nobel Prize for Peace.[2]

The British press had covered King's career quite extensively since the Montgomery Bus Boycott first brought the young Baptist minister to prominence as leader of a year-long nonviolent campaign against segregated seating on the city's buses. One of the first in-depth national features on that protest was an article by celebrated journalist-broadcaster Alistair Cooke in the *Guardian*. Cooke, who also reported from Montgomery on one of his weekly BBC radio programmes *Letter from America*, was a regular and popular source of commentary on US politics and culture for British audiences. Although he was generally sympathetic to black aspirations, he was not initially enamoured of direct action protests and rather empathised

with southern whites trying to cope with the gathering threat to white privilege and their cherished way of life. Certainly, in Spring 1956, he badly
misinterpreted Montgomery and grossly underestimated King, who he described as 'bland' and 'smooth' and dismissed as a 'cats-paw' of the NAACP,
the civil rights organisation he mistakenly believed was orchestrating the
boycott. Harvey Lee Moon, NAACP director of public relations, wrote an-
grily to correct what he felt were Cooke's myriad errors of fact and
interpretation, not least with regard to King, to whom Moon felt Cooke
was being supercilious when describing him as 'an educated man.'[3]

Even before Cooke's article appeared in print, his Montgomery-
themed *Letter from America* had encouraged British listeners, who he seems
to have assumed would all be white, to put themselves in the shoes of white
southerners in the face of recent challenges to segregation. 'Suppose that
half the population of Birmingham (England, not Alabama), or Sheffield,
or Brighton or London was coloured. And suppose it had been so for two
or three hundred years. With the coloured people going to their schools and
you going to yours. Would you at once accede to a law going through Parliament that next autumn your children must go to school with coloured
people?' he asked. It was an unsettling if largely rhetorical question. Cooke
knew very well that, just eight years after the SS *Empire Windrush* had
docked at Tilbury carrying the first shipload of migrating British citizens
from the Caribbean, domestic race relations were showing signs of stress,
with the spectre of miscegenation and interracial sex never far from the centre of white British anxieties. 'What a parent thinks of,' Cooke explained in
patriarchal language that casually equated parenthood with men, 'is that his
children will mingle equally, as scholars and playmates, then, later on as
friends and sweethearts, with coloured people.'[4] Listeners were left to imagine what those sweethearts might get up to together. Over the next decade
or so, journalists and politicians of all ideological stripes followed Cooke in
using America as a way to address—and sometimes to try to shape—British
racial attitudes, laws and practices.

After his initial false step, Cooke, like most other British journalists
who regularly covered the early, primarily southern phase of the modern US
freedom struggle, among them Stanley Burch and Don Iddon for the *Daily
Mail* and Richard Scott and Hella Pick at the *Guardian*, came to respect
King's leadership skills, oratorical prowess and enormous personal courage
in the face of almost daily threats to his life. Moreover, the civil rights movement more generally began to get increasing media attention in Britain. By
May 1956, *Crisis*, the journal of the NAACP, reported with a little bit of
journalistic license that 'Recent events in the Southern revolt against public

school desegregation have received almost as much publicity in the English as in the American press.'[5]

Coverage of the southern campaigns for civil and voting rights continued throughout the 1960s, spiking during the dramatic protests in Birmingham, Alabama in Spring 1963 and the March on Washington in August of the same year, and again during the March 1965 Voting Rights campaign in Selma, Alabama. More generally, stories of nonviolent direct action protests and of the violent responses of some diehard segregationists, of legislative battles in Washington, and of voter registration drives during the Mississippi Freedom Summer of 1964 and across the South featured regularly in the British print and electronic news-media, which also gave plenty of exposure to the occasional visits by high profile African American leaders such as King and Malcolm X.[6]

As the decade wore on, especially as major racial disturbances gripped many American cities during the 'Long Hot Summers' of the mid-to-late 1960s, King was increasingly portrayed in Britain as a voice of calm and reason at a time of rising violence and black nationalism. As early as February 1965, in the immediate aftermath of Malcolm X's murder by fellow Black Muslims loyal to Malcolm's estranged mentor Elijah Muhammad, Stanley Burch wrote in the *Daily Mail* of how 'on the non-violent wing of America's 20 million Negroes discipline is painfully maintained under the powerful influence of Dr. Martin Luther King.' Burch contrasted this strand of black protest with 'a violent wing,' of 'competing, wrangling...black extremists who scorn Martin Luther King as a 20th century Uncle Tom, and deride his passive resistance creed as a monstrous joke.'[7] In August 1966, Alistair Cooke presented King and Stokely Carmichael, the new firebrand Chairman of SNCC and populariser of the "black power" slogan, as 'polar opposites of the present Negro strategy. One will not let the white man rest, but will not stone him either; the other means to take arms against a sea of troubles and by chanting 'black power' achieve it.'[8] Over the next eighteen months this British sense of King as a bulwark against black power militancy grew ever stronger.

Those living in the North East of England had access to much of this national coverage of the early civil rights movement and were well aware of King's role within it. For example, King's appearance on *Face to Face* had aired in Newcastle at 10.25pm on Sunday, October 29, 1961.[9] But perhaps what is even more significant in terms of context for King's 1967 visit and local responses to it, was the extent to which the regional press, particularly Newcastle's two major newspapers, the *Journal* and the *Evening Chronicle*, took a keen interest in US race relations, often using them as a kind of diagnostic mirror with which to examine the current state and future prospects for British race relations.

In May 1954, both the Newcastle *Evening Chronicle* and *Sunderland Echo* reported on white resistance to the Supreme Court's historic *Brown vs Topeka Board of Education* decision, which declared racial segregation in public schools unconstitutional.[10] *Brown* overturned the doctrine of 'separate but equal' facilities for the races on which the Jim Crow system of racial apartheid in the US South had rested since the Court's 1896 *Plessy vs Ferguson* ruling had legitimised a legal fiction that saw far more separation than equality. *Brown*, the culmination of years of litigation by the NAACP, was one of the sparks that ignited a dynamic new phase in the long African American freedom struggle. The Montgomery bus boycott was one example of this new urgency and in March 1956, the *Northern Daily Mail* reported Martin Luther King's call for Montgomery's black citizens to continue their 'boycott of the city's buses,' noting King's invocation of the nonviolent tactics Gandhi had used to, in his words, 'topple the British military machinery,' in India. 'We will fight injustice with passive resistance,' King explained, as the local press worked to acquaint North East readers with his methods.[11]

Bus boycotts in Montgomery and elsewhere were among the many indications of a new militancy in the African American freedom struggle. The *Evening Chronicle* closely followed the rising tide of protest in the late 1950s and early 1960s, often focusing on the violence of white resistance to desegregation.[12] For example, the paper tracked the mob action in Little Rock, Arkansas that greeted efforts to admit nine black students to the city's previously all white Central High School in September 1957. It followed Governor Orval Faubus's use of National Guardsmen to preserve segregation, at least until President Dwight D. Eisenhower mobilised federal troops to protect the terrified but determined black children attending the school. Although there was little direct editorialising on the fledgling Movement, there was no doubt where sympathies lay. Tacit support for the stoic black students and nonviolent protestors was coupled with implicit opposition to white segregationists such as Faubus, and to more violent white supremacists such as John Kaspar, whose arrest in Nashville, where he had plotted with the Ku Klux Klan to bomb a school that admitted a black child, was also reported.[13]

A year later, the *Journal* was still following the Little Rock story, reporting the federal government's effort to get a Supreme Court order that would prohibit Faubus from simply closing down Arkansas public schools rather than succumb to what the Governor called 'forcible integration by Negro children.'[14] It was no coincidence that the story appeared next to the paper's coverage of the Nottingham 'Race Riot.' For many this brief but intense outburst of racialised conflict in the East Midlands in late August 1958, along with the Notting Hill riots in London just a few days later, marked the unofficial birth of a 'race problem' in Britain. The Newcastle press reported widely on both 1958 riots. The Archbishop of Canterbury, Dr Geoffrey Fischer, warned of a country 'Divided by Racial Tensions,' as a *Journal* headline put it. Fischer lamented the difficulties of applying 'the Christian belief in the natural dignity and value of every man and woman because they are created in God's image....in a Communist country, in some parts of Africa or in parts of the United States.'[15]

In Spring 1963, dramatic images of protests in Birmingham, Alabama were beamed around the world. Eugene 'Bull' Connor's brutal policing methods, using high-pressure fire-hoses, German Shepherd dogs and mass incarceration against demonstrators, including young children, came to symbolise the ugliness and immorality of white efforts to preserve segregation. In Newcastle, press support for the Movement in general, and for King and his nonviolent methods in particular, soared. When an agreement between civil rights leaders and the City Commission was finally reached in early May, it was celebrated on the front page of the *Journal* with King's declaration that the campaign had 'come to the climax of a long struggle for justice, freedom and human dignity in the city of Birmingham.'[16]

According to Paul Barry, much of the conversation at the informal coffee morning King attended with students in Newcastle involved questions about his 'I Have a Dream' oration at the August 28, 1963 March for Jobs and Freedom in Washington.[17] That event and King's speech had further increased his international, certainly his British, profile. In Newcastle, 'The greatest rally for Negro rights in [American] history' was headline news. And while it was the 'Dream' section at the end of King's speech that quickly captured the public's imagination, the *Journal* immediately recognised that there was an urgent militancy at the heart of an oft-misunderstood speech that was about much more than a prophetic vision of a harmonious interracial future. The paper focused on King's warnings that 'the whirlwinds of revolt,' would consume America if black rights were not secured and legitimate black aspirations not met. America had written 'a bad cheque' to its citizens of colour, King explained, and they had marched to Washington, and would continue to protest across the South and the entire nation, until the US finally met its 'sacred obligations.'[18]

Like the Birmingham campaign and the March on Washington, the series of marches in Selma, Alabama, in March 1965 to protest the continued denial of black voting rights, also garnered widespread coverage on Tyneside. This was perhaps not surprising, given that the North East had a long tradition supporting extensions of the franchise. As we shall see, this was part of a local radical political heritage dating back at least to the 17th century that intersected with powerful anti-slavery and anti-racist movements in the region and provided an important historical context for King's visit. In 1965, the Tyneside press described the savage beatings and teargas assaults dished out to nonviolent black protesters by Alabama state troopers at the Edmund Pettus Bridge on March 8, during what became known as 'Bloody Sunday.' Those shocking images had ricocheted around the world. They revealed the lengths to which some southern segregationists would go, in many cases supported by local law enforcement agencies, to cling on to white power. Although Martin Luther King was not at the 'Bloody Sunday' march, he hurried to Selma to rally support for a second march from Selma to the state capital in Montgomery, home of segregationist icon Governor George Wallace. The proposed march was planned in defiance of a local court ban on further demonstrations. On March 10, the *Journal* reported 'A huge Negro civil rights march…led by Dr. Martin Luther King,' that included 'scores of white clergymen of several faiths.' It explained how this truncated march, later known as 'Turnaround Tuesday,' ended at the edge of the Edmund Pettus Bridge when 'the marchers knelt in prayer,' on the same spot where 'nearly 80 were injured in a charge by state troopers on Sunday.' Unknown at the time and much to the surprise and anger of many of the protestors, King had struck a behind-the-scenes deal with the Alabama authorities that allowed the demonstrators to return to their churches and homes unmolested if they abandoned the plan to continue to Montgomery.[19]

This, however, was far from the end of matters and the Newcastle papers stuck with the Selma story. The next day, the *Journal* reported King's call for still more national support and Andrew Young's pledge to continue defying court bans on peaceful demonstrations against a profound injustice. Young told protesters 'We are not going to pay any attention to that.' In an example of how editors could juxtapose particular stories to reinforce their sometimes unstated editorial position, the Selma report appeared next to a story about US Army officers from the 547th Engineers Battalion stationed at Darmstadt in West Germany, who attended a fancy dress party dressed as members of the Ku Klux Klan, complete with a burning cross. The paper gave full reign to the concerns of the African American officers and soldiers on the base about such inflammatory behaviour. 'Was this to make us afraid? It doesn't make me afraid,' insisted one incredulous but uncowed solider, Alonze Galloway, who filed an official complaint. 'I want some answers,' he fumed.[20]

One of those who heeded King's call to come to Selma for a third attempt to march to Montgomery was Rev. James Reeb. A northern white Unitarian minister, Reeb and two of his fellow clergymen were brutally beaten by segregationists. The local press respectfully followed Reeb's battle for life, but on March 12, the *Chronicle* sombrely reported that 'Mr. Reeb was the tenth person to die in racial violence in this Deep South state since 1962.'[21] Four days later, the paper gave front page status and extensive internal coverage to President Johnson's call for Congress to support a comprehensive Voting Rights Bill that eventually became the 1965 Voting Rights Act.[22] Later it gave similar prominence to Johnson's executive order to federalise the National Guard to protect the civil rights activists who, after one violently repelled march and one aborted march, were finally able to make their way across the Edmund Pettus Bridge and proceed to Montgomery.[23] Tyneside readers could follow the progress of the five-day trek across Alabama and learn about King's rationale for the protest, which, he explained, was 'to make it clear that we are determined to make brotherhood a reality for all men.'[24]

Noble though that aim was, the Newcastle press reported a series of foiled attempts to bomb or otherwise disrupt the Selma to Montgomery march which reminded readers that the battle for racial justice was fraught with danger and that its outcome remained uncertain. That uncertainty and the fragile, piecemeal nature of progress in the freedom struggle became all too clear when the marchers finally reached Montgomery. On March 26, 1965, the front page of the *Journal* celebrated 'the most massive civil rights demonstration in the racial history of America's South.' The next day, the headlines were all about the murder of Viola Luizzo, a Detroit 'mother of five,' who had come to Alabama to support the protests and was killed by Klansmen while ferrying marchers back to Selma.[25] The local press also covered President Johnson's condemnation of the Klan and the launch of a federal enquiry into its activities in the wake of this latest outrage.[26]

The cumulative effect of local and national print and electronic media coverage of the US civil rights movement in Britain was to make it part of the 1960s zeitgeist and Martin Luther King a household name. Yet extensive media coverage was only one possible mechanism whereby Tynesiders could become informed about and interested in American race relations. An intriguing insight into how that process worked for at least some in the region comes from one of Newcastle's most famous cultural exports during the decade: The Animals rhythm and blues group.

Lead singer Eric Burdon was born in Walker, grandson of the groundsman at the home ground of Newcastle United Football Club, St. James's Park. Growing up, he remembered that 'I was obsessed with race. In South Shields...there is a mosque where Muhammad Ali was married into the Muslim faith—a lot of people don't know that. There was a contingent of Africans living there, East Africans mostly.'[27] When asked about the origins of his interest in race and an unusual sensitivity, for somebody of his generation living in an overwhelmingly white city, to matters of racial injustice, Burdon has given a number of overlapping explanations. In one response, he jokes that it all stemmed from the fact that some of his relatives were coal miners: 'They went to work in the morning white and came back at night black, but they were the same people underneath. I loved them in the morning and I still loved them in the evening. I know it sounds stupid, but I really believe that helped me to see past colour without prejudice.'[28]

A second response stressed Burdon's personal relationships with people of African descent in Newcastle. He admitted that his 'first serious love affair was with an African girl named Doreen.' In the early 1960s, Doreen Caulker was, according to Animals drummer John Steel, 'Eric's big love.' Burdon even celebrated her on record. 'For Miss Caulker' is a smouldering midnight blues featuring some of keyboard player Alan Price's most sumptuous piano. According to Burdon, he 'developed an early reputation for having a lot of black friends, particularly displaced Africans in Newcastle, two of whom were members of the first band I was in, the Pagans.'[29] Personal exposure to some of the abuse that Caulker and his other African friends had to endure, and which he also suffered for dating across racial lines, doubtless sensitised Burdon to the irrational spitefulness of racism.

Burdon quickly learned how prejudices could cluster around ethnic and religious, as well as racial, identities. At school he came across children who had been evacuated from the East End of London during World War Two to the relative safety of Newcastle. They were moved, not simply to escape the Blitz, but also 'because of their accents, people were prejudiced against them. They were outsiders, and one of them happened to be a Jewish German and just because she was German, everyone thought 'Nazi, Nazi, Nazi.' They didn't understand she was a victim of the Nazis.' These early formative experiences convinced Burdon that ignorance was at the heart of intolerance and discrimination. He resolved to learn more about race and race relations. In the absence of 'a university of race….a government department where people can learn racial harmony,' Burdon began to pay attention to various unfolding colonial struggles for independence, recognising the international dimensions of racialised oppression.[30] Indeed, a third factor contributing to Burdon's relatively enlightened racial views in the late 1950s and early 1960s was his teenage experience in Paris with John Steel and some other friends at the time of the Algerian revolution against French rule. 'Snatch squads would come on the buses and grab ahold of Algerian bus conductors and drag them off. It was the real thing – a racial nightmare I knew existed coming to life.'[31]

A fourth and critical influence on Burdon's understanding of race, and especially of the racial situation in the US, came through his love of African American music. Blues and rhythm and blues were crucial influences on the rock and roll and skiffle revolutions that swept Britain in the mid-to-late 1950s. For Burdon and many of his music-obsessed peers, particularly those connected with the British blues revival, black music seemed to provide a direct window onto the African American experience and encouraged some of them to find out more about it.[32]

Writing in 1966 for the African American magazine *Ebony*, Burdon explained how, for his generation of music-loving Geordies, 'People like [Chuck] Berry, [Ray] Charles and [Bo] Diddley did more for the Negro race outside the United States than anybody.' Just a few years previously, Burdon explained 'we were either too young or didn't want to know about the Negroes' troubles in America,' but now, thanks to his musical education, he was someone who 'think(s) about the race situation in America.' Adding Sonny Boy Williamson, Nina Simone, B.B. King, and John Lee Hooker to his list of inspirational artists, Burdon believed that 'If it hadn't been for them I wouldn't have been interested in this country in the first place. I started collecting things—photographs newspaper articles, magazine clippings—to find out why Negroes were being mistreated and often brutally so.'[33]

Eric Burdon's personal experiences and musical enthusiasms fused with a growing awareness of the contemporary African American freedom struggle and a burgeoning admiration for Martin Luther King that was stoked by national and local press coverage. When a journalist from *Melody Maker* spoke to the singer shortly after the Animals' 'House of the Rising Sun' climbed to the top of the British singles charts in the summer of 1964, he reported that Burdon was 'Intensely interested in America's Negro Civil Rights Bill, and keeps a scrapbook of cuttings on the subject.' In fact, he had started that scrapbook years before, about the same time that he wrote 'Blues' across an art journal in his own blood.[34] A similar interest in US race relations, again initially a by-product of their love of African American music, may also explain why three of the Animals—Burdon, Price, and bassist Chas Chandler—chose 'bigotry' as one of their major dislikes in a *New Musical Express* profile at a time when most pop stars were answering similar questions about their pet hates with 'having my photo taken' or 'Brussel sprouts.'[35]

There has never been any simple or necessary correlation between white love of black music and progressive racial attitudes on either side of the Atlantic. This was something which became abundantly clear to the Animals while on tour in Mobile, Alabama, in 1965. Burdon struck up a conversation with a young white girl who had asked him for an autograph. Soul star Otis Redding had played the same venue the previous evening and both singer and fan agreed that Redding's version of 'My Girl' was one of their favourite records of the moment. Burdon asked the girl if she had been to Redding's concert. 'Did I see him?' she replied, incredulously. 'You got to be joking, man, the place was full of niggers.'[36] They learned another lesson about what the Movement was up against in Meridian, Mississippi, when the band's black roadie, Sonny, was denied entry to their motel. Chas Chandler apparently pointed out that the passage of the 1964 Civil Rights Act had outlawed this kind of discrimination—again suggesting both an interest in and understanding of the state of the freedom struggle—but to no avail. Custom and white power, not federal law, continued to dominate the realities of Mississippi race relations and Sonny was forced to sleep in an annexe. 'The next day,' according to Burdon, 'we found the swimming pool was filled with redneck families. All it took was for Sonny to dive in and the place cleared, leaving it for us alone.'[37]

If the experiences of an international pop star can hardly be taken as wholly representative, the kinds of information about Martin Luther King and the civil rights struggle to which Burdon and his bandmates had access while growing up were widely available across the region—and they appear to have had an impact. In early August 1965, a few months after Selma and just as the Voting Rights Act became law, Margaret Blenkinsop, 'a 15½ year old white school girl' from Blyth, a dozen miles up the North Sea coast from Newcastle, wrote an extraordinary letter to King. Blenkinsop told King that 'I really believe that what your movement is doing is right' and that if she 'could help in some small way I would feel honoured.' She then confessed that 'As I am still at school I don't have much time or money but I would be glad to give you some of what I have.'[38]

Meanwhile, among the student body at Newcastle University, King's sonorous voice had become 'instantly recognisable,' according to Brian Lishman, one of those who attended the coffee morning with King.[39] At that meeting, students asked questions, not only about the 'I Have a Dream' speech, but also about efforts to elect black political candidates and the meaning of "black power." This was a concept with which King actually had a good deal of sympathy in so far as it was directed at securing greater black political, cultural and economic power. Yet he disliked the slogan itself, mainly on the grounds that it was too easy to caricature as anti-white, rather than a pro-black, although he also had problems with how some black power advocates rejected nonviolence and embraced armed self-defence. Sharing his conviction that militants such as Stokely Carmichael and H. Rap Brown were 'products of the race problem, not the cause of it,' King bluntly told the students, 'I feel that the doctrine of black supremacy is as evil and dangerous as the doctrine of white supremacy.'[40] The range of topics discussed over coffee in Newcastle indicated keen student interest in and considerable knowledge of the African American freedom struggle. In the impromptu speech he gave at the conclusion of the special congregation arranged in his honour, King would stress the connections and parallels between that struggle and recent developments in British race relations.

CHAPTER FOUR

'We Do Not Have a Copy':
Martin Luther King's Lost Newcastle Speech

That Martin Luther King visited Newcastle was mainly due to the vision of Charles Bosanquet and the persistence of Ernest Bettenson, coupled with the fact that the University's invitation came at very particular moment in both the African American freedom struggle and in King's public and private life. That he spoke in the King's Hall at the end of the degree ceremony was almost entirely due to the charm and diplomatic skills of Vice-Chancellor Bosanquet, coupled with King's basic decency and genuine gratitude to the University. It was certainly something of a coup, since all the correspondence in the preparations for the visit had indicated that he would not speak. 'We are assuming that Dr. King will not be expected to speak when he receives the honorary degree,' wrote Dora McDonald in late September 1967. Bosanquet wrote directly to King on October 3, confirming that, 'we would not expect you to speak when you receive the honorary degree,' although he tentatively added that, 'if on the other hand you would like to say anything to the assembled company (either after the congregation or after lunch), this would greatly please all of us. But I impress on you that this in entirely for you to decide.'[1]

As November 13 approached, however, the Vice-Chancellor predictably found himself inundated with requests from various individuals and groups within the University to be allowed to meet with, or at least to hear, King. Rev. B. Ingliss-Evans, the University's Baptist chaplain, asked if a personal audience might be possible, while Alan Booth, the Convenor of Debates in the Union Society, asked if King's 'schedule would allow for him to address the students in the University' in addition to attending the small informal coffee morning. R. H. Pain of the Department of Biochemistry spoke for many when he wrote that, 'it would be a pity for the University to lose the opportunity of hearing him speak to as large an audience as possible,' and suggested the University's St. Thomas's Church at the Haymarket as a suitable venue.[2]

Bosanquet responded to all these requests in much the same manner. He politely pointed out that King's visit was to be very short and that, 'It is quite impossible to arrange for any other public meeting to be held, and in any case, it was a condition of his coming that he should not be involved in speech making.'³ Yet Bosanquet clearly felt obliged to try to persuade King to say something to the University. In his reply to Dr. Pain, the Vice-Chancellor explained that he had written to King, 'to tell him that a large body of staff and students want to hear him, and to ask him whether he would be willing to speak for a few minutes at the conclusion of the Congregation.' He admitted that he would not know if King was willing to address the King's Hall audience until the two men actually met in Newcastle just a few hours before the ceremony.⁴

Bosanquet's letter to King was waiting for him at the London Hilton Hotel on Sunday, November 12. 'You asked me earlier whether you would be expected to give any address and I replied that in view of the pressure upon you we would not ask you to do this,' Bosanquet wrote. 'But I want to leave you in no doubt that there are a large number of our Faculty and our student body who would wish both to show their support for you by their presence and to receive a message from you. If you would be willing to do this, the opportunity would be at the end of the Congregation but if you would prefer to say nothing, all of us would entirely understand.'⁵

Courted by such a tactful invitation, it is hard to imagine King refusing. But Bosanquet certainly did not presume that he would consent. Thus, as the Vice-Chancellor admitted in his *Annual Report*, published after King's assassination, the University had made no provision to record the events. 'It is a matter of profound regret,' Bosanquet wrote, 'that because we did not expect him to speak no tape recording of his address was made. The terrible tragedy of 4ᵗʰ April in Memphis has greatly increased our sadness that we have only photographs and our memories of that moving scene in the King's Hall.'⁶ For the next twenty-five years, Newcastle University responded to enquiries about King's visit with the information that, 'he made an unprepared speech and unfortunately we do not have a copy.' Anyone hoping to find more information was advised to 'contact *The Guardian* which carried a report of his address.'⁷

In fact, although it had slipped from institutional and popular memory, King's speech had been filmed by the same Tyne Tees Television crew that George Howe had been at such pains to accommodate in November 1967. Clues that the speech might have been recorded were not only peppered across Howe's checklists and briefing papers, but were also to be found in some of the photographs taken on November 13. Some show what appears to be a reporter with a microphone and bundles of cables leading to a clunky reel-to-reel tape recorder hovering next to King as he added his signature to the Honorary Degrees Book. Those images indicated the presence of staff from television or radio, alongside print journalists. In 1992, while searching for more photographs of the occasion in the University's audio-visual collection, housed at that time in the Medical School, I found 16mm film of the events in the King's Hall. The 9.50 minute film was spliced to a separate soundtrack tape and then transferred to video. It contained a substantial portion, roughly one third, of King's speech, a short clip of the Academic Procession into the Hall, and part of the speech by J.H. Burnett, the Public Orator, as he formally recommended King for his Honorary Doctorate. This fragment appears to have been a remnant of the original footage of King's speech, some of which aired locally on the Tyne Tees *6.05* newsmagazine show on the evening of his visit.[8]

As all historians appreciate, the past is never static; history is never truly over and there are always new perspectives to apply to old topics; always more research to do and more evidence to unearth that offer new insights into an unstable past. And so it was in 2015 that additional, probably unbroadcast, film from King's visit came to light. This tiny fragment, just 1.48 minutes long, shows King seated in what appears to be an empty classroom in Newcastle University's Armstrong Building being asked his opinions on the causes of the escalating urban violence in the US and whether there were any lessons Britain could learn from the American situation. Another noteworthy feature of this new discovery was the identity of his interviewer. Clyde Alleyne's presence adds another fascinating layer to the whole story of King's visit.[9] In Spring 1967, Alleyne had become the first regular black television news reporter in the nation, when he was hired to co-host Tyne Tees's *6.05*. Moreover, news of the former Trinidad and Tobago radio announcer's breakthrough appointment had even made the African American press. In May 1967, *Jet* magazine hailed Alleyne as 'England's first Negro television announcer.'[10]

The *Jet* story was another example of how news and ideas about race and race relations were rapidly relayed across the Atlantic, especially after the launch of the Telstar, the world's first telecommunications satellite, in 1962. Although the direction of that flow was largely from the US to Britain, it was not one-way traffic. Whether viewed positively (as with Alleyne's appointment) or negatively (as when the African American press bemoaned racial discrimination in British unions and employment practices, reported on Klan and Klan-like activity, or compared the Nottingham and Notting Hill race riots to events in Little Rock) developments in British race relations were regularly covered in the American, especially the African American, press. Moreover, American civil rights leaders such as King and Malcolm X were compelled by their experiences in Britain—and elsewhere beyond the US—to refine their understandings of how race and racial oppression worked in a global context. Both men, at the premature ends of their lives, arrived at an analysis of racism that down-played the exceptionalism of the American situation and linked it to the workings of modern global capitalism and the operation of various kinds of colonial and neo-colonial power that were often maintained through a combination of economic and military force. Although there remained fundamental differences between the two men, not least around religion, the role of whites in the African American freedom struggle, and nonviolence versus armed self-defence strategies, in the final year of their respective lives both men embraced broadly international socialist solutions to the problems of war and social, economic and racial injustice.[11] In Martin Luther King's case, many of these ideas were evident in what he had to say during his trip to Newcastle.

King's speech at the end of the Congregation demonstrated his superb technique as a public orator. He stood behind a simple lectern, resplendent in his scarlet academic robes, flashed with white silk sleeves and facings. On his head he wore a soft black velvet square cap, topped with a white tuft. One hand was thrust into his trouser pocket, but occasionally it emerged to join the other hand in making gentle emphatic gestures, or to move across the face of the lectern, as if he were tracing the outline of a written text. That text was actually lodged in his memory.

King expertly quilted together a speech from his own extensive back-catalogue of stock rhetorical phrases, occasionally internationalising themes he had previously dealt with principally in American terms and folding in timely remarks on British race relations. The result was something uniquely tailored to the occasion. It was a masterpiece of improvisation, recycling, and responsiveness that made good use of both his training as a Baptist minister and more than a decade as a civil rights leader well-used to making unscripted comments. Delivered in his distinctive, deeply resonant voice, there was a contemplative, measured, almost sombre, quality to the speech. Knowing just how exhausted he was and the gruelling journey he had made to get to Newcastle, it is difficult not to detect signs of physical and emotional fatigue in the surviving footage. Yet, as his speech gathers momentum, King's words seem to transcend this weariness. As the *Courier* student newspaper reported, he captivated a hushed King's Hall 'for over half an hour with a magnificent speech, delivered in the clear, relaxed, yet fervent tones of a master orator.'[12]

Substantively, King said little at Newcastle that he had not said or written elsewhere. A partial exception were his comments on the racial situation in Britain which, not surprisingly, seem to have been the portions of his speech selected by Tyne Tees for broadcast on *6.05* and which were, there-fore, cut from the original film of the speech and are, at present, lost to us. Fortunately, some of what he had to say about British race relations and its parallels with and divergences from the American situation can be recon-structed from the accounts of print journalists and deduced from the surviving fragment of his conversation with Clyde Alleyne.

In the body of his Newcastle speech, King redeployed language and invoked themes that he had used many times before. For example, he drew nervous laughter in the King's Hall from his quip that, 'Well, it may be true that morality cannot be legislated but behaviour can be regulated. It may be true that the law cannot change the heart but it can restrain the heartless. It may be true that the law cannot make a man love me but it can restrain him from lynching me; and I think that is pretty important also!' That line was an old favourite. It had played equally well with British audiences in Lon-don's City Temple Hall on December 7, 1964, when he explained his opposition to those, such as the recently defeated Republican presidential candidate and states' rights champion Barry Goldwater, 'who believe that legislation has no place' in the quest for civil rights and racial equality.[13] This was not the first outing for a phrase that King had carefully filed away in his rhetorical playbook years before. He had written much the same thing in his 1957 article 'Facing the Challenge of a New Age,' for the journal *Phylon* and said virtually the same thing in a June 1962 Commencement Address at Lincoln University in Pennsylvania, and again at Cornell Col-lege, in Mount Vernon, Iowa, four months later.[14]

Notwithstanding the major court victories and legislative triumphs of the 1950s and 1960s, King was eager to impress that the struggle for racial and social justice in America was far from over. His experiences had shown that converting statutory rights into actual rights and equal opportunity of-ten required mass protest. 'Only when the people themselves begin to act are [they] able to transform a law which is on thin paper into thick action,' he told SCLC staff at a retreat in Frogmore, South Carolina, in November 1966. For all their successes in destroying Jim Crow laws in the South, King lamented that 'these legislative and judicial victories did very little to im-prove the lot of millions of Negroes in the teeming ghettoes of the North'; these 'were at best surface changes'—a necessary preface to the even tougher battle for the more fundamental changes that would finally slay what King called the 'monster of racism.'[15] It was with a similar sense of just how far was left to go on the journey to freedom and justice, rather than of how far African Americans had travelled, that King told his Newcastle audience that the plant of freedom was 'still only a bud, not a flower.'[16] Three months earlier, in the aftermath of major race riots in Detroit, King had told the Annual Meeting of the SCLC that, 'The deep rumbling of discontent in our cities is indicative of the fact that the plant of freedom has grown only a bud and not yet a flower.'[17]

Many other fragments of earlier essays and speeches re-surfaced in King's Newcastle speech, either verbatim or in close paraphrase. At the Frogmore retreat, King had spoken of how black and white destinies were bound closely together at least in part to distance himself and his avowedly integrationist organisation from the separatism of some black power advocates. 'There is no separate Black path to power and fulfilment that does not intersect with white roots (sic). And there is no separate White path to power and fulfilment short of social disaster that does not share that power with Black aspirations to freedom and human dignity,' he told his SCLC colleagues. Just one day short of a year later, he repeated virtually the same mantra in the King's Hall. 'There can be no separate black path to power and fulfilment that does not intersect white routes and there can be no separate white path to power and fulfilment short of social disaster that does not recognize the necessity of sharing that power with coloured aspirations for freedom and human dignity.'[18] Yet the context changed the meaning, or at least made it more ambiguous, more complex, even as the words remained much the same. In Britain, notwithstanding the rise of black power sentiment among some minority leaders and organisations, the main target for such Jeremiads was not would-be black separatists, but those British whites who refused to respect minority rights and ambitions.

At another point in his Frogmore speech, King had slipped into philosophical mode to dismiss the 'empirical' foundations for pervasive notions of black inferiority. He argued that 'racism is at bottom based on an ontological affirmation – the affirmation that the very being of a people is inferior.' In Newcastle, he similarly denounced the 'myth of the inferior race…the tragedy of racism is that it is based not on an empirical generalisation but on an ontological affirmation. It is the idea that the very being of a people is inferior.' He declined, however, to add the chilling observation he had shared at Frogmore that 'the ultimate logic of racism is genocide.'[19]

Most crucially, in Newcastle King drew attention to what was, by late 1967, a familiar theme in much of his public speaking and writing: the 'three urgent and indeed great problems that we face not only in the United States of America but all over the world today ... the problem of racism, the problem of poverty and the problem of war.' According to the *Courier*, in his speech King had 'illustrated his themes by incident (sic) from his own life—the prejudice he had found in America, the poverty in India, and the world-wide threat of a nuclear holocaust.'[20] King had been yoking together these elements at least since the Frogmore retreat of November 1966, although there were some subtle shifts in emphasis and vocabulary over the year. At Frogmore, for example, he had explained that 'There is (sic) three basic evils in America: the evil of racism, the evil of excessive materialism, the evil of militarism.' While 'war' and 'militarism' were used fairly interchangeably by King during this period, the switch from a critique of rampant materialism to an indictment of poverty was perhaps more significant. It represented, at least in part, a move from a subjective moral judgement on consumer culture to a more hard-nosed, empirically grounded assessment of one of its tragic correlates: the poverty that flourished amid plenty. An obvious factor in this subtle change of language and emphasis was that by November 1967 King was immersed in planning for the Poor People's Campaign, which by definition prioritised poverty.[21]

It is also worth pondering King's preference in Newcastle for 'problems' over 'evils' to characterise the triumvirate of racism, poverty and war. In other expressions of similar ideas he tended to prefer the more dramatic, emotive, somehow less clinical word 'evils.' For example, in a speech to the Atlanta Hungry Club six months earlier, another address which, like the one from Frogmore, he seems to have intuitively drawn on in Newcastle, King had also excoriated 'the continued existence in the world of three major evils—the evil of racism, the evil of poverty and the evil of war' as 'America's Chief Moral Dilemma.'[22] Maybe the change reflected King's sensitivity to the more secular nature of British society: he may have felt 'evils' carried with it the suggestion of sins before God, rather than man-made and man-judged wickedness and was, therefore, less appropriate for a British audience.

As at Frogmore, the Hungry Club and elsewhere, so in Newcastle, one of King's goals was to emphasise how racism and poverty were inextricably linked to war in an increasingly avaricious, competitive and under-regulated global economy. After a protracted public silence on Vietnam, the last of those themes, war, had become an increasingly pressing issue for King. He first spoke out publicly against US involvement in South East Asia at a rally in Chicago on March 25, 1967 and again, more famously, in his speech at New York's Riverside Church on April 4, 1967. Although not an absolute pacifist, in the sense that he acknowledged the right of self-defence and believed there was such a thing as a 'just war', King had become a passionate advocate and courageous practitioner of nonviolence who was staunchly against American intervention in Vietnam and implacably opposed to the nuclear weapons that cast such a terrifying shadow over the Cold War world. In December 1957, he had written in *Ebony* magazine that, 'I definitely feel that the development and use of nuclear weapons should be banned. It cannot be disputed that a full-scale nuclear war would be utterly catastrophic.' He was convinced that 'the principal objective of all nations must be the total abolition of war. War must be finally eliminated or the whole of mankind will be plunged into the abyss of annihilation.'[23]

Such beliefs had long linked King to international peace activists, including those in Britain's Campaign for Nuclear Disarmament (CND). One of the co-founders of CND, Canon John Collins of St. Paul's Cathedral, had unsuccessfully tried to get King to participate in a four-day mass march from Aldermaston, the site of Britain's Atomic Weapons Establishment, to London, scheduled for Easter 1964 and 'modelled on the Washington Civil Rights March.' Knowing of King's abhorrence of nuclear weapons and rejection of war more generally, Collins believed that his presence 'would give a great boost to the Peace Movement in Britain.'[24]

In the Spring of 1967, as plans for King's visit to Newcastle were coming together and America sunk ever deeper into the unwinnable quagmire of Vietnam, Peggy Duff, another leading British peace and CND activist, tried unsuccessfully to lure King to a conference on the war being organised by the International Conference for Disarmament and Peace (ICDP), of which she was General Secretary, scheduled for later that summer in Stockholm.[25] She also wrote inviting him to an event planned by a coalition of Danish peace activists in Copenhagen on July 4, 1967.[26] Duff had met King in London in December 1964 and played a role in arranging some of his engagements on that visit. Perhaps it was this personal connection that explains why he took time to call Duff about the proposed 1967 European events and arranged to meet her in San Francisco in late May, when Duff was visiting America.[27] Although King was unable to attend any of the events she initially proffered, Duff was apparently encouraged by their face-to-face meeting and continued to write to King on behalf of the ICDP. She certainly saw his forthcoming trip to Newcastle, which he apparently discussed with her in San Francisco, as an opportunity. On September 13, she wrote to ask if King could add an extra day to his trip and visit West German peace activists. She added that 'the ICDP would itself very much appreciate the opportunity to organise a meeting for you in London while you are here.'[28]

Although his November 1967 schedule was too tight to shoehorn in any other events, it was clear that King's credentials as a campaigner for peace and against nuclear weapons were well recognised overseas. Talking briefly to the press in Newcastle after the degree ceremony, King reiterated his opposition to American involvement in Vietnam and his fear that the conflict could escalate into a nuclear war 'which can destroy millions of people and everything we know as civilization.' King called on President Lyndon Johnson to admit that the whole misadventure was a terrible mistake.[29]

King would have found a sympathetic audience for this message on the University campus. In October 1965, the Students' Union debated the motion, 'America should get out of Vietnam now.' The motion was narrowly defeated, primarily on the grounds that it was impractical to demand US withdrawal as a precondition for peace negotiations, but there was widespread criticism of the 'morality of America's action.' A month later the *Courier* reported that 'one of the most enthusiastic forms of protest by students in recent years has been that involving nuclear disarmament.' Among a relatively conservative student body, the Vietnam War and nuclear weapons were major causes for concern by the time King arrived in Newcastle to condemn both.[30] Indeed, across the city and region, there were lively branches of CND, many of them involving people who needed little persuading that somehow racial oppression, economic inequality and militarism were inextricably tied together. 'I was a serious and politically aware youngster, involved in the movements of the time, including the Campaign for Nuclear Disarmament, the Young Socialists and the Anti-Apartheid Movement,' remembered Fiona Clarke.[31]

Speaking to the Hungry Club in Atlanta in May 1967, King had referred to racial injustice as 'still the Negro's burden and America's shame.' Tweaking the language in Newcastle, King deftly internationalised his basic point, describing racism as 'still the colored man's burden and the white man's shame.' He also ended his speech in Newcastle, just as he had done at the Hungry Club, and as he did on many other occasions, with a favourite quote from the Old Testament prophet Amos and his stirring vision of 'the day when all over the world justice will roll down like waters and righteousness like a mighty stream.'[32]

For many who heard King speak in Newcastle, it was a profoundly moving experience. Dorothy Booth, for example, remembered 'being quite spellbound by his speech,' while Vice-Chancellor Bosanquet described it as 'an unprepared but unforgettable address.' Ken Jack, Professor of Chemistry at the University and a member of the Honorary Degree Committee, clearly appreciated the significance of the award in the context of King's domestic tribulations. 'In a time of great difficulty and stress for him, I was very pleased that the University was courageous enough to honour him.'[33]

Local pleasure at the award was almost universal. The only documented expression of disapproval was a bizarre letter advising that, in the light of the FBI's and, by extension, the US government's hostility towards King, the decision to honour him would effectively prevent any Newcastle graduates ever finding employment in America. 'One cannot slap the face metaphorically of the FBI and get away with it,' Edwin Fenwick warned in a letter to the Vice-Chancellor. Although the extent of the Bureau's surveillance and harassment of King and the Movement was not public knowledge at the time, the British press had reported FBI Director J. Edgar Hoover's characterisation of King as 'the most notorious liar in the country,' shortly after King's nomination for the Nobel Peace Prize. Again, it is clear that King's travails in America were no secret to North East observers.[34] Unfazed, Bosanquet wrote back, archly thanking Fenwick for his 'original thoughts about the possible consequences of the action of this University in conferring the honorary degree of DCL upon Dr. Martin Luther King,' and pointedly adding that 'this action has given very great satisfaction to many citizens of the United States which remains a free country.'[35]

Looking back after nearly fifty years, another of those in attendance on the day, Peter H. Woodhead, explained the enduring power of King's speech, particularly in its recognition of the intersecting problems of racism, poverty and war: 'What an analysis, and what foresight, for these words might have been spoken yesterday, and yet right true across the world today. Did he die in vain? I hope not, as his inspiration still lives on, in me for one.'[36] Meredyth Bell (née Patton), the Deputy President of the Students' Representative Council, had met with King over coffee and been deeply impressed by both his presence and his humility—and by the lovely mohair suits King and Young wore. 'I don't think he was a terribly tall man,' she recalled, 'but he seemed it…he seemed to me quite a force to be reckoned with. Yet when you spoke with him he was a very gentle man.' King, Bell explained, had the rare ability to make everyone he spoke to seem as if they were the sole focus of his attention. In the King's Hall, however, as he eased into his 'awesome' speech, King seemed 'like a different person.' Bell was particularly struck by the richness of King's language, especially when he concluded his remarks with a prophetic vision of transforming 'the jangling discords of our nation, and of all the nations of the world, into a beautiful symphony of brotherhood.' As she remembered, 'Because he spoke slowly and meaningfully, you hung on every word. And as his speech developed he had the entire audience rapt.' Moreover, few could miss the central message.

'He wanted the end of poverty, the end of war, and the end of racism. That was what his speech was about,' remembered Bell.[37]

Paul Barry, the *Courier* photographer who took some of the best informal images of the day, was similarly in awe of and inspired by King's speech. 'When he did the ceremony and gave his speech,' Barry remembered, 'the atmosphere was electric…He had a sort of slow manner; he was not delivering his words hurriedly, but he put some sort of meaning into every syllable.' Already interested in the US civil rights movement and CND, Barry responded immediately to King's call 'for all men of good will to work passionately and unrelentingly to get rid of racial injustice, whether it exists in the United States of America, whether it exists in England, or whether it exists in South Africa, wherever it is alive it must be defeated.' Barry joined the campus anti-apartheid movement which sought to end sporting links between the University's rugby team and those at South African universities. When they failed to halt a proposed tour by South African teams, Barry was among a small but dedicated group of demonstrators from Newcastle and Durham Universities who protested at and temporarily disrupted the first match against Orange Free State University.[38] Half a century later, King's words in Newcastle retain their analytical bite—who would argue that racism, poverty and war are not still among the greatest challenges the world faces?—and their inspirational and emotional power. Moreover, that power, doubtless intensified by knowledge that this was the last public address King gave outside of North America and that not six months later he would be felled by an assassin's bullet in Memphis, transcends the boundaries of time and place. In other words, it is not just a legitimate regional pride that makes this such an enduring statement of King's vision of a pathway to a fairer, more compassionate and peaceful world. 'You can tell the occasion meant a great deal to him and you can see he was exhausted. You could hear it in his voice,' commented Kasim Reed, the Mayor of Atlanta, when shown film of King's recovered Newcastle speech by BBC journalist Murphy Cobbing in 2014. 'If you are an excellent orator—and I think he was one of the very best that ever lived—then the occasion will change you and it clearly changed that speech and made it special.' Other Americans who saw the footage were similarly moved. 'It was vintage Martin Luther King Junior—riveting, eloquent and penetrating,' purred Rev. Raphael Warnock, one of King's successors as Pastor of Ebenezer Baptist Church in Atlanta. 'One of the things that strikes me is the way his words are so incredibly relevant all of these years later,' Warnock continued. 'Here's a man who had a schedule busier than many heads of state and I think it was important for him even in the midst of a dogged schedule to make his way across the pond to help the people in that audience, to raise their consciousness around those issues so the reverberations of the movement would continue.'[39]

And yet, while King's Newcastle speech maintains its power to move and motivate, to inform and inspire across oceans and generations, it was very much a product of its time and many of its most significant contemporary resonances were certainly a function of place. In other words, to understand better the full import of King's words and the deeper historic significances of his visit to Newcastle we need to go back, not just to 1967 and a particularly volatile moment in the history of British race relations, but much further back into the history of North East race relations, to the story of the region's interest in and connections to the African American freedom struggle, and to related histories of political radicalism and peace activism in the region. We also need to confront the dark flipside of such enlightened and progressive traditions: a history of racial intolerance, discrimination and occasional violence that in 1967 gave Martin Luther King's message such contemporary significance.

Part Two:

Local Contexts, Global Connections

CHAPTER FIVE

Deep Roots: Slavery, Race and Radicalism in the North East to 1833

It is tempting to view Martin Luther King's 1967 visit as a fascinating but isolated episode in Newcastle's civic life. In fact, his visit forms part of two distinct, yet entwined histories on Tyneside and in the wider North East. The first involves the region's long tradition of political radicalism and support for progressive social movements that included a steady interest in the plight of African Americans, initially as part of powerful surge of anti-slavery activity in the 18th and 19th centuries; the second links to a largely forgotten history of racial, ethnic and religious diversity in the North East in which African American fugitive slaves and abolitionists once played a significant part. The next four chapters explore the social, political and ideological contours of these intersecting histories, since together they created the deep underlying local contexts within which King's visit took place and through which its significance and that of the African American freedom struggle of the 1950s and 1960s were understood.[1]

King's visit extended, rather than initiated a complex relationship between the North East and African American history that stretches back at least as far as the 17th century and connects the region to important facets of Atlantic World and Black Atlantic history. As local historian John Charlton notes, unlike in other port cities such as Bristol and Liverpool, in Newcastle, 'There were no known slave traders, or trade ships or shackled slaves to trouble the conscience.' Nevertheless, local agricultural, industrial and merchant interests were linked by 'hidden chains' to slavery in the British Colonies and in the Americas more generally.[2]

Charlton offers a long list of the region's landed gentry, coal and shipbuilding magnates, and a rising class of merchants and manufacturers who either owned slave plantations in the North American colonies or in the Caribbean, or who kept slaves at home, or who engaged in various kinds of commerce with slaveholding colonies and countries. For example, in the years before the American colonies declared their independence from Britain in 1776, the Delaval family of Seaton Delaval held land in North Carolina and appears to have run a slave plantation in colonial Florida until it was restored to Spanish rule in 1783; at the time of the 1833 Act that abolished slavery in the British Empire, Newcastle's John Altham Graham

Clarke and his brother James owned or co-owned 600 slaves across five plantations in Jamaica; the Trevelyan family of Wallington Hall had interests in seven Grenada plantations that included 1,240 slaves.[3]

In a region where seafaring and shipbuilding were an integral part of the local economy, sailors recruited from the North East frequently served on ships that carried the raw materials produced by slave labour and sometimes slaves themselves. Other seamen worked on ships that transported manufactured goods to and from locations where slavery flourished. Among the more grim cargo were manacles and neck-collars made at the Crowley ironworks by the firm of Swalwell and Winlaton in Gateshead, along with tools that were used on slave plantations. Sometimes this transatlantic commerce took place on ships built on Teesside, Tyneside, or Sunderland, which may have been the most important shipbuilding centre in the country in the 1830s and 1840s, with sixty-five separate yards. Indeed, the Pinkney family of Sunderland, who ran the Neptune Steam Navigation Company, was responsible for the first shipment of slave-produced American cotton to go directly to Manchester spinners rather than via the powerful cotton brokers of Liverpool.[4] Meanwhile, many of the staples of ordinary life and the accoutrements of elite culture in the region depended on slave labour. Whenever North Easterners sipped coffee or tea, sweetening it with sugar, or smoked tobacco, or took a pinch of snuff while enjoying a nip of rum, or added ginger to their cooking, or donned their cotton clothing, they found themselves implicated in a global economy in which slavery played a vital, if sordid part.[5]

The spectacular development of Newcastle as a hub of industrial, commercial, financial and cultural activity in the late 18th and early 19th centuries was ultimately inseparable from the overt and hidden workings of the transatlantic slave trade. Paradoxically, however, during this period Tyneside and the North East also became a bastion of agitation against the slave trade and, in some cases, against the institution of slavery itself. This tension between what might be conveniently, if not wholly satisfactorily, be termed progressive and reactionary responses to slavery, racial differences and minority rights created ripples in the region that could still be felt centuries later. The tug of war between an incipient cosmopolitanism and narrower, more insular and occasionally starkly xenophobic attitudes towards immigrant communities that was evident in Newcastle when Martin Luther King visited had deep roots in the region's racial, economic and political past.

In the North East, interest in the African American freedom struggle was initially part of broader campaigns against the slave trade and chattel slavery that began in earnest with the efforts of local members of the Society of Friends, or Quakers, in the 18th century. Many Quakers prospered on the back of the slave trade or from the products of slave labour. Nevertheless, the belief that all men and women were equal in the eyes of God, emphasis on peaceful methods of conflict resolution, abhorrence of persecution, and commitment to equally shared rights and responsibilities meant that Quakers were philosophically opposed to slavery—an institution that had violence, persecution and gross inequality at its rotten core. After founder George Fox explicitly condemned the inhumane treatment of slaves in 1657 and then called for emancipation in 1671, many Quakers in the North American colonies had begun to divest themselves of their human property. Their brethren in England also began to distance themselves from the institution. In hotbeds of Quakerism like the North East, Friends often emerged at the forefront of anti-slavery campaigns.[6]

This was an age when voting was essentially restricted to men with money and property: as late as 1780, the electorate still constituted less than three percent of the population of England and Wales.[7] Consequently, extra-parliamentary pressure groups such as those organised to oppose the slave trade and sometimes slavery itself, were considered legitimate vehicles for the expression of popular sentiment and exerted substantial influence on local and national politics. Moreover, anti-slavery agitation regularly intersected with campaigns to assert individual and communal rights against the tyranny of unaccountable political power. Providing common, if sometimes shifting, ground among the many putatively 'radical' groups on Tyneside that emerged to challenge the political, social, economic, religious, educational or political status quo—and sometimes all of these things—was what historian Kathleen Wilson describes as a shared 'culture of dissident politics…that contested the politics of deference.'[8]

A notable North East pioneer in this regard was John Lilburne. Born around 1614 in Sunderland and educated at Newcastle Royal Free Grammar School, Lilburne became closely associated with the Levellers, a radical political movement that flourished during the English Civil War agitating for religious tolerance, equality before the law and a vastly extended suffrage. Frequently jailed and sometimes subjected to corporal punishment for his beliefs and criticisms of Parliament, Lilburne was popularly known as 'Freeborn John' to honour his commitment to what he called 'freeborn rights.' Indeed, Lilburne gave the world one of its first systematic philosophical defences of the inviolable human rights with which he believed every person was endowed, as opposed to the civic rights bestowed by Kings, governments and laws. This belief in fundamental human rights would subsequently reappear as a cornerstone of the American Declaration of Independence, but also as a crucial ingredient in anti-slavery arguments, not least among the Society of Friends, which Lilburne joined in 1656.[9]

By the early 18th century there were regular exchanges among Quakers in North America and the North East regarding African slavery, which was becoming firmly embedded in the economic and social life of Britain's colonies. In 1737, for example, Newcastle Quakers were reminded by Friends in New Jersey and Philadelphia that, 'as the Gospel breathes nothing but a spirit of love and liberty to mankind so it has been the early care of Friends to caution against the practice of trading in Negroes which we think it necessary to repeat.'[10]

In 1754, the New Jersey merchant, journalist, and itinerant Quaker preacher John Woolman unequivocally denounced slavery in a pamphlet widely disseminated around the Atlantic World. Woolman's *Some Considerations on the Keeping of Negroes, Recommended to the Professors of Christianity of Every Denomination* opened the floodgates for a transatlantic tsunami of anti-slavery publications by Quaker reformers, including Anthony Benezet's highly influential *Observations on Inslaving, Importing and Purchasing Negroes*. Tied into this international community of Quaker reformers through the workings of the London Yearly Meeting, which yoked together national and local Meetings, Newcastle Friends were warned 'against that iniquitous Practice of *dealing in Negroes*,' and a 'most unnatural Traffic, whereby great Numbers of Mankind, free by Nature, are subjected to inextricable Bondage.' Such practices were 'in direct violation of the Gospel Rule,' and Friends were urged 'to avoid being in any way concerned in reaping unrighteous profits arising from the iniquitous practice of dealing in Negroes and other slaves.'[11]

As Quaker involvement in slavery and the slave trade gradually declined on both sides of the Atlantic, so Friends in the North East began to play an ever more important role in promoting anti-slavery. In Newcastle, families such as the Richardsons—Henry, his wife Anna and sister Ellen—and in Darlington, Joseph and his daughter Elizabeth Pease, were often at the forefront of campaigns against the traffic in human beings. These families also acted as hosts and benefactors to numerous visiting abolitionists and fugitive slaves.

Quakers were not the only anti-slavery activists in a region that had a strong tradition of religious non-conformity. In his 1827 history of Newcastle and Gateshead, Eneas Mackenzie listed 23 'Dissenting' Protestant chapels and meeting houses.[12] Members of these dissenting denominations, notably Unitarians, provided much of the elite leadership for North East abolitionism. Presbyterians and Methodists offered the movement many of its rank and file supporters, drawn heavily, if never exclusively, from the working-class. If Anglicans, the focus of non-conformist religious dissent, were somewhat under-represented in abolitionist campaigns, they were not entirely absent. In 1762, Dr John Sharp, Archdeacon of Northumberland, had 'sounded an alarm throughout the diocese respecting the Slave Trade,' travelling from 'town to town testifying against that enormity.'[13]

The impulses towards anti-slave trade crusades in the North East clearly came from a variety of sources. While elites and the middle-class often led abolitionism, there was also what historian Seymour Drescher terms 'cross-class' enthusiasm for the cause among the region's non-conformists and evangelicals. Indeed, as Drescher notes, religious non-conformism itself came from much the same sources as did anti-slavery activities. There was a reciprocal relationship between the two movements, both of which represented responses to the early phases of British industrialisation, with all the economic, social, cultural, political, and psychological upheaval that process entailed. As Drescher explains, 'Evangelicalism did not create mass abolitionism; rather abolitionism proliferated in the same social and ideological context which was favourable to the growth of non-conformity.'[14]

On Tyneside, this meant that anti-slavery was inextricably linked to the growth of urban Newcastle, a city prospering primarily because of its control of the coal mines located near the River Tyne and of the area's burgeoning shipbuilding and shipping operations. Thanks 'more to immigration than to natural increase,' A.W. Purdue explains that the city's population doubled from 42,760 in 1831 to 89,000 at mid-century. In this fluid environment, artisans and merchants shared the city, albeit in quite distinct neighbourhoods, with rising numbers of skilled, semi-skilled and unskilled industrial labourers. The rapid influx of people created tensions and anxieties as they jockeyed for social and economic status and sometimes simply for space in a city much of which, Purdue notes, 'remained densely populated.'[15]

Space and the right to it certainly animated the activism of Thomas Spence, a radical dissenter and Presbyterian born in Newcastle in 1750. In

1771 Spence campaigned to preserve public access to the city's Town Moor. He subsequently developed a common lands plan, known as the Spence Plan, as part of an assault on what he saw as the dangerous concentration of property, wealth and political power in the hands of landowners and the aristocracy.[16] Spence's denunciation of privately held land, calls for universal suffrage, advocacy of welfare payments for those unable to work, and desire to rid Britain of its hereditary aristocracy, put him on the outermost fringes of late 18th century radicalism. He was, as Michael Srivener suggests, 'a revolutionary who without hesitation recommended the forceful transition of power.'[17] Yet, Spence had much in common with many other Tyneside progressives in his basic opposition to how established authorities, whether aristocratic, religious, political, or economic, exercised largely untrammelled and unaccountable power over the lives of the masses. That lack of agency affronted Enlightenment ideals of natural rights, liberty and justice—concepts articulated by the likes of John Lilburne, enshrined in the American Declaration of Independence and boldly proclaimed, if rather less successfully enacted, during the French Revolution. In Britain, religious nonconformism, the battle for political and educational reform and anti-slavery activism had in common a desire to challenge traditional authority and claim more power for those individuals and communities to which it was routinely denied.[18]

In the late 18th and early 19th centuries, nationally prominent figures such as William Wilberforce, Thomas Clarkson and Granville Sharp were merely the best known of those who made abolitionism one of the most important causes in British popular and electoral politics.[19] The Durham-born civil servant and political reformer Sharp was author in 1769 of arguably the first major anti-slavery text penned by a British author: *A Representation of the Injustice and Dangerous Tendency of Admitting the Least Claim of Private Property in the Persons of Men, in England, In Four Parts.*[20] A maverick who believed that Napoleon was the anti-Christ and that the 'end of days' foretold in the Bible's Book of Revelations were close at hand, Sharp was one of the twelve men, nine Quakers and three Anglicans, who, on May 22 1787, formed the Society for Effecting the Abolition of the Slave Trade in London. Sharp served as its first chairman. He was also partially responsible for the appearance in the North East of Olaudah Equiano, an ex-slave known in his lifetime as Gustavus Vassa. Equiano's visit set a precedent that would be crucial to the region's abolitionist cultures in the mid-19th century, creating a tradition to which Martin Luther King would ultimately be heir in 1967.

A quintessential product and interpreter of the Black Atlantic experience, Equiano has long been the subject of intrigue and no little mystery. Historians continue to debate whether Equiano was born a slave in South Carolina or, as he claimed in his frequently revised autobiography, *The Interesting Narrative of the Life of Olaudah Equiano or Gustavus Vassa, the African*, captured as a child from the Eboe province in the south of modern Nigeria and shipped first to Barbados and then to colonial Virginia. What seems certain, however, is that Equiano ended up working as a barber-cum-valet-cum-deckhand for a prosperous Quaker shipping merchant, Robert Kay, who allowed him to work for himself on the side and supported his efforts to improve his education. In 1767, Equiano purchased his own freedom and settled in England, although he spent much of the next twenty years at sea. [21]

In the 1780s, Equiano became increasingly involved in anti-slavery campaigns. He became a friend and colleague of Sharp, informing the abolitionist about the 1781 Zong massacre in which 133 slaves were murdered by the crew of a slave ship bound for Jamaica. The slaves were thrown overboard to save dwindling water supplies after a series of navigational errors sent the ship off course. The massacre took place partly to save the lives of the ailing crew and some of the human cargo, but mainly to enable the ship's Liverpool-based owners to file an insurance claim for loss of property, which would have been impossible had the slaves reached land before they died. Between them Equiano and Sharp made this grim tale, and the 1783 court cases over the insurance claim by the slave-trading syndicate that sponsored the voyage, a rallying cry for abolitionists. Although the legal proceedings ended on appeal with a ruling that the insurers were not liable to pay compensation, the fact that there was no punishment for those who had killed the slaves helped to galvanise popular opposition to the slave trade. [22]

The Zong affair marked Equiano's emergence as a major, rather exotic figure in British abolitionist circles. Inevitably, given the North East's growing reputation as a bastion of anti-slave trade agitation, he made his way to the region. The 1789 first edition of his memoir was already available in Newcastle, where in 1791 it featured among the 5,416 texts available for loan from R. Fischer's Circulating Library to the literate and relatively prosperous patrons who paid its twelve shillings annual membership fee. That September, Equiano advertised the latest edition of his autobiography in the *Newcastle Daily Chronicle* and gave a series of lectures while lodging at Robert Darnton's bookshop opposite the Turk's Head public house in the

Bigge Market.[23] He also visited St. Anthony's Colliery, where he went under the River Tyne to experience the cramped and dangerous conditions endured by northern miners. It was the sort of gesture that helped to create the idea, not wholly fanciful, if often far too simplistic, of an affinity between the white working-class in the North East and other victims of economic exploitation and political powerlessness; an affinity that might transcend racial differences.

Equiano, like many who followed him to the North East a generation later, appreciated the hospitality—and book sales—he enjoyed in the region. After his departure, he wrote to the *Chronicle* offering:

> warmest thanks of a heart growing with gratitude to you, for your fellow-feeling for the Africans and their cause. Having received marks of kindness, from you who have purchased my interesting narrative, particularly from George Johnson, Esq. of Byker, I am therefore happy that my narrative has afforded pleasure in the perusal; and heartily will all of you every blessing that this world can afford, and every fullness of joy which divine revelation has promised us in the next.[24]

While Equiano was consolidating his status as a highly effective celebrity advocate for abolition, in January 1788, Thomas Clarkson's London Abolition Committee sent requests to the mayor of every city in England to sign a petition against the slave trade for presentation to Parliament. On February 12, the Newcastle Common Council agreed to raise such a petition and a week later approved it for delivery to the House of Commons by John Erasmus Blackett. There was a certain irony in the fact that the Newcastle Common Council at the time was, as John Charlton observes, 'a conservative body of merchants and included two sugar importers.' Nevertheless, 'it was one of the first such bodies in Britain to take such a decision,' influenced, Charlton argues, by strong abolitionist sentiments among the city's powerful trades guilds.[25]

In October 1791, one of the nation's first provincial anti-slavery societies was also founded in Newcastle. The Society in Newcastle for Promoting the Abolition of the Slave-Trade brought together a small but passionate group of religious non-conformists and dissenters. Foremost among them was William Turner, who had taken over the ministry of the Hanover Square Unitarian Chapel in Newcastle in 1781. Both Turner and his Chapel would become central to Tyneside's anti-slavery activities over the next half century. Indeed, as founder of Britain's first Literary and Philosophical Society in Newcastle in 1793 and of various other public educational and cultural institutions around the city, Turner was both a product and an architect of a new kind of enlightened and aspiring middle and literate working-class in the city.[26] These were people who read about, and sometimes participated in, a variety of progressive reform initiatives against established social, political and economic elites and who questioned the sources and legitimacy of their power. Challenging the workings of and ideas behind the slave trade was thus connected to a wider set of challenges to the status quo in the North East, particularly on Tyneside.

Turner's fledgling Society included members of his own Unitarian Chapel, William Batson and Edward Prowitt, Anglicans such as Thomas Allason, the vicar at Heddon on the Wall, a smattering of Methodists and Presbyterians, and a significant number of Quakers, among them Robert Ormston, George Richardson, and the North Shields seaman Henry Taylor. There were at least five Quakers on the committee of ten that oversaw the Society's affairs. One of its first undertakings was to publish 'An Abstract' of all the evidence exposing the horrors of the traffic in human cargo that Clarkson and Wilberforce had presented to a Select Committee of the House of Commons over the previous two years. The pamphlet featured on its cover a striking depiction of a chained and kneeling slave set against a plantation backdrop created by the renowned local engraver and anti-slavery supporter Thomas Bewick and modelled on Josiah Wedgewood's iconic anti-slavery image 'Am I Not a Man and a Brother?'[27]

The Preface to the pamphlet graphically described the abuses suffered by captured Africans at the hands of 'Admirals' and 'slave merchants' during the dreaded middle-passage across the Atlantic—and again at the hands of 'planters' and slave-masters in the British Caribbean and North American colonies once they arrived in the New World. There was clear evidence 'That the slaves *have been insufficiently fed, lodged*, and *clothed*...that their *ears* and *noses* have been *slit* and *cut off*; that they have also been otherwise disfigured, as well as *deprived of limbs and members*; that they have been *suddenly murdered* and *buried*; and that in some cases, where they have run away, rewards have been offered to indifferent persons to bring them to their owners *alive* or *dead*.'[28]

It was significant that the Newcastle campaign to abolish the slave trade was not based solely on revulsion at the barbarity of the system and certainly not primarily on a commitment to ideals of human brotherhood, racial equality, or moral decency—although these were motivations for many abolitionists driven by religious convictions about the inherent sinfulness of the institution and a belief in the equality of all before God. Rather, the clamour to end the slave trade and, for many, ultimately to support slave emancipation was couched in terms of a commitment to democracy and accountability. It was the arbitrariness of the power exercised, often cruelly, by slave traders and slave owners over politically and legally powerless slaves that drove a good deal of abolitionist discourse in the North East. One of the complaints by Newcastle's first anti-slavery Society in 1791 was that slaves 'have been under the power of the master and overseer to an *unreasonable* degree.'[29]

From the outset, then, diverse radical, dissenting and non-conformist elements in the North East, boasting a wide array of formal and informal political affiliations, supported the abolition of the slave trade and sometimes emancipation on a variety of religious, moral, political and legal grounds. When in 1792 William Wilberforce unsuccessfully tried to introduce an Abolition Bill into Parliament, he was supported by Sir Ralph Milbanke, a County Durham Member of Parliament, and Lord Percy, the Duke of Northumberland, whose descendent presided over Martin Luther King's honorary degree ceremony. Petitions supporting Wilberforce and condemning slavery arrived from all over the country, including from Alnwick, Darlington, Durham, North and South Shields, and Wooler in the North East.[30]

There was also a petition from Belford in Northumberland, which exemplified the conspicuous involvement of women in local anti-slavery campaigns. Four-hundred and thirty-three women signed the Belford petition. This activism brought some women into the public sphere of politics and protest. But even those women who remained largely confined to the traditional domestic sphere of hearth and home could use their power over household expenditures to support the abolitionist cause by making decisions about which products to buy or not to buy.[31] There were periodic boycotts, often led by Quakers, of sugar, cotton and rum and other items which bore the stain of slave labour. 'Humanus,' a pseudonymous correspondent to the *Newcastle Courant* in January 1792, explained how, while he was away from home, the women in his family had 'perused a pamphlet entitled "An Address to the People of Great Britain on the Utility of refraining from the use of West India Sugar and Rum." On my return, I was surprised to find that they had entirely left off the use of sugar, and banished it from the tea-table.' It was not the exorbitant price of the sweetener that provoked this boycott. The pamphlet had persuaded the ladies of his household 'that the consumer of an article procured by a horrid traffic, and the most inhuman of their fellow creatures, is in some degree accessory to the crimes attending that pamphlet.'[32]

Here was a commitment to the idea of collective social responsibility for the well-being, or otherwise, of all humankind. It was a concept that Martin Luther King invoked in his Newcastle speech when he insisted that everyone was caught in what he called 'an inescapable network of mutuality.' His insistence that it was the duty of 'all men of good will to work passionately and unrelentingly to get rid of racial injustice…we have got to come to see that the destiny of white and colored persons is tied together,' would have resonated with those on Tyneside who, 170 years earlier, had campaigned against slavery, the most visible and heinous expression of racial injustice in their day.[33] King's gendered language ('all men') betrayed a casual paternalistic sexism that riddled the US civil rights movement of the 1950s and 1960s, along with most American institutions, and left an unwelcome legacy in the belated acknowledgement of the major role played by women in the long African American freedom struggle. By contrast, Humanus's 1792 account was testament to how anti-slavery activism could empower women, who became indispensable to mid-19th century abolitionism.

On March 15, 1807, after two decades of mounting pressure, Parliament passed 'An Act for the Abolition of the Slave Trade' officially ending British involvement in the African Slave Trade. Tyneside abolitionists rejoiced in the fact that one of their own, Charles, later the second Earl, Grey was the Whig government's Foreign Secretary and had played an important role in the passage of the Act. An aristocrat born second son of Charles, the first Earl Grey, in Falloden, Northumberland in 1764, Grey was a pragmatic champion of parliamentary reform. He worked hard to expand the franchise and rid the nation of the kind of unaccountable power, cronyism, and corruption that plagued politics. The undemocratic workings of British politics were exemplified by 'rotten boroughs' where sham elections were foregone conclusions and simply perpetuated the power of landed elites.

As was true of many other, if rather less wealthy, abolitionists Grey's anti-slavery position fused with a more capacious vision of rights and responsibilities. Although he always remained suspicious of ceding too much power to the masses, Grey harboured a deep sense of honour and principal that regularly led him to offer support to the marginalised and oppressed at home and abroad. For example, shortly after the Anti-Slave Trade Act passed, Grey resigned his cabinet post in protest at George III's demand that government officials should sign a personal commitment to oppose the expansion of Catholic rights in Britain.[34] This kind of patrician reformism was another element in the progressive politics of the North East that, in turn, underpinned a measure of interest in and sympathy for the plight of African Americans.

Although the slave trade had been abolished, slavery itself still flourished around the globe. Over the next quarter of a century, anti-slavery agitation maintained its momentum, initially focusing on ending the institution in the British Empire, but after 1833 increasingly directed towards ending slavery in the US. A new national Society for Promoting the Gradual Abolition of Slavery Throughout the British Dominions was founded in early 1823 and, at an April 29 meeting in the Newcastle Guildhall, 2,912 people signed a petition that was presented to the House of Commons as part of an abolition motion debated in Parliament on May 15, 1823.[35] It was one of at least 228 such petitions raised in support of the national Society's position, including from North East sympathisers in Alnwick, Blyth, Chester-le-Street, Darlington, Durham, Gateshead, Hexham, South Shields, Stockton, Sunderland and Tynemouth.[36]

The day before the great debate in Parliament, on May 14, 1823, a Newcastle upon Tyne branch of the national Society was formed; one of the first among some 250 local affiliates. With Sir John Edward Swinburne as president, Thomas Wentworth Beaumont, MP, and Robert Bell, the Mayor of Newcastle, among its Vice Presidents, and Matthew Forster and John Fenwick serving jointly as Secretaries, the Society was funded by private subscriptions, a £3.11s.6d collection from the New Court Chapel following an anti-slavery sermon by Rev. G. Sample, and a generous £5.50s subsidy from the Newcastle Common Council, indicative of local government support for a popular reform cause.[37] Gradualist in its approach, in September 1823 the Society published a pamphlet declaring its intention 'to pursue the best and most efficacious methods within its reach, for the mitigation and progressive extinction of slavery within the British Dominions.'[38] James Losh, a successful Newcastle lawyer, radical reformer and Unitarian ally of William Turner, who together helped to make Brunswick Chapel a centre of local abolitionist activity, was also initially sympathetic to gradualist approaches to ending slavery in the British Colonies. Like most Newcastle abolitionists, however, he was unequivocal in his rejection of 'unfounded assertions of the inferiority of the negro race, and of their incapacity for improvement and civilization.'[39]

Meanwhile, local abolitionists campaigned for politicians who were sympathetic to their cause. Often they couched their appeals in the language of natural rights and yoked them to the campaign to expand the franchise for British men. Somebody signing himself 'A Free Born Briton' insisted that 'No man is worthy of liberty himself who would enslave another,' and petitioned the electors of Northumberland and Newcastle upon Tyne to support abolition in the fiercely contested general election of 1826. This was a campaign so rancorous that it actually culminated in a non-fatal duel on the beach below Bamburgh Castle between Whig candidate John George Lambton and the sitting independent Northumberland Member of Parliament, reformer and local abolitionist leader Thomas Wentworth Beaumont.[40]

With anti-slavery sentiment rising, in 1830 Charles Earl Grey ended twenty-four years out of government, during which time he had served briefly as Member of Parliament for Appleby and as a member of the Whig opposition in the House of Lords. He returned in triumph as Prime Minister. His four years in office would prove important for both the anti-slavery movement and for the advance of political rights for British men. In 1832, Grey introduced and oversaw the passage of the 'Representation of the People Act,' informally known as Great Reform Act. The crowning achievement of his attempts to reform Parliament, the Act restructured English and Welsh politics (separate Acts the same year dealt with Ireland and Scotland): it abolished 143 of 203 old boroughs, established 130 new seats and, according to best estimates, increased the size of the adult male electorate from about 478,000 to 800,000, mainly by adjusting eligibility qualifications relating to property holding.[41]

Grey saw moderate political reform as a means to preserve aristocratic power by enfranchising more members of a rapidly expanding middle-class and forming with them a coalition to stave off challenges from more radical political ideologies and working-class organisations. In the end, the Act still only enfranchised about eight percent of the total English and Welsh population. Continued unrest among the struggling and often disenfranchised agricultural workers who had taken part in the 'Swing Riots' of the early 1830s spoke to the Act's shortcomings. Most factory labourers and all women still lacked the vote. In Newcastle, the Act actually removed about 2,000 voters from the electoral rolls, while adding roughly the same number of new voters from the city's middle-class. Thus it initially produced little change in the size of the electorate, which remained at around 5,000, roughly ten percent of the population.[42] Nevertheless, the Great Reform Act was an important step towards establishing, in principle if not so much in practice, the foundations for a more representative democracy in Britain. Prior to the Act, between 1806 and 1832, the percentage of genuinely contested elections was never higher than thirty-eight percent and usually below thirty percent; in the first election after the Act, seventy-four percent of parliamentary seats were contested.[43]

All of this was important for the entangled histories of abolitionism, race and radicalism in Newcastle. As was the case nationally, a local consequence of the Great Reform Act was that the influence of the middle-classes increased. Following the Act, Tyneside's ambitious and expanding middle-class had, according to historian Peter Cadogan, 'become the practical arbiters of political policy,' diluting the local and national power of, among others, the West Indies planters who had been among slavery's greatest supporters.[44] The West Indies lobby in the House of Commons lost about forty seats in the first post-Reform Act elections, which also returned 104 MPs committed to abolition. Although slave interests remained powerful in the un-reformed House of Lords, the Great Reform Act, which was enthusiastically supported by North East abolitionists, shifted the balance of power and paved the way for the Abolition of Slavery Act that eventually passed on August 29, 1833.[45]

North East anti-slavery activists could take some credit for helping to keep up the public pressure that led to the 1833 Abolition Act. After the end of legal British involvement in the slave trade in 1807, local campaigners had worked towards the gradual abolition of slavery in the British Colonies. By 1830, however, two things had changed. Patience with gradualism was largely exhausted and abolitionists took a broader, more global view of the evil institution: both developments brought US slavery into ever sharper focus. On August 11, 1830, at a meeting in the Brunswick Place Wesleyan Chapel chaired by Thomas Wentworth Beaumont, the organisation that had begun life in 1823 as the Newcastle upon Tyne Society for the Promoting the Gradual Abolition of Slavery Throughout the British Dominions, added new urgency by dropping the word 'Gradual' from its name.[46]

This shift in gears was also reflected in a new frenzy of anti-slavery petitioning and propaganda in the region. In Autumn 1830, meetings were held in Alnwick, Berwick, Bishop Auckland, Darlington, Durham, Hexham, Morpeth, North and South Shields, and Sunderland.[47] According to Sean Creighton, in that year alone at least thirty-five petitions were sent to the House of Lords from the North East. Arriving from, among other places, Sunderland, North and South Shields, Durham, Morpeth, Fawdon, Byker, Whitburn and West Boldon, these petitions bore the signatures of members of the general public, religious congregations and a variety of dedicated abolitionist groups.[48] Shortly before the Whigs and Earl Grey returned to power in December 1830, William Woodman, secretary of the Morpeth Anti-Slavery Society, wrote directly to the Earl and his son, the MP Lord Howick, requesting that they serve as patron of the Society and as one of its vice-presidents, respectively. The letter also urged both men to champion anti-slavery petitions in the Houses of Lords and Commons. Grey and Howick declined their invitations. In so doing they managed to stress both their general opposition to slavery and their cautious approach to abolishing it. 'I am as adverse as anyone to the system of slavery, & shall always be ready to support in my place in parliament any well considered scheme for putting an end to it,' wrote Howick who, like his father, felt that once back in office, factory legislation, amendments to the poor law and, especially, electoral reform should take priority.[49] Undeterred, more petitions followed in 1831, from places such as Houghton Le Spring, Monkwearmouth, Newbottle, and Wolsingham. Meanwhile abolition again became a significant factor in several North East parliamentary elections, where anti-slavery candidates were regularly returned.[50]

Early in 1832, news arrived in Britain of a slave uprising in Jamaica that had occurred just before Christmas 1831. Reports of the brutal suppression of the insurrection by white authorities, and of reprisals against the missionaries who were accused of encouraging the revolt with their subversive teachings about equality before God, further fuelled abolitionist fervour. In Newcastle, as many as 40,000 people may have attended a rally to protest against these events and call for immediate abolition. Across the region, there were mass meetings in Berwick, Darlington, Durham, Gateshead and Sunderland. With the Great Reform Act safely secured in June 1832, local abolitionists doubled their efforts to force an anti-slavery Bill to the front of Grey's legislative agenda. More than a million signatures on over 5,000 petitions reached Parliament. Among the signatories were 6,293 women from Newcastle and Gateshead who, on May 13, 1833, put their names to a 'Petition for the Immediate Abolition of West India Slavery.' It was one of 800 such women's petitions that year, signed by around 300,000 women.[51]

On the eve of the passage of the Abolition of Slavery Act, Rev. G.F.W. Mortimer, headmaster of the Newcastle upon Tyne Grammar School, perfectly captured the moral imperative of the abolitionist cause, while carefully, if somewhat romantically, linking it to an ancient British commitment to law, justice and individual freedom of will and conscience. Mortimer listed the manifold cruelties of the system, with its capricious, unregulated punishment and subjugation of the slave 'to another's will, which is at once the most galling and the most degrading part of Slavery.' He challenged those who argued that immediate emancipation would be too dangerous or too economically ruinous for unprepared slaves and slaveholders alike. Having piled up his 'facts written in blood,' recounted gruesome 'catalogues of guilt, and punishment, and degradation,' and presented his ethical and practical arguments for abolition, Mortimer asked simply, 'who, in the face of this evidence, will be the apologist of Slavery? Who will not join in condemning it as a murderous, a demoralizing, and accursed system? Who will blame us for demanding its immediate extinction?' For men and women like Mortimer, the 'existence of Slavery in any part of the British Empire' was 'a blot upon our free and liberal institutions—a foul and loathesome stain upon the honour of the British Character.'[52]

The Abolition of Slavery Act, which came into effect on August 1, 1834, mandated that all slaves in the British Empire under the age of six would be freed immediately. Many abolitionists were unhappy with the so-called 'apprenticeship' provision, whereby slaves over the age of six were to remain part-slave and part-free for a further four years. During this time they would be paid a wage for the work they did in the portion of the week when they were 'free.' Others were incensed that the government had agreed to provide £20 million in compensation to slave-owners who had lost their 'property.'[53]

Despite such criticisms, the Act, another triumph for Grey and his administration, sounded the death-knell for slavery in the British Empire and there was much rejoicing in the North East. The local press reported a round of celebrations in Newcastle, including 'an elegant cup of tea, in the vestry of New Court Chapel'; a packed public service in the Methodist New Road Wesleyan Chapel; a gathering of 300 people of various denominations, who again took tea together in the Nelson Street Music Hall; and a mass meeting at the Brunswick Chapel, with more than 800 attendees listening to speeches and singing abolitionist hymns. Elsewhere in the region, there were similar events in Berwick, Durham, and North Shields. In South Shields the veteran abolitionist Dr. Thomas Winterburn presided over a celebratory breakfast at the Golden Lion public house in the morning, while in the evening seven different congregations came together to give thanks at the Primitive Methodist Chapel.[54]

Further progressive legislation followed under Earl Grey's administration, notably the passage of the Factory Act that banned the use of children aged under nine years old in industry and restricted the hours that could be worked by those under eighteen. When Grey's tenure as Prime Minister ended in 1834, amid controversies over the question of Irish home rule, public gatherings were held across the region to express gratitude for his service. A meeting at the South Shields Town Hall on August 1 specifically cited Grey's role in helping remove 'the manacle of the Negro' as among his most significant achievements.[55]

Shortly after Grey retired, plans were hatched to commemorate his many contributions to public life. In 1838, a Newcastle city centre monument was completed, with a statue of Grey set a-top an imposing 130 foot column. Whig reformers such as Grey, chastened by the social tumult of the American and then French Revolutions, had skilfully managed incremental and piecemeal change as a means to prevent yet more radical upheaval. Paternalistic at heart, they were never more conservative than in their enthusiasm for limited reform. Nonetheless, the inscription at the base of Grey's Monument lauded a man who, 'During an active political career of nearly half a century was the constant advocate of peace and the fearless and consistent champion of civil and religious liberty.'[56] In remembering Earl Grey this way the city publicly acknowledged the close connection between the struggles for peace and for freedom. That interplay, evoked by Martin Luther King in 1967, would play out in fascinating ways during the remainder of the 19th century as the struggle to end slavery in the US came to occupy a vital place in Tyneside's progressive politics.

CHAPTER SIX

'Brethren in the Cause of Universal Freedom in America':
Peace, Politics and Abolitionism
in the North East before the US Civil War

In the summer of 1838, the same year that Earl Grey's Monument was completed, the apprenticeship system in British colonies set up by the 1833 Abolition of Slavery Act finally ended. Many in the North East had campaigned against 'the sufferings of the so called Negro Apprentices,' and petitioned 'for their immediate and unconditional emancipation,' as the record of a January 1838 anti-slavery meeting at Newcastle's Hood Street Salem Chapel, put it.[1] Consequently, the demise of the apprenticeship system prompted another round of celebrations on Tyneside, at Salem Chapel and in the Turks Head Long Room on the Bigge Market.[2] But while slavery in the British Empire was over, the institution continued elsewhere, not least in the US, which provided a new focus for abolitionist activities in the region. This activism in turn attracted a torrent of charismatic African American visitors to the North East, fugitive slaves and dedicated abolitionists who created the tradition to which Martin Luther King was heir.

Many of those most actively involved in abolitionist circles in the mid-19th century were also at the forefront of North East peace activism. Others supported a variety of 'free trade' positions associated with British radicals and leaders of the Anti-Corn-Law League, John Bright and Richard Cobden. In an Atlantic World where, as Marc-William Palen explains, there were extensive 'ties between free trade, Christianity and abolitionism in the American North and Britain,' until the 1860s 'some of the most prominent transatlantic Cobdenites were a regular *Who's Who* of radical abolitionists.'[3] These campaigners believed that free trade among nations, without government restriction on exports or imports, would stimulate greater economic well-being among all the peoples of the world and, if coupled with a non-interventionist foreign policy, promote greater international understanding and ultimately world peace.

Free trade proved an ambiguous and limited instrument for the promotion of global peace and social justice, since it informed British imperial expansion with its relentless search for new markets to exploit and resources to control whether by force or 'informal Empire.'[4] Still, many of those who supported free trade in the 19th century recognised, as did many of those involved in peace work, and as did Martin Luther King a century later, that war, racism, poverty and economic injustice were interconnected and invariably did violence to the possibility of a more just and harmonious world. The intricate lattice work of interlocking social movements, progressive political crusades and economic theories that surrounded abolitionism in the North East during the 19th century fortified a radical political tradition in which King's analysis of the social ills confronting the world and strategies for change would seem quite familiar.

The Newcastle Auxiliary to the national Peace Society (formally called the London Society for the Promotion of Permanent and Universal Peace) was founded in October 1817. After a period of relative inactivity, the Auxiliary grew during the 1830s when it became increasingly militant in its absolutist rejection of any attempts to justify war. In its 1831 report, the Auxiliary urged 'fellow-townsmen' to embrace the peace movement, believing 'that the day is not very distant when the sublime precepts of the Lord Jesus Christ to his disciples, "Love your enemies, do good to them who hate you," will be clearly seen to be incompatible with war, how specious soever may be the pretext on which it is undertaken.'[5] Six years later, the Newcastle Auxiliary stated its intention was 'simply to shed light on the abstract principles of justice and mercy' for all peoples of the world. It pledged 'to place these principles prominently before the view of men of every rank, and colour, and clime; that all men may see and feel that an appeal to the sword, whether individually, as in the case of duelling; or on a more fearfully extended scale, as in national warfare, is as utterly subversive of the eternal principles of right and wrong…'[6]

In 1842, the Newcastle Peace Society separated from the national Peace Society, frustrated by its cautious moderation, and became an independent entity for eight years. Indeed, as historian David Saunders notes, Newcastle pacifists have always tended to be 'radical even by pacifist standards. Few of them were prepared to contemplate violence of any kind,' a characteristic that he attributes to 'the overwhelmingly Nonconformist (and especially Quaker) aspect of their composition.' Once more, then, Quakers and other religious non-conformists were to the fore, with the Peases in

Via WESTERN UNION CABLES

d fuM 28511

NT27 A LLW23 FAX ATLANTA GA 58 27 1235P EST

RE: AT
NEWCASTLE

1967 FEB 23 8 4

E M BETTENSON

THE UNIVERSITY OF NEWCASTLE UPON TYNE

6 KENSINGTON TERRACE

NEW CASTLE UPON TYNE 2

TEL
TEL

WOULD BE HAPPY AND HONORED TO ACCEPT HONORARY DEGREE IN NOVEMBER

WHEN I WILL BE IN ENGLAND REGRET THAT IT IS NOT POSSIBLE TO

BE THERE IN MAY PLEASE ADVISE IF NOVEMBER IS SATISFACTORY FOR

SPECIAL ONVOCATION

MARTIN LUTHER KING JR

Top: Martin Luther King's February 23, 1967 telegram to Ernest Bettenson, Registrar of the University of Newcastle upon Tyne, was the civil rights leader's first direct communication with the University and confirmed his willingness to travel to Newcastle to receive an Honorary Doctorate in Civil Law. *Behind:* Martin Luther King enjoys a joke with the Duke of Northumberland who, as Chancellor of the University of Newcastle upon Tyne, presided over the ceremony when King received his honorary degree.

1

thank you

WE APPRECIATE
YOUR BUSINESS . . .

Wear this COLORED CASUAL
Hanky · · *Our Compliments !*

COPPEDGE
Cleaners and Laundry Service

440 Forrest Ave., N. E.

1-Hr. Cleaning Service

Good Grooming Is Our Business

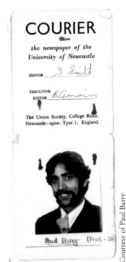

COURIER

the newspaper of the
University of Newcastle

EDITOR ....

EXECUTIVE
EDITOR ....

The Union Society, College Road,
Newcastle - upon - Tyne 1, England.

Top row from left: 1) Edna and Laurence Kane worked for Charles Bosanquet, Vice-Chancellor of the University of Newcastle upon Tyne, and lived at his Adderstone Crescent residence. There, on November 13, 1967, they met Martin Luther King and Andrew Young. *2)* King made a present of this dress handkerchief to Edna Kane as a gesture of thanks for the hospitality – and breakfast – he and Young had enjoyed at Adderstone Crescent. *3)* Paul Barry, a photographer for the *Courier* student newspaper, took some of the best pictures of King's visit to Newcastle. *Middle:* Andrew Young and Martin Luther King attended a coffee morning with students. *Left:* Among the students who met with King and Young were (left) Meredyth Bell (née Patton), Deputy President of the Students' Representative Council, and (right) C.B. 'Nick' Nicholson, President of the Students' Representative Council.

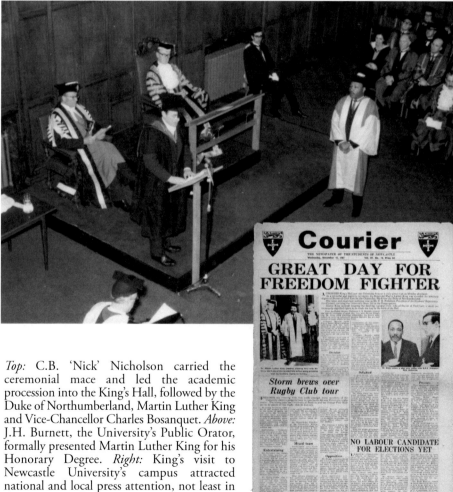

Top: C.B. 'Nick' Nicholson carried the ceremonial mace and led the academic procession into the King's Hall, followed by the Duke of Northumberland, Martin Luther King and Vice-Chancellor Charles Bosanquet. *Above:* J.H. Burnett, the University's Public Orator, formally presented Martin Luther King for his Honorary Degree. *Right:* King's visit to Newcastle University's campus attracted national and local press attention, not least in the *Courier* student newspaper.

334 Auburn Ave., N.E.
Atlanta, Georgia 30303
Telephone 522-1420

Southern Christian Leadership Conference

Martin Luther King Jr., *President*   Ralph Abernathy, *Treasurer*   Andrew J. Young, *Executive Director*

January 30, 1968

Vice Chancellor C. I. C. Bosanquet
The University of Newcastle
Newcastle
ENGLAND

Dear Dr. Bosanquet:

This is a belated note to say that one is always humbled on
the occasion of receiving an honorary degree from such an
outstanding University as Newcastle Upon Tyne, and yet,
in the course of constant criticism and malignment of one's
best efforts, the recognition by an institution of higher
learning of the historic significance of one's work in the
ministry is a tremendous encouragement, far overshadowing
the barbs and arrows from the daily press.

I especially appreciated the warm reception and generous
response of faculty and students on this occasion. My sincerest
appreciation to the members of the Board and faculty who saw
fit to confer this distinguished degree.

I do hope that our paths will cross again sometime in the not
too distant future.

Sincerely,

Martin L. King Jr.

Martin Luther King, Jr.

Km

Copies circulated 6.2.68 to: Chancellor
Registrar
Public Orator
Editor 'Courier'

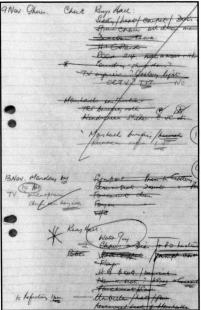

Dear Miss Mellor,

Thank you for your letter. When Dr. Martin Luther King received his
honorary degree in this University on 13th November 1967, he made an
unprepared speech and unfortunately we do not have a copy. However, I
suggest that you contact The Guardian newspaper which carried a report of
his address.

Yours sincerely,

Miss B. Mellor,
Welfare Officer,
H.M. Prison. Leyhill,
Wotton-under-Edge.
GLOUCESTERSHIRE.

Clockwise from top left: 1) University Registrar Ernest Bettenson (left) and Chief Clerk George Howe (right) were instrumental in making arrangements for Martin Luther King's visit to Newcastle. *2)* On January 30, 1968, Martin Luther King wrote a heartfelt letter of thanks to Vice-Chancellor Charles Bosanquet, explaining how much he valued his award from the University. *3)* After receiving his Honorary Degree Martin Luther King gave a spellbinding impromptu speech, focusing on the problems of racism, poverty and war. *4)* Because King was not expected to speak in Newcastle, the University had made no provision to record his remarks and, as this September 1, 1975 response to a query about King's visit shows, for many years it was unaware that occasion had been filmed. *5)* George Howe's handwritten notes from November 9, 1967, clearly indicate (centre left, in red) that he was expecting a TV crew to cover King's Honorary Degree Ceremony.

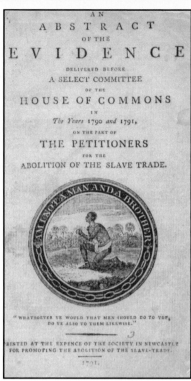

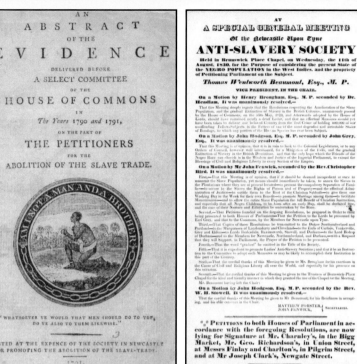

Clockwise from top left: 1) Portrait of ex-slave and abolitionist Olaudah Equiano, who visited Tyneside in 1791. *2)* This anti-slavery tract, published in 1791 by the Society in Newcastle for Promoting the Abolition of the Slave-Trade, featured a version of the famous 'Am I not a Man and a Brother' image by renowned local engraver Thomas Bewick. *3)* A report of a meeting of the Newcastle Upon Tyne Anti-Slavery Society on August 11, 1830. *4)* Darlington-based abolitionist, peace campaigner, suffragist and Chartist Elizabeth Pease was part of a Quaker community vital to radical politics in the North East. *5)* Frederick, Douglass, the most important of all African American abolitionists, visited the North East several times between 1846 and 1886. *6)* Like many visiting black fugitive slaves and abolitionists, William Wells Brown used his own experiences to encourage support for campaigns against slavery in the United States, as in this appearance at the Central Hall, South Shields in the early 1850s. *7)* William Wells Brown.

5

Top row from left: 1) Unitarian minister William Turner was a stalwart of North East abolitionism in the late 18th and early 19th centuries and the main founder of the nation's first Literary and Philosophical Society. *2)* Brunswick Methodist Chapel was a frequent venue for abolitionist meetings in Newcastle. *3)* Harriet Martineau, an influential British critic of slavery in the United States, lived on Tyneside for several years starting in late 1839. *Middle row from left: 1)* Completed in 1838, the monument to Charles Earl Grey in Newcastle city centre celebrated a man described as 'the constant advocate of peace and the fearless and consistent champion of civil and religious liberty.' *2)* Charles Earl Grey, Prime Minister when both the Great Reform Act of 1832 and the Abolition of Slavery Act of 1833 were passed. *3)* William George Armstrong, a Newcastle engineer, entrepreneur and philanthropist, supplied arms to both sides during the American Civil War. *Left:* Politician and journalist Joseph Cowen was at the heart of radical politics on Tyneside from the middle of the 19th century.

SHOCKING LYNCHING SCENE.
A NEGRO BURNED ALIVE.

According to Dalziel's Agency, one of the most shocking cases of lynching in the history of the United States took place on Saturday last at Texarkana, Texas.

On Feb. 15, Mrs Henry Jewell, a farmer's wife, was alone in her home with a five months' old baby, her husband having been called away from home upon business. Shortly after the latter's departure a negro appeared at the door and asked the whereabouts of Mr Jewell. The woman informed him that her husband had gone to the town. The negro said he had a horse he was anxious to sell to Mr Jewell, and left. Mrs Jewell then decided to visit a neighbour, and went out, when the negro, who had been in hiding, sprang from behind a bush and seized the unfortunate woman by the throat. After a desperate struggle the negro dragged the fainting woman to an adjoining barn, where he kept her for an hour, and then fled. When Mr Jewell returned home he found his wife insensible, bearing marks of the terrible maltreatment she had undergone. He gave the alarm, and posses were immediately organised and started in pursuit of the negro. For a week their search was unsuccessful, but on Saturday they came across a coloured man named Coy, whom they suspected of the crime. He was at once confronted with his victim, Mrs Jewell identifying him without the slightest hesitation. It was then decided to hang him forthwith, and, surrounded by an angry mob he was marched through the main streets of the city in the direction of the place selected for his execution.

On the way one of the leaders was about to put a rope round his neck when a shout went up "Burn him!" The cry was immediately taken up and repeated by a hundred throats. When near the Post Office a man who had hold of the rope, which in the meantime had been placed on the prisoner's neck, attempted to mount a telegraph pole with it. He was seized by the foot and dragged to the ground. "Burn him, burn him," was shouted again and again. It was evident that death by fire would be the only thing likely to appease the multitude. Several leading citizens mounted a box and told the mob that if they had decided to burn the wretch they should at least, for the sake of their wives and children, take him outside the city. Another start was then made, and, followed by the howling mob, Coy was taken outside the city limits. When just beyond the track of the Iron Mountain Railway a halt was made. There was a stump of a tree, about 10ft high stood in a large open space. To this the negro was immediately bound with iron fastenings, and then the contents of several cans of kerosene oil were poured over him. "Let his victim apply the match," shouted out someone. "Let Mrs Jewell set fire to him," was shouted back by every man in the crowd.

Then a scene was enacted unparalleled in the history of the country. A clear space had been left round the doomed wretch. Suddenly out of the crowd, and greeted with cheers and shrieks of enthusiasm, Mrs Jewell emerged. She looked pale, but determined, and was supported on either side by a male relation. She walked to the place of execution, where her assailant was pinioned, struck a match, and applied it to the negro's clothes in two places. In a few minutes Coy was wrapped in flames, and ultimately died in fearful agony. Mrs Jewell stood facing him with her arms folded until death terminated his sufferings.

The crowd which actually witnessed and assisted at this horrible scene could not have been less than 4,000; some estimate it as high as 6,000.

It is deemed probable that the local authorities will endeavour to punish the ringleaders.

Clockwise from top left: *1)* A 'shocking lynching scene' in Texas reported in the *Newcastle Courant*, February 27 1892. *2)* Ida B. Wells, African American journalist, newspaper editor, suffragist and international anti-lynching campaigner, received an enthusiastic welcome in Newcastle in April 1894. *3)* Arab seamen, primarily from the Yemen, began to settle in South Shields at the turn of the 20th century. *4)* An Arab procession through South Shields, December 6, 1937. *5)* The South Shields 'race riot' of August 1930 was one of several outbreaks of violence between white, Arab and Somali seaman in that port town during the first half of the 20th century.

7

Girl, 16, says she loves Pakistani

A SIXTEEN-YEAR-OLD girl was said at the Moot Hall juvenile court today to have stayed in a Pakistani's room with him several times.

"I love him dearly and I'm going on loving him," said a statement attributed to her.

She is a snack-bar assistant whose parents are said not to be exercising proper control of her. She is alleged to be in moral danger, and in need of care and attention.

INDIANS IN NEWCASTLE

Children laugh at the turban

'THE OLD CUSTOMS ARE KEEPING PEOPLE BACK'

THE old ways don't matter when you come to Western countries. With these words a Hindu shattered my notion that the Indian community in Newcastle would be keeping alive some of their old customs

The Moslems have a Moslem at Mr. Mohammed's office to Society and a mosque to help any of the community in

Even the hookah is fast in Blenheim street. It is used

Moslems worshipping in the Mosque, Westmorland Road, Newcastle. This is the first time that such a picture has been taken in the City.

Service. Most of them suffer from bronchitis

INDIANS IN NEWCASTLE   . . . . a special investigation

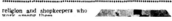

This is the first of a special series of articles by Tony Stride on the Indians in Newcastle—their work, and play, their dress, their customs, how they educate their children, what they hope to achieve in the future. It is a series that will command the attention of every thoughtful reader.

AND they've all got cars y'know . . . It was a Westmorland Road shopkeeper speaking. His tone carried with it a suggestion of a secret envy of an inferior mob.

We were in what some of the locals would not hesi-

From the burning sun of Asia to the smog of Tyneside

doubled in the past ten years.

Estimates varied from "about 900" (a Newcastle detective) to "about 500" (most of the Indians interviewed).

I set out to discover why such numbers desert the Asian sun for Tyneside's smog - ridden slums; and, if they've all got cars, how can they afford them?

To get the truth I tramped the bare boards of the seedy unly old Victorian mansions, let off in single rooms in which two or three eat and sleep—and the deep carpeted

religion and shopkeepers who work among them

credit. And for a few weeks

Darlington and the Richardsons in Newcastle especially prominent. Another Quaker, Gateshead-born lawyer and subsequently Secretary and then President of the Newcastle Literary and Philosophical Society, Robert Spence Watson was a leading light in pacifist circles from the 1860s into the early 20th century, eventually becoming President of a rejuvenated national Peace Society in 1903.[7]

In the mid-19th century, there was considerable overlap between the peace and anti-slavery movements, not just in terms of membership, values and transatlantic orientation, but also tactically, in their shared emphasis on publicity through pamphleteering and the press. *Advocate of Peace*, the official organ of the New York-based American Peace Society, regularly carried notices from the London-based *Herald of Peace*, including accounts of an 1835 lecture tour by Rev. James Hargreaves that took in Stockton, Gateshead and Newcastle.[8] Keenly aware of the value of publicity for peace and anti-slavery work, Anna Richardson edited *The Olive Leaf*, a magazine especially aimed at children. She also edited *The Slave*—an abolitionist periodical she founded with her husband Henry—and *Monthly Illustrations of American Slavery*, which from 1847 served as a kind of international news distribution service on slavery for hundreds of newspapers.[9]

The focus on the US among North East abolitionists increased steadily between 1833 and 1861, the year in which southern slaveholding states seceded from the Union to create the Confederate States of America and precipitated four years of bitter and bloody Civil War. Local interest in American slavery was further stimulated by the procession of black and white American abolitionists and entertainers who visited the region, as well as regular appearances by British anti-slavery campaigners who had toured the US. Indeed, the number and calibre of these visitors reflected the North East's status as a centre of British anti-slavery activity while, cumulatively, they consolidated a regional sense of solidarity with the African American freedom struggle. North East abolitionists worked hard to cultivate these transatlantic networks, hoping to generate international pressure to end the institution or at least to oppose its extension into new territories and states as the US expanded westwards.

The most important white American to court British abolitionists in the middle third of the 19th century was William Lloyd Garrison, co-founder of the American Anti-Slavery Society (AASS) and editor of the leading anti-slavery newspaper of the era, *The Liberator*. Garrison especially targeted female anti-slavery groups in Britain. An advocate of women's suffrage as well as of an immediate end to slavery, Garrison first visited

England, though not the North East, between May and August 1833. He enthused about the extent of British women's involvement in the anti-slavery cause and hoped to inspire similar efforts in the US. His main British allies, Charles Stuart and George Thompson, conducted a reciprocal tour of America in 1834 and worked tirelessly to promote international exchanges of information, ideas and sometimes financial support. In Darlington, for example, the Ladies' Anti-Slavery Society led by Elizabeth Pease responded to an appeal by the Ladies' Association of New England that was itself prompted by a visit from Thompson, to publish a declaration of solidarity with their American abolitionist sisters. The declaration was reproduced in many anti-slavery newspapers. In April 1836, the Newcastle Ladies' Emancipation Society (NLES) was founded after Thompson's March 30 appearance at the Friends' Meeting House on Pilgrim Street, probably accompanied by the ubiquitous Pease. Following in the footsteps of their Darlington colleagues, the NLES also sent a widely circulated expression of support to America in December 1836.[10]

Elizabeth Pease, whose father Joseph had founded the Peace Society in 1817, combined abolitionism with an unflappable commitment to peace, temperance and Chartism—a popular movement inspired, in part, by the desire of artisans and the working-class to secure some of the political rights that the Great Reform Act of 1832 had granted to the middle-class. Having initially concentrated on her work with the Darlington Ladies' Anti-Slavery Society, in June 1840 she travelled to the World Anti-Slavery Convention in London and met with leading American campaigners, including Lucretia Mott and Elizabeth Cady Stanton. Delegations to the conference were also sent from anti-slavery societies in Newcastle, South Shields and Sunderland.[11] The organiser of the Convention was Birmingham-based Quaker and sometime Chartist Joseph Sturge, who used the occasion to promote the British and Foreign Anti-Slavery Society he had launched in April 1839. At a time when women's participation in politics was still widely frowned upon, Sturge declared that Pease and the handful of other women delegates would not be allowed to take part. It mattered little to Sturge that Pease and her Darlington Ladies had been instrumental in helping him establish his Central Negro Emancipation Committee in 1837.

Male opinion on the ruling was split. Lewis Tappan, William Lloyd Garrison's main rival in American abolitionist circles, opposed the involvement of women and had been hostile to the initial open invitation from Sturge. Tappan endorsed a second call for delegates in February 1840 that stipulated only 'gentlemen' need attend. In America, this controversy deep-ened the rift between more radical, immediatist Garrisonians and supporters of Tappan, who broke away from the AASS to form their own American and Foreign Slavery Society in May 1840. As it transpired most of the American delegates who did show up in London in June, including Wendell Phillips, Henry B. Stanton and Garrison himself, supported the women's right to participate. Nonetheless, a shoddy compromise saw Pease and her fellow female delegates seated in a segregated section, away from the main arena of discussion and debate. It was another reminder of how the struggle for African American freedom and equality was always con-nected to other struggles against prejudice and discrimination, in this case those based on gender.[12]

Differences of opinion over the place of women in abolitionism pro-vided just one source of tension within a transatlantic movement that was never wholly in agreement on tactics, timetables or rationales for ending slavery. Generally speaking, however, British abolitionism was less factional and divided than its American counterpart. British abolitionists were prag-matists rather than ideologues. They entertained a variety of tactics to bring about emancipation and wove anti-slavery into a multitude of other pro-gressive causes and humanitarian concerns. Garrison appealed to them by casting the AASS as part of a global struggle against both slavery and a range of other social and economic ills. Perennially wary of direct involvement in American party politics, he favoured moral-suasion and publicity to change popular attitudes towards slavery and bring about unanswerable public pres-sure for emancipation. Again, this approach found favour with British radicals who, with the franchise still severely restricted, were well used to trying to influence government policies through propaganda and extra-Par-liamentary agitation.

In 1834 British abolitionists, many directly inspired by Garrison, cre-ated the British and Foreign Society for the Universal Abolition of Negro Slavery and the Slave Trade. Known colloquially as the Universal Abolition Society (UAS), the organisation prioritised aiding American anti-slavery ac-tivities and opposing continued foreign participation or complicity in the slave trade around the world.[13] North East abolitionists, still bristling at both the 'apprenticeship' provisions and the compensation paid to planters under the 1833 Abolition of Slavery Act, followed suit. They tended to echo Garrison's call for immediate and global emancipation and his emphasis on moral-suasion and propaganda, believing that the issue was of such im-portance that it transcended party politics. As the founding statement of the

Durham branch of the UAS explained in October 1836, its objective was 'to aid by all lawful and peaceful means the exertions which are being made for universal emancipation:- We are not instigated by party politics, - by private motives, - or by any desire of unnecessary interference with the Institutions of other States.' The Society pledged that 'the only weapons we would bring to bear on the Question,' would be 'argument and persuasion, - treaty and convention, - moral and Christian influences.'[14]

Earlier, in Newcastle on March 31, 1836, the city's leading anti-slavery group had undergone yet another name change, affirming its global as well as its immediatist agenda by rebranding itself the Newcastle upon Tyne Society for Abolishing Slavery All Over the World. With veteran activist John Edward Swinburne as President, Thomas Wentworth Beaumont and Robert Ormston among its vice-presidents, and the redoubtable Rev. William Turner on its committee, the reconfigured Society 'devoted itself, by all lawful means, to promote the *immediate* emancipation of the Slave.' George Thompson spoke at the Brunswick Place Wesleyan Chapel meeting when the Society adopted its new name and passed a motion that took direct aim at 'the cruel and abominable system of Slavery at present existing in several of the United States of North America.' The Society recognised, however, that racial prejudice and discrimination was not unique to the slaveholding southern states. It excoriated 'the vile and odious distinction of colour obtaining in them all' and noted how the mistreatment of African Americans contravened the tenets of the much-admired American Declaration of Independence, with its affirmation that 'all men are created equal—and that they are endowed with certain inalienable rights—that among these are life, liberty and the pursuit of happiness.' Slavery also flouted 'the golden rule of the Divine Founder of Christianity, which enjoins, "Whatsoever ye would that men should do to you, do ye even so to them".'[15]

In Newcastle, then, religious conviction fused with a typical enlightenment commitment to the sort of individual rights enshrined in the American Declaration of Independence. This potent blend of political ideology and religiously rooted moral conviction was similar to Garrison's own brand of urgent abolitionism. Indeed, the 1836 resolutions of the reconstituted Newcastle Society ended with an expression of sympathy for its transatlantic 'brethren in the cause of universal freedom in America, under the persecutions to which they are subjected.'[16]

The dynamism of abolitionism in the North East during the three decades after the Abolition of Slavery Act reinforces a point made by historian Richard Huzzey, who has challenged the conventional wisdom that this was 'a period of anti-slavery decline' in Britain. While Huzzey accepts that the gradual rise of pseudo-scientific racism, 'stirrings of imperialism' and the 'fading influence' of national anti-slavery societies might suggest the exhaustion of anti-slavery sentiment and activity, he cautions that 'judging the health of anti-slavery sympathies from the institutional survival of abolitionist organizations is a mistake.' This was, he argues, a period of 'anti-slavery pluralism,' when anti-slavery ideologies and activities intersected with a wide range of other social, political, moral and economic causes to create the powerful, if sometimes fleeting and unstable intellectual synergies and organisational alliances that characterised popular radical politics in Victorian Britain.[17]

Nowhere was this pattern more evident than in the North East where, in the middle third of the 19th century, many radical causes enjoyed a reciprocal, mutually reinforcing relationship with abolitionism. Operating alongside and often in conjunction with pro-free trade and anti-corn-law agitation, perhaps the most important of these causes was Chartism. Chartists in the region, many of them associated with the Radical Reformers of Newcastle group established in 1836 by Feargus O'Connor, or with the Northern Political Union and its successor the National Charter Association, campaigned to expand the suffrage to all men over twenty-one. They also wanted to ensure the integrity of the electoral process by means of secret ballots, annual parliamentary elections, and equal representation for all constituencies.

Following considerable enthusiasm among local radicals, Chartism in the North East had a decidedly chequered career after the early 1840s. Although it once boasted an unusual number of businessmen and elite members of society in its ranks, it failed to preserve this fragile cross-class alliance amid rising levels of public disorder and incendiary—some feared revolutionary—rhetoric. Middle-class reformers increasingly sought to work within, or put pressure on, established political parties, primarily the Whigs. Consequently, Chartism in the North East became largely a militant working-class rallying cry that generated few tangible political rewards until some of its aims were eventually met by the Second Reform Act of 1867 which further expanded the male franchise. Nevertheless, throughout the middle years of the 19th century, many of Chartism's core democratic ideals survived among the region's working-classes in the Miners' Association, the Seaman's United Association and the other nascent labour organisations.[18]

Although Chartists occasionally disrupted anti-slavery meetings to draw attention to their grievances, complaining that middle-class abolitionists were more concerned with the plight of slaves than with the rights of British workers, their democratic ideals and resistance to unaccountable political power meant that many Chartists were also enthusiastic abolitionists. Since neither abolitionism nor Chartism were especially unified movements, generalisations about either are perilous. Still, the transatlantic connections between what Ray Bradbury has termed 'these two great liberatory movements of the nineteenth century,' were plentiful, as demonstrated by the platform Chartists regularly gave, in print and in person, to visiting American abolitionists such as Garrison and Frederick Douglass. Although far from synonymous, Bradbury argues that both movements can be seen as 'part of a wave of questioning upheaval that swept the newly developing capitalist economies of the first half of the nineteenth century.' In the North East, this meant that mid-century abolitionism and Chartism often shared the same rhetoric of individual and collective liberation.[19]

Certainly, when William Garrison first visited the North East in 1846 he discovered a hotbed of abolitionist fervour and radical politics. Accompanied by George Thompson, Garrison arrived in Darlington on October 15 for a meeting with Elizabeth Pease. From Darlington, Garrison and Thompson travelled to Newcastle, arriving on October 17 to address what Garrison later described as 'the most densely crowded and enthusiastic meeting I have yet encountered on this side of the Atlantic.' A public breakfast followed the next day, hosted by the Unitarian minister of the Hanover Square Chapel, Rev. George Harris, while the Mayor of Newcastle, Thomas Emerson Headlam, presided over a public rally.[20]

Before leaving Newcastle, Garrison met briefly with the mother and sister of Harriet Martineau, another important British abolitionist with close connections to the North East. Her mother, Elizabeth Rankin Martineau, was the daughter of a Newcastle grocer and, ironically given Harriet's staunch opposition to slavery, sugar refiner. Although Harriet was born in Norwich in 1802, she moved to the region for health reasons in late 1839. After spending six months living in Newcastle at 28, Eldon Square with her sister Elizabeth and brother-in-law, the eminent doctor Thomas Michael Greenhow, on March 16, 1840 Martineau relocated to 12, Front Street in Tynemouth. She stayed for five years, developing a fierce loyalty for the picturesque coastal town. In February 1843 she teasingly rebuked her friend Fanny Wedgewood for suggesting she lived in urban Newcastle rather than in the small but prosperous town at the mouth of the Tyne. Martineau wrote of how the move had done wonders for her condition: 'I am sure that the general effect on my health must be very great,' but she also admonished, 'Shall I once more say (for the sake of not losing your letters) that we live *not* at *Newcastle* but at *Tynemouth*: and that we have no more to do with Newcastle than with York?'[21]

Martineau's health remained fragile in Tynemouth, but she continued to be a prolific writer, astute analyst of social structures and formidable champion of many progressive causes. Indeed, Martineau was already something of a radical celebrity by the time she returned to her North East roots. In particular, her three volume *Society in America*, published in 1837, was a pioneering work of sociological observation which condemned, among many other American shortcomings, the nation's neglect of women's education and rights, and acceptance of slavery.[22] The following December, Martineau published *The Martyr Age of the United States,* a report on the travails of contemporary American abolitionists. The essay, which originally appeared in the *London and Westminster Review*, was quickly republished by various anti-slavery organisations in Britain and the US, including the Oberlin Institute, a pioneering bi-racial educational facility for men and women in Ohio. Martineau greatly admired Oberlin and in 1840 authorised a reprint of *The Martyr Age* by the Newcastle upon Tyne Emancipation and Aborigines Society that raised £500 for the college.[23]

Another famous, if more fleeting, visitor was Harriet Beecher Stowe, author of the 1852 international bestselling novel *Uncle Tom's Cabin*. Like much of Britain, the North East had succumbed to 'Uncle Tom Mania.' The anti-slavery novel was favourably reviewed and then serialised in the *Chronicle* from late October to Christmas 1852. The paper also advertised an 'Uncle Tom's Cabin Almanack.' This was 'an Abolitionist Memento' whose 'contents will demonstrate the Truth of the Scenes depicted in *Uncle Tom's Cabin*, as drawn from the Lives of celebrated Individuals once in Captivity as Negro Slaves.'[24] Four years later, Stowe visited Newcastle and attended Durham Cathedral in October 1856 while on tour to promote her new novel, *Dred: A Tale of the Dismal Swamp*.[25] In December 1857, *Dred* was adapted for the stage and performed at Newcastle's Theatre Royal and Sunderland's New Lyceum, where the book's abolitionist themes were specially enhanced for the region's enthusiastic anti-slavery audiences by the addition of a new character, Jane, a fugitive slave.[26] By this time, however, the North East had little need for dramatic impersonations of runaway slaves; the region was getting very used to welcoming the real thing.

While there was plenty of racial condescension in some of the language used to exhort whites to support emancipation and, as we shall see in Chapter Eight, the North East was hardly devoid of racist attitudes or racial conflicts, visits from black abolitionists helped to establish the basis for some measure of racial tolerance and understanding in the region. It was during this period that much of the groundwork for the cultures of welcome that would later be widely attributed to and proudly claimed by the region was laid. Crucial in this process was the procession of charismatic African American anti-slavery activists, many of them fugitive slaves, some of them consummate performers with memoirs to hawk and stage shows to promote, who passed through the region. These visitors were living embodiments and emissaries of the Black Atlantic. Successors to Olaudah Equiano, precursors of Martin Luther King and, for many of those they encountered in the North East, representatives of the entire slave population, black abolitionists exposed local whites to aspects of African American thought and culture, challenged racist stereotypes, and made powerful anti-slavery appeals on a variety of ethical, economic, scientific, political and religious grounds.

In the mid-19th century, as the sectional crisis between free and slave-holding states in the US worsened, the parade of black abolitionists arriving in Britain and making their way to the North East lengthened. The successor to the NLES, the Ladies Negro Friend and Emancipation Society of Newcastle (LNFESN) in Newcastle sponsored visits by Charles Lenox Remond, the son of free Massachusetts blacks, and Dr. James Pennington, a Brooklyn-based minister who had escaped slavery in Maryland in 1827 when he was nineteen years old and later became Yale University's first African American student.[27] The Society also paid £25 towards bringing Henry Highland Garnet from New York to England, where he travelled the country, lecturing against the evils of slavery and for a boycott of slave-produced goods. Garnet helped to breathe new life into ethical consumerism campaigns in the North East during the 1840s and 1850s, when new Ladies' Free-Labour Produce Societies appeared in Alnwick, Darlington, Gateshead, Hartlepool, Middlesbrough, North and South Shields, Stockton, Sunderland and Winlaton, many of them spearheaded by Quaker women.[28]

The boycott movement dovetailed perfectly with rising interest in free trade doctrines. Indeed, David Brown has even speculated that 'The rise of free trade abolitionism in Britain in the 1840s and 1850s perhaps pushed the economic side of the abolitionist argument above the moral, even though to many they remained inseparable.'[29] In Newcastle, the LNFESN dedicated itself to 'encouraging the consumption of Free-Labour Produce,' but was also active in petitioning against slavery and raising popular awareness of its barbarity.[30] The Society even offered direct financial support to fugitive and freed slaves. On May 10, 1844, for example, it gave a one-off donation of £4 to support the education of an emancipated woman living in the free state of Illinois, so that she could become a teacher, 'employed in the instruction of some portion of her race.'[31]

Once more, the Richardsons were at the heart of things on Tyneside. Henry and Anna welcomed the entire Garnet family into their home, which was then located at 89, Blandford Street in Newcastle, and arranged an event at the city's Independent Chapel in which a succession of speakers denounced American slavery and in particular the Fugitive Slave Act.[32] This much-reviled Act was part of the Compromise of 1850 that temporarily and partially eased sectional tensions in the US. However, it did so at the cost of appeasing southern slave power by allowing slavery into some of the new western lands secured during the Mexican War of 1846-8 if it was the will of the majority of the people in those territories. Even more odiously, the Act protected the right of slave-owners to pursue their escaped 'property' throughout the entire US.[33]

The Compromise of 1850 was directly responsible for the presence on Tyneside of another escaped slave. James Watkins, originally known as Sam Berry and born on a plantation in Maryland in 1821, had escaped in 1844. Like so many others in his situation, Watkins was 'thrown into the greatest disquietude and peril,' by the enactment of the "American Fugitive Slave Law" in 1850. In 1851 he sought sanctuary in England and the following year published his memoirs, which explained the particular threat of the new Fugitive Slave Law for the benefit of British readers. 'This atrocious and abominable law makes it a great crime, punishable with heavy fines and imprisonment, to be either directly or indirectly a party to the escape of a slave. It also appoints Commissioners and Assistant-Commissioners throughout the so-called Free States, to see after catching the fugitives, and returning them to their owners.'[34] As Watkins pointed out, the Fugitive Slave Act required officials and citizens of free states to cooperate in the return of runaway slaves to their lawful master. On both sides of the Atlantic, this Act, compounded by the 1857 Dred Scott decision, in which the Supreme Court ruled that no slave or former slave in the US could ever be a citizen or enjoy any legal rights that whites needed to respect, intensified abolitionist pressure. Again, by implicating the North and federal authorities in the perpetuation of slavery, it encouraged an understanding that neither slavery nor the racist attitudes on which it depended were exclusively southern vices. This would have significant consequences for North East public opinion when Civil War eventually broke out.

James Watkins was somewhat sceptical about those radicals he encountered in England who glibly proclaimed a common experience among the labourers of the industrial north and the slaves of America. 'Since I have been in England,' he wrote in 1852,

> I have often been surprised to hear working-men declare, that they, too, know what slavery is. They argue, that they are compelled to work very hard and long, for little pay, and this they call 'slavery,' forgetting all the while, that they can, at any time, give a fortnight or month's notice to their employers that they are going to leave, and then, they are at liberty to improve their circumstances, if they can. All this is very different to being placed on the auction block, and knocked off to the highest bidder, with the same case and as little consideration as a piece of old furniture is done in any English marketplace....When I hear people talk thus, I fear they don't comprehend the subject....I prize my freedom above every earthly blessing.[35]

In Newcastle, in October of the same year, the *Chronicle* had also dismissed simplistic analogies between industrial labour and slavery: 'In our minds there is no parallel whatsoever; for however hard our working populations have to toil for their daily bread, at all events they are not bought and sold like cattle.' Grim though conditions and remunerations were for many British factory and agricultural workers, they had a measure of freedom, a range of possibilities for improvement and mobility, and certain protections at law that slaves simply did not enjoy.[36]

By the time Watkins prepared the twenty-third edition of his popular autobiography, this time for publication in Newcastle in 1864, he was highly attuned to British racial attitudes. On one hand, he recognised from personal experience white susceptibility to the seductive pull of racial stereotyping, which allowed them to be simultaneously titillated, fascinated and appalled by the imagined characteristics of non-whites:

> Through the ignorance and the prejudice of a certain portion of this community, we coloured people have been calumniated, and ideas have been disseminated in relation to us, which have no

foundation in fact, but have only originated in the malice of people who have made it their business to misrepresent us; thus, for instance, we often hear English mothers and servants threaten a naughty child with being handed over to 'Black Sam,' or 'The Black Man,' & c.[37]

On the other hand, Watkins joined many of his fellow fugitives in celebrating the warmth, generosity and genuine support he received from many sections of the British public:

> Whilst I have had the honour of being cordially received by the higher classes, and by some of the nobility of this country (and for the encouragement they have given me I am deeply grateful), yet I would not forget the thousands and tens of thousands of the poorer classes, or, as they are called, the 'lower orders,' who have received me with unexampled kindness, and have so nobly rallied round the cause which I advocated, and have shown, in a most decided and unmistakeable manner, their abounding sympathy for the slave, and their utter detestation of the slave's oppressor.[38]

Here again was the invocation of a community of feeling, of interracial solidarity, which progressives in the North East would frequently celebrate as indicative of the region's relatively harmonious race relations and dominant cultures of welcome. As Watkins continued, 'Though these people are spoken of as the 'working' and the 'lower classes,' I have never found their sympathies less warm, their generosity less cheerful, nor the instincts of their hearts less noble, than those who are far above them in worldly wealth and influence.'[39]

Another notable African American visitor who became even more enamoured of the region was William Wells Brown. An ex-slave and author in 1853 of *Clotel, or the President's Daughter*, the first novel published by an African American, Brown believed there was unusual warmth and sincerity in the reception he received on Tyneside. 'Of the places favourable to reformers of all kinds, calculated to elevate and benefit mankind, Newcastle-on-Tyne doubtless takes the lead,' he wrote. 'In no place in the United Kingdom has the American Slave warmer friends than in Newcastle.'[40]

Brown first visited Darlington and then Newcastle in November and December 1849 on what turned out to be a three year-long speaking tour of Europe. His sojourn included a visit to the August 1849 Peace Convention in Paris as a member of the American Peace Committee for a Congress of Nations, again suggesting the intimate connection between international struggles for peace and those for racial justice. Using Newcastle as his base for extensive touring in the north of England, Brown was another guest of Henry and Anna Richardson, by this time living at 5, Summerhill Grove. While in Newcastle, he wrote a new introduction to the fourth, British edition of his *Narrative of William W. Brown, An American Slave*, a best-selling memoir of his experiences of slavery and his escape to freedom initially published in Boston in 1847.[41] In Newcastle, he also arranged with J. Blackwell, publisher of the *Newcastle Courant*, to produce a British version of *The Anti-Slavery Harp*, a compendium of abolitionist songs suitable for use at anti-slavery meetings that would 'bring before the English people, in a cheap form, a few spirited Melodies against Chattel Slavery.'[42]

Blackwell's role here, like that of other abolitionist Tyneside publishers and newspaper proprietors, including Brown and Green, J. Clark, and Joseph Cowen, indicates how progressive politics on Tyneside in general, and anti-slavery activism in particular, depended heavily on a vibrant print and reading culture in the city. Enlightened views in an enlightenment city relied on an informed citizenry. One key to Tyneside radicalism was an expanding literate population and widely available material for it to read, whether in elite, subscriber institutions like the 'Lit and Phil' and the Assembly Rooms, or in public libraries, or in coffee houses dotted around the city, or via a dynamic local press and pamphleteering culture that, as early as the mid-17th century, had earned the city a national reputation as a centre of printing and the book trade.[43]

To keep himself alive as well as to raise consciousness and support for the anti-slavery cause, Brown sold copies of his books and gave many speeches to packed audiences, particularly in Darlington, where he was a guest of the Pease family, and in Newcastle, where his first lecture, at the Nelson Street Lecture Room on December 11, 1849, was filled to overflowing. In Newcastle, Brown 'was received with loud cheers,' and there was unanimous support for a resolution that offered the meeting's 'warmest and most cordial congratulations' to Brown on his visit to the region. Moreover, in a genuinely radical insistence on full equality for non-whites, those assembled flatly repudiated 'the doctrine of the inferiority of the African race, and regarding Mr. Brown as a representative of this oppressed people...unreservedly recognise his right to perfect social, political and religious equality, a right received from the hands of his Creator.'[44] Between 400 and

500 people also attended a public tea at the Newcastle Music Hall on January 3, 1850, when Brown received a specially sewn purse containing twenty sovereigns raised by the local community.[45] In October and November of the same year, again with the support of the Richardsons and some shrewd advertising in the local press, Brown held the first exhibition of an elaborate Panorama which used some of his own sketches and paintings, augmented by the work of others, to depict the evils of American slavery alongside episodes from his own life at the Commercial Sales Room near Grey's Monument.[46] In mid-December 1850, Brown also presented his Panorama at the Seaman's Hall in South Shields and a couple of years later again at the town's Central Hall.[47]

Around the same time, Brown welcomed William Craft to Newcastle, where they shared the spotlight at a March 13, 1851 anti-slavery meeting in the Nelson Street Lecture Room. At the meeting Craft explained how he and his wife Ellen had made a particularly daring escape from slavery in Georgia with Ellen posing as a white master to William's black slave.[48] Although abolitionists had rallied to protect the couple in Boston, after the Fugitive Slave Act they sought refuge first in Canada and then in England. On arrival in Liverpool in late 1850, Ellen was taken ill, but William travelled to meet Brown in Newcastle.[49] Brown, who often appeared at public events alongside the Crafts, acted as a mentor to the couple. So, too, did Harriet Martineau. Following a meeting with the Crafts and Brown at her new Lake District home in Ambleside, Martineau arranged for them to go to Ockham School in Sussex to undergo intensive lessons in reading and writing. Martineau believed this was necessary to prepare them for a life as effective abolitionist propagandists.[50]

The Crafts eventually spent eighteen years in Britain, finally returning to the US in 1868. Before that, however, in August 1863, with the US Civil War raging, William Craft had returned to Tyneside to engage representatives of the British so-called scientific community in one of the most significant and revealing exchanges on the state of racial thought in mid-19th century Britain. On August 27, 1863, renowned British anthropologist Dr James Hunt presented a paper to the annual meeting of the British Association for the Advancement of Science in Newcastle. In his talk on 'The Physical and Mental Characteristics of the Negro' Hunt presented a range of new physiological 'evidence,' especially pertaining to the thickness of black skulls, to support his argument that people of African descent were congenitally inferior to whites in intelligence and higher physical and mental functions to whites. When Hunt finished, Craft rose to mercilessly mock and systematically refute the anatomical evidence upon which Hunt's argument was based. If blacks did, indeed, have thicker skulls, Craft teased, God had doubtless arranged this to protect them from the kind of racist fallacies peddled by Hunt and some other scientists in 19th century Britain. Without thick skulls, Craft suggested '[our] brains would probably have become very much like those of many scientific gentlemen of the present day.'[51]

As he filleted Hunt's decidedly fishy argumentation, Craft paused to offer homilies ('Englishmen were not all Shakespeares') and amusing anecdotes that drew appreciative laughter from the audience. Craft insisted that circumstances, environment and opportunity, not genes, blood, and bone structure were what determined the achievements of different races, at different times, in different places.[52] This was precisely the argument that 'A Free Born Briton' had made when urging North East support for abolitionist candidates in the 1826 election; it was also the same point that Martin Luther King made in Newcastle in 1967 when he dismissed racism as the 'myth of the inferior race; it is the notion that a particular race is worthless and degradated innately…It is the idea that the very being of a people is inferior.'[53]

Taking on Hunt's accusation that the stooped posture of 'negroes' was evidence of their closer proximity to a simian past, Craft sparked cheers by comparing them to local white farm workers: 'As to the [N]egro not being erect, the same thing might be said of agricultural laborers in this country.' Back-breaking field work, not hereditary traits, were the crucial factors here. One report noted how Craft also reminded his audience that 'When Julius Caesar came to this country, he said of the natives that they were such stupid people that they were not fit to make slaves of in Rome (laughter).' He reflected that 'It had taken a long time to make Englishmen what they now were,' adding that there was ample evidence to show that, once free of the bonds of slavery 'negroes… made very rapid progress when placed in advantageous circumstances.' At the end of his speech, Craft was rapturously applauded by an audience who heard in his eloquent, informed and witty performance living refutation of Hunt's theories.[54]

Other African American visitors to the North East and Britain more generally also challenged the myths of inherent black indolence, childishness, primitivism and ignorance that permeated a lot of white European thinking about peoples of African descent. Collectively and individually these visitors provided an important counterweight to racist ideas that increasingly circulated throughout political and popular culture and helped to shape and sustain British imperial policies. The rise of abolitionist senti-ment and fascination with African American visitors in Britain took place as the nation expanded its Empire in Africa, Asia, Australasia and the Car-ibbean often through the forcible subjugation of non-white populations. Moreover, as Vanessa Dickerson explains, 'a century that saw the nation colonise other, often darker-skinned people…also saw Britain contribute its share of so-called empirical evidence to the European underwriting of bio-logical determinism and scientific racism.'[55]

That said, historians have sometimes been too quick to equate the de-velopment of racist ideologies in Britain with the emergence of related, yet distinct forms of scientific racism in the US. In doing so, they have tended to underestimate how Britain's imperial experiences with non-white popu-lations living largely overseas differed from the situation in the US, where whites, especially in the South, shared a nation with a huge black popula-tion, most of whom were enslaved. The enormous dependence of the South on slave labour virtually demanded an elaborate defence of African and Af-rican American slavery on racial grounds. During the early 19th century, pseudo-scientific justifications for slavery on the grounds of inherent and immutable black inferiority became ever more ardent in the South as a means to counter mounting abolitionist opposition in the North and over-seas. Although scientific racism rarely went unchallenged, even in the South—and even among some of those who supported slavery—it none-theless exerted considerable influence on sectional and national attitudes towards the prospect of emancipation.

In Georgian and early Victorian Britain, by contrast, although racial stereotyping was commonplace and permeated the conception and conduct of imperial policies, often with appalling consequences for indigenous peo-ples of Africa, Asia and Australasia who were their victims, during the first half of the 19th century such beliefs remained somewhat fluid compared with those in the US. To be sure, there was plenty of white racial prejudice and many racially circumscribed impediments to non-white social, eco-nomic and political rights and opportunity in Britain and its Empire. Yet, British racism had not yet become fully systematised or linked to the kind of scientific racism that often dominated southern US defences of slavery and underpinned apocalyptic warnings about the consequences for civilisa-tion and its self-appointed white custodians of emancipation. In the 18th and early 19th centuries, even the spectre of 'race-mixing' between whites and the tens of thousands of black people living in Britain seemed to inspire less white fear and opprobrium than it did in the US, where the dread prospect of interracial sex, loomed large in the demonology of white racism.[56]

The asymmetric development of racial science and racist ideologies in the US and Britain had significant consequences for the black abolitionists who visited Newcastle and the North East in the mid-19th century. In the US, African Americans and their white allies were working to dismantle widely understood and firmly held racist myths; in Britain they were often working to prevent such myths becoming embedded in popular consciousness and political culture. This they did by arguing that racism, especially scientific racism, was rooted, not in legitimate science, but rather in white social, economic and political imperatives to justify slavery. In short, in 1863, Craft's environmental explanations for the plight of African Americans were far more familiar and credible to the majority of whites in Newcastle and across Britain than was Hunt's nominally scientific insistence on innate racial difference.

Resisting the rise and steady encrustation of racist ideas in Victorian Britain was no easy task. The needs of empire increasingly served a similar function as did slavery in the US as a driver of the kind of spurious racial science that would later flourish in the eugenics movement. Moreover, by the mid-19th century, blackface minstrelsy, with its broad caricatures of African America life and demeaning portrayals of black intelligence, had become the most popular entertainment form in the Atlantic World. James Watkins had decried the vogue for minstrelsy for precisely these reasons. 'We have public exhibitions in pot-houses and low singing rooms of men who black their faces, and perform such outlandish antics as were never seen amongst the negroes, and who profess to imitate, but who in reality only caricature men of my race.'[57]

Victorian Tynesiders enjoyed minstrelsy immensely. Following a successful British tour in 1836 by Thomas Dartmouth ('Daddy') Rice, the creator of the staple blackface minstrel character Jim Crow, who would subsequently lend his name to the system of racial apartheid in the postbellum US South, and then, in 1843, by the Christy Minstrels, Newcastle ballad and broadsheet publishers W. & T. Fordyce and W.R. Walker both published collections of minstrel tunes. The Fordyce company's *Jim Crow's Song Book* even included a song called 'Jim Crow's Visit to Newcastle', while Walker's firm, based in Newcastle's Royal Arcade, put out 'The Banjo Songster' featuring songs such as 'Dere's Someone in De House Wid Dinah' and later published 'Miss Lucy Neal', a particularly vile piece of racial caricature involving graphic violence, callous murder and wanton promiscuity.[58]

Throughout the 19th century and well into the 20th century, minstrel shows and other stage presentations further exposed Tynesiders to stereotypes about African Americans—perpetually happy, superstitious, ignorant, full of childish mischief and often enjoying life in an idyllic Old South. In Newcastle, Cobb and Chapman, self-declared 'Delineators of Negro Life,' appeared at the Victoria Music Hall in 1861; William Ceda's 'Troupe of Negro Minstrels' played the Oxford Music Hall in 1868; in September 1893, the vogue for burnt-cork minstrelsy during the summer prompted the *Newcastle Courant* to declare 'the present season has been essentially a Nigger's season'; when the revue *In Dixieland* played at the Empire Theatre in February 1914, it was praised for 'embodying southern songs, southern dances, and impersonations of Southern characters—a lifelike picture of the Negro as he and she is'; *The Sugar Baby* musical revue ran at the Empire in early 1918, featuring the 'negro eccentrics' Harry Scott and Eddie Whaley.[59] Although Scott and Whaley were Kentucky-born African Americans, they performed in Newcastle and Sunderland in the blackface minstrel tradition.[60] Indeed, they would later become stalwarts of the BBC's popular *Kentucky Minstrels* radio show that ran from 1933 to 1950, and even headlined in a 1934 film of the same name (possibly the first blacks to star in a British feature film).[61] Thus, they joined a succession of minstrel performers who helped to weave one distorted thread into the tapestry of British ideas about peoples of African descent. Fortunately, there were other, rather different threads in that tapestry.

Away from the stage, fugitive slaves and abolitionists passing through the North East helped to discredit the idea that there was anything sunny about slave life in the Old South. Their presence also counteracted the derogatory stereotypes that were central to minstrelsy and white racism. One of the most ubiquitous figures in the region was Moses Roper, a North Carolina-born slave who, after many attempts, finally escaped slavery in 1834, arriving in Britain for the first of several visits in late November 1835. Roper's relentless touring on behalf of the abolitionist cause and to promote his own memoirs included speeches at Alnwick, Darlington, Durham, Felling, Hartlepool, Morpeth and Newcastle.[62] Charles Lenox Remond had initially accompanied William Lloyd Garrison to the World Anti-Slavery Convention in London in 1840. Sponsored by the Newcastle LNFESN, Remond's lengthy speaking tour of Britain and Ireland included a week-long stay with Elizabeth Pease in Spring 1841. In Darlington he gave three lectures, in addition to a talk before what he described as 'a very large and intelligent assembly in the Flag Lane Chapel, Sunderland.' He also spoke in

Durham, Gateshead, North and South Shields, and Newcastle, where he was yet another guest of Anna, Henry and Ellen Richardson.[63] On May 2, Pease wrote enthusiastically to *The Liberator* of how Remond 'is exciting a warm interest in the question of American slavery, by his powerful and convincing appeals.'[64]

A decade later, Henry 'Box' Brown blurred easy distinctions between entertainment and education on the issue of slavery. Brown toured Britain to promote the first English edition of his autobiography with a stage show that told the remarkable tale of how he had literally mailed himself to freedom in Philadelphia in a box. Brown was not averse to shipping himself around Britain in what he claimed was the very same box in order to drum up publicity for his performances. Brown's 'Panorama of Slave Life,' ran for a week in Newcastle in October 1852 and the following month in North and South Shields. It combined harrowing depictions of slave life with the uplifting story of Brown's own ingenious escape from a Virginia plantation to simultaneously stir support for the abolitionist cause and stimulate sales of his memoir.[65]

The most important of the many African American abolitionists who came through the North East was Frederick Douglass, who had escaped slavery in 1838 and spent nineteen months in Britain starting in 1845. Throughout this period he toured Britain and Ireland extensively and spent considerable time on Tyneside, staying with the Richardson family. He spoke in the region on at least sixteen separate occasions at venues in Cullercoats (where his speech on February 25, 1860, was in an infant schoolroom opened by his fellow abolitionist Henry Highland Garnet), Darlington, Hexham, Newcastle, North Shields, and Sunderland, leaving an indelible impression on many who heard him. Among his fans was the radical journalist and politician Joseph Cowen, who was destined to play a major role in promoting support for the Union and opposition to the Confederacy during the US Civil War.[66] Like many fugitive slaves before him, Douglass was struck by the intensity of the region's anti-slavery passions. In late December 1846, he told a cheering crowd at the Nelson Street Music Hall in Newcastle of his pleasure at seeing 'so large an audience assembled for so noble a cause,' and of his joy 'that Newcastle had a heart that could feel for three millions of oppressed slaves in the United States.' Douglass predicted this would be 'the first of a series of meetings in the north, to arouse again the gigantic energies' of local abolitionists 'and to direct those energies against the enslavement of humanity, though 3,000 miles away.' Tyneside,

Douglass assured an enraptured audience, was ready 'to blow the trumpet of freedom once more across the Atlantic.'[67]

When Douglass returned to America in April 1847, it was as a free man. The Richardsons had raised the money to purchase his freedom. Working through abolitionists Ellis Gray Lorin and Walter Lowrie in Boston and New York respectively, on December 12, 1846, Hugh Auld, brother of Thomas Auld, who was Douglass' 'master,' registered the bill of manumission that formally made Frederick Baily, as Douglass was known, a freeman. The cost was $711.66, or about £150. The decision to purchase Douglass's freedom was not without its critics. Some felt that the purchase legitimised the very notion that a human being could ever be owned by another human being, to be treated and disposed of just like any other item of property.

While the propriety and ethics of his purchase were being debated by American and British abolitionists, Douglass concluded his lengthy exile in Britain. Despite the fatigue caused by an endless round of speaking engagements, he continued to impress, inspire and influence wherever he appeared. On the eve of his return to the US, Elizabeth Pease wrote to *The Liberator*, expressing her thanks for finally getting the chance to meet with and listen to Douglass. 'Much had I longed to see this remarkable man, and highly raised were my expectations; but they were more than realised,' Pease gushed. She added that Douglass was 'A living contradiction…to that base opinion, which is so abhorrent to every humane and Christian feeling, that the blacks are an inferior race.'[68]

In fact, anti-slavery sentiment was by no means incompatible with a strong sense of white racial superiority, a paternalistic desire to 'raise up' an underdeveloped, if not necessarily congenitally inferior race. Some earnest white abolitionists had serious reservations about the desirability of granting blacks full social or political equality. Differences of opinion about the intellectual capacity and moral character of peoples of African descent and related doubts about their suitability for full citizenship even threatened the relationships between British Quakers and some of their American counterparts who considered slaves 'fit for freedom but not for friendship.' British Friends like the Richardsons and Peases were appalled at tales of segregated Quaker Meetings in the US. Pease was instrumental in spreading word of the so-called 'Negro pews' by publishing a pamphlet in Darlington decrying the racial discrimination and prejudice demonstrated by American Quakers, notwithstanding their opposition to slavery.[69]

Pease's widely circulated pamphlet offered insights into a world in which, although slavery was increasingly deemed unacceptable, racial prejudice and discrimination were gaining ground. A few weeks after Pease finally met with Frederick Douglass, he sailed home from Liverpool aboard the *Cambria*. He was forced to travel in steerage despite having a first-class ticket paid for by his friends in Britain and Ireland, including his sometime host in Newcastle, Henry Richardson. The *Newcastle Guardian* expressed widespread local condemnation of these 'Disgraceful Proceedings.'[70] It was a salutary reminder that racism was not wholly dependent on slavery and would have a long and ignominious history, on both sides of the Atlantic, long after that institution was dead.[71]

CHAPTER SEVEN

'God Bless the Policy of Emancipation!':
The North East and the African American Freedom
Struggle from the Civil War to the Rise of Jim Crow

Frederick Douglass returned to the North East on two more occasions. In February and March 1860, he gave speeches in Newcastle, Hexham, Morpeth and North Shields, often taking time to defend the actions of the militant abolitionist John Brown. In December 1859, Brown had been executed for leading an October raid on a government armoury at Harper's Ferry in Virginia, from which he hoped to secure weapons for an armed slave revolt. Douglass fled to England because of the discovery of letters to him from Brown, courting his support for the raid and slave rebellion. Although Douglass wanted no part of the plan, which he rightly thought was doomed to failure, he nonetheless defended Brown's actions. Douglass was convinced that there was already a war raging in the US over slavery—thereby justifying Brown's actions—and that moral-suasion may have outlived its usefulness. Sounding remarkably like the martyred Brown, in Newcastle Douglass proclaimed that what was needed was the forcible overthrow of slave power by an army of slaves and their abolitionist comrades. This was not quite what his pacifist Quaker friends were expecting. It is, however, an indication that there were always alternatives to the peaceful, political and legislative approaches to social change that dominated Tyneside's anti-slavery campaigns, just as a century later there were always those who questioned the efficacy of Martin Luther King's nonviolent direct action strategies to make freedom and equality of opportunity a lived reality for African Americans.[1]

When Douglass visited Britain for the final time in 1886, on a trip he admitted 'was in some respects sentimental,' he did so primarily to meet again the 'two ladies who were mainly instrumental in giving me the chance of devoting my life to the cause of freedom. These were Ellen and Anna Richardson, of Newcastle-upon-Tyne…without any suggestion from me they…bought me out of slavery, secured a bill of sale of my body, made a present of myself to myself, and thus enabled me to return to the United States, and resume my work for the emancipation of the slaves.'[2]

The final phase of the long struggle for emancipation to which Douglass had devoted himself began when Abraham Lincoln, a Republican 'free-soiler' opposed to the expansion of slavery, was elected US President. In January 1861, seven southern slaveholding states seceded from the Union. In April, South Carolina secessionists attacked a federal government fortress at Fort Sumter in Charleston Bay, sparking the Civil War. North East abolitionists were broadly supportive of the Union against the Confederacy, which eventually included eleven slaveholding states. Yet, this was not always an automatic or simple choice. Growing opposition to slavery co-existed with considerable admiration for the South and many of its perceived values. The South's emphasis on community and a stable social structure—albeit one that rested on the awful reality of human bondage— was often contrasted with the rampant individualism, social friction and avarice associated with the more urban, industrialised and competitive North. There was also an acute awareness that British trade, industry and consumption depended heavily on commerce with the South. Moreover, the Confederacy worked hard to attract support and possibly even intervention from Britain by presenting itself as the aggrieved party, as victim of an unresponsive and unrepresentative Republican administration that was operating in direct contradiction to southern—that is *white* southern— interests. Just as the thirteen American Colonies had once felt compelled to rebel against Britain to secure their rights and establish a representative government, so the Confederacy courted international support by casting secession as the only honourable response to the tyranny of the North, where industrialists, free-soilers and abolitionist zealots were directing a hostile federal policy against the beleaguered South.[3]

In the North East, anti-slavery sentiment had always intersected with widespread distrust of centralised and unaccountable governmental power. Agitation for an expansion of the franchise had continued after the Great Reform Act of 1832, helping to create the pressure that eventually led to the Second Reform Act of 1867. In this political climate, Confederate arguments found some traction. There was a good deal of elation at the early military success of the plucky underdog South against the mighty Union forces. Although racial ideologies in Britain remained somewhat in flux, the South's appeals to transatlantic white solidarity also earned some support as the Confederacy positioned itself as an Anglo-Saxon bulwark against the horrifying prospect of a newly freed black population of millions. Put crudely, in the North East at the start of the war, elites generally supported the South; radicals were initially torn between their loathing of slavery and suspicion of Union motives, which included both a sense that Lincoln may have overstepped legitimate authority in his treatment of the South and a profound disappointment that he initially refused to make emancipation a war aim; between these two poles, the general population vacillated and joined most British observers in recoiling from the wholesale slaughter of one of the first truly modern wars.

North East debates over which side to support in the US Civil War were crystalized and then shattered by two crucial events. On October 7, 1862 the Liberal government's Chancellor of the Exchequer William Gladstone came to Newcastle and spoke about the conflict at the Town Hall. Although his family's fortune derived principally from slavery, Gladstone was a long-time opponent of the institution. Yet, as for most Liberals, slavery was not central to his initial analysis of the Civil War or understanding of its ramifications for Britain. He used his speech to acknowledge that the Confederate President Jefferson Davis had not just created an army and a navy, but also 'a nation.' The emergence of an independent South was, he suggested—erroneously as it happened—a 'certainty.' Regardless of the Confederacy's commitment to slavery, Gladstone implied that it should be welcomed into the community of nations.[4] Gladstone's speech galvanised local radicals and abolitionists who were adamantly opposed to the very notion of a slave nation, let alone British recognition of the Confederacy as a legitimate new state. Inadvertently, Gladstone's Newcastle speech moved the slavery issue much closer to the heart of regional and national debates over who to support in the Civil War.

One person for whom such matters appeared to be of little immediate consequence was William George Armstrong. An entrepreneurial Newcastle engineer and armaments manufacturer, Armstrong happily supplied both the Union and the Confederacy with state-of-the-art weaponry made in his Elswick factory. It was Armstrong, in some ways a rather enlightened and philanthropic industrialist, who in 1871 founded Armstrong College (initially called the College of Physical Science), a precursor to Newcastle University. There was a deep irony in the fact that Martin Luther King should receive his Honorary Doctorate and rail against the horrors of war in a building named after a man whose wealth was in large part built on a genius for developing new technologies of mass killing.[5]

By happenstance, on the same day that Gladstone spoke in Newcastle, news reached Britain—although probably not Gladstone himself—of a second event that also pushed slavery to the forefront of discussions about the Civil War and turned the tide of British public opinion against the

South. On September 22, 1862 Abraham Lincoln issued his Preliminary Emancipation Proclamation, later formalised on January 1, 1863. All slaves were to be freed if Confederate forces did not cease hostilities. In the wake of these events at home and abroad, the South's fight was increasingly viewed in Britain as an unpalatable and indefensible attempt to preserve slavery rather than as a principled fight over states' rights and popular sovereignty. As historian Peter O'Connor explains, after the Emancipation Proclamation 'Although it was still possible to advocate for the South through pre-war notions of politics and ethnicity...the complexities of the pre-war South were eroded, to be replaced with a simple slavery-versus-freedom dichotomy—a choice that, for most of the British population, was no choice at all.'[6]

In Newcastle, news of the Emancipation Proclamation was greeted by a massive celebration at the Nelson Street Music Hall, with crowds overflowing into adjacent streets. Partly responsible for the popular jubilation was Joseph Cowen, a crusading radical journalist and later (from 1874 to 1886) Liberal Member of Parliament for Newcastle. Cowen played a crucial role in rousing opposition to the Confederacy and inspiring a new wave of anti-slavery zeal on Tyneside. Although his later enthusiasm for British imperialism sometimes sat awkwardly with the views of his fellow parliamentary Liberals, Cowen's anti-slavery activities, in conjunction with his support for universal suffrage, better working conditions for the region's miners, expanded working-class education, and free public libraries, placed him at the centre of the region's radical politics. In 1859, Cowen had also purchased what quickly became one of the most influential provincial newspapers in Britain: the *Newcastle Daily Chronicle*.[7]

Cowen used the *Chronicle* to launch repeated attacks on the Confederacy and stir popular support for its defeat and slave emancipation. Most radical of all, he and his staff agitated for full acceptance into American society of the freed slaves. As they railed against the South and its heinous institution, Cowen and his principle journalists, W.E. Adams and Richard Reed, helped to change the tone and focus of anti-slavery rhetoric and campaigning, influencing debate on the War and slavery far beyond the North East. Encouraged in part by the continued presence of black and white abolitionists in the region, these North East radicals promoted both racial equality and a community of interests among all those who faced exploitation and disenfranchisement by masters, bosses and political elites. Thus the War inspired a renewed, if tentative, emphasis on a class-based solidarity that could, potentially at least, transcend racial differences.[8]

The most widely circulated expression of wartime Tyneside radical-ism was an 1863 pamphlet, *The Slaveholders' War*, written by W.E. Adams. A Chartist journalist and subsequently editor of the *Newcastle Weekly Chronicle*, Adams was among the co-founders, with Cowen and Rev. M. Miller from Darlington, of the Union and Emancipation Society of the North of England, headquartered in Manchester. The pamphlet's sub-title, *An Argument for the North and The Negro*, signalled how closely a Union victory had become aligned with the idea of freedom for American slaves. After starting with a lengthy discourse on the illegality of southern secession from the Union, which made Confederates 'to all intents and purposes, re-bels—rebels moreover to a Government which they themselves had helped to set up,' Adams offered a brief history of the sectional crises over the ex-pansion of slavery that had ultimately led to the conflict. He dismissed all pretence that southern slaveholders had any other objective in seceding than the 'permanent establishment of all the evils that slavery has brought upon the world.' For the Confederate slaveholder, Adams insisted, slavery 'has more than a mere commercial values in his eyes; it is part of his morality to believe in it, of his philosophy to justify it, of his religion to maintain it. Nay, it is not only the true and just system of society for the South; he holds that it is the only true and just system of society for all the world.'[9]

Perhaps most strikingly, Adams explicitly linked the fight for abolition and black rights in the US to the battle for political rights in Britain. On October 16, 1863, in a talk at the Church of the Divine Unity in Newcastle, the visiting Boston-born socialist reformer and abolitionist Rev. William Henry Channing had painted the Civil War as a struggle for democratic accountability and political freedoms. Appealing for British support against the Confederacy, he described the War as a clash 'between an oligarchy based on the institution of slavery, and a people possessing free institu-tions.'[10] Adams likewise felt the American conflict over slavery could be pressed into the service of the campaign for greater political rights and free-doms in Britain. Having pilloried those, notably some associated with the London *Times* newspaper, who continued to try to 'defend slavery on the grounds of a biblical sanction'—an effort he derided as having 'the effect, not of exalting slavery, but of degrading the Bible'—Adams reminded his readers of the fear and hostility that had greeted Earl Grey's Great Reform Act of 1832. The 'same foolish forebodings are indulged in now whenever a further extension of the suffrage is asked and advocated,' he complained. Addressing similar forebodings about the impact of freeing millions of slaves, he concluded that 'Fear is the great obstacle to progress, as daring is the great redresser of wrongs.' The story here, Adams suggested, was not simply the truism that those in power seldom give up their power without a struggle; it was also an acknowledgement that fear and fear-mongering invariably stalks any effort to enact progressive reforms that might empower previously marginalised or powerless sections of society.[11]

Sitting at the centre of this radical network, Joseph Cowen's influence was considerable and international. When William Lloyd Garrison could not contribute his usual editorial for *The Liberator* in late August 1864, the Boston abolitionist paper simply reprinted a glowing endorsement of Garrison that Cowen had penned for the *Chronicle* on August 22. The piece was prefaced by a short biography in which Cowen's newspaper was described as 'the exponent and advocate of the most advanced and radical opinions in England.' Cowen, *The Liberator* assured its readers, 'takes a deep interest in the great struggle for universal freedom and republican principles which now agitates America.'[12]

Cowen was close at hand when Garrison visited Newcastle for the final time between July 6 and 10, 1867. He stayed with Newcastle Town Council member John Mawson. Writing after receiving the shocking news of Mawson's death in a nitro-glycerine explosion in December the same year, Garrison described his friend and fellow abolitionist as 'one of the most affectionate, loving, magnetic persons I ever knew, and had one of the most charming homes at Gateshead into which I have ever entered.' Garrison had been greeted rapturously on Tyneside during his valedictory visit. On July 9, 'the apostle of negro emancipation,' as the *Chronicle* described him, was feted at what Garrison described as a 'grand reception' in the Assembly Rooms. 'In honouring such a man,' the newspaper commented, perhaps a little smugly, though not without some justification, 'Newcastle has honoured itself.'[13] There was also a second welcoming address, from the North Shields Reform League, read by Cowen himself.[14]

By this time, the Civil War had ended in victory for the Union forces and, on April 14, 1865, Lincoln had been assassinated. Whatever doubts radicals in the North East might have harboured about the late President's handling of the secession crisis, or about his decision to suspend *habeas corpus* during the conflict, or even about his motivations for freeing the slaves, which some saw purely as an act of military expedience, were forgotten in an outpouring of grief that emphasised Lincoln's role as 'the Great Emancipator.'[15] In early May 1865, letters of condolence flooded into the office of Charles Adams, the US Ambassador in London, from all over Britain, including city councils in Berwick, Darlington, Gateshead, Morpeth, Newcastle, South Shields and Sunderland. In Newcastle, on May 3 representatives of the Council adopted a resolution proposed by Joseph Cowen 'to give utterance to the feelings of grief and horror with which it has heard of the assassination of President Lincoln.' The following day, a specially convened public meeting in the Town Hall unanimously agreed to send a similar message to Charles Adams, 'for transmission to his Excellency the President of the United States, Mrs Lincoln, and the Hon. W.H. Seward' (Lincoln's Secretary of the Treasury, who was also hurt in the assassination attack). The resolution was proposed by Rev. W. Walters and seconded by William Lloyd Garrison's doomed abolitionist friend, Councillor John Mawson.[16]

Across the region, similar resolutions were approved, all expressing shock, sorrow and support for Lincoln's commitment to, as the President had put it in his Gettysburg Address, a 'rebirth of freedom' in a US finally rid of slavery. 'We have ever felt towards him while alive a personal friendship,' wrote J. Martin, pastor of the United Methodist Free Church in West Hartlepool, 'and now that he is no more of this world we love his memory…We have faith in the future of United States, and we say God prosper and bless the American people! God bless the policy of Emancipation.'[17] A mass meeting at Darlington's Central Hall unanimously resolved to express 'to the President and People of the United States its horror and detestation of the crime,' adding its prayers 'that this awful event may strengthen their determination to uproot and utterly destroy the Slave Institution, and to re-construct and consolidate their Union upon the basis of Free Labor and Political Liberty.'[18] Here, in distilled form, was the ideological crucible in which the North East's popular support for African American freedom and for Lincoln's brand of republicanism had been hammered out: regardless of moral or humanitarian concerns, slavery affronted a popular commitment to both the rights of labour and the right to political representation. After his death, British radicals and labour leaders continued to tie calls for extending the suffrage to what they believed to be Lincoln's capacious conception of democracy—albeit that women were still excluded from this vision and that his plans for the postbellum political status of ex-slaves had been unclear.[19]

Following Lincoln's death, Andrew Johnson assumed the Presidency and the US embarked on a period of Reconstruction. Initially, Reconstruction saw considerable advances for southern black civil and voting rights thanks to a combination of federal legislation, notably the 14th and 15th

Amendments to the Constitution, and the protection offered against white supremacist groups such as the Ku Klux Klan by federal troops stationed in the region. By 1877, however, Reconstruction was over. With the withdrawal of federal protection, always precarious African American rights began to disappear amid a rising tide of regional and national white racism and xenophobia. Racial and religious intolerance in the US was accentuated by changing patterns of immigration which saw increasing numbers of non-White Anglo Saxon Protestant (WASP) arriving from eastern and southern Europe. White nationalism was also intensified by the US's first major imperial adventures in the Pacific and Caribbean which brought the nation into conflict with non-white and non-WASP peoples in places such as Cuba and the Philippines. By the time the US Supreme Court legitimised racial segregation in its 1896 *Plessy vs Ferguson* decision, most black voters had already been purged from the electoral rolls in the South.[20]

Terror, custom, laws, and economic oppression combined in a poisonous mix that defined the Jim Crow era for millions of African Americans. Many sought a better life in the cities of the north and west during several major migrations in the early 20th century. Beyond the South, some found greater opportunity and there were fewer overt, legally sanctioned prohibitions on movement, work and voting. In truth, however, the US was a Jim Crow country, with deep reservoirs of racism and discrimination that crimped black lives and stymied black aspirations throughout the entire nation. As Martin Luther King pointed out in his 'I Have a Dream' speech, one hundred years after the end of slavery, the promise of freedom and justice for all Americans articulated in the Declaration of Independence and reaffirmed by Abraham Lincoln in his Gettysburg Address remained unfulfilled for African Americans.[21] It was in order to confront this world of denied or abridged citizenship rights, racial violence and economic marginalisation that the civil rights movement emerged in the 1950s and 1960s.

The post-Civil War travails of African Americans during Reconstruction and into the Jim Crow era never quite captured the imagination or stirred the indignation of a mass of North East citizens in the way that abolitionism and slavery once had, or in the way that the civil rights campaigns of the 1950s and 1960s would do once more. Yet, the region was neither wholly ignorant of, nor indifferent to, the state of race relations in the US. Return visits by the likes of Fredrick Douglass and William Lloyd Garrison kept the ongoing African American struggle for equal rights firmly in view during the decades after Emancipation. The region also hosted appearances by the Fisk Jubilee Singers as part of a 'gospel invasion' that swept Britain in 1873, when their visit coincided with an extended mission by American evangelist Dwight M. Moody and his musical collaborator Ira Sankey.[22] The Singers, who hailed from the black Fisk University in Nashville, mainly performed concertised spirituals and were extraordinarily effective ambassadors for their University and for the African American cause more generally. In November 1873, they worked in the North East alongside the Moody and Sankey Revival, giving concerts in Sunderland and Newcastle, where the enthralled audience included the Congregationalist Minister Henry Thomas Robjohns. As one of the Singers noted, Robjohns 'had so thoroughly worked up the public interest that every seat was sold.' As the Minister himself recalled, 'The Jubilee Singers had been specially prayed for. A moment's pause, and there went up in sweet, low notes a chorus as of angels.'[23] Appeals by the Fisk Jubilee Singers for support for their institution and for black education more generally helped raise public awareness of the many political, economic and social challenges faced by newly freed African Americans.

Among those challenges was the terrible violence meted out by some white southerners who resorted to terrorism and lynch law to keep newly freed blacks firmly in their place at the bottom of society. In September 1868, Tynesiders could read about the 'Thirty Negroes Killed in a Riot' in Camilla, Georgia when white Democrats had rounded on newly enfranchised black Republican voters. Reports on further race riots in Georgia and Louisiana followed in October.[24] In Spring 1871, the *Journal* described 'Anarchy in the Southern States' as federal authorities struggled to halt the spread of racist violence across the region.[25] Two years later it reported on 'something like a war of the races' at Colfax, Louisiana, where armed whites killed as many as 150 African Americans in the wake of a disputed election for Governor. According to Eric Foner, this was the 'bloodiest single instance of racial carnage in the Reconstruction era.'[26] In some ways, however, this was merely the prelude to the grim era that became known as 'the nadir' of African American history.

When Reconstruction ended, the US federal government abrogated virtually all responsibility for protecting the civil and voting rights of southern black citizens against a variety of discriminatory Jim Crow practices that were increasingly enshrined in law. In 1900, the *Newcastle Courant* reported on the widespread use of property qualifications and literacy tests to remove most African Americans from the political process. 'The restrictions are so ingeniously arranged that they hit the illiterate black far more than the illiterate white man,' the paper explained.[27] There was also widespread recognition in the North East that laws to supress black voting and limit social and economic opportunities were underpinned by the perpetual threat of white violence. Jim Crow rested on a culture of terror and intimidation. In particular, white violence was directed against black men accused of sexual crimes against white women. In 1892, the *Courant* reported on a 'shocking lynching scene' in Texarkana, Texas, when a crowd numbering at least a thousand—and according to some estimates five or six times that number—assembled to watch Mrs. Henry Jewell set fire to Edward Coy, an African American accused of assaulting her. Coy had been captured and taken to jail, but a vigilante posse decided that no trial was necessary. Coy was tied to a stake and doused with oil before Jewell was invited to apply the torch. It subsequently emerged that Coy and Jewell had been in a consensual relationship for at least a year prior to the lynching. In the toxic environment of the Jim Crow South, such liaisons were both illegal and taboo. If discovered, interracial sex often meant lethal retribution against black men and perpetual shame and social ostracism for white women. In this climate, the discovery of illicit interracial relationships between white women and black men often sparked false accusations of rape as women sought to save face. Although it was by no means the only or even the main reason why more than 4,000 black men, women and children were lynched between 1880 and 1950, the dread spectre of interracial sex haunted the white imagination and underscored a ferocious commitment to segregation.[28]

The celebrated African American anti-lynching campaigner Ida B. Wells focused on this racial-sexual dynamic when she came to Newcastle in April 1894, following in the footsteps of the black abolitionists and fugitive slaves who had regularly put the North East on their itinerary a generation earlier. Wells, 'a bright, intelligent, young lady of 'colour',' according to the *Newcastle Daily Leader*, came 'bearing a message from Frederick Douglas (sic), whose freedom from slavery,' the paper was keen to remind its readers, 'was bought by Newcastle friends.' Speaking at the Wesleyan Chapel in Brunswick Place and two days later at Ryehill Baptist Church, Wells told of her own horrendous experiences of racial violence in Memphis. Wells had attempted to use her *Free Speech* newspaper to expose and bring to justice the whites who had lynched three of her friends, apparently because their increasingly successful grocery business had aroused the resentment and anger of rival white businessmen. Wells' newspaper had been supressed and she was forced to flee her hometown in fear of her life. Thereafter, she became an internationally renowned, if perpetually frustrated, champion of anti-lynching legislation. In Newcastle, as in many other British cities, she horrified audiences with gruesome tales of how whites, especially in the South, tortured and killed African Americans without fear of punishment. In 1893 alone, Wells explained, at least 158 men and four women had been lynched. As the *Newcastle Daily Leader* noted, southern white men sought to justify their actions 'by declaring lynching to be a necessity because the honour of their women and children was violated by black men.' Moreover, the paper echoed Wells' concern that lynching 'mania' was spreading to all parts of the US. Wells, the report explained, had come to Britain, and to Newcastle, appealing for 'justice and money' and hoping 'to get the press, the pulpit and the public to cry out against these lynchings.' Confident that the city's cultures of welcome were still alive, the paper had 'no doubt many humanitarians will, in Newcastle….help the stranger in her cause.'[29]

Tynesiders were shocked and appalled by the lack of due process and the sheer barbarity of the lynchings described by Wells and reported in the local press, which continued to cover outrages such as the January 1914 lynching of five men, 'hung from a single tree,' in Sylvester, Georgia, and the extra-legal murder of two 'Negroes burned at the stake' in Sulphur Springs, Texas, in August 1915.[30] Nevertheless, as we shall see in the next chapter, white, especially male white, hostility to relations between non-white men and white women, also had their counterparts in the North East of England.

The postbellum period saw continued efforts to compare and con-trast the plight of African Americans with that of local workers. As early as December 1864, with the Civil War entering its final stages, journalist George Julian Harney championed the cause of the North and lambasted the neutrality of Lord Russell's British government, but also pondered the long term implications of the War for the extension of the suffrage, among blacks and whites, on both sides of the Atlantic. Harney shared his thoughts with the readers of the *Newcastle Weekly Chronicle* in a series of 'American Matters' and 'American Notes and Boston Notions' columns. From 1864 to 1888, the radical Tyneside Chartist and staunch republican wrote from his new home in Boston. Never was he more enthusiastic than when de-scribing the sight of free blacks voting alongside white citizens; yet he pointedly compared this exercise in democracy, in which 'the Negro is equal to the White man "before the law",' with the continued denial of working-class voting rights in Britain.[31]

The scare quotes Harney placed around the phrase 'before the law' are not easy to interpret, but there is at least a possibility that he was making a distinction between ideas of legal equality and social equality. The former proposition was relatively easy for Harney and his Tyneside readers to accept. The whole campaign against slavery had been, in part, a battle to address and destroy an abhorrent legal anomaly that allowed one human being to be owned by another; the denial of black political rights could also be viewed as primarily a legal, constitutional matter. By contrast, even though during the Civil War, Harney, Cowen and other radicals had appeared to champion the idea of a genuine social equality that transcended racial differences, such notions would prove a harder pill to swallow for many whites on both sides of the Atlantic.

At the moment of Lincoln's assassination, with the Civil War and slavery coming towards an end, there were already signs that racial enlightenment among even the most eminent radicals and ardent abolitionists on Tyneside had its limits. Certainly, some of the rhetoric around Lincoln's death suggested that, after what Newcastle's Sheriff W. Lockley Harle called 'the Cain-like mark of slavery—that black cloud on the majestic brow of America,' had been 'obliterated,' it was a transatlantic alliance of whites in Britain and the US that would emerge to dominate, not just Atlantic, but global affairs. 'The two great nations of Anglo-Saxons would [henceforth] be united together, and on common principles and with common love should lead the civilisation of the world,' Harle concluded at the Newcastle Town Hall meeting that issued letters of condolence on Lincoln's death. At the same meeting, Joseph Cowen proposed that while 'All friends of freedom had lost a friend' with Lincoln's death, it was 'the Anglo-Saxon race in both countries,' who 'would be united' in their pursuit of prosperity and desire to spread their beneficent influence across the world.[32]

Notwithstanding these stirrings of the kind of transatlantic WASP solidarity and hubris that would underpin imperial adventures by Britain and the US, there was still genuine enthusiasm for emancipation and for the expansion of black civil and voting rights in America. In August 1865, just four months after the end of the Civil War and Lincoln's assassination, Harney reported on an abolitionist meeting where Wendell Phillips, Charles Burleigh, Stephen S. Foster, Abby Kelly Foster, Andrew T. Foss, Tyneside favourite William Wells Brown, 'and a coloured lady, Mrs. F. W. Harper,' all spoke and issued a resolution about the conditions under which the former Confederate states might be readmitted to the Union. Far from resting on their laurels with the end of slavery, these abolitionists insisted that 'any organisation of the rebel States which does not rest on the principle of the absolute equality of every man before the law, and the recognition of the full civil rights of every citizen was a practical surrender of the North to the South; and that viewing such reconstruction as the essential triumph of the slave power, we pledge ourselves to agitation to crush it…' Harney urged Tyneside readers 'to remember that if "slavery is dead," the spirit of slavery still lives, and the Abolitionists and friends of equal rights and equal laws in this republic have still claims on the sympathy and cooperation of the good and true of every land.'[33]

Harney continued to monitor the struggle of freedmen to secure and protect their civil and voting rights amid rising agitation in the North East in support of another round of British political reform. He reported 'Negroes voting in Virginia' in March 1867, alongside news from South Carolina that 'A meeting of blacks and whites has been held at Charleston to organise a Republican Party in the city.'[34] He invoked the enfranchisement of African Americans (men only, of course) and their passionate embrace of politics to agitate for further expansion of the franchise at home. In Britain, he explained, 'Our interest in American politics has been mainly that of a desire to see the disenthralment of an oppressed and cruelly wronged race.' Characterizing this as a hard-won 'victory for humanity,' as opposed to simply a victory for enslaved African Americans, he hailed the six years since Lincoln's election as nothing short of a 'revolution.' But, he asked, at the very moment when the Second Reform Act was making its way through Parliament, 'Will the British working man occupy as proud a political position as that now held by the Negroes of the States, within six years to come? There is a stinging humiliation for us Englishmen in the very question.'[35]

One hundred years later Martin Luther King came to Newcastle and added his voice to those in Britain who, like Harney, continued to use America's racial troubles to argue for stronger legislation to protect the rights of coloured citizens. But Harney had also used a transatlantic comparison to insist on the need to extend and protect the rights of British whites. In 1967, there were many whites in Britain, including some in the North East, who followed Harney's example by looking closely at the escalating racial tensions and violence in the US to argue for immigration restriction, sometimes for the repatriation of racial and ethnic minorities, and for measures to preserve white privilege against the perceived threat of growing numbers of non-white citizens. In this respect, they tapped into a far more parochial and reactionary tradition within North East race relations. It was a tradition in which the US regularly functioned as a cautionary tale, a horror story evoked to support the idea that racial differences were

insurmountable and that a racially, ethnically, or religiously diverse population imperilled a kind of 'Britishness' that was, despite historical realities
to the contrary, conceived as fundamentally white and Christian.

CHAPTER EIGHT

The Challenges of Diversity: Cultures of Welcome, Cultures of Hate

In May 1917, the epic motion picture *Birth of a Nation* opened in Newcastle. A technically pioneering but profoundly racist piece of cinema, the film presented as historical fact a poisonous myth about how the Ku Klux Klan had saved the postbellum US South from the tyranny of black political domination and the abomination of forced racial integration at the hands of rapacious African American freedmen. In an enthusiastic review, the *Journal* described the Klan as a noble organisation, founded 'with the chivalrous intention of protecting women and children from attacks by Indians and outlaw Negroes.' The paper proudly proclaimed that 'its ranks included Tynesiders who were very active and useful members.'[1] Although Tyneside press reaction to the Klan and its outrages, both during Reconstruction and after the emergence of a second Klan in 1915, was generally hostile, the *Journal's* review suggested some kind of latent sympathy for the organisation and nostalgia for a time when white power reigned unchallenged. It also hinted at a counter-narrative to the dominant story of Tyneside as a place of deep sympathy, support and welcome for peoples of colour.

In his study of slavery and anti-slavery in the North East John Charlton rightly points out that 'The belief, held by many, that North East England was free from the taint of involvement in the appalling system that was slavery is without foundation.' Nevertheless, he concludes on the kind of celebratory note that has characterised most studies of the region's race relations. 'Once the evil of slavery was properly understood in the North East,' Charlton suggests, 'men and women in the region became leading advocates of its abolition.'[2] This is an attractive scenario which casts education and a basic sense of human decency as the keys to racially progressive and inclusive attitudes across the region. Once the evils of slavery, and by extension the racist myths upon which it depended, were exposed, North Easterners had rallied to help hasten its demise.

During the 18th and 19th centuries local anti-slavery sentiment and political radicalism had flourished in a region where the permanent population was overwhelmingly white and nominally English. However, the very notion of an 'English' identity is an elusive, somewhat chimerical concept, complicated by intricate relationships with Irish, Scots, and Welsh identities, not to mention French-Norman influences after 1066, older Germanic, Scandinavian and Roman strains before that, and a largely forgotten heritage from Africa and Asia.[3] Moreover, from the late 18th to the early 20th centuries, the population of the North East, as in much of Britain at a time of growing urbanisation and industrialisation, was highly mobile. For many people, migration was a way of life not an exception; notwithstanding strong family ties and local loyalties, in Britain, especially in its cities, it was perfectly common to live, work and play in the company of strangers. In 1851 as many as two-thirds of British adults lived in areas other than those in which they were born. By 1911, over a third of the population in the North East had either been born outside England or were the children of migrants; in Newcastle, slightly over one third of residents were not born in the city.[4]

Consequently, if there is more than a grain of truth in traditional depictions of the North East as home to a peculiarly intense and iconoclastic brand of provincial white 'English-ness,' there was always a more cosmopolitan side to the region; always exceptions that complicated the region's reputation as home to an unalloyed whiteness. Thanks to the pioneering research of historians such as Charlton, Sean Creighton, Richard Lawless, Dave Renton and Nigel Todd the story is slowly emerging of the many non-white, non-British visitors to the area and of those, including African American slaves and ex-slaves, who settled permanently in the North East during the 18th and 19th centuries. In 1777, for example, a teenaged Bill Richmond had beaten up three British soldiers in a tavern in New York, which was then under British occupation during the American War of Independence. Either as a consequence of his pugilistic prowess or because he was the son of a washerwoman working for General Hugh Percy, son of the Duke of Northumberland, Percy brought him back to England, probably to the family's ancestral seat at Alnwick, before sending him to school in Yorkshire.[5]

Other people of African descent also found homes in the region under a variety of circumstances. Elizabeth Montagu, an abolitionist, literary critic, and Northumberland coal mine owner, was one of the most remarkable and richest women of the mid-18th century. No great fan of Newcastle she described the city as 'horrible, like the ways of thrift it is narrow, dark and dirty,' but nonetheless lived for a while at East Denton Hall on the West Road, attended by a black servant called Tom.[6] A more permanent resident was Mary Ann Mackham, who arrived in North Shields in the early 1830s after escaping slavery in Richmond, Virginia. In 1841 she married local rope-maker James Blyth and they lived on Howard Street. In 1881 Mackham was a widow, living in Nelson Street, North Shields; a decade later, she was living with what appear to be relatives of her late spouse in South Benwell, Newcastle. In 1893, she died and was buried in Preston Cemetery, North Shields.[7]

Migrants, permanent and temporary, from the African Diaspora were not the only foreigners to take up residence in the region and help forge its distinctive cultures. The most significant and self-consciously non-English group to settle in the North East in the 19th century were the Irish, who were especially visible on Tyneside. In 1851, the Irish accounted for 8.6 and 8.1 percent of the total populations in Gateshead and Newcastle respectively.[8] Although they were often subjected to tremendous abuse and discrimination in mainland Britain on the grounds of religion, ethnicity and politics, Tyneside seemed generally hospitable to the economic refugees who fled Ireland and starvation in the wake of the dreadful 'potato famines' that ravaged the country between 1845 and 1851. By mid-century Newcastle had the fourth largest proportion of Irish relative to its overall population of any city in England and Wales.[9]

The strong Irish presence was another reflection of what historian Joan Hugman describes as 'the relative absence of sectarianism' on Tyneside, where the religious non-conformism that fuelled a good deal of anti-slavery activity was extended to tolerance for Roman Catholicism. The Irish also exerted a significant influence on local politics. Irish nationalists often found support among radicals who opposed coercive power and non-representative governments. As Hugman explains, Joseph Cowen's *Chronicle* operated at times as a '*bona fide* Irish newspaper.' It extensively covered Irish politics and endorsed the fight for Home Rule. Indeed, in August 1873, the first Irish Home Rule Conference was held in Newcastle. By 1881 the Liberal administration of Prime Minister William Gladstone judged the *Chronicle* to be 'just as seditious as the Irish nationalist press' and tried to restrict its distribution. From the perspective of Tyneside's community relations, Hugman suggests, the most significant feature was that 'This stress on collective rather than ethnic goals became a rallying point for all sections of the community.'[10]

On Tyneside, Hugman argues, ethnic and religious differences were largely ignored in favour of shared, broadly progressive and anti-imperialist coalitions. Class solidarity among the region's workers, coupled with the North East's strong, cross-class radical traditions tended to trump ethnic rivalries and religious tensions. Again, the dominant narrative here is of

Tyneside as essentially a bastion of unusually good interfaith, interethnic and interracial relations. Forged in the 18th and 19th centuries, that viewpoint persisted into the 20th century, etched into the popular imagination by a steady stream of feel-good stories of interracial cooperation and goodwill. For example, when Charles Johnson, a septuagenarian African American night watchman at the Swan Hunter shipbuilding company, died in January 1936, 'friends and colleagues' as well as 'many representatives of the firm,' attended his funeral at Heaton Cemetery. There was even a warm obituary in *The Shipyard*, the works magazine, for 'a well-known and popular man.' However, barely concealed behind what appears to have been genuine sadness at Johnson's passing were hints of the condescension and restricted opportunities regularly encountered by people of colour, even on Tyneside. According to the obituary, Johnson had 'proved his faithfulness by his long genuine service' at Swan Hunter; he never failed to offer 'a cheerful word and smile' for all who passed through the main gate to the Wallsend yard. This language had uncomfortable echoes of minstrelsy and how plantation owners in the Old South routinely described their grinning, loyal, happy-go-lucky slaves. By the time he died, the Alabama native may have been well-thought of, respected even, by his workmates and bosses, but he had been patrolling the main Wallsend shipyard gate at night, doing one of the most menial and lowest paid jobs in the company, for four decades. The obituary even got his name wrong, calling him 'Johnstone': for years he had been unimaginatively known to his co-workers and employers simply as 'Black Charlie.'[11]

Despite such mixed-signals regarding the nature of local white racial attitudes and the extent of the opportunities available to non-whites, the notion that powerful cultures of welcome dominated Tyneside's response to newcomers endured. It persisted even after World War Two when the numbers of outsiders of various races, ethnicities and religions began to rise and the area began to see its first major communities of colour, mostly from South Asia. A 1957 study by Sidney Collins compared race relations in three major British ports—Cardiff, Liverpool and Newcastle—and concluded that, despite scattered evidence of racial discrimination and conflict, conditions and attitudes were more favourable for immigrants on Tyneside according to almost any index one might reasonably apply.[12]

A decade later, just months before Martin Luther King's visit, the Tyneside branch of CARD produced a report on *Colour Discrimination in Newcastle upon Tyne* which admitted that most of the immigrants questioned 'didn't seem to regard discrimination as a problem.'[13] For much of the decade Tyneside, in particular South Shields where a significant community of Arab seamen, at first primarily from Yemen, had sprung up in the late 19th and early 20th centuries, was presented to national British audiences as, in the words of David Bean, writing in the *Guardian* in the Spring of 1961, 'a study in integration; a place where colour prejudice died years ago.' Reporting on the experiences of the local Muslim community, which by this time comprised 'Arabs, Somalis and Pakistanis' congregated mainly in the town's Laygate area, Bean even noted a good deal of inter-marriage with the white population: 'The majority of South Shields Moslems are seamen, and many of them have white wives.' Bean painted a fairly idyllic picture of peaceful integration and a vision for the future. 'You can see it best in the children; the way they stream out of school together like a human rainbow...oblivious to colour,' he enthused.[14]

One of Bean's interviewees was Kashmiri-born café owner and community activist Sayed Shah. Shah was similarly positive about South Shields race relations, pointing to common interests among hard-working whites and equally hard-working non-whites in a seaport and shipbuilding town that had been buffeted since World War One by a succession of economic set-backs. When Bean visited, Shah was busy raising money for a new religious centre. Stressing the significance of Islam in uniting the diverse non-white populations in the town, which white commentators tended to lump together, Shah hoped that the new centre would dispel local misassumptions about Muslims and their faith. This, he said, was a 'place where not only our own children will be taught, but where all people may come and go freely to see what our religion is about. In that way we will achieve even greater understanding.' Contact, communication and education: these were the keys to racial and religious tolerance, Shah maintained, confidently declaring, 'We are here an example of what other multiracial communities will achieve soon.'[15] Seven years later, a week after Martin Luther King's murder, two days after the introduction of a new Race Relations Bill, and at a very different moment in British and Tyneside racial history, journalist Maureen Knight returned to South Shields to report once again on 'The Town Where Colour Doesn't Count.' The piece was part of a trio of newspaper articles on race relations that concluded 'the further north you travel, the better it is.'[16]

And yet, as Knight appreciated, this positive picture did not represent the whole story of race relations in the North East, or even South Shields, either historically or in the 1960s. Beneath the surface of apparent or relative racial tranquillity lay other, less cheery and more reactionary undercurrents marked by bigotry, discrimination and occasional but intense eruptions of racial violence. It was this uglier side of the North East's racial history that threatened to gain the upper hand in the late 1960s. Part of an increasingly intemperate national debate about immigration and domestic race relations that played out against the backdrop of a dramatic deterioration in American race relations, this was the context that made King's 1967 visit so timely and gave it such contemporary significance.

Racial tension, conflict and violence were nothing new to the 1960s: they had always been part of a discordant counterpoint to the region's relative racial harmony and progressive traditions. For example, not everyone in the North East, certainly not all of those who benefitted financially from slavery or the slave trade, was sympathetic to the abolitionist cause in the 19th century. In a fairly common piece of pro-slavery sophistry, some argued that agitation for an immediate end to slavery actually threatened the well-being of the slaves, who would be left destitute, without employment or care, in addition to being detrimental to the financial interests and physical safety of whites. The contention was, as one contributor to the *Journal* explained in 1832, that emancipation would 'lead to the abandonment of the estates and the slaves' situation will be highly dangerous to public tranquillity.'[17]

The previous year, just as North East anti-slavery activists moved into high gear and sometimes proclaimed a belief in the shared brotherhood of all mankind, two drunken white seamen, William Craggs and George Mallet, beat up and then murdered their black shipmate, Africanus Maxwell, by throwing him off the Union Quay in North Shields in the early hours of July 13. A policeman, Thomas Richmond, had encountered a bloodied Maxwell earlier in the evening when he pleaded, unsuccessfully, for the constable to protect him and take his two assailants into custody. After Maxwell wandered off, Richmond heard one of the white men reject his companion's suggestion to return to their ship, the sloop *Orestes*, with the threat 'we will have more of him first.' Witness Hannah Holmes heard Maxwell pleading 'I don't want to fight. I want to go back on board my ship.' Another witness, Jane Martin, saw Mallet throw the helpless Maxwell over the quay, where he broke his neck and died thirty-six hours later. Although the background to the altercation and its precise racial dynamic remained unclear, the evidence that Maxwell had been murdered was compelling. It was even clearer, however, that black life was cheap on Tyneside. It took the jury 'about 3 or 4 minutes' to return not guilty verdicts against Craggs and Mallet. The

Judge simply cautioned the two white men 'with an admonition against drunkenness and bad company.'[18]

This was by no means the only example of the racially skewed workings of the criminal justice system on Tyneside. In March 1927, Chief Magistrate Alderman W.J. Robertson presided over a court case relating to a 'stabbing affray' among six South Shields Arab seamen who had got into an argument over job opportunities on the *Maid of Andros* steamer. Robertson agreed with both defence and prosecution lawyers, that 'although there has been stabbing left and right,' it was not worth wasting valuable court time trying to work out who were the aggressors and who were the victims since, as the prosecuting lawyer put it, 'no white people had been involved and the injuries were among their own people.' Robertson brought the trial to a speedy conclusion by sentencing defendants and plaintiffs alike to be bound over to keep the peace for twelve months at a cost of £10 should they fail to do so.[19]

Cases like this revealed racial bias lurking in local courts. Meanwhile, a succession of lurid stories of rampant dockside violence among Yemeni and occasionally Somali sailors fed white racial stereotypes about non-whites. Although port towns were notoriously rough locales regardless of racial or ethnic factors, the cumulative effect of multiple reports of non-white violence in South Shields was to reinforce popular ideas about a basic lack of decency, civility and restraint among the Arab and African men who comprised the vast majority of the migrant population. Those stereotypes were especially potent when they intersected with sensational tales of sexual impropriety, especially ones involving relationships with white women. All these factors came together in August 1912, when Ali Hassan was accused of assaulting a local white woman called Mary Ellen Said who, with her Arab husband, ran one of South Shields' most important boarding houses for seamen. Hassan, who also had a white wife, Maud Dean, hoped to set up a rival boarding house and this economic competition appeared to be at the root of the incident. Although the evidence was far from conclusive, and Hassan insisted that 'we never hit a woman in my country,' he was found guilty of assault and fined twenty shillings plus costs.[20]

White attitudes towards those local white women who took Arab men as partners often implied a kind of racial treachery, or suggested that the women were guilty of a similarly transgressive and unsettling sexual non-conformity. Some were castigated for an equally unfeminine, venal thirst for the money that Arab seamen were willing to lavish on them. More often than not, however, they were depicted as victims of predatory and unscrupulous Arab men who would stop at nothing to be with white women. In May 1917, the *Shields Daily News* reported how jealousy over a white woman had prompted Mahomed Ali to stab his romantic rival, Said Ali, causing grievous bodily harm.[21] More shocking, and more troubling in terms of its evocation of white female complicity in servicing Arab lust, was the story of Hamid Ali, also known as Mohammad Kassen. In July 1923, Ali was charged with 'having carnally known a girl of 14-years, Margaret Ann Frazer.' Prurient interest in this tragic case was further stoked when the girl's grandmother was charged with 'having encouraged Kassen in the commission of the offence.'[22]

A month later, Hassan Mohammad was executed at Durham Jail for the murder of Janet Nagi, the white Jarrow-born widow of another Arab seaman who, following a period when they had dated, fatefully rejected Mohammad's advances. The initial front-page report of the killing in the *Shields Daily News* was headlined 'Arab's Crime.' As in a slew of similar headlines ('Arab and Girl'; 'An Arab Melee'; 'An Arab's Death'; 'Two Arabs and a Women'; 'Arab v Soldier'), the language neatly attributed a propensity for predatory sex and violence not to named individuals but to an entire racial group. In reviewing the Nagi murder case, the South Shields Deputy Coroner seized the opportunity to publicly denounce interracial liaisons. 'It seems a great pity that white women should marry men of a different nationality altogether,' he explained, adding that 'it seems to me that steps should be taken to prevent these unions if possible.' Thus press, popular opinion and white officialdom combined to depict Arab men as morally as well as intellectually inferior to whites, while their relationships with white women were often viewed as an assault on both decency and white racial purity.[23]

During the interwar years, racial prejudice and racial conflict in South Shields, across the North East and throughout Britain became inextricably linked to moral panics about broader changes in female sexuality, social mores, and the dreaded spectre of interracial sex and interracial marriage. Such anxieties fed upon the popularity of eugenic arguments about how unions between whites and non-whites threatened the supposed racial purity and superiority of the white race. This kind of pseudo-science, successor to the sort of ideas that James Hunt had advanced to such public derision and William Craft's stinging rebuke during the British Association for the Advancement of Science meeting in Newcastle in August 1863, had acquired much greater traction among the white nations of the Atlantic World during the imperial expansions of the late 19th and early 20th centuries. Interracial sex, it was claimed, would lead to a glut of unwanted, intellectually deficient and physically damaged 'half-caste' children. Mixed-race relationships were vehemently denounced as contrary to nature and probably to the teachings of the Bible. But it was also believed that such liaisons reflected and encouraged a culture of sexual immorality that was traditionally associated in white imaginations with non-whites, be they African, Asian or Middle-Eastern.[24] In a simplistic but enormously powerful white western calculus, black was historically the colour of sin and immorality; white was the colour of purity and virtue. These colour-coded values often informed white British and American attitudes towards non-white populations at home and abroad.[25]

When simmering racial tensions, incomprehension around cultural and religious difference, and pervasive white fears of miscegenation were compounded by economic distress, they sometimes boiled over into violent conflict. In August 1918, the local press reported, somewhat hyperbolically, on 'A South Shields Riot,' sparked when Thomas Press, an ex-soldier, and seaman Charles Edgar, led an attack by white men on Arab seamen and Arab-owned boarding houses.[26] Worse was to follow. As in many British ports immediately following World War One, there were serious racial disturbances in South Shields in 1919, beginning in mid-January when a crowd of white men, again including returning ex-servicemen, launched a premeditated attacked on an Arab shop in Waterloo Vale. For several weeks, sporadic battles between whites and Arabs continued to flare up, alongside several all-white confrontations between the police and ex-servicemen.[27]

The immediate catalyst for this unrest appears to have been the employment of Arab seamen at a time of depression and high unemployment among recently demobilised white sailors and other military personnel. Tensions were intensified by the wartime influx of Arabs into the town's previously all-white Laygate district. At the outbreak of World War One in 1914, there had only been a couple of dozen permanent Yemeni residents in South Shields. What had passed for fairly good race relations in the earliest years of Arab settlement was thus largely circumstantial, made possible because of the small numbers involved and the seafaring nature of the work the Arabs did. Mostly serving as firemen aboard merchant ships, they were often not even in the town—and when they were, they all lived together, virtually quarantined in the town's Holborn area. During the War, however, as casualties depleted the available manpower for the British Merchant

Navy, the number of South Shields Arabs swelled to 3,000. As many as 700 of those who served as firemen aboard merchant vessels working out of the port may have lost their lives during the conflict. 'Not,' as local historian Barry Carr tartly observes, 'that this sacrifice was recorded on the War Memorials and Rolls of Honour that sprouted up in practically every street. As a memory, the sacrifice was confined to the Arab community.'[28] Tyneside Arabs, most of them British subjects from the Yemeni port-city of Aden, may have risked and even given their lives to defend the British Empire, but they clearly did not conform to official or popular views on Tyneside of what it meant to be British.

Rising numbers meant that the post-War Arab community was both more conspicuous and more widely dispersed as it spread from its historic base in Holborn to Laygate. In response, a territorial kind of white working-class racism, exacerbated by the desperate struggle to find employment and secure a living wage, escalated. When court cases were held at Durham Assizes in connection with the interracial violence of early 1919, J.B. Fye, a veteran of the National Union of Seamen (NUS) and official of the Cooks' and Stewards' Union, was convicted on a charge of using language likely to cause a breach of the peace. Fye was a bullish opponent of the use of Arab labour on British ships and hostile to their very presence in the town. He had urged an angry crowd of white seamen to physically prevent nine Arab firemen signing up for service on the SS *Trowalland*. 'Don't let these Arabs sign on the ship,' he told the white mob; 'Come out you black _____. You are not going to join the ship,' he warned the Arabs, all of whom were fully paid up members of the NUS. When one of the Arabs asked Fye why he objected to fellow union members working on the ship, Fye replied, 'You black_____ this ship is not for you.' The insult so offended the Arab that he hit Fye who in turn promptly knocked him to the ground. This incited a full-fledged battle between the white mob and the badly outnumbered Arabs, who were pursued back into Holborn.[29] So much for simplistic notions of interracial working-class solidarity and an inherently progressive labour movement on Tyneside. As throughout history, class identities and allegiances mattered; but they were sometimes simply less important in determining attitudes and actions than other identities and allegiances, including those based on race, national origin and religion.

As if to confirm the linkage between poverty and racism that Martin Luther King emphasised in his Newcastle speech, when the Great Depression of the 1930s devastated a region heavily dependent on shipbuilding and maritime trade, racial and other inter-group tensions in the region soared again. Much of this hatred was directed towards local Jewish communities and individuals such as Albert Gompertz, a Labour councillor from South Shields (and in the 1950s, Mayor of the town), who had been very supportive of the local Arabs in their battles against official and unofficial hostility. There had been Jewish communities in the North East since at least the 18th century and the area's first Synagogue opened in Sunderland in 1781. During the interwar period around 3,000 Jewish people lived on Tyneside, with concentrations in Gosforth, Jesmond, Kenton and the beginnings of what would become a major Orthodox community in Gateshead. These groups were targeted by the paramilitary Blackshirts associated with Sir Oswald Mosley's British Union of Fascists (BUF). On Tyneside, the BUF briefly found sufficient support for its anti-Semitic bile that in May 1934 the *Journal* lamented how Newcastle, home to one of the first BUF branch offices, was 'becoming one of the storm centres of aggressive Fascism in Great Britain.'[30]

Across the North East, there were significant pockets of fascist support among members of Rotary Clubs on Tyneside and in Durham and among students at Armstrong College in Newcastle. In October 1934, a women's branch of the BUF opened in Gateshead, where former local MP John Beckett was a leading figure in national fascist circles, serving as Secretary of the British People's Party and eventually joining Mosley and his other 'Fascist lieutenants' in prison in May 1940. Elsewhere, a portrait of Italian fascist dictator Benito Mussolini temporarily hung alongside a painting of King George VI in the Newcastle Assembly Rooms and the Italian vice-consul in Newcastle, Signor N. Tognoli, encouraged young members of the Italian community in the North East to join local Fascist Clubs offering them the chance to attend Fascist Summer Camps in Italy.[31]

Ultimately, however, the appeal of fascism in the North East proved sorely limited. Or, perhaps more precisely, in the 1930s there were sufficient concerted efforts to counter the militaristic brand of hyper-nationalism and scapegoating typical of fascism. This time, local unions played an important and positive role in revitalising the region's cultures of welcome against the BUF and similar organisations. As in the anti-slavery activities of the previous century, local women played a major role in this effort. The formidable 'Red' Ellen Wilkinson, a Labour MP for Middlesbrough and from 1935 for Jarrow, won fame as an organiser of the famous 1936 Jarrow Crusade of unemployed workers from Tyneside to Parliament. But just as she fought to improve the economic condition of her constituents and, in particular, to expand the employment opportunities available to women, she also waged a similarly determined—and in her mind related—battle against fascism at home and abroad. Many other local women joined her in anti-fascist mobilisations, often combining their opposition to fascism with activism for world peace. A 4,000-strong 'Demonstration against War and Fascism' in South Shields in September 1935, for example, was led by 900 women. The protestors approved a resolution that called on the government to support League of Nation efforts to 'cancel out the dual brutes, Fascism and War.' Prominent in these campaigns were Gateshead Labour Councillor Ruth Dodds, Sunderland-based Leah Manning, who was president of the National Union of Teachers and joint-secretary of the Coordinating Committee against War and Fascism, as well as members of the Bolden Colliery Labour Women's Section and the Co-operative Women's Guild.[32]

Many local women also joined Manning, who was a leading figure in the National Joint Committee for Spanish Relief, in efforts to give refuge to Basque children imperilled by the Spanish Civil War, when General Francisco Franco's fascist forces overthrew the elected Republican government. In June 1937, shortly after the Basque capital Guernica was destroyed by aerial bombardment, the North East gave sanctuary to around 325 of the 4,000 Basque children evacuated to Britain. About half the young refugees were taken into Catholic convents and homes around the North East, mainly in Newcastle and Darlington, but they also found shelter in private homes and refuges set up in Tynemouth and Hexham. Somewhat removed from the region's pacifist tradition, around 100 men and women from the North East, thirty-five of whom were killed in action, also joined the International Brigade, believing that the governments of Britain and other democracies were not doing enough to halt the rise of Franco and his fascist allies in Europe.[33]

Also crucial to anti-fascist activities were local branches of the Communist-controlled National Unemployed Workers' Movement (NUWM). The NUWM coordinated lobbying, petitioning, demonstrations and marches, including the Jarrow Crusade, and liaised with the Labour Party and Trades Union Congress, in an effort to dramatise the terrible effects of the Depression on core British industries and their workforces. Like many on the political Left, the NUWM understood that mass unemployment, acute economic distress, coupled with inadequate government responses to those problems, created a fertile environment for fascism, with its propensity for vicious racial, ethnic and religious scapegoating. In the mid-to-late 1930s, BUF attempts to hold recruitment rallies in Harbour View, South Shields, at the Westgate Road monument to Joseph Cowen in Newcastle, at Gateshead's Town Hall and Windmill Hills, on the Newcastle Town Moor, and at the Palace Theatre in South Shields were all met with massive vocal and occasionally violent resistance from a coalition of anti-fascist organisations, including the NUWM, the Labour Party, the more radical Independent Labour Party, the Socialist League, the Communist Party, sundry unions and various Jewish community groups. As one contemporary observer told local historian Nigel Todd, 'there was always one event that brought the Communists and most of their critics together. This was the arrival of Sir Oswald Mosley's Blackshirts.'[34] Tyneside anti-fascism, which tended to go hand-in-hand with a rejection of racist dogma, was thus a rallying point for representatives of minority groups, radicals and liberals who were often at loggerheads with each other over goals, priorities and tactics.

Much the same scenario unfolded immediately after World War Two when a revival of Mosley-ism, this time in the form of his Union Movement, inspired another wave of attacks and vandalism against Jewish homes and synagogues. A small but dedicated group of men formed the Newcastle Combat Group to counter the resurgence of anti-Semitism, but it was soon declared redundant by the Jewish Representative Council, which was keen to emphasise the isolated nature of the incidents. More generally, Tyneside and the greater North East continued to be a tough market when it came to organising sustained racist activism. This was partly because knowledge of the Holocaust and of Nazi crimes against other ethnic minorities had sensitised many people to the perils of fascism and the horrific consequences of allowing racist ideologies to go unchallenged. But it was also partly because the region's cultures of welcome really did exist, not as some kind of preternatural indigenous form of racial tolerance, but as a historic process in which enough people in the region, whether inspired by faith, philosophy, education, self-interest or political ideology were willing to mobilise against the scaremongering and stereotyping that underpinned racial prejudice, discrimination and violence.

Paradoxically, however, the fact that racist insurgencies in the North East were usually suppressed quite quickly had an unfortunate unintended consequence. Because local government, minority groups, labour unions and other predominantly white progressive organisations tended to dismiss dramatic eruptions of racial animosity as aberrations, as spontaneous, irrational events that ran counter to North East traditions of tolerance and inclusivity, the very real problems that affected the region's migrant communities specifically on account of their race, ethnicity or religion often went unrecognised or unaddressed. Similarly, the tendency to characterise outbreaks of white racial or religious bigotry and violence as exceptional meant there was a reluctance to confront their underlying causes in white communities.[35]

These deeper systemic issues would become even more conspicuous from the mid-20th century when the non-white population of the North East began to rise. However, there were already plenty of portents of the kind of difficulties that lay ahead during the interwar period. In 1930, for example, there was another series of racially charged incidents in South Shields. Since the 1919 riots, Arab seamen had continued to be the target of racist abuse and stereotyping in the local press. This had helped to perpetuate a climate of fear, mistrust and open hatred that sometimes expressed itself in verbal and physical assaults whenever Arabs ventured beyond the relative security of their Holborn and Laygate enclaves. The Arab community's preference to keep itself largely to itself in the face of this abuse encouraged further misunderstandings about its culture and religion. Pragmatic insularity was often interpreted as an unwillingness or inability to integrate into the broader South Shields society. It was precisely this problem that Sayed Shah was still trying to address in the early 1960s, when he dreamed of welcoming non-Muslims to his new religious centre in South Shields and educating them about Islam and his community's culture. A few years later, when Martin Luther King came to Newcastle, the local press was awash with similar debates about the ability or desire of Tyneside's immigrant groups to integrate into mainstream white-dominated society and about the capacity or willingness of the region's white to accept these migrants into that society—and on what terms.

In August 1930, the violence in South Shields was sparked by an incendiary blend of economic crisis, ideological rivalries and power struggles within the seamen's union movement, but fuelled by racial animosity and the perennial fears of 'race-mixing.' It is worth pausing to look more closely at those events, since similar ingredients contributed to racial tensions in the post-war period. In 1930, the Communist-backed Seamen's Minority Movement was fighting for the abolition of the NUS's PC 5 form. This document confirmed that its bearer was a fully paid-up member of the NUS and, therefore, entitled by law to ship out of British ports. Unlike their white rivals, South Shields' Arab sailors, often subsidised by the boarding house masters who were a powerful and sometimes sinister force in the operation of port labour markets, tended to be fully paid-up PC 5-carrying members of the NUS—this despite the fact that the NUS had long waged a racist campaign against the port's Yemeni and Somali seamen and boarding house masters, calling for their repatriation. Because of their loyalty to the NUS, these migrants were sometimes the target for the anger of white seamen who were keen to break the stranglehold of the Union and abolish the PC 5. But, paradoxically, Arab seamen were also courted by the Minority Movement in its campaign against the NUS, which it viewed as a corrupt extension of major shipping interests, rather than as a defender of workers' rights.[36]

Tensions came to a head over NUS plans to introduce a rota system that applied only to Arab and Somali seamen and severely restricted their opportunities to work. The Union hoped that this discriminatory sop to white seamen, who retained unrestricted opportunities to join ships as long as they held a PC 5, would undermine the appeal of the Minority Movement by effectively segregating non-white seamen and ensuring greater white employment. Ironically, however, despite its flagrant racism, the rota system did at least guarantee the legal right of non-white workers to serve on British vessels. Somewhat disingenuously, the NUS hoped that this gesture would guarantee a cohort of loyal black members who could act as strike-breakers in the event, which seemed likely, of an industrial dispute between ship owners and the white sailors aligned with the Minority Movement. Perhaps not surprisingly, after decades of mistreatment by the NUS, most Arab and Somali seamen refused to be pawns in the Union's latest racialised games. They generally supported the efforts of Minority Movement to nullify the effect of the rota system and refused to sign on to ships under its provisions. However, when it became clear that some white NUS members were taking positions as firemen that were traditionally the preserve of Arab and Somali seamen, Minority Movement leaders deliberately stoked anger against these 'scabs' and set the scene for violent confrontation.

Arab-white violence broke out again at Mill Dam on August 2, 1930: some of it spontaneous; much of it, on both sides, well-organised. At Durham Assizes, where many of the combatants later stood trial, Mr. Justice Roche singled out John Dowell, an unemployed Boldon miner, for special attention. Dowell had been brought in by the Minority Movement and was, along with two local seamen, William Harrison and Peter O'Donnell, at the heart of the physical confrontations. Describing them as 'dupes of the professional agitators…who did stir up the Arabs,' Roche sentenced the men to six months hard labour. Meanwhile, Ali Said, one of the boarding house masters, was identified as 'the main organizer of these Arab attacks' on the white seamen. His punishment was much harsher than that of his white counterparts. Said was sentenced to sixteen months hard labour and, along with fourteen other Arabs, recommended for deportation. In passing judgement, Justice Roche invoked the economic coordinates of this violence, but saw the Arab presence itself as root cause of the problem. The Arabs, he felt, were particularly unwelcome 'at a time when there is obvious slackness of trade and when it is very difficult to get ships. These men in idleness are dangerous here.' He also went out of his way to voice the sexual tensions that underpinned so much racial animosity by insisting on the 'undesirability of the Arabs marrying white women.'[37]

Following the 1930 'riot' the fortunes of the South Shields immigrant community generally improved. The local press, particularly the *Shields Daily News*, began to take a more active role in defusing communal tensions by promoting understanding, rather than simply sustaining racist stereotypes about non-whites. In January 1931, for example, it went out of its way to educate readers about the meaning of Ramadan, as observed by local 'Arab, Somali and Mohammedan Indian' residents. The annual commemoration of the first revelation of the Qu'ran to the prophet Muhammad was depicted as a thoroughly respectable act of religious devotion and civility: 'Besides fasting Ramadan is observed by special prayer at the end of the day in addition to the ordinary period of prayer during the day, and by greater strictness of conduct in avoiding swearing or anything wrongful.'[38] It may also have helped that local children increasingly mingled in the same schools. By the mid-1930s, the attendance register for the Cone Street School in South Shields showed Derhin Abdullah and Irene Ahmed listed alongside Andrew Adams and Audrey Allen; Abas Mohamed sat in class with Joseph Mills.[39]

As Barry Carr notes, this kind of integration was a cornerstone of 'the apparent racial harmony that so intrigued visitors to the town thirty years later.'[40] It was, however, a somewhat flawed, a-historical vision that erased memories of the battles fought against racism and other forms of bigotry in the past in order to present an idealised, sanitised vision of the region's harmonious present. Commentators who trumpeted without qualification Tyneside's racial progressivism regularly underplayed the historic struggles of the region's minorities for acceptance, civil rights, and equal economic and educational opportunities. They also tended to ignore the equally strenuous efforts of some whites to preserve racial privilege and deny a succession of immigrant groups those rights and opportunities, let alone respect and acceptance. Perhaps most crucially, romantic visions of Tyneside's good race relations failed to recognise that efforts to eradicate racism, or at least to protect minorities from its worst effects, were ongoing, not completed, projects. This would be an important lesson in a region that became increasingly diverse after World War Two and where interracial harmony was still occasionally ruptured by outbursts of violence, prejudice and ill-feeling.

One such outburst occurred in 1945, in the midst of post-war demobilisation and a short sharp economic downturn. Once more, the location was that model of good race relations, South Shields, with economics, race and sexual tensions again to the fore. The newly formed Tyneside Inter-Racial League complained of an 'open campaign of discrimination against the coloured people' of South Shields by the local police. Chief Constable T.B. Humphrey had declared his intention to 'clean up certain cafes in the town,' which he claimed were centres of crime and vice. He then proceeded to target almost exclusively immigrant cafes. When the first cases against two Indian café proprietors were heard, a local magistrate levied fines of £5 against the men for permitting prostitutes to assemble on their premises. The judgement was then overturned on appeal by a Quarter Session judge who ordered the police to pay costs. After this chastening reversal and a public rebuke of its racially motivated arrests, the police resorted to more summary methods. Humphrey dusted off an obscure wartime defence regulation that enabled the police to close any café or business merely on suspicion that unlawful practices might be taking place there. In these cases, local white, often highly partisan magistrates heard any appeals against the police, with the café owners effectively becoming the plaintiffs; they had to prove both inappropriate police actions and their own innocence, which was rarely assumed. In their first swoop under this regime, police closed down Ali Hassan Cassim's café on the suspicion that prostitutes and their clients were being served food on the premises. When Cassim appealed, police were unable to prove that any of Cassim's customers were prostitutes and admitted that no law had actually been broken in the café. Yet Cassim was still found guilty—guilty, that is, of being suspected of something that the police could not prove. His appeal was dismissed and he was charged £25 costs, adding further financial insult to the economic injury of having had his business shut down. Procedurally, there was no right of appeal from local courts to the Quarter Sessions in these cases and several other immigrant-owned cafés were also shut down.[41]

South Shields was not the only place on Tyneside where race relations continued to be shaped by white anxieties around morality and interracial sex, especially as some of the old core industries—mining, shipbuilding and heavy engineering—that once provided much male employment in the region entered a period of slow but inexorable decline. This cocktail of concerns particularly afflicted British white working-class men in areas like the North East where blue-collar work was at the heart of masculine identity, self-respect and a cornerstone of family and community life. Immigrants, perceived as unwelcome rivals for jobs, houses and even female attention, represented another potential threat to a brand of white patriarchal authority and male self-esteem that was already being challenged as women secured the vote, gained better access to education, became more active in the job market and took greater control over their sexual and reproductive lives.

'Notwithstanding the widespread Negro associations with white women in the British Isles, and a public tolerance seemingly, Englishmen have a deeply ingrained horrors of such relations,' wrote the African American journalist Roi Ottley of his time in England during the mid-1940s. 'English white women vigorously defended their marriages to Negroes. They usually are successful in reconciling parents to their unions,' he added, but 'Feeling against blacks run high among English workingmen in periods of unemployment—a fact intensified by the crackling hostility provoked by sex rivalry.'[42]

A decade or so later, in 1958 the non-white population of Britain stood at around 190,000 or roughly 0.35 percent in a population of 55 million.[43] Although still low in absolute and proportionate terms, the growing non-white population and the racial violence in Nottingham and Notting Hill during August and September that year had increased white worries around basic bread-and-butter issues such as access to jobs, healthcare and housing. A national opinion poll in early September revealed that although 48 percent of respondents were in favour of non-white Commonwealth citizens being allowed to compete for jobs in Britain, 37 percent were against it; 54 percent opposed migrants being given places alongside whites on the waiting lists for local council housing; 65 percent already favoured restrictions on immigration to Britain from the 'New' Commonwealth. A massive 71 percent of white respondents still disapproved of interracial marriages, with responses more or less evenly spread in terms of location and gender.[44]

On Tyneside and across the North East, similar patterns were apparent. Even though Sydney Collins painted a generally positive picture of the experiences of African, Arab, and West Indian seamen in the late 1950s, he observed that 'white persons show disapproval of mixed sex relations in a number of ways,' adding that 'it is a common feature of British society for whites to stare at, or, occasionally, to make uncomplimentary remarks about a mixed couple seen together.'[45] One Middlesbrough Councillor openly campaigned against what she considered to be an unwelcome influx of Asian immigrants to the area on the well-trodden grounds that they represented a serious threat to the virtue of her white female constituents, for whom, she claimed, 'a dark skin holds a strange fascination.'[46] In late February 1958, magistrates at the Moot Hall Juvenile Court in Newcastle gave a sixteen year old white female snack assistant 'whose parents are said not to be exercising proper control of her,' a one year supervision order, the basis for which appeared to be her love for a Pakistani bus conductor. The magistrate felt that this racial transgression offered clear evidence that the girl was 'in moral danger, and in need of care and attention.' Underpinning this racialised moral disquiet was the dreaded spectre of mixed-blood off-spring—a paranoia given an ironic twist when the same edition of the *Chronicle* also reported favourably from the US on efforts in Georgia to quash a 'proposed bill to segregate blood supplies.'[47]

Some of these white anxieties found a focal point on local buses, a common site of racial tensions and minority protest in Britain just as they were in America. Martin Luther King had first emerged as a civil rights leader during the Montgomery Bus Boycott, assuming leadership of a campaign that demanded the hire of more black drivers, more courteous treatment of black customers by white drivers and, eventually, for completely desegregated seating. In addition to their general resistance to any integration, southern white segregationists were particularly alarmed by the prospect of white women having to share bus seats with black male passengers: a kind of intimacy in a confined space that played on their paranoia about interracial sex.

On Tyneside buses that issue tended to lurk in the background while economic concerns were pushed to the fore. In February 1958, the same month that one white Newcastle teenager found herself in court for loving a non-white bus conductor, a mass meeting of white bus workers sent a delegation to the management of the Newcastle Corporation Transport Undertaking, which controlled the city's buses. The delegation alleged that Indians and Pakistanis were being hired ahead of 'local men.' Apparently unable to accept the notion that these non-whites were now actually 'local men' themselves, the white busmen asked the Corporation to respond to rumours that 'coloured personnel' working as drivers and conductors were not subject to such exacting examinations as their white colleagues and were getting more overtime. However, a motion to work to rule in protest against the employment of any 'coloured people' was defeated, and Sid Hills, regional secretary of the Transport and General Workers Union, announced the Union's refusal to 'countenance a colour bar.' Hills tellingly, if condescendingly, blamed the agitation for a ban on 'what one might call the poor white element,' among Newcastle's bus crews. Councillor Dennis Larrow, Vice-Chairman of the Newcastle Transport Committee, had the distinct 'impression from various sources that the white people are not too happy about the present situation' and was surprised that the complaints had not come sooner. Larrow blamed the 'lack of white recruits' for the situation. Frank Taylor, General Manager of the Transport Undertaking, denied the allegations of special treatment for non-white workers, but still decided that the best way to defuse the situation was by pandering to white complaints. He announced the hire of twenty-two new white employees and offered reassurances that no more coloured workers would be employed as long as suitable white applicants were available.[48]

Although white bus workers insisted that their grievances were 'more concerned with the ability of the staff than the colour of skin,' it was hard not to detect the racist dimensions of an unedifying squabble over the hiring and treatment of coloured bus workers. As Hills explained, the dispute flared at a time when, having eschewed work on the buses in search of better opportunities, an economic downturn meant that 'quite a large number of white people were joining the staff, possibly because they feared the unemployment situation.'[49] Asian and Caribbean immigrants had been broadly accepted when they took the kinds of low-paid unskilled jobs that white workers hoped to leave behind. But in times of economic squeeze, when upward mobility was limited and those low-level jobs were the only ones available, immigrants were viewed far less favourably.

As ever, there were always powerful voices on Tyneside that protested the demonisation of newer migrants and encouraged greater understanding of their cultures and the difficulties they faced. The local press provides a useful insight into changing race relations and racial attitudes on Tyneside throughout the 1950s and 1960s. Generally speaking, Newcastle's *Evening Chronicle* and *Journal* were sympathetic to immigrant groups, gave them positive exposure and tried to demystify them for their predominantly white readership in the belief that knowledge and information would quell racial acrimony born of ignorance and myth. Across the region, newcomers were widely, if by no means universally, reported on respectfully as new, different, sometime puzzling, yet far from intrinsically threatening additions to the population, prompting Dave Renton's conclusion that 'The North East press remained far friendlier to migrants than its London counterpart.'[50]

Nevertheless, immigrants of colour on Tyneside were still regularly cast as a 'problem' to be solved by local government and the white community. Moreover, some of the most probing journalism uncovered a mix of latent and overt prejudice lurking behind even positive stories of interracial harmony and minority achievement. Particularly revealing in this respect was a series of four substantial articles on 'Indians in Newcastle' by Tony Stride that appeared in the *Chronicle* in late February 1958.[51]

The title was somewhat misleading since Stride's brief extended far beyond the Indian community. Although he sometimes slipped into using 'Indians' as a catch-all term for all South Asian immigrants, Stride drew important distinctions within that diverse group, not least by offering a potted history of the 1947 partition of newly independent India into two nations: a predominantly Muslim Pakistan and an India dominated by Hindus and Sikhs. 'I spoke to Moslems, Hindus, Sikhs, and to the Newcastle school teachers, ministers of religion and shopkeepers who work among them,' Stride explained, all in an earnest quest to cut through the 'misconceptions and warped notions that abound' among local whites. Stride was astonished when 'One well-educated woman said to me quite seriously: "I suppose they live on grass and nuts".' She was trying to explain how, according to some of the whites that Stride interviewed, substantial numbers of Pakistanis and Indian residents were apparently able to own cars—in 1958, not something many working-class whites on Tyneside could boast—despite living in substandard accommodation and earning meagre wages. Many worked as pedlars, door-to-door salesmen who specialised in selling fabrics to other Asians and across the city. These pedlars acted in essence as agents for Asian wholesalers, who were themselves doing rather well economically, thereby creating a source of interracial resentment. 'And they've all got cars y'know,' said a white Westmorland Road shopkeeper. 'His tone,' Stride felt, 'carried with it a suggestion of secret envy of an inferior mob.'[52]

Economic rivalries, underlying racism, ignorance and unfamiliarity with the newcomers' religious and social cultures continued to foment white suspicion and occasionally hostility towards their new neighbours. Still, Stride felt obliged to reaffirm the notion that Tyneside was doing far better than most other areas of Britain in terms of race relations and opening up job opportunities for minorities—even if most of the examples he offered were of unskilled workers in bakeries, factories or on the railways, doing the kinds of manual and menial labour generally deemed acceptable for immigrants. Two years previously, he noted, the first Indian had been hired as a bus conductor in Newcastle. 'In view of the cool, not to say hostile, reception accorded them in other parts of the country at the outset, incidents may have been anticipated,' wrote Stride. 'Yet, judged by the Letters to the Editor, the travelling public would seem to prefer the Indians.' There were about fifty 'Indian' bus conductors and a handful of drivers, Stride reported. According to Mohamed Zar, this was 'better than peddling,' which he felt was close to 'begging.' Working on the buses was thus considered a step up, if a modest one. Yet, it actually extended the history of restricted employment options for minorities. Immigrants 'do not come here from India to be bus conductors,' Zar pointed out. 'But when they arrive there is hardly any other job open to them.' Zar, who Stride was at pains to point out had 'an English wife and three lively children'—noting elsewhere that 'about twelve Indians in Newcastle have English wives'—had once owned his own business.[53]

The third of Stride's articles focused on schools in Newcastle's West End. Potentially, education offered prospects of a better career for all the children living in this economically deprived part of the city, while mixed-race schools could promote greater interracial and interfaith understanding, and encourage social integration. Stride was struck by the emphasis that Indian and Pakistani parents put on education, even to the point of falsifying the ages of their offspring so that they could get more years of schooling. What was also apparent, was that a mix of cultural insensitivity and racial stereotyping permeated these schools and shaped the expectations of many of the white staff. Gordon Dowson of the Bell Terrace School rather disdainfully told Stripe that, 'If we get them (immigrant children) early enough they stand nearly as good a chance as the English children.' Dowson went on to explain how 'we've had one boy who has been here three years, and if he has another three years here he would be no better,' raising the possibility that he believed that these children, because of their race, not their circumstances or language deficiencies, might just not be as smart as white British children. Dowson added that even in a subject such as arithmetic, for which 'most of the children show a natural bent,' their talents were 'of the mechanical kind, not the thinking kind.'[54]

In fact, a report on the educational attainment of Indian and Pakistani boys in five West End schools in the 1960s found that, despite a 'climate of animosity' that gave them 'a marked sense of not belonging,' they consistently performed better than their white English peers, largely thanks to strong parental and communal support for education and ambition. These young Indian and Pakistani men, J.H. Taylor of Benfield School reported, 'were on their way up and out'–to universities and polytechnics, or into apprenticeships and careers. Their relative success and upward mobility only deepened resentment and suspicion among some poor whites who felt left behind.[55]

Stride found other signs of cultural and racial tension in West End schools. When it came to post-games showers at St. Paul's, a state-aided Church of England school which had about thirty Asian students in a student population of 300, the few Sikh boys who showed up wearing turbans 'were tactfully told that they must change their hair style or wear a bathing cap.' In deference to their faith, they chose to wear the bathing cap. Gordon Dowson was convinced that 'If parents would let their children dress like the other children they would forge ahead much quicker.' The message was that social acceptance would be much easier if only immigrants would abandon some of the most conspicuous outward signs of their difference and become more like the white population. Even if Sikhs, Muslims and Hindus had been willing to abandon these aspects of their religion and culture, they could not erase their skin-colour, the clearest marker of their difference. Tolerance of diversity had its limits. In the late 1950s, it was assumed on Tyneside that integration, if it was to happen at all, would happen on white British, nominally Christian terms: it would be less about multiculturalism than about assimilation.[56]

Stride believed that some old immigrant customs and practices were fading and that a measure of assimilation was indeed taking place through a mixture of external pressure and internal preferences. The traditional Hookah was smoked less; herbal remedies were falling out of favour as access to modern medicine became available via the National Health Service. The biggest changes, however, were in religious practices and beliefs, particularly among the young—which was actually also broadly true among young white British Catholics and Protestants during the late 1950s and 1960s, when formal church attendance and traditional religious beliefs also declined.[57]

According to Stride the 200 Hindus in Newcastle were the least devoted of the new immigrant groups to their native religion. Of course, there were exceptions and Diwali celebrations took place each October. Nonetheless, Stride's assumption 'that the Indian community would be keeping alive some of their old customs and adhering to religious beliefs which dominate their native country' had been 'shattered.' One young Hindu told him that he felt such customs 'are just a sort of myth. They are keeping people back.' A Hindu Society had been founded in the mid-1950s to curate those traditions and teach Hindi to children, but it had floundered.[58]

Stride found Indian Sikhs, also numbering around 200, rather more devout than the Hindus. 'They meet every Sunday for prayer,' he reported, and there were several major festivals and celebrations throughout the year, including the Basakhi in April and the Gur Parb in October. Here, too, some of the old sartorial and religious customs had lapsed under pressure from white society. 'Children point and laugh at us, so most of the Sikhs over here have abandoned the turban,' explained Indar Singh, who believed this lack of respect and sensitivity came from the fact that local white children rarely went to any church, unless it was on a school trip. Despite the mandatory religious instruction they got in school each day, English children, Singh felt, 'are lost as regards faith.'[59]

The area's Muslim community had a 'Moslem Society and a mosque in Westmorland Road—the Jamait-ul-Muslimin.' Although Stride felt that attendance at the prayer meetings every Friday and on one Sunday each month was patchy, he appreciated the importance of religious leaders in the life of the community, where they commanded 'universal respect.' In what Stride and his editors clearly considered a breakthrough for greater communal understanding, the *Chronicle* published a photograph of worshippers inside the Mosque, proudly announcing that 'This is the first time that such a picture has been taken in the City.'[60]

For all the missteps and occasional tone-deafness on cultural and religious matters, Stride's articles represented a sincere effort to educate and inform local whites about their new neighbours. He worked hard to offer Tyneside readers a complex, nuanced, if inevitably still subjective account of the religious and national diversity within an Asian immigrant community that was frequently reduced to one-dimensional stereotypes. Although shaped and mediated by a white journalist, the articles also allowed a variety of non-white voices to articulate what it was like for immigrants to try to make their way in a strange and sometimes hostile new world without completely abandoning, even as they adapted, their traditional cultures—and to do all this with a measure of pride and dignity intact. Stride was also prescient in what he wrote at the end of his final instalment. 'Nearly every Indian and Pakistani I met vowed he would go back to his own country one day. It is their dream. But will they? I very much doubt it.'[61] The new immigrants were here to stay.

Following the 'Indians in Newcastle' series, Miss Patricia Geraghty wrote a supportive but cautionary letter to the *Chronicle*. 'From first hand reports of their experiences it would appeared that some Northumbrians are more tolerant than people from other parts of England,' she wrote, 'but there are still far too many practicing the colour bar we like to think is non-existent here.' Geraghty urged vigilance against latent as well as overt prejudice towards the Indians and Africans who lived, either permanently or temporarily, in the region. Referring explicitly to the city's growing number of overseas students, Geraghty described a 'Northumbrian Club' in Nigeria, 'where students who have been in Newcastle meet to discuss their impressions of life there, and to reminisce over student days. What a tribute to our country it would be if those impressions were always of tolerance and welcome, instead of shut doors and condescending attitude!' Geraghty concluded her homily with a nod to the global, Cold War contexts within which post-war British and American race relations were being redefined. 'Perhaps if more people could be made to see these students as the youth of a continent which will in the future be of great influence in the world, instead of imagining them as members of an uncivilized tribe, the situation for them could be made easier.'[62]

A few months later, in the midst of the racial disturbances in Nottingham and Notting Hill, an editorial in the *Journal* tried to chart a course through the changing landscape of British race relations. 'Resentment is not new,' the paper rightly noted, before suggesting that racial tensions were more pronounced 'in inland towns which, before the war, had negligible communities of coloured people.' The argument was that coastal 'port area populations,' such as those along the North East coast, 'have had time to develop a sense of proportion' and find a way to negotiate racial differences. Although the editorial endorsed the idea that 'All good Christians accept coloured men as brothers in Christ,' it admitted that 'very, very few will accept them as brothers-in-law in families.' Prejudice, the paper conceded, was an unpleasant reality of life, even in the North East where the 'coloured elements generally "keep themselves to themselves".'[63]

The editorial pointed out that there were few signs of the kind of formal colour bars or 'open racial clashes' evident in other British cities and towns, where 'trouble has usually begun with the intimate association of white women with coloured men.' Nonetheless, the newspaper warned that 'it is unwise and even dangerous to ignore' the 'strength and rigidity' of white racial prejudices. 'Even more dangerous is wish-thinking that there is no undercurrent of feeling against coloured men who are, or may soon be competing for jobs in Britain…Let us face the situation squarely. More coloured immigrants are coming in than can now be placed in economic employment.' To defuse this explosive mix of economic and sexual rivalries, the *Journal* joined the growing call for immigration restriction and even deportation of the 'bad citizens among [coloured migrants]: the vice racketeers, the drug peddlers, and the parasites on the Welfare State.' The editorial conceded such 'bad citizens' were rare among 'the well-behaved and deserving majority' of immigrants and called on Tynesiders to 'make a broader-minded effort to assimilate the immigrants within our gates.' Nevertheless, it urged the government to 'control the future inflow' before Britain was, to use a phrase that increasingly dominated discussions of immigration and race relations, 'swamped.'[64]

The *Journal*'s heartfelt editorial reflected shifting attitudes towards immigration and revealed the extent to which the region was embroiled in national debates on the subject. As the 1950s ended, coloured immigrants and their children were increasingly cast as problems that could only be solved by tightening entry regulations. Despite taking care to acknowledge that most immigrants were good upstanding citizens, the *Journal* had linked non-white immigrants to vice, crime and an indolence that put an unsupportable strain on the welfare state and social services. On the same day the *Journal* editorial appeared, the *Chronicle* reported on plans being mooted by the Conservative Government's Home Secretary R.A. Butler to hire 'coloured detectives' who could 'be employed in coloured community areas, including Tyneside, to track down coloured immigrants, mostly men, who turn to vice or violence and incense the local white communities.'[65] Much as in the treatment of South Shields Arabs in the early 20th century, members of Tyneside's non-white communities were once again being portrayed as especially prone to vice and violence and as a threat to the social, moral and economic order, with whites the victims of their crimes and provocations.

In September 1958, the *Journal* had not entirely absolved Tyneside whites of responsibility for creating the 'race problem.' Yet, it still clung precariously to the notion that somehow a port area like Tyneside, with its longer history of transnational connections and tentative, fraught multiculturalism, might yet offer an inspirational template for better, more open, sympathetic and tolerant attitudes towards immigrant communities. It was this stubborn optimism that David Bean had picked up on and showcased for a national readership in the *Guardian* in March 1961 when he hailed South Shields as a shining example of interracial amity—albeit with scant regard for the very real history of racial animosity in that seafaring and ship-building town.

If Bean had lingered just a few months longer in the North East, he would have had a salutary lesson about the fragility of the region's apparent racial harmony. In August 1961, the most significant outbreak of racial violence in the North East during the 1960s took place in another of the region's major port towns, Middlesbrough. A teenaged white apprentice moulder, John Hunt, was killed in an altercation with Hassan Said, an Arab seaman. In the three days of disturbances that followed, local whites, sometimes in mobs 500-strong, attacked Arabs and Pakistanis and their properties around the Cannon Street area, gathering support in local pubs and marching to the chant of 'Let's get a wog.' Press coverage of the confrontations quickly declared this a race riot and often blamed racist young white 'hooligans' for the violence. The official report from R. Davison, the city's chief constable, generally concurred, but it also emphasised that the incidents had taken place in a particularly impoverished section of the city where violence of all kinds was quite commonplace, not least against the local police, as had happened during the August 1961 riots.[66]

The Middlesbrough riots contained two familiar themes. First, cheap housing stock meant that immigrants had been attracted to the down-at-heel Cannon Street area where a few had done rather well by setting up businesses that catered primarily to their own community. This success caused economic resentment among local whites that all-too-easily mapped onto barely suppressed racial prejudices. Second, the spectre of miscegenation hovered over the riot. The main establishment targeted and set on fire during the disturbances was the Taj Mahal café run by Mrs. Meah, a white Englishwoman married to a Pakistani man. Mr. Mulreany, a ringleader among the rioters, had taken very public and very vocal offense against Mrs. Meah and her business. Mulreany had actually been present when John Hunt was fatally stabbed by Hassan Said. Said's motives were always unclear, but Chief Constable Davison seemed to hint that Mulreany's presence may have been significant. Certainly, after the initial incident Mulreany publically vowed to attack the Taj Mahal as a reprisal. Once again, white anxieties about race-mixing had combined with economic rivalries and endemic poverty to create a maelstrom of white anger that spilled over into a major racial confrontation. It was, as Dave Renton puts it, 'the closest the North East came in the entire post-war period to a mass anti-foreigner pogrom.' Such incidents indicate the perils of glib generalisations about the racial attitudes of the white community in the North East, or about any other community for that matter. While the region continued to enjoy its reputation for relatively progressive race relations, the Cannon Street riots, in Renton's words, 'remind us that white society was not some given "neutral". The people of the North East were capable of tremendous generosity. They were also capable of great violence.'[67]

Moreover, as Martin Luther King recognised only too well, racial violence, indeed racism and violence, were much more likely to occur in areas marked by poverty, with all its attendant disadvantages, frustrations and pressures. This was a key part of the message he brought to Newcastle in 1967, arriving at a moment when race relations on both sides of the Atlantic were in a particularly parlous state.

Part Three:

Take a Look at America

CHAPTER NINE

'The Developing Darkness':
Martin Luther King and the Intersection of North East, British and US Race Relations in the 1960s

Martin Luther King's visit to Newcastle in November 1967 and his murder in Memphis in April 1968 coincided with the climax of a particularly fraught period in British race relations that profoundly shaped local and national reactions to both events. Indeed, for over a decade the American racial situation had been examined more closely than ever before by journalists, politicians and lay commentators hoping to understand, predict and even shape the course of British race relations as the sun finally set on the British Empire. The 1956 Suez Crisis had seriously damaged British prestige and power in the Middle-East while a wave of independence movements against former colonial powers in Africa, recognised by Conservative Prime Minister Harold MacMillan in February 1960 as evidence that 'the wind of change is blowing through this continent,' meant that Britain had to come to terms with declining influence in world economic and political affairs.[1]

With the loss of Empire came the new challenges—and the new opportunities—posed by leadership of a diverse Commonwealth. Immigration from that Commonwealth had increased steadily during the 1950s, not least as a consequence of the 1952 McCarran-Walter Act, which severely restricted the entry of British West Indians into the US and encouraged them to look to Britain for better opportunities. With members of the Commonwealth granted full citizenship rights, as opposed to merely subject status, by the British Nationality Act of 1948, immigrants from the Caribbean, India and Pakistan made up the bulk of the non-white people who came to Britain. Although there were some tensions, these citizens of colour were initially courted and cautiously accepted as a solution to labour shortages and as workers willing to fill the lowest paid and least attractive jobs in an economy finally beginning to recover after years of austerity.[2]

In the North East, local business leaders welcomed a new pool of potential employees and consumers, seeing them as vital to the region's economic prospects. 'If the North East's plans for continued economic growth are [to be] realised then it can be expected that greater numbers of immigrants will make their way here,' explained J.E.T. Aldridge in the *Voice of North East Industry.* Moreover, Aldridge was careful to pre-empt any racist stereotyping of the new arrivals. 'Any conception of other racial groups being inherently inferior in intelligence to our own is unfounded,' he insisted. 'As with white workers, aptitudes and application to the work situation will vary with the individual.'[3]

In 1962, however, in the midst of a brief economic slump and rising fears that traditional British culture was about to be swamped by unregulated immigration from what was known euphemistically as the New Commonwealth (to differentiate it from the 'white' Commonwealth of Australia, Canada, and New Zealand, and the non-coloured portions of Rhodesia and South Africa), the Conservative government passed a Commonwealth Immigrants Act. This measure significantly restricted the ease of access to Britain for her Afro-Caribbean, African and Asian Commonwealth citizens.

It was not only the Conservative Party that favoured immigration controls. Both major parties initially worked hard to keep serious discussions of race and race relations off the political agenda, fearing that it would exacerbate, rather than alleviate, white popular anxieties and disrupt the relative smooth operation of consensus politics in the 1950s and early 1960s. However, having initially encouraged Commonwealth immigrants, as well as migrant European workers under the European Volunteer Workers Scheme (EVWS), to solve domestic labour shortages, Labour and Conservatives alike increasingly viewed the entry of Commonwealth citizens of colour as a 'problem.' That problem was to be solved principally by more rigorous policing of national borders, ideally without jeopardising the many economic and geo-political advantages that the Commonwealth offered Britain.[4] When it returned to power in 1964, the Labour government upheld the 1962 Commonwealth Immigrants Act. In August 1965, it presented a White Paper calling both for the further tightening of entry controls and for the Home Secretary to be given discretionary powers to deport illegal aliens. Eventually, on March 1, 1968, again under Labour, another Commonwealth Immigrants Act was passed, this one far more stringent than the 1962 version. Designed specifically to restrict the entry of coloured Commonwealth immigrants, the 1968 Act was, as the European Convention on Human Rights later declared, both an affront to human dignity and overtly discriminatory on racial grounds.[5]

If one impulse in British race relations legislation in the 1960s was towards immigration restriction, another was directed toward the protection of immigrant rights against the effects of habitual and institutional racism. Whereas successive administrations had initiated a range of social, publicity and educational programmes to help ease the way for European workers entering Britain after World War Two under the EVWS, coloured immigrants from the Commonwealth received no such assistance. At the national level there was little government investment in helping the white British population understand, respect or accept their new neighbours; little was done to help the migrants settle into a challenging and at times hostile new world. Consequently, as Kathleen Paul writes, 'social pressures and conflicts, especially between working-class whites and migrants were allowed to fester...policy makers manifested their own conviction that the 'coloured immigrants' were a problem simply because they were in the country in the first place.'[6]

In this context, even the more progressive anti-racist legislation of the 1960s was still conceived primarily as a way to solve, or at least to mitigate the 'problems' posed by an increasingly diverse population. In 1965, the Labour government, having carefully paraded its restrictionist credentials in its White Paper calling for limits on immigration, succeeded in passing a Race Relations Act. Modelled on the 1964 Civil Rights Act in the US that had ended statutory or *de jure* racial discrimination while leaving in place a good deal of actual, structural or *de facto* discrimination, the 1965 Race Relations Act created a Race Relations Board to conciliate between those accused of discriminatory practices and their victims.[7] Unfortunately, the Board had few powers of enforcement. The Act provided no protection against discrimination in crucial areas such as housing and employment. Even before its passage, minority organisations and sympathetic politicians were calling for a new Race Relations Act, with a much wider brief to combat racial discrimination and imbued with far more effective powers of enforcement and punishment.

Meanwhile, reactionary forces in Britain became ever more vocal and, thanks to groups such as the British National Party (BNP), the League of Empire Loyalists (LEL) and the Racial Preservation Society (RPS), better organised. Most of these new organisations demanded the repatriation of all coloured immigrants and complained that the Race Relations Act threatened basic freedoms of expression, which usually meant the freedom of British whites to express their racial views, even if that meant insulting or discriminating against people of colour. Just ten weeks after the 1965 Race Relations Act went into effect, a *Daily Mail* report on the newly founded RPS exposed the toxicity of its racist views. Founded by James Doyle of the Brighton Kemp Town Conservative Association and Robin Beauclair, the

RPS spread its message via a four-page newspaper that the *Mail* denounced as 'grotesquely lopsided. They concentrate on disease, murder, rape, prostitution and vice, frequently citing American reports.'[8]

That was not the RPS's only debt to the US. It also promoted the ideas of Professor Wesley Critz George, a North Carolina eugenicist who believed in the innate biological inferiority of all non-whites. Following the Supreme Court's landmark 1954 *Brown* school desegregation ruling, George became an important figure in the propaganda wing of the southern white campaign of Massive Resistance against integration. George's pseudo-scientific ideas about white superiority and the threat to health and morality posed by contact with non-whites permeated RPS ideology. 'We should not have them in from the health point of view. We quarantine dogs yet we let in people with leprosy,' Beauclair explained before launching into a diatribe about the dangers of transmitting genetic deficiencies, of which Africans had plenty, he claimed, through cross-racial blood-transfusions–a fallacy which the *Daily Mail* exposed with a statement from the National Blood Transfusion Service. Migrant Poles and Hungarians, Beauclair generously admitted, had turned out to be 'jolly nice people…They're good English people now.' But they were white; there was no such capacity or prospect for Asians and West Indians coming to Britain. 'The race struggle is a struggle for breeding grounds,' Beauclair pontificated, in language of which George would have been proud. He added ominously that 'In North America the Negro is winning…Good luck to him. But, please, not in this little island.'[9] This was both a figurative and literal appeal to a 'Little Englander' mentality historically associated with xenophobia, excessive nationalism, and a fear of cosmopolitanism. It conjured up a beguiling vision of ethnic, racial and cultural purity, unsullied by centuries of migrations, conquests and imperial adventures and the intricately mixed-lineages they produced. This was, as David Olusoga writes, 'a vision of England that did not match the realities of the nation as it was…and a vision that required much of the history of the past four hundred years to be set aside.'[10]

Just as progressive forces in Britain looked to the US and the civil rights struggle for clues as to how to avoid or reduce racial conflict through the recognition and protection of minority rights, so some of the rising stars of British white nationalism also looked across the Atlantic and saw a salutary lesson: the health, integrity and privileges of the 'white race' were being compromised by African Americans and the sort of backsliding white sympathisers the RPS condemned as 'Leftist', 'race-mixers', 'communists' and 'do-gooders.'[11] In February 1967 members of the RPS joined members of broadly similar nationalistic groups such as the BNP and the LEL to form the National Front (NF). The NF was destined to become the most vocal, conspicuous and well-supported British anti-immigrant organisation of the next decade or so. In the North East, however, despite trying to recruit support, periodically offering candidates in local elections and conducting or condoning a series of terrifying attacks on non-white residents and their property, the NF struggled to gain significant traction. That failure was due, in part, to the emergence of an array of ad hoc and more formal anti-fascist and anti-racist groups. These local organisations, the latest custodians of the region's 'cultures of welcome,' heirs to those who had rallied against the Oswald Mosley's BUF in the 1930s and his post-War Union Movement, included the union-backed Anti-Fascist Committee, founded in North Shields in 1972, and several local branches of the national Anti-Nazi League established in late 1977 and early 1978.[12]

A decade earlier, King had arrived in Newcastle at a moment when overlapping debates about the wisdom of a new Race Relations Act and the desirability of far tighter immigration controls were well and truly joined. In April 1967, a widely publicised report by the independent Political and Economic Planning Ltd (PEP) had exposed the pervasiveness and intensity of discrimination against coloured citizens in Britain. In the same month, the Race Relations Board also published its annual report, in which it stated that 'no effort should be too great to prevent the development of American patterns of *de facto* segregation in this country. Similarities in housing patterns and employment already exist in fact.'[13]

It was not just the Race Relations Board that invoked the deteriorating racial situation in America as a portent of what might soon happen in Britain if immigrant grievances were not addressed. Throughout 1967 and 1968, the British government and media repeatedly referred to the stalling of the civil rights movement, the emergence of black power and the escalation of racial tensions as a cautionary tale. In late July 1967, as Newcastle University was trying to finalise arrangements for King's visit, the Tyneside press joined the national electronic and print media in reporting a summer of rioting in Detroit, New York, Birmingham, New Haven, Newark, and other urban centres. 'Race Wars Flare Across America,' screamed the front page of the *Journal* on July 24, 1967. Coverage of the Detroit riot, the worst of the 1960s with forty-three fatalities and an estimated $40-45 million worth of property damaged or destroyed, continued for days until the military was deployed to 'crush rioters.' The following week, the same paper reported that in Washington 'Mobs Riot Near the White House.'[14] Even in the generally temperate Tyneside press, the tone of the reporting was increasingly apocalyptic.

The Detroit riots coincided with a visit to England by Stokely Carmichael, one of the most charismatic and controversial of the black power leaders who provided a militant alternative to King and the mainstream civil rights movement in America. At a time when CARD, the foremost British civil rights organisation, was splintering into broadly identifiable moderate and radical factions, Carmichael met with several black British radicals. These included Michael de Freitas, also known as Abdul Malik or Michael X, in deference to the African American nationalist Malcolm X, who had himself visited England twice, in late 1964 and early 1965.[15] In 1965 Michael X had founded the Racial Action Adjustment Society (RAAS), a loose alliance of British citizens of West Indian, Guianese, African, Pakistani and Indian heritage. Whereas King, his nonviolent protest methods and overarching vision of universal brotherhood had provided the initial inspiration for activists in CARD and other civil rights groups—not least Catholic civil rights campaigners in Northern Ireland—by the late 1960s, figures like Carmichael offered compelling new role models for many young black British radicals.[16]

One of those figures was Obi Egbuna, a Biafra-born writer who in 1967 founded Britain's first putative black power group, the Universal Coloured People's Association (UCPA). Egbuna had met with Carmichael and under his influence published a British reworking of the American's seminal *Black Power* manifesto. Like Carmichael, with his growing interest in Pan-African solidarity, but also like King, with his increasing emphasis on the global interplay of racism, economic injustice and war, the UCPA had a genuinely transnational vision, taking inspiration from struggles against colonial oppression in Africa, Asia and the Middle-East. Because, as Stephen Tuck explains, Britain 'did not have formal Jim Crow segregation…the classic tactics of the American civil rights movement, such as mass confrontations with white-supremacist sheriffs, were not readily transferrable…Black Power, with its explicit international vision was a better fit for those angered by immigration restrictions and frustrated by the moderate response of major black equality organizations.'[17] The British situation for non-white citizens in the late 1960s was not really analogous to that facing African Americans. As Tuck points out, in Britain, non-whites still constituted less than three percent of the British population, and half of them 'were from Asia with their own long-established cultural traditions, and virtually none owned guns.'[18] Nevertheless, the UPCA, like other British ethnic militants, took much of its language and ideology, and some of its tactical cues from the black power movement in America. Meanwhile, other minority groups continued to draw inspiration from the nonviolent direct action tactics and integrationist goals popularly associated with Martin Luther King. As Tuck puts it, 'In short, American styling was a strategic choice by British activists to strengthen their campaigns and to legitimize their own complaints.'[19]

In the summer of 1967, the British government viewed Carmichael with much the same suspicion as did its American counterpart. Carmichael's espousal of black pride and Pan-African identity and his influence on the community activists he met in London drew an almost hysterical response from the British press, which consistently reduced his pro-black sentiments to anti-white hatred and thus fuelled mounting public concern about the growth of black power in Britain. Those concerns often bled into a wider white resentment whenever British minorities drew attention to racial injustice and discrimination.[20] Questions were raised in Parliament about Carmichael's allegedly subversive presence and Labour Home Secretary Roy Jenkins decided to withdraw his entry permit. 'Having considered a report on this man's recent activities,' Jenkins explained, 'I have decided that his presence here is not conductive to the public good. He has now left and I do not propose to allow him to re-enter the country.'[21]

The combination of Carmichael's visit, the distressing images of racial conflict beamed in from urban America, the radicalisation of many existing British immigrant organisations and the formation of others with avowedly radical and occasionally revolutionary programmes had several consequences for British popular and governmental opinion. One was that Martin Luther King was increasingly depicted as a voice of reason and moderation amid the incendiary rhetoric and occasionally violent manifestations of black power.[22] This perception was more a matter of tactics and tone than of goals, since by 1967 King was committed to fighting militarism, economic injustice and racism through a form of democratic socialism. Nevertheless, unlike some more nationalistic black militants, he continued to espouse the virtues of interracial cooperation and nonviolence in pursuit of his radical goals. In November 1967, King's enthusiastic reception, particularly among whites, nationally and in the North East, turned on a keen understanding of this contrast.

King's perceived moderation was pressed into the service of many, sometimes quite contradictory arguments in British debates about race and immigration. Immediately following King's trip to Newcastle, the House of Commons debated the new Race Relations Bill. Sir Cyril Osborne was a veteran Conservative MP who had represented the rural Louth, Lincolnshire, constituency since 1945 and spent much of that time railing against foreigners of one sort or another. Osborne informed the House that 'Yesterday a most moderate coloured leader from America—Dr. Martin Luther King—received an honorary degree from Newcastle University...he said, "All our troubles could soon be yours." He said that we had the makings of a Selma or a Watts situation in this country. This is the thing that should worry Honourable Members on both sides of the Committee.' Osborne continued, 'Let me quote exactly what Dr. Martin Luther King said about this problem. He said: "Britain is in the same situation as many of the northern cities of America were at the turn of the century. They did not have legal segregation, but there were latent prejudices in the white community."' Instead of focusing on King's call for education to counter the ignorance that bred such prejudices, or legislation to curtail their discriminatory impact on minorities, Osborne quoted from a brief press conference King had given in London the day after his Newcastle visit to support the case for further restrictions on immigration. 'I beg the Government to place greater restrictions on immigration because otherwise it will automatically cause the situation to arise that has occurred in America and which no one there seems to be able to solve at the moment.'[23]

David Winnick, the Labour MP for Croydon South, took a rather different message from King's words and example. 'Does not the honourable Member agree that to a large extent the trouble in America has been caused by years or even centuries of discrimination against non-whites, and that this is part of the trouble at the moment? Only now are the Negroes in America beginning to get their legitimate legal rights as human beings.' Osborne did not deny such discrimination existed, but he fell back on the mantra that the real problem in Britain was that there were simply too many immigrants of the wrong colour and, therefore, of the wrong pedigree entering the country. 'The more colour that is brought into the country, with its poverty and its background, the greater the danger that the tragedies that did so much harm in America will be repeated here. It is because of this that I have pleaded all these years for some restriction.'[24]

Osborne had, indeed, been making such pleas for years. A few months earlier, as Carmichael's trip and the Detroit riots captured the headlines, he had asked the Home Secretary if 'in view of the half million unemployed, and the danger there will be over one million unemployed next winter...he will introduce legislation to amend the Commonwealth Immigrants Act, and forbid all immigration until Her Majesty's Government's policy of full employment has been achieved.'[25] Roy Jenkins rejected the premise of Osborne's question—that unemployment would double over the next year—and stated simply that he had no intention of amending the Commonwealth Immigrants Act at this time. Instead, he joined David Winnick and others, mainly but not exclusively on the British Left, in arguing for further legislative safeguards for minority rights. Again with one eye on America, Jenkins contended that legislation to outlaw discriminatory housing and employment practices, if vigorously enforced, might obviate the need for black power militancy in Britain and prevent racial violence along American lines. As early as 1966, in a May 23 speech to the National Committee for Commonwealth Immigrants in London made to welcome Mark Bonham Carter as the first Chairman of the Race Relations Board, Jenkins had promoted a progressive vision of a multicultural Britain in which both 'host' and 'migrant' cultures could flourish and strengthen each other. In a phrase that subsequently found its way into countless sociology textbooks, Jenkins explained how he did 'not regard [integration] as meaning the loss, by immigrants, of their own national characteristics and culture...I define integration, therefore, not as a flattening process of assimilation but as equal opportunity, accompanied by cultural diversity, in an atmosphere of mutual tolerance.'[26]

Jenkins had put the finishing touches to this speech, which some of his aides dubbed his 'We Shall Overcome Speech,' while visiting King's College, part of the University of Cambridge. In it he also insisted that any self-respecting modern British university should be at the forefront of efforts to create this kind of diverse, mutually respectful society. 'Where in the world,' he asked rhetorically, 'is there a university which could preserve its fame, or a cultural centre which could keep its eminence, or a metropolis which could hold its drawing power, if it were to turn inwards and serve only its own hinterland and its own racial group?'[27] Jenkins' remarks were widely praised and even more widely publicised. He repeated them frequently over the next few months, the period during which his Labour Party colleague and Newcastle University chemistry professor Lord William Wynne-Jones resolved to nominate Martin Luther King for an honorary doctorate at his institution.[28]

There is no definitive evidence connecting Jenkins's May speech and Wynne-Jones's proposal that Newcastle University should publicly honour King. Still, Vice-Chancellor Bosanquet certainly intended to use honorary degrees to signal Newcastle University's engagement with the great social issues of the day—and recent events in America and Britain had combined to make race relations one of the most pressing of those issues. In a similar vein, Jenkins had suggested that universities could do much to allay public fears of multiculturalism and demonstrate the social, cultural, intellectual and economic benefits of immigration and labour mobility. The Home Secretary concluded his speech by conceding the existence of widespread 'community prejudice' in Britain, 'whether it springs from fear or inadequacy or less reputable motives.' He pledged to support further legislation to outlaw discrimination, once more invoking the US to explain his position. 'American experience, though it can sometimes be misleading in this field, shows clearly that this is not a problem which solves itself without positive action.' He admitted that 'unless we can solve it this will be a major blot on our record for the rest of this century, a constant source of weakness abroad, a handicap to full economic development.'[29]

Roy Jenkins helped to prepare the way for what in October 1968 eventually became a new Race Relations Act. One of the foundations for this new legislation was another PEP report, prepared by a committee chaired by Professor Harry Street and published just days before King visited Newcastle. Street and his team of researchers had conducted an international survey of anti-discrimination legislation to advise the government on how best to extend and improve the 1965 Race Relations Act in order to address discrimination in housing, employment, financial institutions, and various public accommodations and services. The majority of case studies in the Street Report came from the US. Fifty-nine pages, or nearly half of the report, drew on examples from the US and Canada.[30]

Everywhere one looked in the run up to King's visit it seemed as if British responses to its own racial problems were being formulated in the context of understandings and misunderstandings of the American situation. As a *Guardian* editorial noted on the day King flew into London, the civil rights leader's presence 'coincided with an upheaval in the Campaign Against Racial Discrimination…with the sentencing of Michael X, Britain's main black power spokesman to a year in prison, and with the Street Report on the necessity of strong laws to fight racial discrimination. All three phenomena—CARD, Michael X, and the Street Report—have their links with America's own experience of race relations.'[31] King understood and went out of his way to encourage this sense of interconnectedness, of entwined destinies. Commenting briefly to the press on his arrival at Heathrow Airport on November 12, he said 'England has to be eternally vigilant and extremely concerned so that the problem will not grow and develop in greater dimension, because it could become as serious as in the United States.'[32] Some people feared that had already happened.

In Newcastle the following day, as he presented King for his Honorary Doctorate, J. H. Burnett, the University's Public Orator, also made very explicit use of the American analogy to emphasise the relevance of King's work for a nation struggling to resolve its own racial problems and pondering the wisdom and nature of further legislation:

> Every one of us will, I am sure, realise the parallel between Dr. King's present concerns in America and the situation in Britain today. Despite this country's great public traditions of freedom, ghettos are springing up in our cities, discrimination is daily exercised in employment, those activities which the Englishman regards as the least lucrative and attractive are becoming the tasks of the non-English, and we have had to enact a Race Relations Bill in an attempt to regulate our behaviour.

Burnett then called upon the Chancellor to bestow the award on King, 'not only because this University wishes to honour a great and good man, not only because in so doing we are acting on behalf of all universities and of all right-thinking men and women in Britain, but because every one of us shares with him the common problem of living with our neighbours and of ensuring the dignity and freedom of all men.'[33]

This noble commitment to the common cause of eradicating prejudice and ending discrimination took place in a city which still had a relatively small immigrant population, certainly compared to places like Birmingham, Bradford, High Wycombe, Huddersfield, London, Nottingham, Slough, West Bromwich and Wolverhampton, where absolute and/or proportionate numbers of 'New Commonwealth' immigrants were much higher. Nevertheless, Tynesiders were hardly indifferent to or isolated from national debates on restriction and protection, particularly as the local Asian presence continued to rise. In late 1966, Sudha Telang, a local Indian woman, was appointed on a temporary contract to research 'immigration problems in the city' for the Newcastle City Planning Department.[34] In 1967, her report estimated that there were around 3,400 'coloured immigrants' on Tyneside, including roughly 400 students studying at Newcastle University—a figure that begs the question of why the University found it so difficult to find a more diverse group to meet with King for coffee on November 13. Overall, the coloured immigrant population on Tyneside was almost twice as large as recorded by the 1961 Census. A subsequent report compiled by Sheila Patterson put the number of 'New Commonwealth Migrants' in Newcastle in 1967 closer to 5,000 out of a population of 260,750. By way of comparison, a similar-sized city such as Leicester in the East Midlands had 6,000 migrants out of a total of 267,050; Bradford in West Yorkshire, a particular magnet for Asian immigrants, had some 12,500 migrants among a population of 298,220. On Tyneside, Telang found the areas of greatest non-white concentration were in 'Jesmond, the west end of the City and, to a smaller extent, Heaton.' Most came from India and Pakistan; around 400 were from the Caribbean; others had origins in Yemen, Somalia and West Africa—descendants and heirs of the Arab and African seamen who had first found homes in South Shields during the early 20th century. Telang's report concluded that 'Commonwealth and Colonial immigrants' represented only 0.9 percent of the total Newcastle population, less still on the south bank of the Tyne in Gateshead. Even Patterson's higher figure of 5,000 constituted less than two percent of Newcastle's inhabitants.[35]

Reviewing Telang's demographic and sociological survey, Wilfred Burns, the City's Chief Planning Officer, was unequivocal in stating that in Newcastle,

> The coloured immigrant, like certain other groups in society, is discriminated against either consciously or unconsciously...the fact of underprivilege for the majority of the immigrants is indisputable. Their housing standards are low...and for one reason or another they do not have ready access to the widest choice of housing area. Similarly, the widest opportunities of employment do not seem to be available, although it is fair to say that unemployment is not a problem. There may be prejudice too in the field of education, motor insurance and so on.[36]

Burns's understanding that racial prejudice and discrimination were genuine problems on Tyneside was typical of local government responses during the 1950s and 1960s. Newcastle City Council sometimes struggled to offer effective leadership and find appropriate solutions to rising interracial tensions, or to address the particular problems faced by immigrant communities in the region. It could also be oblivious to intra-communal differences within minority groups as well as to struggles for power among them. Dave Renton, the foremost historian of post-World War Two race relations in the North East, is probably right to argue that while local government agencies 'often played a more positive role than that of national agencies...their priority was still not to support migration but to manage it.'[37]

Nonetheless, Newcastle City Council and its specialist agencies such as the Special Committee as to Commonwealth Immigrants (SCCI) and the Tyne and Wear Community Relations Council (CRC), the local iteration of a national network of CRCs, worked consistently hard to combat discrimination and reduce racial conflict. Generally speaking the Council honoured the region's more progressive traditions of racial and religious tolerance in testing times. In early 1961, for example, the Council had returned policy recommendations from its Parliamentary and General Purposes Committee for dealing with racial and religious discrimination in clubs and recreational facilities in Council-owned properties, arguing that it was not stringent enough. The Council wanted the regulations extended to outlaw discrimination in any businesses or accommodations on land leased from or operated by the Newcastle Corporation. In March 1961, the Committee revised and strengthened the language in accordance with the Council's wishes.[38]

The Council also consulted with and gave practical support to a plethora of increasingly active local community organisations. Indeed, one of the key developments in Tyneside race relations during the 1960s was the growing significance of voices from within migrant communities themselves. At its September 1966 meeting, the SCCI resolved to enlist more minority representatives, initially inviting Dr. Basu (Indian), Neville Pierre (Trinidad and Tobago) and Mr. M. Khwaja and Mrs. Ahmad (both Pakistani) to join the Committee.[39] Whether involved with the SCCI, or the local CRC, or in grassroots community organisations such as the Indian Forum, the Pakistan League, Tyneside CARD or Jamiat al-Muslimeen, a Muslim presence in the city from the mid-1930s, Tyneside's racial and religious minorities became increasingly prominent actors in the fight against discrimination.[40]

In September 1967, the Council created the Commonwealth Immigrants Working Group (CIWG) to replace the somewhat ad hoc and under-resourced SCCI. In introducing the new provisions, Basil McLeod, a Councillor from the city's St. Nicholas Ward and CIWG chair, cautiously revisited the familiar notion that race relations on Tyneside were basically very good and might even prove inspirational to other parts of the country.

'Newcastle upon Tyne is not faced with the intense racial difficulties such as are experienced in some other big cities in this country,' McLeod suggested. 'It has, however, a substantial immigrant population and it has the opportunity to secure a high degree of racial integration that could be a model for other areas where the problems are more difficult.'[41] There was, nevertheless, a significant break with the past in the Council's acknowledgement that good race relations needed to be actively nurtured, not passively awaited: as an elected body sworn to serve the entire community, the Council accepted that it bore some responsibility for securing equal rights and opportunities for minorities until such time as discriminatory practices and, perhaps ultimately prejudice itself, disappeared. Nobody in 1967 was holding their breath for either of things to happen.

Not surprisingly, the Labour-dominated Council echoed the sentiments of Home Secretary Roy Jenkins in its conception of how to handle local race relations. 'There are often conflicting view as to what integration means and it is as well to set down clearly the goals that should be pursued,' McLeod explained. 'Integration does not mean uniformity or the abandonment of group cultures. It accepts that all people have equal rights and this includes the right to be different. It means creating a relationship between different sections of the community in which these differences are accepted as contributing to the life of the community in general.'[42] It was this emphasis on the potential benefits of immigration and diversity, rather than a relentless focus on its challenges and problems, that aligned the Council, not only with Roy Jenkins's thinking, but also with Tyneside's historic cultures of welcome.

The CIWG comprised 'six members of the Council, one member of the Newcastle Council of Social Services, one representative of the Campaign Against Racial Discrimination and four members of the immigrant community (one Indian, one Pakistani, one Sikh, one West Indian), all with equal voting rights.' With a budget of £2,000, most of which was earmarked for a full-time community liaison officer (an appointment the Council struggled to make), the Group was dedicated to securing fair and equitable treatment for all citizens of Newcastle, regardless of colour. It focused particularly on housing, employment, social and cultural provisions and education, where special measures were proposed 'to ensure that the language difficulties are overcome to the maximum extent possible.'[43] Although somewhat mechanistic in its diversity-by-numbers approach to membership, the CIWG represented a sincere effort by city leaders to embrace Tyneside's growing multicultural identity and encourage the local population to do the same.

This commitment was further in evidence when the Council enthusiastically received Sudha Telang's 1967 report on immigrant life on Tyneside at a meeting held just three weeks after King's visit. The Council focussed on the Report's evidence of prejudice, discrimination and social and economic marginalisation, rather than complacently pointing to the often quite positive picture of harmonious race relations, immigrant achievement and upward mobility that Telang presented. The Council reaffirmed its determination to intervene against discrimination in housing, health and employment practices and to address the particular educational, health and recreational needs of migrant communities.[44]

Benwell Councillor Connie Lewcock tapped into the longstanding belief among Tyneside progressives that education and publicity were the best ways to expose social evils and rally public and governmental efforts to confront them. Lewcock, a former Suffragette and veteran of the anti-Fascist mobilisations of the 1930s, personified the enduring significance of women in Tyneside's progressive politics. She urged widespread distribution and serious contemplation of Telang's findings: 'I hope the people of Newcastle will avail themselves of the information in this report and will make it known amongst themselves and amongst their neighbours.' Then suddenly, in the middle of a fairly staid Council meeting, Lewcock switched to an entirely different, more passionate, homiletic, register. 'I am quite sure that if we accept this report as a formality and we do not accept it in our hearts and in our actions every day the report will be a failure and all that we have said here today will be valueless,' she warned. In almost preacherly mode, Lewcock concluded with words of which Martin Luther King would doubtless have approved. Indeed, he may even have inspired them when, just a few weeks earlier and less than a mile away from the Council chambers which were then located at the Town Hall in the Bigg Market, he had spoken of the 'inescapable network of mutuality' which bound together all mankind and of his vision of a 'beautiful symphony of brotherhood' throughout the world. 'If we believe in the brotherhood of man,' Lewcock insisted, 'we have got to start living it the next time we meet our brother whatever he is like and wherever he lives.'[45]

Newcastle City Council's attempts to improve the economic and social prospects for Tyneside's migrant communities dovetailed with broader efforts to deal with economic problems that continued to afflict the region and provided such potentially fertile ground for interracial strife. It was no coincidence that Sudha Telang's Report emanated from the City Planning Department, the division of the Council most intimately involved in trying to halt and reverse the area's declining fortunes. Economically and to some extent culturally and socially, the region seemed off-the-pace, out of step with the boom-times enjoyed by many sections of British society. By the mid-1960s, London was swinging and, as Dominic Sandbrook evocatively exaggerates, 'Britain was enjoying a reckless surge of growth and prosperity, and as shoppers strolled down their local high streets...they were sur-rounded by all the trappings of the affluent society: car and television showrooms, crowded supermarkets, teenagers chatting over their mopeds, radios blaring out the latest hits by the Beatles and the Rolling Stones.'[46]

The North East had not greatly benefitted from this fitful, unevenly shared and ultimately quite precarious economic boom. Five days after King appeared in Newcastle, Labour Prime Minister Harold Wilson had to de-value the worth of the British pound by fourteen percent to make British goods more attractive overseas and address both a crippling balance of trade deficit and mounting government debts.[47] The new levels of prosperity un-doubtedly enjoyed by many in the 1960s were driven mainly by a mix of new service, creative, leisure, financial and technological industries, not by the older heavy industries, notably mining, shipping and shipbuilding, which had traditionally underpinned the North East economy. In 1961, for example, twenty-nine percent of Newcastle's population was still employed in manufacturing of one sort or another, but the proportion was rapidly dwindling and three decades later it stood at just thirteen percent.[48]

The loss of jobs in shipbuilding and related trades was devastating, es-pecially on Tyneside where roughly one in five workers was employed in the industry in 1962 as opposed to one in ten across the region. Between 1959 and 1966, six North East shipyards closed as a result of overseas com-petition, mainly from Japan, Germany and Sweden. Although the region still launched fifty-one percent of all British ships, the total tonnage under construction was falling and the industry in the North East effectively shrank by twenty-five percent during this period.[49] In fact, on the same day that King arrived in Newcastle, the Tyne and Blyth District Committee of the Confederation of Shipbuilding and Engineering Unions was making plans to go to London to lobby the government to protest the sacking of 600 workers at two Vickers shipbuilding works in Elswick and Scotswood.[50]

It was a similar story in another of the region's signature industries: mining. Although the coal industry, which had been nationalised in 1947, remained important, between 1950 and 1960 22,000 miners left work in the North East's pits. By 1954, no coal was being exported to customers outside Europe; a decade later, no coal was being sent to France or Germany, while London, one of the greatest consumers of North East coal, had begun cleaning up its act, getting rid of its famous smog by developing smokeless zones. As demand and production fell, the first major round of pit closures hit the region. The number of collieries in the Durham coalfields dropped from 127 in 1947 to 38 by 1969 and there were other closures in Northumberland. As a consequence, the number of coal berths on the River Tyne fell from 34 in 1946 to 16 by the mid-1960s.[51] Although unemployment in the North East in the late 1960s remained quite low, averaging 2.6 percent, this was still considerably above the national average of 1.6 percent. Even more telling, the average weekly income in the North East was just eighty percent of the national average. Poor wages and the threat of further job-losses in key employment sectors created economically grounded anxieties that intensified the likelihood of racial friction with newcomers amid the scramble for a job and a living wage.[52]

It was in this context of escalating economic woes that Newcastle's City Council launched a major programme of urban redevelopment and economic modernisation. The programme was spearheaded by Wilfred Burns in the City Planning Office and the visionary, if sadly corrupt, T. Dan Smith, Newcastle City Council Leader from 1960 to 1965 and from 1966 until 1970 Chair of the North East Regional Planning Council.[53] A 1963 White Paper prepared for the Board of Trade by Lord Hailsham with a good deal of input from North East planners and businessmen, had identified the area from the Tees to the Tyne as 'a growth zone' and authorised special development funds.[54] Three years later, a 1966 government report on the nation's shipbuilding industry generated further financial support for North East economic regeneration schemes.[55]

On Tyneside, the reforms initiated by Smith and Burns continued into the early 1970s. Results were decidedly mixed. While old dilapidated slums and outdoor lavatories gradually disappeared from tightly packed and unsanitary terraced streets, so too did long-established communities, with many residents rehoused in soulless tower blocks. Dozens of elegant city centre Georgian and Victorian buildings, admittedly many of them in awful disrepair, were razed to make way for new shopping outlets and office blocks as the planners sought to rebrand Newcastle as 'the Brasilia of the North.' Beyond the city centre, new suburbs grew, as did new towns such as Killingworth and Cramlington which became home to large numbers of displaced former miners. Across the greater Tyneside area, transportation links were improved and the old Woolsington Airport was expanded to cater to intercontinental freight and holiday traffic. Meanwhile, the Council itself, housed from 1968 in an impressive new Civic Centre near the Haymarket, became one of the city's major employers, overseeing a seventy-one percent increase in the number of staff employed in public administration.[56]

Few of these developments addressed the worsening plight of the city's already embattled West End. Once the site of many engineering works and armaments factories, the area had become home to growing numbers of South Asian immigrants attracted by the low cost of the housing stock. They shared the neighbourhood with a frustrated, disillusioned and increasingly impoverished white community. With local government and private sector resources devoted mainly to city centre renewal and suburban development, this part of the city, one where economic revitalisation was vitally needed, was poorly served. Rising non-white migration into this area at a time of deepening economic distress and social deprivation created a potentially explosive situation.[57]

Whatever the final verdict on the urban planning and economic redevelopment schemes of the 1960s and early 1970s, the crucial point here is that the number of non-white immigrants on Tyneside rose, not rapidly but unmistakably and, in certain sections of the city quite significantly, during a period of profound and deeply disconcerting social and economic change for many white residents. This was a moment when old communities, old patterns of employment, even the old places in which people had lived, worked and played for many years, were vanishing. Such disruptions would have been unsettling at any time, but especially when compounded by relatively high levels of poverty and worries about future employment prospects. In the late 1960s, this sense of dislocation, deprivation and loss among many local whites could easily manifest itself in resentment of newcomers and strangers, especially those who appeared to be doing quite well—and even more especially when they appeared to be getting special attention from local government to address their particular needs.

In this environment, Tyneside's brittle tradition of better-than-usual race relations was severely tested. In 1967, the Tyneside branch of CARD under the leadership of Chris Mullard produced its own report on *Colour Discrimination in Newcastle upon Tyne* based on a study of eighty-eight Asians living in the West End. The Report found that most of the immigrants questioned 'didn't seem to regard discrimination as a problem.' Paradoxically, however, it catalogued multiple examples of discrimination at work, on the street, in securing loans, and when trying to buy or rent property. The report concluded that problems for Tyneside immigrants were probably greater than those questioned were willing to admit and speculated that tensions with local whites were likely to increase in the future. The real test of Tyneside's reputation for racial tolerance, CARD suggested, would come when the next generation of immigrants tried to take their place in the mainstream of Newcastle's economic and social life, rather than forging their economic, cultural and social lives largely within relatively circumscribed racial and religious enclaves: that was when local white willingness to support genuine equality of opportunity in the face of palpable racial and cultural differences would become clearer.[58]

The City Planning Officer's 1967 Report, informed by Sudha Telang's findings, made much the same point. Addressing whites on Tyneside, clearly cast as the chief potential source of any racial difficulties, Wilfred Burns and his colleagues insisted that 'if we are to accommodate immigrants of a different culture from our own then we have to be prepared to see flexibility in our own social system.' The Report also reiterated that 'integration…does not mean that new cultures should, as matter of social policy, be assimilated into the blood stream of native British society so that the new elements are diffused (although some assimilation is bound to occur with second and future generation immigrants). It does mean, however, that social policies should be so framed to allow minority groups to continue to express themselves and so add to the enrichment and variety of city life.'[59]

In 1967, then, Burns and the majority of Newcastle City Council welcomed and tried to promote the kind of multiculturalism espoused by Roy Jenkins, who hoped that passage of the latest Race Relations Bill would end racial discrimination and encourage the development of a more tolerant and equitable society. Not everyone on Tyneside was quite so enthusiastic. Just six days before Martin Luther King's visit, D. C. H. Fulton wrote to the *Journal* insisting that he was 'opposed to persecution in all its forms. I deplore the bigotry, fear and sometimes hatred that motivates thousands—possibly millions—of British citizens who discriminate against coloured people.' Yet, like many others Fulton questioned the wisdom of a new Race Relations Act which would attempt to 'legislate against prejudice.' This was, he felt, the 'equivalent of saying, "Love these people or I'll break your arms'." There was a danger, he claimed, that any act designed explicitly to protect immigrants from discriminatory practices would mean that 'in the U.K. the coloured immigrant will have more rights at law than the natural-born Englishman.'[60]

The arguments that protection of minority rights necessarily came at the expense of white rights and that it was impossible to legislate away folkways and deep-rooted racial prejudices were ones with which Martin Luther King was all too familiar. Both had been touchstones of white southern resistance to legislative attempts to end segregation and disenfranchisement in the US and would later animate white objections to affirmative action policies designed to redress the effects of centuries of racial discrimination. That is why in Newcastle, King, who according to Vice-Chancellor Charles Bosanquet appeared well informed on the British situation, was at such pains to extol the virtues of stringent laws to curtail the worst practical manifestations of racial prejudice. 'While the law may not change the hearts of men, it does change the habits of men if it is vigorously enforced,' he explained. 'And through changes in habits, pretty soon attitudinal changes will take place and even the heart may be changed in the process.'[61]

King believed that in the absence of formal segregation Britain was in danger of becoming inured to the devastating effects of latent racism and structural discrimination. 'Britain is now in the position that the northern cities of America have passed through,' King said, echoing the warnings of the Race Relations Board's Annual Report just a few months earlier. 'There is no legal segregation, but there is a latent prejudice leading to discrimination in housing and jobs. It is from this that a black ghetto is developing in Britain.'[62] King had emphasised the same theme at his breakfast meeting with the Vice Chancellor, counselling, in Bosanquet's words, that the British 'should bestir ourselves to ensure early and full acceptance of coloured people in Britain as completely equal citizens. If we delayed, then we should see the creation of areas of coloured poverty and the lightning flashes of mistrust and intolerance that might be the first signs of the coming storms of violence.'[63]

Clearly, King felt that this was a crucial message to bring to Britain in 1967. He repeated it again at the brief press conference immediately following the degree ceremony, when he warned that British racial problems might 'get much more acute if there is not eternal vigilance on the part of the Government and of people of goodwill in dealing with the problems before they explode.'[64] Responding to a question about recent US race riots, King reminded Tyne Tees reporter Clyde Alleyne that it was only ever a tiny minority of African Americans who were involved in violence and that 'violent revolts grow out of revolting conditions.' If gross inequalities in wealth, housing and education persisted, King feared that 'despair and deep bitterness' would drive more to violence. To prevent the likelihood of a similar catastrophe in Britain, King urged his hosts to 'take a look at America, so to speak, and avoid some of the problems that have developed there. Because I think there are similarities and through strong legislation, vigorously enforced on the housing question, the jobs question, and the schools question, England could avoid many of the dark nights we have passed in America.'[65]

Back in London en route home to Atlanta, King spoke even more ominously to journalists of the 'developing darkness' of racism in British society where he saw 'some ghettos emerging and some prejudice existing.'[66] The *Daily Mail* reported King's warnings about the 'prejudices and half-truths' regarding British immigrants that needed to be corrected by 'strong legislation and a determined education policy.' Reverting to the sort of language he used to denounce some of the more violent and nihilistic expressions of black power militancy, King insisted that 'We must not yield to the politics of despair.' But he admitted that 'If we cannot change the breeding grounds of prejudice—the slums, the poverty and inadequate education—then violence and chaos will result.' King concluded by 'urging the policy makers in Britain and every individual in the country to deal with the problem now.' If they did not, he warned, 'All our troubles could soon be yours.'[67] By the time he was murdered in April 1968, these words would sound grimly prophetic.

In Newcastle, King's message sparked an immediate response. A lengthy *Evening Chronicle* editorial acknowledged King's exemplary credentials for speaking out against the evils of discrimination based on either race or religion. The paper feared that 'it is possible that, because we have seen little that even remotely resembles the explosive American reaction to the evils of segregation and second-class citizenship, proper weight will not be given to the warning which he delivered when he received an honorary degree at the hands of the Duke Of Northumberland.' The editorial continued, 'Tynesiders in particular may not be prepared to concede that racial ghettos are beginning to develop possibly because few have any real appreciation of what the term 'ghetto' implies, but in the main because they have failed to perceive what has grown up gradually and quietly in the absence of active intolerance or discrimination on a measurable scale.' Without a major immigrant population on the scale of cities such as Wolverhampton, Bradford or London there was, the paper suggested, a complacency bordering on smugness about the region's reputation for racial tolerance that blinded many whites to the travails of immigrants and to the prejudice and discrimination they endured. 'Tyneside has its ghettos. Make no mistake about that. How else can areas of generally sub-standard accommodation occupied almost exclusively by immigrant minorities be described!'[68]

So far, so enlightened. But the editorial then proceeded to identify the immigrants themselves as one of the main reasons for the emergence of these nascent ghettos which, 'owe their existence more to the reluctance of minorities to make the effort to adapt to a new environment and their passive acceptance of inferior conditions than to any positive discriminatory activity on the part of the rest of the community.'[69] This was a complex matter, where cause and effect were not always easy to disentangle. As social historian Kevin Myers notes, for some non-whites, particularly a new generation who came of age in the late 1960s and 1970s, 'liberal and radical attempts to promote a more pluralist Britain had limited appeal…Faced with discrimination and racist hostility at school, on the streets and in the labour market, increasing numbers of young black Britons were dissatisfied with those who preached piecemeal progress through patient communication with white society or else explained racism as a secondary phenomenon of capitalist relations.'[70] In keeping with Myers' analysis, there really was a certain amount of voluntary insularity among Tyneside's immigrant groups, who sometimes did prefer to live, worship, study, work and play in the safety of their own neighbourhoods and who viewed the rhetoric of multiculturalism with suspicion in the face of racist realities. Nevertheless, the *Evening Chronicle* veered dangerously close to blaming the victims of racism for their own marginalisation.

In its final comments, however, the paper retreated from disavowing the role of underlying social and economic factors, coupled with the attitudes of many local whites, for creating most of the problems faced by immigrant communities. Somewhat defensively it still insisted that 'active racialism does not account for the plight of these minorities,' but accepted that this 'does not absolve the community from its fundamental responsibilities.' Going further, the paper argued that 'A clear racial conscience involved accepting a duty to encourage full integration by recognising the possibility that latent prejudice may have contributed to the situation which exists and taking steps to redress it.'[71]

This call to action and conscience connected the paper to the better angels of white Tyneside's responses to centuries of encounters with outsiders. 'Simply to tolerate racial or religious minorities can never be fully satisfactory,' the *Evening Chronicle* insisted. 'We need many more manifestations of their unreserved acceptance than we have so far seen if we are to overcome their innate diffidence towards coming to terms with strange, sometimes bewildering conditions.' The editorial concluded by urging white Tynesiders to answer King's plea to do better by their fellow citizens. 'We may not have tried to deprive them of their right to dignity and parity, but if we have not involved ourselves in showing them the way to complete integration we have failed in our duty as sorely as if we had been guilty of the worst type of discrimination.'[72]

Of course, the underlying assumption here was that the eventual assimilation and acculturation of immigrants to 'traditional British' culture was the best possible outcome for both migrants and the host nation. There was little in the editorial to suggest that multiculturalism might actually be a positive force in British society as Roy Jenkins and some City Council leaders had suggested and as King always maintained with regard to the contributions of African Americans to the history and culture of the US. In the decades after World War Two official and white popular conceptions of how a variety of Commonwealth migrants related to concepts of 'British-ness' invariably drew a clear distinction between those immigrants popularly considered to be of 'real' British stock—whites from Australia, New Zealand and southern Africa—and migrants of colour who, notwithstanding their citizenship status under the 1948 Nationality Act, were often still considered as merely British subjects. As Kathleen Paul explains, whether living overseas or in Britain, 'Dark-skinned Africans, West Indians or Asians…[were] considered members of the political community of British-ness only'; they were not generally considered part of 'an exclusive familial community defined by blood and culture' which consisted of 'white skinned residents of the United Kingdom, who were always presumed to be of European descent.'[73]

In all of this, there remained little appreciation that 'British identity' was an elusive, decidedly mongrel and multicultural affair, whose chief characteristics were largely the product of white imagination enabled by white power. Not only was British-ness in an awkward, ever-evolving relationship with English, Irish, Scottish and Welsh identities, but it was also cross-cut by differences of class, status, gender, religion, region, and sub-region. Moreover, many of the most cherished 'British' values, ideas, and institutions were relatively modern traditions, invented in the Victorian era precisely to promote or consolidate a decidedly fragile sense of nationhood and common purpose. Many of the cultural traits, habits and symbols that by the 1960s had come to epitomise British-ness had roots in places that were, or at least began life as, emphatically non-British, often imported or imposed as the result of imperial and colonial manoeuvres of one sort or another. Even the name 'Britain' was foreign, a variation on the Latin term used by the Romans; tea was from India or China; Jewish immigrants from Spain first brought to Britain the practice of frying battered fish, although Italians in London may have been responsible for adding fried sliced potatoes to make that British culinary staple fish and chips; Queen Elizabeth II was mainly of German extraction, her husband Prince Phillip was Greek and their grandsons, William and Harry would later have Indian blood through their mother, the iconic 'English rose' Lady Diana Spencer; historically vast numbers of British citizens were of French-Norman, Norse, and, whisper it gently, African, Asian and Middle-Eastern lineages, among many other racial, ethnic and religious heritages that mingled messily to create the British population.[74] Such historical and biological truths had relatively little influence on popular attitudes or governmental policy towards immigration which, in Kevin Myers phrase, 'slowly became racialised and then ethnicised.' By the late 1960s, he argues, 'ideas about races and ethnicities, about skin colour, language and cultural traditions,' were fast becoming 'key markers for identifying those who belonged in Britain and those who did not.'[75]

As the issues raised by King's remarks entered the realm of public debate, Rev. John Muir responded to the *Evening Chronicle* editorial by suggesting that the Newcastle community-at-large was rather more responsible for the ghettoisation of its immigrants than the paper had allowed. He, too, raised the spectre of racial unrest in America to make his appeal to white Tynesiders in words that virtually paraphrased what King had said when he arrived at Heathrow on his way to Newcastle: 'Unless all sections of the community make positive efforts to achieve integration,' Muir warned, 'the situation could very well become just as serious and violent as in the United States.'[76]

While some Tynesiders, like Muir, used King's visit to consider the problems of how to protect minority rights and encourage full and equitable immigrant participation in a society with many different core beliefs, customs and values, others were already of the opinion that such efforts were doomed to failure. Immigrants were and always would be undesirable aliens. Restrictions on further arrivals and possibly repatriation of those already in Britain were the only appropriate responses in the midst of increasingly dire warnings about the imminent arrival of thousands of new immigrants who would swamp British society, take British jobs and houses and generally destroy 'traditional British values.'

Sometimes local antagonisms towards immigrant communities took novel form. There had been a tiny, initially somewhat transient Chinese presence on Tyneside since at least the 1880s when the Armstrong-Whitworth shipyards at Elswick prepared four vessels for the Chinese navy. The Chinese population in the North East slowly increased after World War Two as British passport holders and students began to arrive from Hong Kong, Singapore, Malaysia, as well as from mainland China and Taiwan. In 1949, Newcastle's first Chinese restaurant, the Marlborough Café, opened on the Scotswood Road; in 1962 there were fifteen such establishments in the city. By 1967, Tyneside's still modestly sized, but quite well-established Chinese community was working hard to make a success of its laundry, restaurant and other businesses.[77]

But not everyone was happy. One local took such exception to the cost of a Chinese meal containing what he described as 'the 'miniest' king prawns I have ever seen,' that he felt moved to share his anger with readers of the *Evening Chronicle*. C. Arthur criticised the inability of the 'Chinese gentleman in charge,' to understand his complaint and quickly moved on to a more general rant against the Chinese, their cuisine, and their apparent financial success. 'These bland, prosperous, conveyors of Oriental 'cooking' have lost my custom,' he fumed. 'It's too much to hope, I suppose, that they might make a contribution from their exorbitant profit to some fund to encourage a higher standard of literacy.'[78] A few days later, however, Mrs. J.K. Moffat came to the defence of the Chinese and their restaurants against Arthur's charges of usury, rudeness and mix of linguistic and culinary incompetence. She commended Tyneside's Chinese restauranteurs for their 'efficient and courteous service' and insisted that the 'lavish, well-cooked and hot' helpings represented extremely good value for money.[79]

And so it was in the months after King's visit that white Tynesiders debated the merits and faults, great and small, of their new and not-so-new neighbours. As so often in the region's history, for the majority of the 1960s, the ebb of racial prejudice was quickly followed by the flow of racial tolerance. When bigotry raised its head, there were still strong countervailing voices raised in opposition to it. Racial stereotypes were certainly in play—how could it be any other way when the *Black and White Minstrel Show* was still a fixture on British television, with its barely updated version of the kind of blackface minstrelsy that had been wildly popular in the region a century earlier? Or when 'Gollywogs' still adorned the labels of Robertson's marmalade jars? Or when you could still buy Darkie Toothpaste and, as an appalled Andrew Young noted on his return to America from Newcastle, 'a shoe polish called "Nigger",' adding that the English 'have no sensitivity on this question.'[80]

There were always concerted efforts to counteract such demeaning racial stereotypes and misrepresentations on Tyneside, not least from within migrant communities themselves. The local press and local government also continued to work sincerely, if not always with a sure touch, to offer constructive, progressive leadership in the field of race relations. They grappled with, rather than ignored, the existence of racial prejudice and discrimination and tried to understand and address those phenomena in the context of the economic and social problems affecting many parts of the region. The fabled cultures of welcome just about endured. In the spring of 1968, however, it seemed as if the polarities might be reversed: it was prejudice and discrimination that appeared to be ascendant with understanding, compassion and tolerance in retreat. Martin Luther King was again involved in the chain of events that dramatically raised the intensity of 'restriction versus protection' debates and sparked yet another soul-searching re-examination of Tyneside's race relations.

CHAPTER TEN

From Righteous Streams to Rivers of Blood:
Martin Luther King, Enoch Powell and
Race Relations on Tyneside, 1968

On April 4, 1968, Martin Luther King was shot dead in Memphis. Registrar Ernest Bettenson announced that Newcastle University 'deeply deplored' the killing and that 'we are flying our flag at half-mast to show our deepest regret and sympathy for Dr. King's family, who have suffered terribly in the course of his career.'[1] Shockwaves reverberated around the region. Local Royal Mail worker Peter O'Donnell had followed King's career closely and was so moved by his death that he sent a personal letter of condolence to Coretta Scott King. O'Donnell received back a postcard from King's widow thanking him for his thoughtfulness.[2] The Newcastle press gave his King's assassination remarkably full coverage. For months it closely followed the murder hunt that ended with the arrest of James Earl Ray in London and his subsequent trial and conviction. On April 6, a front page headline in the *Journal* declared 'America on Brink of Race War,' while an editorial reiterated the common view that King represented sanity, reason and civility amid the nihilistic violence and anger of black power. According to the paper 'Dr. King was an effective brake on the achievements of militants like Stokely Carmichael and the advocates of Black Power.' As rioting broke out across America once more, the Newcastle press joined the rest of Britain in asking again if racial conflict in the US 'could swell to proportions hitherto unknown and sweep beyond the shores of the New World.' To prevent that, the *Journal* turned to King's own words in Newcastle and called for 'men of goodwill everywhere,' to 'unite behind the principles of peace and social justice for which Martin Luther King stood.'[3]

News of King's murder and the ensuing riots generated two distinct, though not wholly incompatible responses in Britain, both designed to avert the possibility of similar unrest. One was an intensified clamour for a new Race Relations Act which would more effectively protect minority rights, allay racial grievances and thus undermine the growth of militancy. On April 9, 1968, the Labour government finally introduced the bill it had been promising since Roy Jenkins—who had been succeeded as Home Secretary by James Callaghan—had touted it the previous July. The same day, a supportive statement appeared in the *Journal*. Written with the shock of King's murder still reverberating around the city, the statement again channelled King's message in Newcastle. As the city stared uncertainly into its own racial future, the paper endorsed more stringent anti-discrimination legislation. 'It can be argued, as it was against successive civil rights acts in America, that you cannot legislate against racial prejudice. This misses the point. The purpose of legislation is not to make people hold certain views, but to prevent them practicing discrimination. We cannot afford to repeat the American mistake of doing too little too late.'[4]

The second response was to demand an end to immigration, possibly even the repatriation of non-white Commonwealth citizens in order to reclaim Britain as a white country. In Birmingham on April 20, 1968, Enoch Powell, Shadow Minister of Defence in Edward Heath's opposition cabinet, delivered one of the most infamous speeches in modern British politics. He denounced the proposed Race Relations Act and condemned the laxity of existing immigration controls, despite the draconian provisions of the revised Commonwealth Immigrants Act passed earlier in the year. Using highly emotive language that conjured up images of an impending race war in Britain, Powell insisted that to enact this bill was to 'risk throwing a match onto gunpowder.' As befitted a gifted classical scholar, Powell announced, 'I am filled with foreboding. Like the Roman, I seem to see "the River Tiber foaming with much blood."'[5]

Powell had been consolidating his views on the need for immigration restriction and repatriation for several years. But it was the American situation, coupled with exaggerated reports of vast numbers of East Kenyan Asians waiting to migrate to Britain, that provided the catalyst for his increasingly radical public statements. In October 1967, Powell had made his first visit to the US and was deeply disturbed by the racial antagonism and violence he found in northern cities, particularly in a riot-torn Detroit. Safely back in England, he allegedly told an American friend, 'Integration of races of totally disparate origins and culture is one of the great myths of our time. It has never worked throughout history. The United States lost its only real opportunity of solving its racial problems when it failed after the Civil War to partition the Old Confederacy into a South Africa and a Liberia.'[6]

In his 'Rivers of Blood' speech Powell presented the American situation as a portent of what awaited Britain if it did not arrest and ideally reverse the growth of its non-white population: a population which still constituted less than 2.3 percent of the total British population in 1968; comprised less than ten percent in the cities where the immigrant population was most dense; and rarely accounted for more than fifty percent in any statistical unit bigger than a street. Despite the numbers, Powell spoke despairingly of replicating 'that tragic and intractable phenomenon which we watch with horror on the other side of the Atlantic.' The American racial crisis, he suggested, was unavoidable, 'interwoven with the history and existence of the States itself.' In Britain, however, he charged that a crisis 'is coming upon us here by our own volition and our own neglect. Indeed, it has all but come. In numerical terms, it will be of American proportions by the end of the century.'[7]

Powell was censured and dismissed from Edward Heath's shadow cabinet for his inflammatory remarks. But it was quickly apparent that he had articulated deeply felt prejudices and genuine fears among many British whites. Polling data revealed that the percentage of British people who favoured unlimited entry for 'new Commonwealth' workers had fallen from thirty-seven percent in 1956 to ten percent in 1964 and plummeted further to just one percent in 1968.[8] Powell received more than 110,000 letters commenting on his speech, of which barely 2,000 expressed disapproval and most were very enthusiastic. Throughout the country, workers walked off their jobs and held demonstrations to express sympathy with Powell. A Gallup Poll conducted in late April 1968 indicated a seventy-four percent approval rate for Powell; the Opinion Research Corporation put the proportion even higher at eighty-two percent.[9]

And what of Tyneside, that widely acclaimed bastion of good race relations where, on April 9, the same day that the government introduced its new Race Relations Bill, the *Journal* published the first in a major three-part series on local race relations by Maureen Knight under the headline 'The Farther North You go the Better it is'?[10] There, too, Powell's speech had touched a raw nerve. Just south of the Tyne, 500 workers at the Dunlop plant on the Team Valley Industrial Estate in Gateshead walked off the job in support of Powell and raised a petition opposing any new Race Relations legislation. This happened despite the fact that Gateshead had one of the lowest proportions of immigrants in the region and that the Dunlop works did not employ a single non-white worker. 'The general feeling among the men is that they would not work with coloured staff,' the *Evening Chronicle* reported. The workers feared that the proposed Bill, with its provision against discriminatory hiring practices, might provide an opportunity for coloured workers to force their way in and deprive whites of employment.[11]

As nationally, letters to the Tyneside press were overwhelmingly supportive of Powell. 'At last a politician makes a bold and courageous speech on the coloured immigration problem,' enthused Alan Nicholson.[12] 'Everyone with whom I have discussed the speech agrees that no more coloured immigrants should be admitted to Britain at present, and I support this view entirely,' wrote Mrs Layne of Gosforth.'[13] Seven factory workers from Birtley in County Durham, co-signed a letter to the *Journal*, condemning the proposed Race Relations Bill as 'the ultimate in irresponsibility' and praising Powell for speaking 'down-to-earth common sense...we applaud his stand and are right behind him.'[14] Local Labour Party loyalist, J. Short, wrote in strong support of the Conservative Powell on this issue, believing that 'he is only expressing the views of the ordinary, and many professional, people of Britain. He simply wants to avoid serious trouble, which is inevitable if something drastic isn't done now.' Short's distinction between 'ordinary' and 'professional' people was an awkward way of expressing an important truth: Powell's views drew white support, as well as condemnation, from across obvious class and party political lines. 'I do not wish harm to any man, no matter what his colour or creed,' Short continued in what was a quite familiar prelude to pejorative or ill-informed remarks about the impact of immigrants on British society, 'as long as he doesn't interfere with other nations' way of life.' Because of their backgrounds and colour, these particular citizens were not conceived as truly part of the British 'way of life'; instead they were seen as opposed to, or compromising it. 'This "open door" policy in this country can lead to nothing but serious problems in a much shorter time than it has taken to develop in America,' Short concluded.[15]

Repeatedly, the American situation offered Tynesiders a crucial lens through which to view Powell's comments. 'He's dead right about the darkies,' wrote R.T. Oxford. 'It's already too late to avoid completely the fate that is overtaking the United States, but we can try to mitigate the inevitable consequences of the folly of succeeding misguided administrations by inducing as many foreign-born members of our population as possible to return.'[16] Mrs. B. Hunter was similarly forthright. 'Those who were against this Race Bill will be even more so now,' she explained. 'We put up with the coloured people for years when there were not many of them, but to have them taking our houses, jobs, school places etc. will be going just too far.'[17]

Equally upset was Mrs. R.A. Boyes, who regretted Powell's dismissal 'for expressing the worries that many ordinary people like myself feel if this Government persists in pressing Bills like the "Race Relations Bill" through Parliament.' Having recently left council housing to become a proud home-owner, Mrs. Boyes articulated the loss of power that many whites felt would accompany the passage of an Act that they saw as eroding their rights in order to protect and even privilege the rights of minorities. The Act would, Boyes claimed somewhat melodramatically, rob her of the 'one last liberty of selling our house to whom we wished.' Boyes subscribed to the increasingly popular idea that legislating against racial discrimination would simply diminish white rights and power. In the fierce battle for economic security and social mobility on Tyneside, she showed no interest in the argument that this might ultimately be a progressive step, let alone an ethically commendable one, in so far as it sought to ensure equitable treatment for all citizens, regardless of colour. In fact, Boyes had nothing but contempt for those who supported race relations legislation and warned that their misguided attempts to legislate equality would stir up ever more racial resentment among whites. 'The unfortunate thing about this particular Bill, and ones like it,' she argued, 'is that the people whom they are intended to protect will find themselves unnecessarily disliked and distrusted.'[18] Tyneside's non-white immigrants could not win: they were pilloried and demonised if they kept themselves to themselves, but many in the white community were far from ready to accept them on equal terms as neighbours or co-workers, and felt aggrieved whenever local or national government intervened to protect them from racial discrimination.

Throughout Britain, Powell's incendiary rhetoric and erudite scaremongering had thrown into sharper relief a previously amorphous, ill-defined sense of white British identity. This newly discovered British-ness was something to be celebrated and protected against all manner of foreign threats, not least by joining Powell in venerating a glorious, ethnically and racially unalloyed, if largely mythical past. As Bill Schwartz concluded, 'Sizeable numbers of those caught up in the turmoil of Powellism discovered themselves, anew, to be white. These ethnic discoveries were imaginative acts. But to work they needed historical memories in order that they might live in the imagination, for memory is not only the past recollected, but a means of becoming.'[19]

By no means all Tynesiders agreed with Powell. While pro-Powell correspondence dominated the letters pages of the local press immediately following his remarks on April 20, in a letter to the *Journal* on April 24 Joan

Hoggard sounded a rather different note. Hoggard explicitly invoked Martin Luther King and his idea that 'we are all one' and, focusing on the socioeconomic coordinates of racism, saw Powell's speech and the support it inspired as indicative of the 'Hatred...that can result from leaving unsolved the problem of coloured overcrowding and racial intolerance.'[20] By the end of April and start of May 1968 other more progressive voices had come to the fore. Condemning Powell's 'demagogic' arguments, a *Journal* editorial accused him of encouraging 'unintelligent people to believe that Britain's problems could be summed up on one word "colour" ...He has enabled silly people to take refuge in a fairy-tale world of evil black goblins.' Tellingly, the editorial couched the factory walk-out in Gateshead and signs of significant support for Powell as a betrayal of the North East's progressive heritage: this was a region where 'a more realistic and responsible attitude to important social and political issues was thought to exist.'[21] Speaking at a May Day 'Campaign for Equality' rally held at Rutherford College of Technology in Newcastle, Ted Fletcher, the Labour MP for Darlington, denounced Powell's 'racialist' speech as 'shocking.' He added that 'I can say without hesitation that if the word Jew had been substituted for the word immigrant it would have read like a speech made by Dr. Goebbel (sic) to a Nazi party meeting in the 30s.'[22]

'It has been my privilege to know and respect many of the coloured community on Tyneside,' affirmed Will George, once a Committee Member and Chair of Tyneside's branch of CARD, who argued that immigrants 'have been most patient over serious problems of housing, education and employment.' He believed that Powell's speech and the 'spate of obvious racialism' it provoked in the region 'has disturbed and created unhappy feelings among immigrants' which now included 'many frightened people.' An export salesmen, George had travelled the world, including the US, and used his experience as the basis for public talks designed 'to inform, educate and persuade Tyneside people in wide organisational groups that we must accept responsibility to promote harmony and understanding to and from our coloured community.'[23]

In Gateshead, Peter E. Oliver was appalled that white workers should walk out in support of Powell and to protest a non-existent problem. In fact, he was incredulous that so many locals had succumbed to Powell's racist rallying call and posed a series of facetious rhetorical questions to his fellow Tynesiders: 'How far has the colour problem grown in Gateshead recently? Not very far by observations I have made. Why have men from Birtley got to complain about the rise of coloured population? Has Birtley

Page 8

Clockwise from top left: 1) William Joyce (left) and Sir Oswald Mosley (second left) among fascists at the Haymarket, Newcastle in July 1934 following a rally on the Town Moor. *2) 3) & 4)* Articles in the Newcastle papers in 1958 captured some of the local white anxieties caused when immigration from the 'New' (as in non-white) Commonwealth began to increase. *5)* Doreen Caulker, for a while girlfriend of Animals' lead singer Eric Burdon, was among those in Tyneside's non-white community who helped to reshape the region's identity – not least its popular culture – in the late 1950s and 1960s. *6)* Eric Burdon and the rest of the Animals rhythm and blues group grew up on Tyneside besotted with African American music and took a keen interest in the American civil rights movement.

Page 9

Clockwise from top left: 1) Martin Luther King speaking to a newspaper reporter in Newcastle, where he was asked about the lessons Britain could learn from America's racial problems. *2)* Labour Government Home Secretary Roy Jenkins proposed legislation to protect minority rights and recognised the desirability, as well as the inevitability, of greater diversity in modern Britain. *3)* Disgraced former Council Leader T. Dan Smith was the driving force behind much of the urban redevelopment in Newcastle during the late 1960s and 1970s. *4)* Malcolm X was an inspiration to many of those, in Britain as well as the United States, who embraced various kinds of Black Power doctrines in the mid-to-late 1960s. *5)* During his meeting with Newcastle University students, Martin Luther King was repeatedly asked about his views on Black Power.

THE JOURNAL

America on brink of race war

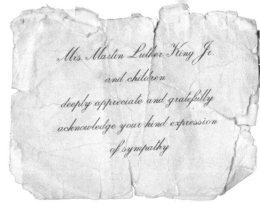

Mrs. Martin Luther King Jr. and children deeply appreciate and gratefully acknowledge your kind expression of sympathy

THE UNIVERSITY OF NEWCASTLE UPON TYNE

MEMORIAL SERVICE

for

Dr. Martin Luther King

Friday April 26 1968   5. 30 pm

APR

FRI 26 Miss Blair's B'day; gave her "The Career Woman's booking Book". Warm & sunny; saw white butterfly in gdn., lunchtime. Completed (& posted) Income Tax Rtn. Pete. had apt'n of tennis, in for tea onwards. Parcel of Di's clo. (postage 4/6) arr'd fm. Shropshire - couldn't bring same on m.c. *Memorial Service (LUTHER KING) a mem'l Service for the late Dr. Martin Luther King, the Amer. Civil Rights Leader & Nobel Laureate, held in St. Thomas' Church, Ncl.u.T. at 5·30 pm. to-day.

Clockwise from top left: 1) This front page from the *Journal* was typical of the extensive local coverage of the violence that engulfed the United States following Martin Luther King's murder on April 4, 1968. *2)* Forest Hall postal worker Peter O'Donnell was so moved by King's murder that he wrote in sympathy to Coretta Scott King and received back this expression of gratitude for his thoughtfulness. *3)* Newcastle University organised a Memorial Service for Martin Luther King at St. Thomas's Church, Haymarket. *4)* Laurence Kane's diary entry for Friday, April 26, 1967 shows that he was among those who attended the Memorial Service for King that day. *5)* Vice-Chancellor Charles Bosanquet had a good rapport with Martin Luther King in Newcastle and gave a moving eulogy at King's Memorial Service. *6)* Chris Mullard, a passionate campaigner for minority rights on Tyneside during the late 1960s and early 1970s.

Clockwise from top left: 1) President Jimmy Carter with Newcastle's Lord Mayor Hugh White and Prime Minister Jim Callaghan at the city's Civic Centre on May 6, 1977. *2)* Carter visited Washington, County Durham, ancestral home of George Washington. *3)* A commemorative album of BBC Radio Newcastle's coverage of Carter's visit. *4)* After four days on Tyneside in July 1977, boxing legend Muhammad Ali carries his 11-month old daughter, Hana, though adoring crowds at Newcastle Airport. *5)* Ali grabs a moment of peace during his frantic Tyneside visit.

Asian shops bore brunt of Meadow Well looting

Newcastle Journal

MEMBERS of the Asian community fell victim to the rioters after months of harassment on the Meadow Well estate, it was revealed yesterday.

Asians bore the brunt of much of the violence seeing their shops burnt and stock looted by rampaging youths.

Local councillors say the vast majority of residents are shocked and ashamed at the treatment dished out to the shop owners who provide a vital community service.

And they spoke of the Asian community's determination to continue trading.

Monday's riots may have started as a move against the police and emergency services but it appears on the estate itself shops run by the Asian community were selected as targets for attack.

Coun Rita Stringfellow, who chairs North Tyneside Council Community Committee said: "The residents I spoke to were shocked and

By PAUL ROBERTSON

and were genuine in their offers of support for the Asian community who have suffered problems here for some considerable time.

"If the Meadow Well loses its shops then the vitality of the area goes and the most vulnerable groups would suffer. We must do our utmost to support and help the Asian community."

Molly Woodhouse, chairman of Meadow Well's Collingwood working party believes the racial attacks were mostly down to people not living on the estate.

"Most residents have very good relations with the Asian community who play a vital role on the estate," she said.

David Chandler, Tyne and Wear Racial Equality Council information officer said: "It is a shame that such a small minority who have abused and attacked the Asian community have led to

Allstar Picture Library / Alamy Stock Photo

Clockwise from top left: 1) When rioting broke out on the Meadow Well estate in North Shields in September 1991, the press reported on how civil disorder rooted in poverty quickly took on ugly racial overtones. *2)* Conference organiser Brian Ward, civil rights veteran Julian Bond, former Mayor of Cincinnati J. Kenneth Blackwell and the Dean of the Faculty of Arts at Newcastle University Jeremy Patterson at the 1993 Martin Luther King Memorial Conference. *3)* Newcastle University Vice-Chancellor James Wright, Pulitzer Prize-winning cartoonist Doug Marlette, Cambridge University's Paul Mellon Professor of American History Tony Badger and Brian Ward at the 1993 Martin Luther King Memorial Conference. *4)* On May 8, 1998, Brian Ward, Harry Belafonte and Julian Bond in front of the plaque Belafonte had just unveiled in the Newcastle University Students Union to mark his and Martin Luther King's receipt of an Honorary Doctorate. *5)* Newcastle United goalkeeper Shaka Hislop was an early supporter of the Show Racism the Red Card movement that started on Tyneside in the early 1990s.

Courtesy of Bernie Donohoe/Journey to Justice

The Journal 🦁

Newcastle University honours four at winter congregation ceremony

FOUR eminent social and political figures were honoured by a university at its winter congregation ceremony.

Newcastle Journal

Rakesh Mittal, Shami Chakrabarti and W.G. (Garry) Runciman

Courtesy of Bernie Donohoe/Journey to Justice

Courtesy of Bernie Donohoe/Journey to Justice

Clockwise from top left: 1) Shami Chakrabarti, founder of Liberty, Britain's leading human rights organisation, received an Honorary Doctorate from Newcastle University in January 2012. *2)* Brian Ward was among those who spoke at the opening of Journey to Justice's 'Footsteps to Freedom in the North East' program in April 2015. *3)* Part of 'Footsteps to Freedom' was an exhibition at the Discovery Museum in Newcastle on links between the American civil rights movement and North East campaigns for social justice. *4)* Carrie Supple, the founder of Journey to Justice. *5)* Raphael Warnock, pastor at Ebenezer Baptist Church in Atlanta, where Martin Luther King also served, with Murphy Cobbing, the BBC Newcastle radio producer who helped to revive interest in King's 1967 visit to Newcastle.

Courtesy of Murphy Cobbing

Newcastle Chronicle

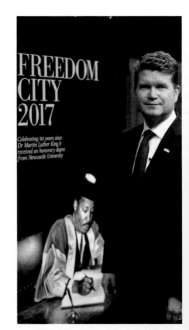

Clockwise from top left: 1) The 'Decency 1 Hatred 0' headline in the *Newcastle Chronicle* for November 24, 2015 celebrated Tyneside's historic 'cultures of welcome' as travellers on a Metro intervened to protect two local young Muslim women from racist abuse. *2)* In November 2015, Matthew J. Barzun the US Ambassador to the United Kingdom, attended the official launch of Freedom City 2017 in the Newcastle Mining Institute. *3) & 4)* Christ Church Church of England Primary School in Shieldfield has one of the most diverse student bodies on Tyneside and sent its choir to participate in a November 2016 event to mark the 49th anniversary of Martin Luther King's visit to Newcastle. *5)* A strong supporter of Freedom City 2017 and powerful voice on issues of social and economic justice, Wallsend born Chi Onwurah became Newcastle's first black Member of Parliament when she won the Newcastle Central seat for the Labour Party in 2010.

Aleksandra Dogramadzi

Randall Stephens

Brian Ward

Theresa Easton

Clockwise from top left: 1) Erv (left) and Fred Phethean (right) perform with The Crossings Band, a fluid collective of local musicians formed in 2009 that is dedicated to supporting asylum seekers, refugees and migrants in the North East. *2)* On January 20, 2017, Grey's Monument in Newcastle was the scene of a major protest against newly inaugurated US President Donald Trump. *3)* Local artist and activist Theresa Easton made a series of foldaway anti-Trump posters, including this one welcoming refugees in English and Arabic. *4)* Prior to addressing an anti-Trump rally in Newcastle, Rev. Jeffrey Brown, pastor of the Twelfth Baptist Church in Boston, visits the house in Summerhill Grove where Frederick Douglass and many other fugitive slaves had once stayed as guests of the Richardson family.

Martin Luther King, Newcastle upon Tyne, November 13, 1967.

got a coloured resident? How many people in the North-East have really got fears of their job because of coloured immigrants? Very few.' Oliver recognised, perhaps without fully understanding, that enthusiasm for Powell on Tyneside in the absence of a sizeable minority population and with little direct threat to white employment prospects, was basically a function of underlying racism and economic uncertainty, compounded by ignorance about the immigrants who did live in the region. His prescription to deal with a changing world and the palpable evils of racism fell back on the tried and trusted notion that knowledge was a great antidote to bigotry and a spur to action against discrimination. 'I am sure that if the people of the North-East took a greater interest in the plight of other people, both Commonwealth and British, they would see that their own troubles were resolved in a better spirit and lasting effect.' Despite the clumsy differentiation between 'British' and 'Commonwealth' people to distinguish white and non-white citizens, Oliver was groping towards an affirmation of what King had spoken of in England as the need for education and a recognition of the 'network of mutuality' that bound people together across racial lines. In the Poor Peoples' Campaign, King and his allies had tried to forge a multi-racial, multi-ethnic coalition of the poor. Oliver seemed to be calling for similar recognition of a shared plight, maybe even a shared destiny, among working people of all colours on Tyneside.[24]

Jessie M. Scott-Batey was at the forefront of more direct action efforts to combat the rise of Powellism on Tyneside. In a jointly authored letter to the *Evening Chronicle* she used words that again echoed King's Newcastle speech as she implored 'People of good will everywhere,' to 'do all they can now to create an atmosphere of tolerance and understanding in which all races can live together harmoniously.' A co-organiser of two anti-racist marches in May, she also organised a conference for Sunday May 26, 1968 'at which some of the problems can be explored in depth by experts.' Emphasising that her campaign was 'non-political and non-sectarian,' Scott-Batey arranged for a variety of 'prominent people' in the region to sign a 'declaration reaffirming their belief in Human Rights.' Thus Scott-Batey shifted the focus of debate, much as King was wont to do in his last years, away from minority rights, per se, towards a more capacious vision of a struggle for human rights, within which non-whites often faced particular problems that needed special and immediate attention. Continuing Tyneside's strong tradition of female activism and leadership, Scott-Batey hoped 'to restore some common sense and humanity to the situation, and to assure those working in the race relations field that they are not without support.'[25]

There were other stirrings of organised working-class, union, socialist and student opposition to Powell's message. Since the late 1950s, the Newcastle and District Trades Council—an important coordinating body for small and new unions in the region that was founded in 1873—had demonstrated the kind of global perspective that King endorsed. In 1957, it sent a motion to the National Council for Civil Liberties calling for pressure to be put on the South African government to change its apartheid policies. It raised money for the African Trials Defence Fund to support those arrested for challenging apartheid and later campaigned against South Africa's ban on black unions. The Trades Council had also joined the Newcastle City Council and Newcastle University students in calling for a boycott of goods produced under apartheid, extending the tradition established by the region's boycotts of slave-produced goods in the 18th and 19th centuries.[26]

In May 1968, the Trades Council issued a statement denouncing Powell and condemning the role of 'the press and the Tories in creating and encouraging racism.'[27] Elsewhere, a local Communist Party official described the speech as 'a shocking display of ignorance and prejudice. ... It was an incitement to race hatred and violence. Made in America by a white racialist, we would all have denounced it.'[28] When Powell was invited to speak by the Conservative Student Society at Rutherford College, which in 1969 became part of the newly created Newcastle Polytechnic, forerunner of Northumbria University, students from Rutherford's Left Wing Society and Newcastle University's Socialist Society tried, unsuccessfully, to halt the lecture.[29]

Despite these public expressions of opposition it was clear that there was widespread sympathy for Powell's views. This was alarming for white progressives but even more so for coloured minorities in the region. On May 9, a series of local council elections across the North East resulted in what the *Evening Chronicle* called 'a disastrous election night' for the Labour Party which lost thirty-six seats to Conservative and Independent candidates.[30] Amid broader economic and social anxieties in the region, the relationship between these election results and anti-immigrant sentiment was far from straightforward. Yet it was surely part of the mix that accounted for this dramatic swing to the right. As the *Chronicle* editorialised, thanks to 'the current controversy over racialism…Even moderate opinion has been ill-influenced in recent weeks.'[31] In Newcastle proper there was a 5.5 percent swing to Conservatives, but in some former working class Labour strongholds, such as Scotswood and Byker (where a thirteen percent swing unseated seven year incumbent Eric Harding), the shift was far more pronounced. By the time all the votes had been counted, Conservatives had won overall control of Newcastle City Council with a majority of thirteen.[32]

With its changed composition, fissures within the Council on the issue of race and immigration became deeper and wider. On July 3, 1968, when Labour Councillor Jeremy Beecham introduced a motion to disband the CIWG, which he believed had been rendered redundant by the creation of a local Race Relations Board and Community Relations Council under the new Race Relations Act, it opened up a rancorous debate around the wisdom of that Act and the virtues, or otherwise, of Enoch Powell's views on immigration. 'It may well be that some of us agree with Enoch Powell. I can say that with confidence. I myself agree with Enoch Powell,' announced Conservative Councillor John Morpeth amid cries of 'shame' from some of his colleagues. But Morpeth was not alone in believing that more than enough had already been done for immigrants. 'Don't let us get carried away by the question of colour and the need to look after coloured people,' advised Conservative Council Leader Arthur Grey. 'Coloured people don't want to be integrated,' he insisted. The new Community Relations Council, rather like the new Race Relations Act, was a waste of time and effort, addressing a 'problem which is non-existent.' Grey mocked laws and organisations that sought to promote integration. 'Are we going to reach the silly and stupid position where we knock on the door and say, "You have got to be integrated or else?",' he asked, drawing applause from sympathetic Councillors who shared his belief that Newcastle had no racial problems, certainly none that could be addressed through laws or the formation of yet more committees. Although Beecham's motion to end the CIWG and support the new structures passed by thirty-eight votes to twenty-eight, there were worrying signs of a retreat from the Council's previous commitment to trying to ensure equality of opportunity for racial minorities while actively encouraging integration and better race relations with the white community.[33]

The man who eventually and somewhat improbably emerged as the region's first Community Relations Officer was Chris Mullard. A forceful and controversial figure, Mullard was born in Hampshire but had begun his political life in earnest working in London with CARD, for whom he eventually served as national secretary. In 1967 he moved north to Tyneside, where he replaced Will George as local CARD chairman. Mullard acted as a lightning rod for white racial anxieties during this period, but he was also a controversial figure among some of the region's immigrant groups. Unflinching in his condemnation of racist whites and critiques of the racial inequalities embedded within British social, political, educational and economic structures, Mullard was barely less hostile to those he called 'Prejudiced patronisers'—people of all races who talked the talk of equality but who counselled endless patience on the part of minorities and seldom acted to make racial equality a lived reality. As Mullard put it in his autobiography, he had all but given up on the goodwill of white people to secure meaningful racial progress and decided 'What I had to do was work with black people rather than talk about them.'[34]

Mullard's time in the North East was stormy. He faced opposition from a variety of local and national politicians, was harassed by the Northumbria police, and had a permanently strained relationship with the national Community Relations Council. Indeed, Mullard was quite sceptical about the whole community relations approach to race relations, viewing it as a way for the establishment to contain, rather than to aid, non-white aspirations. It was, he felt, designed to mute, manage or co-opt more militant black voices. Mullard also polarised opinion within Tyneside's diverse communities of colour. Although they often shared similar experiences, immigrant communities were far from homogenous and had their own inter- and intra-communal tensions and rivalries around class, caste, race, religion and gender that were difficult to navigate, let alone reconcile. Despite these challenges, when he resigned in September 1973, Mullard took pride in having encouraged more concerted efforts among the region's immigrant communities to meet racism head-on and campaign for equal social, economic and educational opportunities. Moreover, although his relationships with white progressives could be turbulent, he never rejected alliances with anyone he felt was seriously committed to the struggle against racial injustice. As he explained to Dave Renton, at his most successful he 'deconstructed notions of Geordyism and North Eastism, repackaging them in terms of anti-racism.'[35]

One of Mullard's first attempts to do just that came when he joined Jessie Scott-Batey in organising a march against Powellism on May 11, 1968 that was due to culminate with a mass rally on the Town Moor. The experience revealed just how difficult his task would be. Opposition to the planned protest came from the Lord Mayor's office, the City Council and from several groups representing the city's Hindu, Muslim and Sikh communities. Among them was the Indian Association of Newcastle, whose leader H.K. Narang feared that the march 'would simply help to create a bad atmosphere and possibly lead to trouble.'[36]

The local press was similarly hostile, further undermining the prospects of success for a protest for that appeared to be attracting little popular support anyway. The *Evening Chronicle* called plans for the rally 'at best ill-considered and at worst dangerous to the point of criminal folly.' The paper used precisely the same arguments that white liberals in America had once used to urge Martin Luther King and the civil rights movement to abandon nonviolent direct action tactics and take protests off the streets lest they antagonise the very whites whose racial prejudices and commitment to white supremacy they were trying to expose and challenge. While insisting that it respected the sincerity of CARD and applauded 'the views it maintains on intolerance and bigotry,' the paper chastised the organisation for its impatience and tactics. For good measure, it also accused CARD of undermining the work of the CIWG with its militancy. 'Admittedly, the form of protest which [CARD] has decided on is, by definition, non-violent,' the paper conceded, 'but it may well be construed by rabid racialists as a serious provocation and thus invite violence.'[37]

Martin Luther King had responded to repeated white—and occasionally black—disapproval of his own 'provocative' direct action tactics by reaffirming his commitment to peaceful methods of publically protesting racial injustice. As he had frequently explained, perhaps most famously in his 1963 'Letter from a Birmingham City Jail,' the strategy was to 'establish such creative tension that a community that has constantly refused to negotiate is forced to confront the issue. It seeks so to dramatize the issue that it can no longer be ignored.'[38] Similarly, Mullard and his colleagues wanted to expose 'rabid racialists' for what they were while at the same time drawing attention to the discriminatory effects of their racism on Tyneside minorities. These tactics promised to flag the existence of racial prejudice and injustice on Tyneside, but they also exposed the limits of white racial liberalism. The *Evening Chronicle* warned that the march would generate 'Schisms in the ranks of the integrationists,' and would be 'hailed with glee by their segregationist opponents and used to discomfort reasonable and rational people.'[39] In truth, the editorial and the responses of many other broadly progressive elements in the area to the proposed CARD protest demonstrated that such schisms already existed.

Basil McLeod, Chair of the CIWG, was blunt. 'If they refuse to call it off, I ask the public to ignore it and treat it with the contempt it deserves,' he said, dismissively adding, 'Generally speaking we have a good relationship with the immigrant community, and we don't want people like CARD upsetting it.' McLeod also shared rumours that unidentified black power agitators from Leeds were to be involved in the protest. 'Any rumour concerning Black Power is rather worrying,' he said. 'They arouse people's feelings passionately on each side and this is a very dangerous situation.' Indeed McLeod felt that 'The Black Power movement appears to be composed of fanatics, whose presence could easily lead to violence.' Although a CARD representative dismissed this as 'just a stupid rumour—a ludicrous load of old codswallop,' the spectre of outside agitation and of a militant, perhaps violent, black power conspiracy, so familiar in the rhetoric of reactionary white responses to new modes of African American protest in the US during the late 1960s, was becoming part of Tyneside's anxiety about the sources and direction of local racial protests.[40]

In a final desperate effort to persuade Mullard and Scott-Batey to call off the march, the *Evening Chronicle* offered to print any statement provided by CARD. With Powellism on the rise Mullard refused to take the deal and, as he put it, 'sell ourselves out.'[41] The heart of the problem was two diametrically opposed responses to the challenges posed by Powell's remarks among those who claimed to have the best interests of immigrants and good race relations at heart. In one camp, the local press, the CIWG and the City Council urged more patience and a less confrontational mode of articulating immigrant grievances. 'The feeling that was aroused after Enoch Powell's speech was enough to make anybody cautious,' explained Basil McLeod.[42] Even Will George, the ex-Chair of CARD attempted to have the march cancelled, claiming that Mullard had effectively hijacked its original, far less militant intention, which was simply to showcase the significant part that immigrants played in the life of the city.[43]

Mullard, Scott-Batey and their supporters were in no mood to delay or compromise. They insisted that Powell's comments and the alarming levels of sympathy they had attracted on Tyneside demanded an immediate and highly visible response: the campaign for racial equality and against the kind of racial bigotry and intolerance associated with Enoch Powell was not something to be deferred or diluted for fear of inciting a white backlash that already appeared to be underway. It was an important moment to show that Tyneside had significant reserves of people of goodwill who would protest Powellism in support of the area's minorities. The organisers were to be disappointed.

One of the most frustrating and dispiriting aspects of the anti-Powell protests was that Tyneside's own immigrant communities largely rejected direct action campaigning. In part, this was because of an enduring sense among local minorities that, all things considered, life on Tyneside really was not too bad. 'We are quite happy living in this region,' observed O.P. Bindra, general secretary of the Newcastle Hindu Temple, when explaining his community's lack of enthusiasm for the march.[44] While such statements may have involved a certain amount of denial and dissembling in order to avoid controversy, there was a genuine feeling that, while race relations were far from perfect on Tyneside, they could be much worse. Moreover, as H.K. Narang had suggested, there was a fear that participating in protests against Powellism could intensify hostility to coloured minorities.

According to the *Journal*, the Saturday May 11 march and rally on the Town Moor drew a crowd of between one and two hundred people, far less than the 2,000 the organisers had expected. Whether in a fit of pique that its overtures to CARD and advice to cancel the protest had been ignored, or simply because by the afternoon of Monday May 13, when its next edition appeared, Saturday's event was old—and, given the low turnout, not especially noteworthy—news, the *Evening Chronicle* declined to report on a demonstration it had done so much to discourage.[45]

Later in the month, Jessie Scott-Batey hosted a rather different meeting 'to stand up and be counted against Powell and racialism in the country' at Rutherford College. Again, attendance was disappointing. On May 26, barely 100 people gathered to hear speeches by Scott-Batey, Eric Hackett, the headmaster of Slatyford Comprehensive School, John Rex, Professor of Social Theory and Institutions at Durham University, Sheffield University law professor Roy Marshall, and former Council Leader T. Dan Smith. Newcastle University's Vice-Chancellor Charles Bosanquet was among several other 'influential people' invited to the meeting who declined to attend. As Scott-Batey rather ruefully explained, 'Some of those we asked have said that they agree with our aims, but don't want to be publicly associated with us.' There were no representatives from Tyneside's immigrant communities on the programme.[46]

Scott-Batey was right that not everyone who stayed away from these public protests necessarily agreed with Powell; certainly not those from the region's own non-white communities. Nonetheless, the failure to mobilise a significant and coherent Tyneside movement against 'Powellism,' coupled with the evidence of considerable white sympathy for his views, gave pause for thought among Tyneside's white racial progressives. Even Maureen Knight's generally flattering articles on the area's race relations warned against complacency and uncovered plenty of prejudice and discrimination. 'The conclusion that no colour bar exists in the North-East is true. At least on the surface,' she wrote. 'True, the Commonwealth immigrant never sees

"No Coloreds" advertisements in this region. But working as bus conductors and drivers are a research chemist, an accountant, a handful of engineers and teachers who cannot find jobs with their professional qualifications...Job hunting is tougher if you happen to be coloured.' One West Indian woman told Knight that 'Only one in 10 employers will take you. Now at the Employment Exchange we ask them to tell a prospective employer that we are coloured to save a wasted journey.' Several interviewees noted—and Knight agreed—that, although the additional protections of the new Race Relations Act were welcome, actually proving that racial prejudice affected hiring decisions was often problematic.[47]

Knight also discovered a blend of misplaced envy and facile scapegoating as some poor whites blamed their economic difficulties and social deprivation on immigrants rather than on the structural economic and social problems that beset much of the region at a time when the effects of deindustrialisation were biting ever deeper. 'It was a nice street before They came here,' one woman told Knight, who drily noted that the woman 'had lived in the same place for thirty years and did not notice its decline–until the immigrants arrived.'[48]

Enoch Powell's speech had unleashed precisely the sort of latent prejudices against which Martin Luther King had warned in Newcastle. As political analyst Arthur Aughey points out, Powell effectively narrowed the range of reasonable and informed debate on race, making it difficult for anyone 'to speak openly about concerns with immigration or multiculturalism for fear of being labelled either racist or xenophobic.'[49] In this climate, discussions about the causes and implications of major demographic, economic, social and cultural changes, discussions which certainly should have involved consideration of the nation's changing racial, religious and cultural profile, were supressed or distorted. Irrational fears about immigrants and the threats they supposedly posed to white economic and social status, and to nebulous ideas of 'English' or 'British' values, were allowed to fester, mutate and acquire the status of truth. The resurgence of these kinds of views threatened to overwhelm the sort of tentative self-scrutiny about Tyneside's racial practices and attitudes that had been prompted first by King's visit and then by his death. Consequently, while there remains more than a kernel of truth in Barry Carr's generalisation that the 'whole ethos of Tyneside working-class culture was anathema to the bullying on which racism is built,' and that in such an environment, relatively good race relations had 'evolved without laws or regulations, committees or reports,' popular white enthusiasm for Powell invites a rather more cautious conclusion.[50]

Like the fugitive African American slave James Watkins, writing in Newcastle more than a century earlier, Martin Luther King never romanticised the white working-class, Geordie or American, as a natural repository of racial tolerance and brotherhood. No class—and, for that matter, no race—has ever had a monopoly on progressive or reactionary, tolerant or bigoted racial views. King did recognise, however, that at times and in places of acute social upheaval and economic distress, when the competition for jobs, decent housing, adequate education, and access to health care and other social services was intense, those whites who felt economically insecure, socially frustrated or politically impotent could be highly susceptible to the lure of racism to try to explain away their travails.

The same groups could also be very susceptible to the appeal of racial chauvinism. Glorifying whiteness, protecting its privileges, and fixating on the notion that it lay at the heart of American or British national identities offered a way for some whites to protect their status and bolster a sense of pride and self-respect. In the 1960s, many whites on both sides of the Atlantic regularly rallied to protect the advantages that their skin colour had historically conferred on them against the perceived threat of racial equality. Their anger and resistance was especially marked whenever efforts to promote that equality relied on government legislation and enforcement. Government action to curtail discrimination was frequently seen as an act of political, even racial treachery, or as an example of 'reverse discrimination' that extended unfair advantages to non-whites who were already widely viewed with suspicion if not outright hostility. Moreover, there were always plenty of individuals and organisations who, for a variety of political, financial and ideological reasons, were happy to encourage the search for scapegoats to blame for what were really deeply rooted economic, social and political problems. Matters were further complicated by the fact that in the late 1960s, on both sides of the Atlantic, there were minority groups who, in the face of decades, even centuries of white prejudice and discrimination, abandoned faith in interracial cooperation, rejected integration and sought separatist paths to whatever measure of freedom and opportunity they could grasp.

Martin Luther King was not among those who despaired of interracial paths to a more just, equitable and peaceful world. In King's mind, the need to enlighten people on matters of racial and human justice transcended barriers of nationality, race, religion and class. That said, in the US during 1967 and early 1968, he focussed on helping the black and white poor to recognise their common interests with other exploited and dispossessed groups—

not least as poor whites and African Americans were bearing a disproportionate burden of the Vietnam War, a conflict which, in honouring King
four days after his death, the Rev. E. Harriott of St. Andrew's Catholic
Church on Worswick Street in Newcastle, described as a 'ghastly frieze
hanging at the back of our minds whether we are actively involved in it or
not.'[51] King saw that 'evil war' as yet another manifestation of the militarism, racism and poverty that were yoked together in the service of an
unfettered global capitalism that was relentless and ruthless in its quest for
control over capital, raw materials, labour and markets. As King explained
in his final and most radical presidential address to the SCLC annual conference in Atlanta in August 1967:

> A nation that will keep people in slavery for 244 years will
> 'thingify' them—make them things. Therefore, they will exploit
> them, and poor people generally economically. And a nation that
> will exploit economically will have to have foreign investments
> and everything else, and will have to use its military might to pro-
> tect them. All these problems are tied together. What I am saying
> today is that we must go from this convention and say, 'America,
> you must be born again.'[52]

The poor and working-class were imagined by King, along with the
labour movement, as potentially crucial agents in the kind of peaceful revolution he envisioned for America. They needed to be encouraged to act in
concert across racial, ethnic and religious lines to address shared grievances
that were rooted in the inequitable operation of unregulated capitalism. It
was this task which lay at the heart of King's hopes for the Poor People's
Campaign and his advocacy of democratic socialism. 'We must honestly
face the fact that the movement must address itself to the question of restructuring the whole of American society,' King insisted. 'There are forty
million poor people here, and one day we must ask the question, "Why are
there forty million poor people in America?" And when you begin to ask
that question, you are raising a question about the economic system, about
a broader distribution of wealth. When you ask that question, you begin to
question the capitalistic economy.'[53]

This was a global analysis, not one simply tailored to the American
situation. Throughout his final year, as riots and violence erupted all around
him and all over the world, King reaffirmed his steadfast commitment to
nonviolence and his religiously anchored belief in the ultimate power of love

to overcome injustice and inequality. 'I have also decided to stick with love, for I know that love is ultimately the only answer to mankind's problems,' he told the SCLC faithful in Atlanta in August 1967, adding 'And I'm going to talk about it everywhere I go… hate is too great a burden to bear.'[54] One of the places he talked about it was in Newcastle where he explained so eloquently that 'there can be no separate black path to power and fulfilment that does not intersect white routes and there can be no separate white path to power and fulfilment short of social disaster that does not recognise the necessity of sharing that power with coloured aspirations for freedom and human dignity.' By cultivating this sense of common destiny and shared humanity, King devoutly believed it was still possible 'to transform the jangling discords of our nation, and of all the nations of the world, into a beautiful symphony of brotherhood, and speed up the day when all over the world justice will roll down like waters and righteousness like a mighty stream.'[55] This was God's ultimate plan for the world. It was a marvellous, inspirational vision, worthy of Amos, the Old Testament prophet from who he borrowed this favourite line.

Yet, the support for Powell in Britain and the 'conservative backlash' of the so-called silent—and largely white—majority in America that swept Republican Richard Nixon into the White House in November 1968 on a wave of hostility to further government efforts to promote genuine equality of opportunity for African Americans, suggested that King's vision still lay somewhere in the far distant future. In the meantime, as King consistently argued, there was a lot to commend expansively conceived and robustly enforced laws that made racial discrimination illegal.

Part Four:

Legacies and Lessons

CHAPTER ELEVEN

Tending the Cords of Memory:
The Road to Freedom City 2017

At 11am on Tuesday, November 1, 2016, Chi Onwurah, Labour MP for Newcastle Central and Shadow Minister for Business, Energy and Industrial Strategy, opened a debate in the Westminster Hall of the Houses of Parliament. Onwurah had called the debate to allow the House of Commons to hear plans for Freedom City 2017. This was a multi-faceted, multi-partner project in Newcastle-Gateshead spearheaded by Newcastle University to mark the fiftieth anniversary of Martin Luther King's appearance on its campus. Outlining the circumstances of King's visit and summarising his speech, Onwurah sketched out an ambitious 'three-year programme of international artistic and political significance,' in which '[w]orld-renowned artists and local communities will come together to produce new artworks responding to Dr. King's iconic speech and legacy.'[1]

Onwurah, born in Wallsend the daughter of a white mother from Garth Heads on the Newcastle Quayside and a Nigerian father who had met his wife while a medical student at Newcastle University in the 1950s, spoke passionately of the enduring significance of King's visit and of his words. 'The battle against injustice is by no means over. Some fifty years after Dr. King came to Newcastle, it is still the wealth and status of a child's parents that will determine his or her potential to a greater extent than almost anything else,' she explained. 'I want every child in Newcastle and beyond to know not only that Martin Luther King came to Newcastle, but that he came for them, to speak to them. Those three themes of poverty, racism and war not only speak to them but are to be answered by them—by every child and every adult in Newcastle and throughout the country.'[2]

Here, then, was a commitment, not just to commemorate a past event of local historical significance, but also to reissue the call to action that King had made in Newcastle. Freedom City 2017, with its blend of cultural, artistic, academic, civic, school and community engagement projects, had been created with a triple agenda:

- To bring Dr King's legacy to life for a new generation in order to equip them with knowledge and skills and empower them to contribute towards tackling the great problems of war, poverty and racism;
- To enable artists to create internationally significant work inspired by the themes of Dr King's acceptance speech and galvanise the region's cultural venues and landmark sites as hosts to a global audience;
- To stimulate academic research and debate that will likewise contribute towards finding solutions.[3]

A year earlier, the US Ambassador, Matthew J. Barzun, had publically launched the initiative in the North East at a November 13, 2015 event in the Newcastle Mining Institute.[4] When Onwurah unveiled further details for a national audience a year later it was in the very different climate of a post-Brexit world. And by January 16, 2017, Martin Luther King Day in America, when even more of the Freedom City 2017 programme was revealed for an international audience at another Westminster event involving Onwurah and Barzun, Donald Trump was five days away from being sworn in as US President. Trump had chosen to usher in Martin Luther King Day with a petulant and ill-informed Twitter attack on Georgia's veteran African American Congressman John Lewis. A former Chair of SNCC, Lewis was the last surviving civil rights leader who had spoken alongside King at the 1963 March on Washington. During the 1960s, Lewis, the son of Alabama sharecroppers, had been beaten and jailed on numerous occasions in the struggle to make the ideals of the US a reality for all its citizens; during the 1960s, the millionaire's son Donald Trump was beginning a career in real estate that later landed him in court on charges of racially discriminatory practices.[5]

On January 20, 2017, the day of Trump's inauguration in Washington, a crowd of several hundred protestors, drawn together under the Newcastle Unites umbrella, gathered at the memorial to Earl Grey, the architect of the Great Reform Act and the Abolition of Slavery Act. They were stirred into action by the racism that, along with sexism, Islamophobia, a jaw-dropping indifference to or lack of understanding of many crucial security and environmental issues, and a basic disdain for truth, expertise, evidence and civility, they found at the heart of Trump's presidential campaign. 'Say no to Racism, Fascism and Islamophobia,' read one banner, draped at the foot of Grey's Monument. A much smaller band of Trump supporters showed up, too, some of them apparently associated with the ultra-right English Defence League. Alongside the Stars and Stripes, they carried the Confederate battle flag, still a potent, internationally understood symbol of white supremacy.[6]

A few weeks later, President Trump issued an Executive Order temporarily banning entry to the US of anyone from seven majority-Muslim countries (Iran, Iraq, Libya, Somalia, Sudan, Syria and Yemen) and indefinitely barring refugees from war-torn Syria. Trump claimed the ban was in the interests of national security, providing a bulwark against possible terrorist attacks by radical Islamic fundamentalists. However, the fact that since 1975 not one American had been killed in the US as a result of attacks by anyone from the targeted nations, combined with the Islamophobic comments Trump had made during his campaign, when he openly boasted that he would introduce a Muslim ban, inspired protests across America—not least among members of the federal judiciary who queried the constitutionality of a ban that discriminated against a particular class of people on the grounds of their religion. Those protests spread around the world, including many British cities.[7] On January 30, 2017 more than 2,000 demonstrators gathered at Earl Grey's Monument to condemn Trump's policy.[8]

On February 20, another crowd assembled at the same historic site for another 'Stop Trump' rally. By this time more than 40,000 people in the North East had signed a petition against a proposed state visit to the United Kingdom by the new US President. 'Love Newcastle: Hate Racism, Fascism and Islamophobia,' read one banner; 'Donald Trump Go Away: Racist, Sexist, Anti-Gay,' rhymed another. Theresa Easton, a locally based artist-activist, produced a series of handy fold-out anti-Trump posters and placards, some in both Arabic and English: 'Laundry is the ONLY thing that should be separated by COLOUR' one declared. Here was clear evidence that developments in US politics continued to reverberate across the Atlantic, helping to shape Tyneside's own political culture. Indeed, there was one very tangible human example of how the anti-Trump protests reinforced the ties that had long bound Tyneside to struggles for racial equality and social justice in the US: Rev. Jeffrey Brown was among those who addressed the rally.[9]

Associate Pastor at the Twelfth Baptist Church in Boston, Brown was co-architect of the so-called 'Boston miracle' of the 1990s that dramatically reduced gang violence and youth homicides in that city. In the 19th century, Twelfth Baptist Church had been attended by numerous ex-slaves and black abolitionists, including Frederick Douglass and William Wells Brown; it was such a hub of anti-slavery activity that it was dubbed 'the Fugitive Slave Church.' Martin Luther King had apprenticed in the same church while a doctoral student in Boston in the 1950s. During his visit to Newcastle, Jeffrey Brown visited the house at 5, Summerhill Grove where Douglass, Brown and so many other abolitionists had been guests of the Richardson family; he delivered a sermon at Heaton Baptist Church; and he gave a public lecture at Newcastle University as part of the Freedom City 2017 celebrations. In concluding his lecture, Brown urged people of conscience to remember Martin Luther King's warning that 'injustice anywhere is a threat to justice everywhere.' That sentiment, Brown insisted 'still holds as true today as it did when Martin Luther King said it,' adding with a pointed pun on the fractious state of contemporary politics, that he also shared King's faith that, ultimately, 'Love always trumps hate.'[10]

While Trump campaigned in the US, a fraught and intemperate 2016 referendum on British membership of the European Union saw some of those who supported a 'leave' vote make crude racist, Islamophobic and xenophobic appeals to the British electorate. They effectively hijacked the opportunity for reasoned and informed debate on knotty issues relating to economics, labour mobility, migration, security, and state sovereignty. Too often immigrants, refugees and asylum seekers were offered up as easy targets for the anger and frustrations of those who were anxious about their economic and social status, national security, and lack of an effective and representative political voice. The ugly campaign helped to license appalling levels of racial, ethnic and religious bigotry. In England and Wales there was a forty-one percent increase in 'hate crimes' immediately following the vote compared with figures for the previous July.[11]

In the midst of this changing and, for many, increasingly alarming and fractured, world, King's message assumed ever greater significance and appeal. As Sajid Javid, the Conservative Government's Secretary of State for Communities and Local Government, said in applauding plans for Freedom City 2017, 'We would all do well to remember what [King] taught us, and one thing that he said is that we must live together as brothers or we all perish as fools. We can all learn from that, no matter who we are, whether in the US or the UK.'[12]

Responding to Onwurah's November 2016 Westminster Hall speech, Marcus Jones, the Conservative Under-Secretary of State for Communities and Local Government, acknowledged that 'the spike in hate crime and racist incidents taking place in communities after the vote to leave the

EU…The scenes and behaviour we saw over the summer—including offensive graffiti and abuse hurled at people because they are members of ethnic minorities or because of their nationality—were absolutely despicable and shameful.' While Jones was still eager to cast Britain as 'a successful multi-ethnic and multi-faith country,' and insisted that 'We can all be proud of the UK's world-class equalities legislation,' he appreciated that this was 'not enough on its own. We must all champion equality and recognise and challenge discrimination.' To that end, the Government had presented a new 'hate crime action plan' and 'launched a race disparity audit' to examine racial differences in treatment and outcomes for people of different backgrounds across the entire range of public services, including childcare, criminal justice, education, employment, and health.[13] Rhetoric and policy, law and implementation have not always been aligned when it comes to matters of social and economic justice. Nevertheless, the recognition that strong governmental action and robust, vigorously enforced anti-discrimination legislation were needed alongside anti-racist educational initiatives was not too far removed from King's formula for confronting systemic inequalities and advancing the long-term goal of eradicating racial prejudice.

In one of the most moving and personal passages of her Westminster Hall speech, Chi Onwurah admitted that, as a child 'growing up in Newcastle I was not aware of [Dr. King's visit],' even though 'His life is an inspiration for individuals across the world, including me.' She described how, aged about ten, her 'earliest memory of him' was 'reading the 'I Have a Dream' speech for the first time. I remember exactly where I was—Boots in Eldon Square, Newcastle.'[14] There was an irony in the fact that a city-centre store should have a poster featuring excerpts from King's most famous speech at a time when in Newcastle memories of the city's unique connections to the civil rights leader had all-but disappeared. Decades later, most local school children, their teachers and the general public, were no more aware of this part of their history than Onwurah had been in the mid-1970s.

So what had happened? Why, for all the powerful impact of King's oratory on those who heard him in 1967, for all the extensive local media coverage of his visit and of his murder, and for all that his life and words had served as an important framing device for local discussions about race relations in the late 1960s, was King's visit so little remembered in Newcastle—the only place in Britain beyond London that he ever visited? Why, as King's posthumous reputation as a globally significant champion of freedom, peace and justice soared, did the sole British University to grant him

an honorary doctorate only fitfully cultivate his legacy and, more prosai-
cally, fail to capitalise on the publicity and recruitment potential of its
unique links to this iconic figure? The answers to these riddles are not clear-
cut. But what is certain is that this neglect and amnesia seemed unlikely in
the immediate aftermath of King's assassination on April 4, 1968.

Shocked and saddened at news of King's murder, the University flew
its flags at half-mast, issued heartfelt statements of regret and arranged a
Memorial Service for 5.30pm on April 26, 1968 in St. Thomas's Church
near the Haymarket. The Students Union helped Registrar Ernest Bettenson publicise the Service by making lunchtime tannoy announcements on
campus. The Service opened with the simple, yet profound statement that
the occasion was 'to give thanks to God for the life of Martin Luther King,
for his work for peace, equality and justice for all races, and to pray that his
example may inspire others to continue the work for which he gave his life.'
The lessons were read by two officers from the Union, President Paul
Brooks and Rudyard Ceres, a black physiology student who on the Saturday
before King visited Newcastle had won the University's Alan McQuillan
Individual Speaking Trophy for his debating skills. Their participation
maintained the connection to students that had been so important to Vice-
Chancellor Charles Bosanquet just five months earlier. 'God declares to his
people that true goodness consists in justice and love for all men,' Brooks
read from the Book of Isaiah. Bosanquet himself gave a warm, deeply respectful address, humanising King by describing the simple breakfast they
had shared at his residence. Bosanquet revealed 'one good reason why
[King] could not stay longer in Britain was that he had promised to be at
home in Atlanta a few days later for his daughter's twelfth birthday'–his
youngest daughter, Yolanda, was born on November 17, 1955. He also reminded the congregation of how King had 'talked of the interrelated issues
of racial equality, of poverty, and of the war in Vietnam,' and of how he
had urged British people to 'bestir ourselves to ensure early and full acceptance of coloured people in Britain as completely equal citizens.
Bosanquet emphasised the prescience and relevance of King's words. 'The
speech of Mr. Enoch Powell and the demonstrations of support for his views
give added urgency to these warnings,' he said.[15]

On April 30, Bosanquet sent the University's condolences to Andrew
Young, informing him of the Memorial Service and sending copies of the
programme and of his address. Amid the 'universal grief and indignation of
people in this country' at the 'horrifying news,' the Vice-Chancellor wrote
that 'These feelings were particularly strong in this University where we

have such vivid memories of his and your presence amongst us for a few hours on November 13.'[16] Given this strength of feeling, there was an immediate call for the University community to come up with ideas and raise money for a fitting tribute. As Bosanquet explained at the Memorial Service, 'Many of us in the University are thinking of ways of ensuring that the University of Newcastle does not forget this very great man who was for barely five months one of our most distinguished members.'[17]

Professor Barbara Strang of the English Department proposed that, in addition to a plaque honouring King on campus, 'any funds received should be spent on his home ground.' Her idea was for a Newcastle-sponsored 'annual prize for a student in his own university'—although since King held no university position, it was not entirely clear what this meant or how it would work.[18] Another, literally more concrete, suggestion came from Jon Gower Davies, a lecturer in Social Sciences. Davies had actually participated in civil rights efforts in Mississippi before coming to Newcastle University. Thus he pre-empted the backstory to *Our Friends in the North*, one of the most critically acclaimed British television series of the mid-1990s, in which Nicky Hutchinson, played by future *Doctor Who*-actor Christopher Eccleston, had also recently returned to the North East from Mississippi.[19] Davies felt that 'the University is under a special obligation to establish some memorial to Dr. Martin Luther King, a man who must surely be the greatest of our honorary graduands.' He proposed that a building, specifically the Claremont Bridge Building, be renamed in King's honour.[20]

The two ideas that gained most traction among the University's senior management were to 'put up a tablet in an appropriate place (King's Hall or Council Room or foyer of the Armstrong Building) recording the fact that M.L.K received an honorary degree here on November 13th, 1967,' and 'to endow a Martin Luther King Lecture...on an appropriate theme (race relations, removal of poverty, peace between nations).'[21] By June 1968, plans for a plaque had been shelved, but the idea of a Memorial Lecture Series was gaining support. Bosanquet initially hoped that the lecture could 'be delivered every third year in memory of the late Dr. Martin Luther King. We think it appropriate that this University should in every way endeavour to continue the work for which he gave his life.' Contributions to support the lecture series were solicited from University staff, who found a fundraising letter from the Vice-Chancellor included in their June 1968 pay packets. On October 9, students were also courted via the first edition of the *Courier* for the new academic year. The appeal suggested 'that contributions should normally not exceed 5s from a student or £1 from a member of staff. But if anyone is moved to give a larger sum, this will be most welcome.'[22]

Following the retirement of Charles Bosanquet at the end of September 1968, the public lecture series was formally recognised by the University Senate and Council under his successor as Vice-Chancellor, Henry Miller, who had been a co-signatory of the original fundraising approaches to staff and students. The campus-wide call for support generated £143 4s, which was added to £200 from the University. The terms of the fund meant that the core capital could not be touched, but the income from interest could be put towards lectures on appropriate themes.[23]

The first Martin Luther King Lecture took place on October 12, 1972, when Trevor Huddleston, then Bishop of Stepney and a leading anti-apartheid campaigner, spoke on 'Race Relations in a Hungry World.'[24] On January 22, 1976, Hugh Tinker, a former Director of the Institute of Race Relations and an expert in conflict resolution, Gandhian ideas and Asian politics delivered a talk entitled 'Whatever happened to Non-Violence.' Tinker, who had spent considerable time in America, drew on his personal association with 'many of Martin Luther King's associates in the Deep South,' to examine 'how far non-violence had made an impression upon a ....violent society.'[25]

When the University formally established the Martin Luther King Lecture series, the plans were more ambitious than Bosanquet had initially imagined. The University wanted a lecture to occur 'no less frequently than every other year…on a subject with which the late Dr. King was closely associated.'[26] For a mix of logistical and financial reasons, however, this schedule quickly proved impossible to sustain. The Lectures were certainly infrequent enough that when the journalist and editor of the *Observer* newspaper Conor Cruise O'Brien spoke on 'Southern Africa (The International Implications of Racial Politics in Southern Africa)' in the Curtis Auditorium on March 6, 1980, the *Courier* mistakenly hailed it as the 'Inaugural Martin Luther King Lecture' when it was actually the third such event.[27]

Two more lectures followed in the 1980s, one by John Alderson, the Chief Constable of Devon and Cornwall and, perhaps more appropriately, one by John Hume, a key figure in the Northern Ireland movement for Catholic Civil Rights and later a Member of Parliament and Leader of the Social Democratic Labour Party. 'I regard it as an honour that the University should see fit to approach me on this matter,' Hume wrote in accepting the invitation and acknowledging the enduring transatlantic significance of King's example. 'I have always tried to uphold the methods and reasoning of Martin Luther King to our young people in Northern Ireland.'[28] In 1998, Hume was co-recipient of the Nobel Peace Prize for his work with David Trimble of the Protestant Ulster Unionist Party on the 'Good Friday Agreement' that sought a peaceful resolution to the sectarian conflict in Northern Ireland. In Oslo, Hume ended his acceptance speech with 'a quotation of total hope, the words of a former Laureate, one of my great heroes of this century, Martin Luther King Jr. "We shall overcome".'[29]

During the late 1980s there were attempts to organise Martin Luther King Lectures by South African Archbishop and anti-apartheid activist Desmond Tutu (who was asked twice) and former US President and honorary Geordie Jimmy Carter. These approaches came to nothing and the fund was not drawn on again until May 1998. During that hiatus, the lecture series was pretty much forgotten. It lingered as little more than a ghostly account code on a spreadsheet until early 2017 when Umbereen Rafiq, the University's Public Lectures and Events Manager, found details of the original plans for the Lecture Series amid some old files archived in deep storage in Team Valley.[30]

With the Martin Luther King Lecture series waxing, waning and then disappearing, and in the absence of any physical monuments to King's visit, the quarter century after King's death saw memories of the occasion slip slowly from institutional and public consciousness. This creeping amnesia was also due to the fact that the 1967 visit had been very much a University, rather than a truly civic, event. Notwithstanding the presence at the degree ceremony of the Sheriff and Mayor as representatives of the City of Newcastle, and of many University academic and administrative staff who were either locally born or who remained in the area for many years afterwards, the vast majority of those who talked with King or heard him speak came from the student body. This was an inherently, if by no means wholly, transient group. When they graduated, many students left Newcastle and took their memories of King's visit with them. Moreover, although Chris Mullard of CARD maintained that he was among those who met King in Newcastle, this may have been the total sum of representation from Tyneside's minority communities. Consequently, the event made relatively little impact on some of the local people who might have been most keen to keep memories of the visit and King's message alive.[31]

It is instructive to contrast this erasure, or at least substantial erosion of popular memories of King's visit, with local responses to visits by two other eminent Americans a decade later: President Jimmy Carter and boxing legend Muhammad Ali. On May 6, 1977, Carter's appearances outside the Civic Centre in Newcastle, in Sunderland, where he visited the Corning Glass factory, and at Washington Old Hall in County Durham, the ancestral home of the first US President George Washington, were much more visible to the general public. There was extensive newspaper, radio and television coverage when Carter was awarded the Freedom of the City of Newcastle by Mayor Hugh White in front of a huge crowd, with some estimates suggesting as many as 250,000 locals lined the streets as the President made his way around the region. In Newcastle Mayor White even obliquely invoked the city's cultures of welcome when he told 'Wor Jimmy,' as the press affectionately dubbed Carter, 'Mr. President, Sir, you are a Georgian. You have now become a Geordie.' Afterwards, a public monument to the visit was erected outside the Civic Centre. There were even commemorative mugs made in Washington, where Carter planted a tulip poplar tree on the village green. The international Friendship Force, set up in collaboration with First Lady Rosalynn Carter, included Newcastle and its twin city Atlanta as charter members and continued to operate into the early 21st century. 'I will always remember the hospitality and friendship— and the incredible welcome,' Carter wrote in a letter of thanks to Hugh White shortly after his visit. By this time, a long-playing album had also been issued, featuring highlights from the extensive BBC Radio Newcastle coverage of Carter's visit, with proceeds going to the Friendship Force.[32]

Memories of the visit were rekindled when Carter returned to the area with his family in 1987. As Carter fondly remembered, 'we were permitted to have an American Independence Day parade on July 4th, perhaps the only time this has occurred on the streets of England.'[33] He was still creating local news in August 2013, writing to Newcastle City Council Leader Nick Forbes to thank him personally for sending a framed photograph of his 1977 visit. In May 2017, Councillor David Faulkner coordinated well publicised and well attended events to mark the 40th anniversary of Carter's visit at the Newcastle City Library and Civic Centre, where the commemorative stone was carefully restored to its original splendour. Once again Carter mailed the City Council with warm greetings and recollections of his visits to the region. The initial high level of public engagement in the event, coupled with the physical reminders of the visit (mugs, monuments and a tree), and a steady stream of news stories and connections, meant that the occasion became deeply lodged in local memory.[34]

Much the same thing happened when, in mid-July 1977, Muhammad Ali, the latest in the long line of African Americans to enchant the North

East, spent four extremely high-profile days on Tyneside. As a Conscientious Objector to the war in Vietnam who had lost his heavyweight world title, not in the ring, but for refusing to accept the military draft, the boxer was linked, if slightly ambiguously given his profession, to King and the region's traditions of peace activism. His itinerary included an open top bus tour of South Shields past crowds standing ten-people deep, a blessing of his wedding vows in the town's Al Azhar Mosque that attracted 7,000 locals of all faiths, a charity darts match before a packed crowd at Gypsies Green Stadium, visits to the West End Boys' Club, the Grainger Park Boys' Club and Washington Sports Centre to spar with some local boxers, a formal banquet at the Newcastle Civic Centre and another swish gala dinner at the Mayfair Ballroom.[35]

On Saturday July 16, 900 people gathered in the middle of the afternoon in the Eldon Square Recreation Centre to watch Ali in conversation with British television boxing commentator Reg Gutteridge. Many more people, nationally as well as in the North East, watched the broadcast on ITV's *World of Sport*. The format of the show allowed members of the public to ask Ali questions, the first of which called for his general impressions of the region and its people. Ali was a gracious guest. He was deeply appreciative of the support he had received in Britain when he was stripped of his world title and boxing license for refusing to serve in Vietnam. In Newcastle, he gravitated towards the language of peace and brotherhood to summarise his thoughts about Tyneside. 'Well, the greatest impression that I've had since I've been here, is the peace that's in the city. The serenity. The unity.' After mocking the ways in which the US police were heavily armed as if permanently primed for war against its own citizens, especially its citizens of colour, Ali enthused about what he perceived to be the absence of violence, particularly racial violence, on Tyneside. 'This,' he gushed 'is like heaven compared to America.' Having described the appallingly banal routineness of lethal violence in America's inner-cities, the Muslim Ali praised what he clearly saw as evidence of a serious commitment to nonviolence and faith-based brotherhood. 'What has impressed me,' he explained, is 'so many people who are actually practicing the Christian religion: living it not just practicing it; but living it. You all practice what people in my country only preach.'[36]

Through all of this, there was no sign that Ali was remotely aware that one of the greatest advocates of a faith-based commitment to peace and nonviolence, and a fellow African American, had spoken of those very matters in the same city just a decade before. Nor was there any hint that Ali had been told that he was extending a long line of African American visitors to the region, who had also come to call for peace, freedom and justice. Nevertheless, Ali managed to sound remarkably like William Wells Brown when he told the Eldon Square audience that his reception on Tyneside was warmer than any he had received in the western world. 'Being a black man, I get these kinds of receptions all through Africa and Asia,' Ali explained. 'But this is the first time in a European country that I have ever had so much fanfare and people admiring me and loving me and coming out to meet me and greet me like this.'[37]

Once it was over, memories of Ali's Tyneside trip were kept alive by at least two documentary films, one for the BBC North East and Cumbria's *Inside Out* programme, another directed by Tina Gharavi. The visit was also the subject of a book by Russell Routledge and of newspaper retrospectives as significant anniversaries rolled around and odd reminiscences of Ali's visit resurfaced. In June 2016, Ian Pleasant, who at the age of twelve had met Ali at the Gosforth Park Hotel where his father worked as a bodyguard, was reunited with a special Muhammad Ali coin that the boxer had given him, but which had somehow ended up in Italy.[38]

The duration and public-facing aspect of the visits by Ali and Carter immediately helped to embed both episodes in the local imagination. Subsequently, popular memories of the visits were regularly replenished by films, recordings, television features, newspaper articles and, in the case of Carter, physical markers, in the case of Ali, film documentaries. This was never likely to be the case for King's brief, rather closeted time in Newcastle, especially as until 1992 there was no film footage of the occasion available. Back in April 1968, Jon Davies had appreciated this potential dilemma when he urged the University to think bigger and more imaginatively than an on-campus lecture series and a plaque ('I'm certainly not very keen on tablets,' he wrote to the Vice-Chancellor). Still pushing for the University to rename the Claremont Bridge Building, which spanned a major city centre road, Davies argued that 'Re-naming the building would, I think, reach more of a public or city audience than the tablet, which would come to the attention primarily of University people.'[39]

As things transpired, the University struggled to find an effective way to commemorate King and honour his legacy for the next twenty-five years. Paul Miskin and Gordon Sharp started degrees at Newcastle University in 1969 but, as they explained to Adam Sharp, they were completely oblivious to the fact that their University had awarded King an honorary degree just two years previously. In a small informal 2017 survey of residents in the

Summerhill area where the Richardson family had once lived, Sharp discovered far more public awareness of Ali's visit than of King's. In fact, more people knew that seminal US rock guitarist Jimi Hendrix had been in the city in 1967, living briefly at 35, Second Avenue in Heaton with his manager and ex-Animals' bassist Chas Chandler while gigging around the region, than knew that Martin Luther King had been in Newcastle the same year.[40]

From this point on, I confess once more to being closer to the unfolding of events than is usual for a historian trying to explain them. In 1992, as a junior lecturer in American History at Newcastle University and charged with teaching a final year Special Subject on Martin Luther King and the Civil Rights Movement, I began to research the circumstances of King's forgotten visit to campus and unearthed film of King's extempore speech. Excited about this discovery, I persuaded my Head of Department John Derry, the Dean of the Faculty of Arts Jeremy Paterson and the Vice-Chancellor James Wright, that this was an important part of the University's and the City's heritage that merited celebration. It did no harm in making the case for King's local relevance that in 1992 Robert Colls and Bill Lancaster concluded the Preface of their pioneering study *Geordies* by quoting 'an old man's words to Martin Luther King in the midst of the black civil rights struggle in the United States: "We ain't what we ought to be and we ain't what we want to be and we ain't what we're going to be. But thank God we ain't what we was."'[41] There was no sign that the authors knew that King had ever been among Geordies in the heart of Newcastle.

In late October 1993, the University, with additional support from Newcastle City Council and the Lord Mayor's Office, the US Embassy, and sundry corporate sponsors, staged the first Martin Luther King Memorial Conference. At the core of the three-day event were academic papers on various aspects of King's career delivered by a range of international scholars. These papers formed the basis for a book, *The Making of Martin Luther King and the Civil Rights Movement*, edited by myself and Tony Badger, who had only departed Newcastle's History department in 1991 to take up the Paul Mellon Chair in American History at the University of Cambridge. The volume was, in retrospect, quite pioneering in presenting a suite of essays by George Fredrickson, Tariq Modood and Mike Sewell that focused on the transnational dimensions of the Movement and of King's career. The newly unearthed film of King's Newcastle speech was shown and a copy of it, along with a selection of some of the documents relating to King's visit, was deposited with Clayborne Carson, the historian in charge of the Martin

Luther King Papers Project at Stanford University and also a speaker at the Conference. In an attempt to institutionalise its links to King, the University briefly became a minor sponsor of the monumental King Papers Project.[42]

The Conference also moved off campus into the city, to reignite popular memories—or, more often, to create new knowledge—of King's visit and his call for spirited opposition to racism, poverty and war. There were public lectures by civil rights veteran Julian Bond, conservative black Republican and former mayor of Cincinnati J. Kenneth Blackwell, and Pulitzer Prize-winning cartoonist Doug Marlette. In collaboration with the Conference, the People's Gallery at the Discovery Museum hosted an exhibit, the centrepiece of which was the first British showing of Marlette's tragically hilarious drawings on 'Race in America.' These were complimented by a touring photographic exhibit on King and the civil rights movement. Another photographic show, 'Race in the West End,' depicted the experiences of minorities in one of Tyneside's most racially, ethnically and religiously diverse neighbourhoods. The Durham-based African American singer-critic-author Sandi Russell—herself another incarnation of the North East's place within a modern Black Atlantic world—performed *Render Me My Song*, her captivating one-woman show on African American female writers. Claudia Menza and Charles Frye staged their *Claudia and Charles Show*, a funny but pointed meditation on interracial affairs. The bands Fun-da-Mental and Transglobal Underground rocked the Students Union in honour of King.[43]

The Conference took place when memories of the Rodney King Riots in Los Angeles in Spring 1992 were strong. Those riots, which followed the acquittal of the police who had beaten King the previous year, highlighted the ongoing iniquities faced by African Americans in matters of law enforcement and criminal justice and indicated that many of the social and economic advances of the 1960s had stalled. Indeed, for many in an urban underclass of impoverished African Americans who had not made it into an impressively expanding black middle-class, conditions and opportunities had worsened significantly during the 1980s and early 1990s.[44] Closer to home, the evisceration of already struggling local mining, shipbuilding and engineering industries during the years when Margaret Thatcher's Conservatives were in power, had taken a terrible toll on the social and economic health of the North East. This exacerbated the sort of social unrest and interracial tensions that erupted into violence and destruction of property in several British cities, notably Toxteth in Liverpool, but also in Birmingham, Manchester, London and Leeds during the 1980s.[45]

Tyneside generally avoided the rioting of the 1980s, but in September 1991 it was shaken by serious disorder on the Meadow Well Estate in North Shields and disturbances elsewhere in the region. The underlying causes of the Meadow Well riots, which principally involved local white male youths, were acute unemployment, widespread social deprivation, hard-core poverty, sub-standard educational and training opportunities, crime and sheer boredom. These problems were intensified by simmering tensions with the local police that finally boiled over when two 'joy-riders,' Dale Robson and Colin Atkins, died trying to escape police in a stolen car. As King would have predicted, in the aftermath of this tragedy white anger and frustrations at a basic lack of social, economic and educational opportunity quickly found an outlet in racial violence. Ashfak Ahmed's fish and chip shop on Avon Road was fire-bombed and he vowed 'I will now leave Meadow Well and never come back…The racism is too much. We were just lucky no-one was burned alive in their homes.'[46]

Not everyone agreed that the disorders had a racial dimension. Local doctor Manju Malik insisted that 'There has been no real racist feeling on the estate,' and argued that 'The attacks have mainly been on Indian shops, but that is because most of the shops in the area are owned by Indians.' Still, the fact remained that a civil disturbance rooted in poverty and social deprivation had, as previously in Tyneside's past, taken on racial overtones. Hari Shukla of the Racial Equality Council and North Tyneside Council certainly believed there was a racial dynamic to the patterns of looting and violence. He helped to dispatch social workers and housing officers to deal with the trauma and shock felt by many Asian residents who, as the *Journal* reported, 'fell victim to the rioters after months of harassment.'[47] When trials in connection with the rioting were held the following July, it became equally clear that, although racism did not spark the lawlessness, it shaped the way the riots unfolded.[48]

Between May 8 and 10, 1998 a second Martin Luther King Memorial Conference followed much the same template as the first. An academic programme spawned another book, this time focused on *Media, Culture and the Modern African American Freedom Struggle*. The academic aspect of the event was supplemented by an art exhibition on 'Africa in the European Imagination: Visions of the Kongo, Angola and Matamba, 1600-1750,' at the Hatton Gallery on Newcastle University's campus and a first British showing for the award-winning documentary *At The River I Stand* about the 1968 sanitation workers' strike that Martin Luther King was supporting in Memphis at the time of his assassination. There were also two public lectures, both part-financed from the Martin Luther King Lecture account that had been untapped since the mid-1980s. The first lecture was by a returning Julian Bond; the second was an 'Audience with Harry Belafonte,' when I joined Bond to interview the charismatic singer-actor-humanitarian and civil rights activist in a packed-to-overflowing King's Hall. In the same venue, on May 8, 1998, Belafonte, one of King's closest friends, advisors and benefactors, received an Honorary Doctorate in Civil Law. Belafonte unveiled a plaque in the Cochrane Lounge of the Students' Union Building that commemorated both his award and King's. The University chose the location carefully to 'encourage current and future students to find out more about Dr King and his contribution to the civil rights struggle.' Pausing to read the inscription Belafonte mused, '1967 was a very troubled and diffi-cult time in the history of our movement, and for Dr King personally. I remember talking to Dr King about coming here. It meant a lot to him, the way he was received and the way this University responded to him.' Belafonte added that he was 'particularly touched by this because most of the universities in the United States do not have a plaque to honour Dr King, and I'm not sure many people in the university system care that much, which is very sad.'[49]

Having staged two highly successful and highly visible Memorial Con-ferences, rediscovered the Martin Luther King Lecture Fund and mounted a commemorative plaque, by the end of the 1990s the University was be-ginning to develop the kind of permanent, living, outward-facing memorial to King, his work and his message that some had envisioned in 1968. But then interest and commitment seems to have waned once more; memories of the connection to King fell back into a curious kind of institutional and public limbo. Again, this was less a matter of wilful neglect than of happen-stance, but it provides a revealing insight into how public memory—and amnesia—can work.

Several factors seemed to have been involved. My own departure from Newcastle University in 2000 to take up a post at the University of Florida probably diminished the likelihood of at least a third Memorial Conference, which was being tentatively planned for 2003 to keep up the five-year cy-cle—if just two events can properly be termed 'a cycle.' Also important was the retirement of James Wright as Vice-Chancellor. Like Bosanquet before him, Wright's interest in using King to signal the University's commitment to addressing major contemporary social challenges had enabled the Memorial Conferences. As institutional attention wandered, even the plaque that Belafonte had unveiled was removed during renovations to the Students Union. The plaque was never reinstalled; its whereabouts are still unknown.

Such losses were of no small consequence. Scholars of social memory and cultural heritage recognise that things like plaques and other 'sites of memory' help to nurture and sustain popular interest in the events, movements and actors of the past.[50] Statues, monuments, named rooms, named buildings, named streets, named bridges, named parks, named ships, along with films, books, plays, newspaper and magazine articles, and countless other kinds of physical objects and events can keep popular memories of the past alive in particular places and for particular audiences; they also shape the nature of those memories. Repetition helps, too. Regularly staged events to honour individuals, organisations, movements, or other historic themes and moments can help to cement them into popular consciousness. Festivals, memorial concerts, television, radio or print retrospectives, artistic and cultural tributes, days of commemoration such as King Day in the US or Remembrance Sunday in Britain, and even themed academic conferences and public lectures: these are the kinds of things that help to fix aspects of the past in the public imagination and create a collective, if rarely uniform, sense of their meaning and importance.

With the partial exception of a handful of lectures and the 1993 and 1998 Martin Luther King Memorial Conferences and their associated events, for the best part of half a century there was little of this kind of public commemoration of King's Newcastle visit.[51] By contrast, William Lloyd Garrison had his name enshrined on a city centre wall, sharing a modest plaque by the entrance to Grainger Market on Nelson Street with Lajos Kossuth, the Hungarian nationalist leader, and Giuseppe Garibaldi, one of the architects of Italian independence, both of whom had also visited the city in the mid-19th century.[52]

Successful commemorations are usually created and maintained by individuals, organisations or institutions with a political, economic, philosophical, artistic, or emotional stake in the aspect of the past, or the particular historical figure, or the organisation being honoured. On Tyneside, the three groups who stood to gain most from cultivating public memories of King's visit and spreading his message were Newcastle University, the City Council, and local minority groups. Until Freedom City 2017, the University only periodically took up that challenge; the City

Council supported any public-facing initiatives coming from the University, but never took the lead; as for Tyneside's minorities, partly as a consequence of the lack of community involvement in the original visit, but partly as a consequence of the subsequent lack of any regular city-wide or school-centred celebrations of that event or the creation of a public monument, as Chi Onwurah could testify, there was no more knowledge of King's presence in Newcastle among the city's minority communities than there was across Tyneside more generally.

With no commemorative infrastructure or public memorials in place, the period after the 1998 Conference was relatively fallow in terms of celebrating King's visit. Yet civic, institutional and personal memories of King's visit never entirely disappeared. Sometimes those memories were embodied in individuals like Melanie Reed of Newcastle University's media, communications and public relations operations, who was involved in both Memorial Conferences in the 1990s. Reed provided a measure of human continuity and institutional memory when the University embraced the idea of Freedom City 2017. Moreover, during the late 1990s and early 2000s, the region witnessed an enormous amount of good work to support social justice and peace, and to confront poverty and racism, which was very much in keeping with King's vision, even if he was not always directly invoked.

A shining example was Show Racism the Red Card (SRRC), founded by Ged Grebby in North Tyneside in 1996. Initially, SRRC was partly funded by a gift from Newcastle United's goalkeeper Shaka Hislop. Born in the London Borough of Hackney of Caribbean (Trinidad and Tobago) heritage, and educated in Washington DC at the prestigious, historically black Howard University, Hislop was a latter-day personification of the kind of Black Atlantic sojourner, a representative of the African Diaspora that had long been part of Tyneside's economic, cultural and racial history. Filling up his car with petrol in 1995, Hislop was appalled, but also puzzled, when he was subjected to a volley of racist abuse by local white youths who, upon recognising him as the popular new goalkeeper for their beloved 'Toon,' instantly changed their attitudes and even asked him for autographs. Here was the tragedy of racism incarnate; its poisonous stupidity exposed; the need for education demonstrated. Hislop gave a donation to what would become SRRC, which blossomed into an educational charity seeking 'to combat racism through enabling role models, who are predominately but not exclusively footballers, to present an anti-racist message to young people and others.' By running a variety of campaigns and events, providing educational resources for schools, local government authorities and sports clubs, and putting on training sessions for teachers, students and coaches, SRRC became a national phenomenon. Expanding its reach far beyond the world of football and adding homophobia and other kinds of bigotry to its remit, by 2016, the organisation was training about 50,000 individuals to recognise and resist prejudice each year.[53]

Occasionally, memories of King's time on Tyneside were stirred more explicitly. In 2007 Newcastle University marked the 40th anniversary of the visit with a couple of stories in its *Arches* alumni magazine. One article dealt with the basic circumstances of King's visit; the other was a short interview with Harry Belafonte by editor Dan Howarth. Appropriately, the features appeared in a special issue dedicated to the theme of 'Helping to Make Poverty History.' The University's fundraising efforts in that campaign were explicitly aligned with King's characterisation of poverty as 'one of the great and grave problems of our world' (sic)—which accurately captured the gist of what King had said in Newcastle, if rather butchering the actual wording. A foreword by Mark Scrimshaw, a Newcastle history graduate, Chair of the Alumni Association, and a BBC producer who had made a documentary feature on race relations in the region to tie in with the 1993 Martin Luther King Memorial Conference, deftly linked the anti-poverty campaign to historic traditions of progressive politics on Tyneside.[54]

In 2011 Nick Megoran of Newcastle University and Andii Bowsher of Northumbria University set up the Martin Luther King Peace Committee (MLKPC), a joint enterprise working across the city's two universities. The MLKPC explicitly honoured King's devotion to peace and nonviolent conflict resolution—a crucial component of his activist career and of his remarks in Newcastle—through monthly prayer meetings and work with other pacifist groups in the area, including the Newcastle Stop the War Coalition, the Northern Region of CND and the Hexham Quakers. In 2014, it collaborated with local schools, to produce an extraordinarily successful online teaching resources pack on the World War One Christmas Truces to coincide with their 100th anniversary. The MLKPC also coordinated a 2016 conference to mark the 200th anniversary of the Peace Society, an organisation with deep roots in the North East whose work regularly intersected with anti-racism initiatives.[55]

The MLKPC's efforts formed part of a series of initiatives and events, some planned, some serendipitous, that collectively signalled renewed public and institutional interest in King's visit and led ultimately to Freedom City 2017. In October 2012, having returned to Newcastle to lead a new

American Studies programme at Northumbria University, I was invited by Melanie Reed to talk about King's time in Newcastle and introduce the film of his speech in the King's Hall. The occasion was organised by the black caucus of the National Union of Journalists, whose conference was being held in Newcastle that year. The Claudia Jones Memorial Lecture honoured the pioneering radical Afro-Caribbean journalist who, in 1958, had founded Britain's first black newspaper, the *West Indian Gazette*. Among the other speakers that night were Chi Onwurah and the Rev. Gerald Durley, a colleague of Martin Luther King in the SCLC. The *Chronicle* covered the event, excitedly reporting the new discovery of 'long lost footage' of King in Newcastle, a mere twenty years after it had resurfaced.[56]

Also in the audience was BBC journalist-producer Murphy Cobbing, who was instrumental in rekindling interest in King's visit. Cobbing had become fascinated by King's trip after hearing about it from Shami Chakrabarti, founder and director of Liberty, the leading British-based Human Rights advocacy group. Chakrabarti had been shown footage of King's speech when she gave a lecture at the University in 2011. A year later, when she was awarded her own Honorary Doctorate, Chakrabarti linked her work to King's campaigns for social justice. 'This is a massive, massive honour, and this is special for two reasons. Firstly, because I am so pleased and happy to be in Newcastle, but secondly, because this was Dr Luther King's English University,' she explained. 'To be given the same honour as him, Doctor of Civil Law, in the same place, as a fellow civil rights campaigner, makes it incredibly special to me.'[57] Linkages and lineages were beginning to be sketched out and celebrated once more; public curiosity was piqued; long-dormant popular memories began to stir. And, persuaded that I had previously only scratched the surface of the local details and transatlantic significances of King's visit and its aftermath, I began working on this book, collaborating with a wide range of media and cultural partners to maximise the impact of that research.

One of the first fruits of that labour was a thirty-minute BBC Radio Newcastle documentary on King's visit produced by Murphy Cobbing that aired on January 1, 2013. The programme found national exposure when it was picked up by BBC Radio 4 as a 'Pick of the Week.' In 2014, Cobbing also had the inspired idea to travel to the US to share footage of King's 'lost' speech with American audiences, including Andrew Young. Perhaps not surprisingly given the brevity and the circumstances of the 1967 trip, Young remembered nothing about it. But like most of those who saw the Newcastle speech, he was moved by King's words and eager to stress their contemporary relevance. 'What I find is, every time I listen to Martin Luther King, no matter how many times I've heard him, it always reminds me of something that yet needs to be done. We are still not finished with his struggle,' he told Cobbing. Some of Cobbing's interviews found their way into a series of short features for BBC Radio Newcastle.[58]

More of Cobbing's interview material was repurposed for *A King's Speech–Martin Luther King on Tyneside*, a BBC North East Television documentary on which Cobbing worked with David Morrison. Narrated by well-known comedian-actor-humanitarian Lenny Henry, the documentary was initially broadcast in the North East and Cumbria on June 1, 2014. Having advised on and appeared in *A King's Speech*, I also showed up in a short feature on BBC One's popular early evening magazine programme *The One Show*.[59] At the end of the year, the documentary won a Royal Television Society Award for Best Factual Programme for the North East and Borders region.[60] By now, irresistible momentum was gathering. The thirst for knowledge about King's visit and how it fitted into broader relations among Britain, the North East and the African American freedom struggle was intensifying.

In Spring 2015, Tyneside was the focal point for the pilot project of Journey to Justice, an ambitious educational and community activism initiative founded by Carrie Supple. Journey to Justice highlighted parallels and connections between the US civil rights movement and UK movements for racial and social justice. The objective was to inspire community groups around Britain, particularly those involving young people, to find constructive ways to battle racism and other social problems. In a refreshing example of the synergy between academic research and public service, Journey to Justice's decision to make Tyneside the testing ground for its work came largely because it complemented the themes of a conference held at Northumbria University to mark the 50th anniversary of the 1965 demonstrations in Selma, Alabama and the passage of the Voting Rights Act. There was a small exhibition on King's visit at the Great North Museum: Hancock, and I acted as academic advisor for a larger one on the US civil rights movement and its transatlantic reverberations at the Discovery Museum. With an eclectic range of cultural and educational activities across the region, Journey to Justice's appearance on Tyneside alongside the Selma conference, revived memories of the 1990s Martin Luther King Memorial Conferences. Media coverage was plentiful and around 4,000 people visited the Discovery and Great North Museum: Hancock exhibits, confirming a public appetite for discovering the region's historic links to King and the African American freedom struggle. In the final project report, it was noted that among the most popular suggestions and comments from visitors to the Discovery Museum was a desire to learn 'More about Martin Luther King's visit to Tyneside.'[61]

Several other factors also helped to pave the way to Freedom City 2017. At the most mundane level, there was simply more potential for marking the 50th 'Golden' anniversary of King's visit than for any previous anniversary. But that alone does not explain the eagerness to re-engage with and revive King's legacy of which Freedom City 2017 was both a vehicle and an expression. While for nearly half a century it had a decidedly mixed record when it came to tending the cords of memory regarding King's visit, the crucial factor was Newcastle University's determination to support the celebrations. In the mid-1960s, Charles Bosanquet had been fully aware of the publicity and recruitment potential of honouring celebrated public figures like King, yet he was equally interested in using such events to showcase the University's commitment to meeting the great social challenges of the day. Much the same dynamic was in play in the 21st century. Protracted conversations about appropriate corporate 'branding' and occasional preciousness about 'ownership' of the events sometimes seemed at odds with King's message and betrayed the fact that the University hoped to gain a good deal of publicity, considerable kudos and conceivably improved recruitment and revenue as a result of its investment of time, money and human resources in Freedom City 2017. Yet, it would be unfair to imply that these were the only, or even the main, considerations. The broad goals of Freedom City 2017 aligned with longstanding goals in the University's Mission Statement, which included a desire 'to play a leading role in the economic, social and cultural development of the North East of England.' This commitment to 'social responsibility,' much the same as the one Bosanquet had championed, had already been given institutional substance by the creation of the Newcastle University Institute for Social Renewal.[62]

Moreover, while the events of 1967 were restricted primarily to the University, Freedom City 2017 was opened up to a much wider range of civic institutions, community organisations, educational establishments and cultural partners. This increased the chance that the vast array of events either taking place explicitly under its umbrella or following more loosely in its slipstream would have more enduring impact.[63] The key visionaries, and in many ways the authors of Freedom City 2017, were the Newcastle-born brothers, Adam and Patrick Collerton. Adam, a local music promoter (co-founder of the city's Jumpin' Hot Club and Northern Roots) as well as community activist, and his brother Patrick, a film and television director based in Bristol and London, were co-creative directors and the driving forces behind plans for a series of major cultural and media events. Pro-Vice-Chancellor for Engagement and Internationalisation Richard Davies and Engagement Manager Andrea Henderson oversaw the ambitious project from the University's end,

An Arts Council grant of £595,190 to Northern Roots and the Newcastle Gateshead Initiative (NGI) helped, in the words of NGI's Culture and Major Events Director Carol Bell, fund 'a city-wide celebration of Dr King's visit to Newcastle upon Tyne through 'large-scale outdoor events, thought provoking theatre, inspiring exhibitions, uplifting music performances, world class academic research and more.' Putting Freedom City 2017 into the context of Newcastle's 'proud history of social justice,' Richard Davies welcomed the grant as 'a strong endorsement of the aims of Freedom City 2017,' that, crucially, 'will help a new generation engage in Dr. King's legacy.'[64] Additional support of various kinds came from Newcastle City Council, Northumbria University and other benefactors.

Across the region and across a variety of platforms, Freedom City 2017 promised to put in place the kinds of educational, cultural, artistic, monumental, and communal building blocks necessary to finally make King, his visit and his legacy a permanent part of popular consciousness on Tyneside. An impressive statue of King was commissioned from Nigel Boonham for Newcastle University's campus. At the University's Robinson Library, I co-curated a new exhibition on King's visit using some of the archival materials upon which this book is based. At the Great North Museum: Hancock, *Freedom!* was a creative response to King's Newcastle speech by filmmakers Geetha Jayaraman and Ian McDonald who explored its international relevance after fifty years. The Museum also hosted 'Not As It Is Written: Black Pittsburgh in Voice and Image,' a sister exhibition on race in Pittsburgh, Pennsylvania—like Newcastle a former coal-mining and industrial centre. Developed by Newcastle University historian Ben Houston, the exhibition prompted visitors to consider continuing transatlantic parallels, links and differences in terms of race and, culture and economics. Houston also worked with Megan Hunt and myself under Nick Megoran's leadership to create a teaching resources pack that used King's visit, speech and career as a vehicle for classroom lessons and school assemblies on race, poverty, war, peace, and the uses and abuses of state power.

Dozens of local community, educational, labour and cultural organisations, whether formally supported by or informally aligned with Freedom

City 2017, also planned activities inspired by King's visit and speech. A series of Café Culture talks discussed matters of current social and political importance, replicating the coffee house and reading room culture that was so central to the abolitionists, peace advocates, political agitators and economic reformers of Tyneside in the 18th and 19th centuries; the annual Tyne and Wear May Day rally of unionists in Exhibition Park took as its theme 'No to War, Poverty and Racism!'; Juice, Newcastle's annual festival for families and young people, showcased King and the civil rights movement; the Baltic Centre for Contemporary Art hosted 'Starless Midnight,' a year-long programme of artistic responses to modern civil rights issues by an array of international artists; Seven Stories, the National Centre for Children's Books located in the Ouseburn, ran 'Rhyme Scene,' in which local young people used poetry to develop stories and conversations around freedom and justice; Matthew Grenby, Paul Peart-Smith and Lydia Wysocki oversaw the creation of *Tyneside Radicals*, a comic book designed to introduce children to the story of King's visit and place it within Tyneside's historic traditions of progressive politics; the Newcastle Centre for the Literary Arts curated *The Mighty Stream*, an anthology of poetry inspired by Martin Luther King's message, in partnership with Georgetown University in Washington DC; dramatic performances speaking to the key themes of King's speech were held at the Theatre Royal, the Live Theatre and Northern Stage, by the Bravo 22 Company troupe of military veterans, locally based Angolan refugee Joana Geronimo, and the Market Theatre from Johannesburg, respectively; the Friends of Summerhill community group secured permission to put a blue commemorative plaque on the old Richardson family house, celebrating their role as campaigners for peace and racial justice and marking the site where Frederick Douglass and so many other fugitive slaves had stayed in the 19th century; South Shields Museum put on an exhibition documenting Muhammad Ali's 1977 visit to the town; a special Freedom City 2017 cruise set off from the Tyne to Amsterdam featuring music by Akala, the Wailers, Black Uhuru, Martha Reeves and the North East's own Voices of Virtue Gospel Choir; Tim Supple, Roy Williams and Mike Griffith planned a mass participation event, Freedom on the Tyne, on the Quayside that brought together stories of human rights struggles from around the globe. [65]

Cumulatively, the sheer ambition, scope and reach of Freedom City 2017 dwarfed any previous attempts to honour Martin Luther King in Britain, let alone on Tyneside. Finally, there was a fitting tribute to King's visit, his activism, and his broader vision of human rights, freedom, justice and peace. Stevie Wonder, the legendary Motown Records recording artist and activist, knew a thing or two about commemorating Martin Luther King's life and legacy, having been at the heart of the campaign to secure a US national public holiday for King in the 1980s. In July 2016, Wonder told the organisers of Freedom City 2017 that if they truly wanted to honour King they needed to 'ensure that the celebrations brought everyone together, irrespective of their race, color, religion or who they choose to love.' It was, Wonder believed, King's prophetic vision of the essential unity of all humankind that needed to be remembered, respected and reasserted.[66]

Ultimately, only time will tell if Freedom City 2017 was successful in making King's visit a permanent fixture in local memory and what kind of impact it may have on politics and community relations in the North East. The goal was to keep alive King's vision and reaffirm his call to progressive social activism by, as Carol Bell of NGI put it, creating 'new ways for arts and cultural organisations to engage hard to reach groups and present, commission and produce work that reflects our diverse communities.'[67] That diversity, reflected in an increasingly interconnected and multicultural world, made Tyneside a vastly different place in 2017 from the one Martin Luther King had visited half a century earlier. As we shall see in the final chapter, the social, economic, cultural and political challenges raised by those demographic changes only increased the relevance of King's message and confirmed the timeliness of Freedom City 2017.

CHAPTER TWELVE

Echoes and Arcs: Martin Luther King,
Race, Religion and Politics on Tyneside in the 21ˢᵗ Century

Taken as a whole, the North East in the early 21ˢᵗ century continued to be 'whiter' than just about every other region in Britain: 95.3 percent of the roughly 2.6 million inhabitants were classified as 'white' according to the 2011 Census. In Tyne and Wear, which includes Sunderland, as well as Gateshead, Newcastle and both the North and South Tyneside local authorities, the white proportion was a little lower at 93.5 percent. In Newcastle upon Tyne itself, however, only 85.6 percent of the population was classified as white. Put another way, while in 1967, the non-white population in Newcastle was less than two percent, by 2011 it had risen to more than fourteen percent. 1.9 percent of that population was characterised as of African descent, 2.2 percent as Chinese, 0.9 percent as Arab, and 0.5 percent as belonging to an 'other ethnic group.' People of South Asian origin made up the biggest non-white segment of the population with a combined 5.8 percent of the population, which translated as 16,128 out of Newcastle's 280,177 inhabitants.[1]

These non-whites were often second and sometimes third generation Geordies and they faced somewhat different challenges to those their parents and grandparents had confronted. There were even some signs of outmarriage, with 1.6 percent of Newcastle's population, 4,279 people, officially classified as 'mixed-race.' Moreover, the overall racial and ethnic mix on Tyneside was becoming increasingly diverse. In 2011, Newcastle was the most favoured destination for Vietnamese migrants to Britain. One thousand Poles came to Gateshead in 2011, joining growing numbers of nominally 'white' migrants to the North East. Most of the new arrivals were economically motivated; many came from Eastern Europe, but there was also a substantial influx of Spaniards to Redcar, Stockton, Cleveland and North Tyneside; more than 1,000 Australians settled in Northumberland; 3,000 Americans arrived in County Durham (600 of them as students); 145 Libyans came to Middlesbrough; 6,000 new Chinese migrants arrived in Newcastle, about a third of them to study at Newcastle University; 1,620

Chinese also settled in Sunderland. Despite this mobility, however, only Newcastle experienced a rate of immigration that was higher than the national average, at 20 migrants per thousand inhabitants. The rate for the North East as a whole was only around 5.5 per thousand head of population, barely half the English average of 11.3.[2]

Amid this increased diversity some things remained sadly familiar. As Chi Onwurah noted in her November 2016 Westminster Hall speech, race and class still profoundly shaped social and economic opportunities for migrant communities and greatly influenced their experiences at home, school, work and play.[3] Racism and other kinds of intolerance and discrimination had certainly not vanished from the region, any more than they had disappeared from the nation or any other part of the globe. Ged Grebby of Show Racism the Red Card believed that 'The big rise in racism both regionally and nationally is Islamophobia,' extending a trend in which religious and cultural differences were often as important as skin-colour in animating prejudice and discrimination.[4]

Legitimate, but often misdirected, concerns over security in the face of a global terrorist threat from radical Muslim fundamentalists who were disavowed by the majority of those who followed Islam meant that Islamophobia took its toll on community relations across the country. One expression of this rising anxiety was the Conservative Government's widely reviled Prevent programme, which risked collapsing an 'anti-radicalisation' agenda into a dangerously vindictive demonisation of Islam that was likely to intensify, rather than to reduce interracial and interfaith tensions among British children and adults.[5]

Far more effective were local initiatives, such as the BME (Black Minority Ethnic) Education Group Conference held at Westgate Hill Primary School in October 2015. Nabilla Ali, a Pakistani-born journalist living in Newcastle, who had been through the trauma of having a family member join a terrorist group, certainly did not underestimate the threat of radicalisation. But in speaking to the Conference and launching a programme of teacher workshops, Ali cut through the more parochial, proscriptive and accusatory aspects of Prevent and its ahistorical emphasis on so-called 'British values,' to call for more rounded, less xenophobic educational initiatives appropriate to the realities of the 21st century. 'I have always wanted to fight against extremism and being a Muslim I know it is a religion of peace,' she said. 'There is no room, absolutely no room, for extremism, radicalisation or terrorism in Islam.' A successful anti-radicalisation programme, Ali insisted, was one which educated and enlightened non-Muslims about the nature of Islam as practised by the vast majority of its adherents. 'We have to involve all of the children, non-Muslims as well as Muslims. I want Muslims not to get radicalised and non-Muslims to treat Muslims as equal citizens.'[6] Ali sounded remarkably like Sayed Shah had in 1961, when he invited non-Muslims to his new community centre in South Shields in an effort to demystify Islam.[7]

In the spring and summer of 2016, tensions around Islam and immigration were exploited and intensified during the Brexit debates over British membership of the European Union. Popular movements on the extreme and sometimes brazenly racist right, found common ground with other groups from across the political spectrum who expressed potentially non-racist, but too often highly racialised concerns about identity, sovereignty, economic status, and political accountability. It was not necessary to be anti-Islam, anti-immigration or racist to vote 'leave'; but those who did so could not avoid the fact that they were aligned with many people whose desire to leave the European Union was often rooted in national chauvinism or racial, ethnic and religious bigotry. Even in Newcastle, that much-heralded bastion of harmonious race relations, untroubled religious diversity, and exuberant non-conformism, Newcastle City Council Leader Nick Forbes declared the referendum 'the most nasty, divisive election in all my time in politics.' When it was over 'remain' campaigners won only a slender majority (50.7 percent to 49.3 percent). The rest of Tyne and Wear, like the vast majority of the North East, voted overwhelmingly to leave.[8]

Although pollsters were shocked, perhaps this was predictable. Throughout Britain, the foreign-born population had risen considerably since the early 1990s from roughly 4.86 million in 1991 to around 6.9 million by 2011.[9] Many of those people were asylum seekers and refugees fleeing war, persecution, terror and poverty in places such as Afghanistan and Angola, Iran and Iraq, Pakistan and Eritrea. By 2005, the North East was home to 5,170 formally registered asylum seekers, constituting around 0.2 percent of the region's population and encompassing more than 100 different nationalities. Newcastle had Britain's fifth highest number of asylum seekers in National Asylum Support Services accommodation assigned by the Home Office, most of them in the West End, Cruddas Park, Byker and Walker. The number of asylum seekers arriving locally dropped between 2008 and 2011, when it stood at 480 persons, but rose again modestly thereafter, when the bloody Syrian civil war created a massive international humanitarian crisis. In Britain, Gateshead was second only to Coventry as the city accepting the most Syrian refugees (107) in the year to

June 2016; regionally, the North East ranked second to Scotland for accepting the most refugees (302). Still, by the time of the Brexit vote, the number of asylum seekers and refugees entering the region was actually declining again. In the summer of 2016, the Home Office housed less than half the number of asylum seekers in Newcastle that it had accommodated in 2004.[10]

Despite the low and falling numbers of new migrants and a national policy that meant Britain accepted far fewer refugees and asylum seekers, proportionately and absolutely, than many other European nations, the latest wave of newcomers received a mixed reception in the North East. This was attributable, in part, to the economic distress that followed the worldwide recession of 2008 that had itself been largely enabled by inadequate national and international regulation of global financial operations and corporate business dealings. In Britain and the US, as elsewhere, far from providing a salutary lesson, the period after the 2008 crash was marked by a shoring up of the very economic and financial institutions that had caused the crisis and a further increase in wealth and income inequality. In the US the richest 10 percent of households in 2015 held 76 percent of the nation's wealth; the bottom 50 percent of households commanded just 1 percent of the nation's wealth. Economically speaking America was, according to the leading business magazine *Fortune*, 'the richest and the most unequal country' on earth. The same data suggested that Britain was the world's third most unequal nation with 20 percent of wage earners accounting for 40 percent of national income and the top 10 percent of British households controlling 45 percent of the country's wealth. By most meaningful indices, the western world was more economically unequal than at any time since the mid-20th century and the new millennium was characterised by the 'haves' putting evermore distance between themselves and the 'have nots.' The poor were left to get proportionately poorer while a once relatively secure and upwardly mobile middle-class felt increasingly vulnerable, squeezed, and frustrated.[11]

It was this imbalance, the collateral human damage and systemic economic injustice associated with the workings of unfettered global capitalism against which Martin Luther King had so often railed. Five decades after his death, deepening economic inequality helped to explain the rise of populist movements in various western democracies. They flourished by offering up crude jingoism and racial, ethnic or religious scapegoats to those fearful about their economic futures, anxious about a perceived loss of social status, and angry at the lack of effective mainstream political responses to their plight. 'Popular movements on the left and the right have demonstrated a dangerous willingness to revert to political small mindedness, to the same nationalist, protectionist, and isolationist agendas that led the world to consume itself in war during the last century,' said outgoing US Vice-President Joe Biden at the January 2017 World Economic Forum meeting in Davos, Switzerland. 'As we have seen time and again throughout history demagogues and autocrats have emerged seeking to capitalise on people's insecurities. In this case, using Islamophobic, anti-Semitic, or xenophobic rhetoric to stoke fear, sow division, and advance their own narrow agendas.' Biden was looking homewards, towards then President-elect Donald Trump, but also towards a post-Brexit Britain, Vladimir Putin's Russia and other places where right-wing politicians have made dangerous but tragically effective hyper-nationalist appeals. 'The impulse to hunker down, shut the gates, build walls, and exit at this moment is precisely the wrong answer. It offers a false sense of security in an interconnected world,' concluded Biden in words that echoed King's recognition of the 'network of mutuality' that already bound the world together in 1967. For King, this interconnectedness demanded better efforts to make those relationships work in peaceful, just and equitable ways, not to disregard them, or manipulate them in a politics based on ignorance, suspicion, blame and hatred.[12]

In Britain, the post-2008 period of austerity was punctuated by much talk about government support for the creation of 'a Northern Powerhouse' that conjured up memories of T. Dan Smith's vaulting ambition of the 1960s and 1970s. Yet, by 2017 little material support for the North East had appeared: 'the north' often seemed to mean Manchester, occasionally Leeds, while some in Westminster appeared to have difficulty contemplating anything north of Birmingham as part of their remit. Local government staff and public services were decimated by central government cuts that stripped some £200 million from the Newcastle City Council's budget between 2010 and 2016, with another £30 million in cuts required for 2016-17. In November 2016, there were reports that 1,800 Council employees faced a reduction in pay with another 100 facing redundancy.[13] Related cutbacks to social services disproportionately affected the poorest and most vulnerable sections of North East society. Although there were some tremendous regional success stories in the leisure, education, technology and cultural sectors, the general economic situation and outlook for the region remained bleak. In August 2015, the *Evening Chronicle* reported that disposable household income-per-head in the region was the lowest in the country, lagging £2,632 behind the national average.[14] The following

March, the unemployment rate of 7.8 percent was the worst in the nation, far above the national average of 5.1 percent.[15]

In the face of economic uncertainty for many, serious poverty for some, and pinched social and educational opportunities for far too many, intercommunal racial, ethnic and religious tensions escalated once more. A report in August 2010 revealed that 42 of 100 asylum seekers interviewed in Newcastle had experienced at least one racist incident in the previous twelve months. The perennially disadvantaged sections of Benwell, Walker and Byker were the worst areas. The same year, Northumbria Police received over 1,000 reports of racial incidents.[16] Between 2005 and 2015 3,908 hate crimes, including racist, religious, homophobic and disablist crimes, were reported to the combined Agencies Against Racist Crime and Harassment service in Newcastle and Sunderland. The number of unreported incidents was anyone's guess. Overall, the majority of hate crimes (54 percent) fell into the category of offensive or abusive language and coercive or threatening behaviour; 32 percent involved material damage to property (18 percent) or physical attacks (14 percent). In Newcastle, Benwell, Byker, Walker and Elswick, the sites of some of the greatest levels of poverty, again had the worst records.[17]

These figures painted a pretty gloomy picture. Yet, as Joe Sharkey points out in *Akenside Syndrome*, his smart, affectionate, yet commendably unromantic investigation of contemporary 'Geordie Identity,' this had nothing to do with innate prejudices. In assessing this kind of evidence, Sharkey maintained, 'the most appropriate link to establish is surely that of racism and poverty, not racism and the working class *per se.*'[18] Although Sharkey made no mention of King, his speech, or his visit to Tyneside, this was precisely the connection the civil rights leader had been so keen to make in 1967.

Given that a 2009 report indicated 'forty percent of the residents of Newcastle live in the most deprived areas of England,' Sharkey actually found it remarkable that there was not even more racial friction and violence across the city. Like many before him he concluded that traditions of working-class solidarity and strong unionism had combined to diminish, if never wholly eradicate, the appeal of racism and racial scapegoating. Historically, the relative geographic isolation of the region, he suggested, had reduced the level of contact with 'foreigners' that other cities, especially port cites, experienced. Paradoxically, while this insularity meant that even modest increases in migrant numbers could create excessive alarm and reactionary responses, it had also allowed strong, principled anti-racist traditions to flourish in the 19ᵗʰ and early 20ᵗʰ centuries in the absence of any real sense of 'threat.' These deeply embedded traditions acted as a partial brake on the growth of racism in the region and provided the foundations for a succession of local anti-racist movements. Sharkey also argued that the region's working-classes were more likely than its middle or upper classes to have direct contact with migrant groups, especially in the early days of settlement when migrants tended to congregate in poorer areas where they could afford rents and property, as had happened in the West End of Newcastle in the 1960s and 1970s. Those intimate relationships, Sharkey believed, helped to undermine stereotypes, increase understanding and even promote cross-cultural friendships.[19]

Sharkey's analysis has many merits, but it is not without its problems. As we have seen, Tyneside was always rather more diverse than he allows, without denying his basic point that it was and remains an overwhelmingly 'white' part of the world. More importantly, while local unions may once have joined political radicals and religiously motivated groups in promoting anti-racism, their power was much reduced following the bitter battles with Margaret Thatcher's Conservative government in the 1980s. Since then, organised labour has exerted a rather diminished influence on the region's politics, consciousness and consciences compared with previous eras—when its record on racial matters was not always as progressive as Sharkey and others sometimes imply. Close proximity among working-class people from different backgrounds in shared or adjacent neighbourhoods may, as Sharkey suggests, sometimes promote greater understanding, tolerance and even cooperation across racial, ethnic and religious lines. But Tyneside's racial history is full of instances where that proximity led to fierce and sometimes violent conflicts among racial, ethnic and religious groups over territory, jobs, resources and even potential marriage partners.

Without wishing to exaggerate the levels of integration in Newcastle's more ritzy neighbourhoods or among its professional and white collar inhabitants, Sharkey may also underestimate the significance of increasing interracial contact among Newcastle's middle and upper classes, particularly among those professionals involved in sectors such as local government, medicine, schools and higher education. Of course, racism is hardly unknown among the better educated, professional, middle and upper classes. Indeed, historically those groups have had much to gain from keeping the poor and working-classes divided along lines of race, ethnicity and religion. Still, as Ged Grebby explained, at Show Racism the Red Card 'We tend to say racism is across the board; it's across class, it's across geography. We would argue that the working-class hasn't been overtly any more racist than the ruling class.'[20] And this is more or less where Sharkey, like Dave Renton and others before him, ends up, sensibly warning against the dangers of simplifying or homogenising the diverse experiences of different racial, ethnic and religious groups, or sub-sets of those groups, across the North East and over time. It is, however, equally important not to overgeneralise about the kinds of responses each of those groups has encountered from Tyneside whites or, for that matter, from other minority groups, among whom relations have sometimes been extremely fraught.[21]

So how, then, are we to sum up race relations on Tyneside and in the North East, and evaluate the relevance of Martin Luther King's visit and his message, in the 21st century? This book has been especially concerned not to romanticise or exaggerate Tyneside's reputation for racial tolerance, which has occasionally been linked too simplistically to idealised notions of a natural interracial, interethnic and interfaith working-class solidarity. That kind of thinking and celebratory analysis can too easily slip into complacency and disavowal of ongoing prejudice and discrimination. It also makes for bad history on any number of grounds. Class, alongside—and intersecting with—status, gender, religion, culture, race, ethnicity and nationality, has certainly been a key factor in the region's past and will doubtless continue to help shape its future. Yet, the working-class has never been a homogenous social, ideological or political entity; moreover, the working-class can hardly boast an unblemished record on matters of racial tolerance or progressive social attitudes. Notions of a unified middle-class or upper-class are similarly problematic and reductive—and it is clear that elites from the North East's religious, press, educational, political and business communities have regularly taken leading roles in local struggles against racism and other forms of bigotry.[22] Ultimately, when it comes to promoting tolerance and fighting discrimination, the region has produced heroes, villains and a host of disengaged bystanders from among men and women of every class and just about every imaginable religious, racial and ethnic group.

And yet, when all these important caveats are put in place, all these cautionary notes are sounded, and all the ambiguous evidence is sifted, there remains evidence that the North East, perhaps Tyneside in particular, really does have remarkably resilient and quite pervasive cultures of welcome. Moreover, it is part of the strength of that tradition that it is not rooted in a single class or section of the community. Rather, it has become an important strand, somewhat threadbare and frayed at times, in the social and civic fabric of the region. Successive generations, facing different challenges, have produced sufficient numbers of local people dedicated to fighting against racism and bigotry and for a better, more just and equitable society that they have just about been able to keep the forces of intolerance at bay.

In recent times, Tyneside's best traditions of inclusivity were formally recognised when the City Council secured 'City of Sanctuary' status for Newcastle in 2014. The award followed, as Deputy Council Leader Joyce McCarty explained, evidence of 'a strong desire…from our communities' to extend the city's 'enviable reputation for being a friendly city which welcomes people from all backgrounds.'[23] Although they had rarely settled permanently, 150 years earlier, fugitive slaves had come from the US to the city and the region because they too saw it as a place of sanctuary, a place they were likely to be welcomed and treated with respect as fellow human beings.

At a time of enormous social and political flux and brutal financial constraints, when central government funding cuts left local authorities struggling to meet their basic statutory obligations, Newcastle City Council continued to promote diversity and equality agendas. It resisted the pull towards what the Nobel Prize-winning economist Amartya Sen decried as a divisive tendency in Britain towards 'plural monoculturalism'—a habit of trying to shoehorn diverse groups and individuals into neat little stereotypes, often crudely defined by their religious affiliation, or by their racial, ethnic and national backgrounds. As Sen put it, 'Being defined by one group identity over all others, overlooking whether you're working class or capitalist, left or right, what your language group is and your literary tastes are,' is crude, simplistic and ultimately 'interferes with people's freedom to make their own choices.'[24]

The local Council, supported in the main by the local press, has tried to encourage an appreciation that multiculturalism is a genuinely valuable and probably inevitable feature of the modern world. Britain and its constituent nations have always been far more polyglot than many of those who have called for immigration restriction, or celebrated a fictionally pure British identity and lineage are willing or able to acknowledge. As Alistair Moffat concludes in his investigation of the nation's genetic history, for several thousand years 'Britain has been the destination for millions of genetic journeys…it is an unfinished story…The British will keep arriving. For this long narrative shows something unarguable. We are all the descendants of immigrants, people who brought their DNA, their culture and their future to the farthest north-west edge of Europe.'[25]

In the face of new levels of diversity, however, perhaps the strongest links to the North East's historic cultures of welcome came in the form of a plethora of informal, semi-formal and government-approved organisations and charities dedicated to supporting migrants and promoting understanding and cooperation. The Newcastle City Council, for example, made a strong commitment to aiding refugees and asylum seekers from the Syrian civil war through programmes such as the Syrian Vulnerable Person Resettlement Scheme. While the arrival of new migrants sparked resentment among some, it also sparked popular expressions of sympathy and support. Dozens of grassroots groups emerged to work within migrant communities and across racial, ethnic and religious lines. Action Foundation was founded as a regional church-based charity dedicated to fighting social exclusion; the Comfrey Project was set up to involve refugees and asylum-seekers in allotment gardening and other useful crafts; Crossings was conceived as a fluid musical agglomeration of newly arrived asylum seekers, refugees and supportive local musicians; the West End Refugee Service in Newcastle and the region-wide North of England Refugee Service established in 1989 offered practical help with language education, housing concerns and legal issues; the snappily named SMART (Supporting Migrants, Asylum-Seekers and Refugees Together) focused on the particular needs of young migrants; the Regional Refugee Forum North East was one of several groups led by asylum seekers and refugees themselves, dedicated to ensuring that they become 'full and active members of the regional community'; the goal of JET (Jobs Education Training) was to 'enable local people from the Black, Asian, Minority Ethnic communities including asylum seekers and refugees to overcome disadvantage and fulfil their potential by accessing training opportunities, improving skills, seeking employment and integrating in their community.'[26]

There were also strong signs of local resistance to the recruitment efforts of ultra-right wing white nationalists groups like the English Defence League and the UK branch of Pegida. An anti-Islamic spin-off from a German neo-Nazi party with far-right British allies, Pegida chose Newcastle for its first British rally in February 2015, encouraged by the area's heavily white demographics and high poverty levels. Pegida supporters were outnumbered five to one by a 2,000-strong counter-demonstration organised by Newcastle Unites. Among those to condemn Pegida and denounce its goals was the local youth circus group, Circus Central. Based in Shieldfield, Circus Central used the hall of Christ Church Church of England Primary School to practise.[27] During the 2016-17 academic year, that school taught roughly 135 pupils from twenty-two different countries, only thirty-seven of whom had English as their first language; the other ninety-eight children shared twenty-six other first languages and a multitude of ethnic and religious affiliations. They also spanned a wide range of socio-economic categories. These were the children of local whites, asylum-seekers, refugees, and long-established minority groups whose backgrounds ranged from labourers to salesmen, from medical workers to chefs, from students to university professors, and from the long-term unemployed to business entrepreneurs.[28]

Equally significant, the diversity at Christ Church has been replicated, albeit unevenly and often to a lesser extent, across much of Tyneside—and not just in the historic 'ethnic enclaves' of South Shields or the West End of Newcastle. In the 2016-17 school year, at Ravenswood Primary School in Heaton, 121 of the school's 636 students, born in eighteen different countries, shared twenty-five first languages other than English. In the generally well-heeled suburb of Jesmond, West Jesmond Primary School similarly reported that for 268 of its 612 pupils, who claimed at least twenty-seven different countries of birth, English was spoken in addition to thirty-seven other languages. In the leafy and overwhelmingly middle-class suburb of Gosforth, 26.7 percent of the 228 pupils at Broadway East First School also had English as an additional language to the twelve other native tongues spoken by children from at least ten different countries of birth.[29]

It would be disingenuous to pretend that this racial, cultural and religious cocktail does not generate its share of inter- and intra-group tensions and occasional outbreaks of racial or religious abuse in the playground. Yet the general sense among school staff is that the children, far more than the adults, get along pretty well. By and large, they have not yet learned from their elders and lessers how to hate or discriminate according to race, ethnicity or religion. Dislike and resentment of their classmates is far more likely to be truly personal as the children really do follow Martin Luther King's injunction at the climax of his 'I Have a Dream' speech, to judge each other by the content of their character—and occasionally by their football club allegiances or favourite singers—rather than according to the colour of their skin or their religious beliefs and practices.

On November 11, 2016, a choir from Christ Church performed 'Refuge' and other songs of friendship and care for the environment in Newcastle University's King's Hall at an event to mark the 49th anniversary of King's visit and publicise some of the forthcoming events of Freedom

City 2017. Five months later, on April 27, 2017, the school joined Ravenswood, West Jesmond and other members of the Ouseburn Learning Trust for its annual spring concert in the Newcastle City Hall. The event brought together hundreds of local children and took King's life and his visit to Newcastle as the inspiration for a programme of 'Songs of Protest and Hope' that included versions of Michael Jackson's 'Black and White,' the 1960s civil rights anthem 'Ain't Gonna Let Nobody Turn Me Round,' Bob Dylan's 'Blowing in the Wind,' and 'Carry Me Home' by contemporary indie-country duo Ward Thomas. Without exaggerating the significance of such stirring musical expressions of youthful interracial, interethnic, interfaith and interclass unity and purposefulness, they appeared to offer an uplifting glimpse into, or at least renewed hope for, the future of an increasingly diverse multicultural Tyneside.

The experience of Ruhi Rahman was also seized upon as evidence that local cultures of welcome were still alive and well. On November 22, 2015 Rahman, a young Newcastle-born Muslim woman, was travelling with her sister on the Metro line from Newcastle to Whitley Bay, when she was racially and religiously abused by a white man. The man demanded she give up her seat for him, shouting that 'this is my country' and warning other passengers that the burka-wearing woman might 'bomb the train.' A group of fellow travellers, many of them football fans not in the best of moods after watching Newcastle United lose 3-0 at home to Leicester City, came to her aid. They demanded that her tormentor shut up and leave the train at the next stop. When the man got off at Palmersville, the carriage erupted into spontaneous applause. As Rahman told the press, 'I'd never seen anything like it.' She explained that it 'was the true Geordie spirit that shone through,' adding, 'I have never been so proud of being a Geordie.' This was a crucial point about the whole bittersweet episode, and one which reinforced Amartya Sen's warning about the perils of reducing complex identities in modern Britain to any single factor, be it race, ethnicity, religion, nationality, gender, sexual orientation or class: Rahman clearly identified as, among many other things, a Geordie.[30]

Rahman's pride in her Tyneside identity, as well as her female and Muslim identities, and the fact that she was comfortable embracing them all simultaneously, transformed the story. It could have been simply another heartening example of how the majority of white Tynesiders tended to reject naked expressions of bigotry towards outsiders. The football-style headline in the *Evening Chronicle* proudly reported 'Decency 1, Hatred 0,' but the newspaper also joined Rahman in presenting this as an example of

Geordies rescuing one of their own, rather than coming to the aid of an outsider. The episode was used to extol a shared commitment to decency, respect and inclusivity. Rahman's story made national news; she even appeared on BBC TV's *Good Morning Britain*. Once more Tyneside was held up to the British public as a place where racism and religious intolerance struggled to put down deep roots and rarely sprouted for long. Of course, this was the best possible, most progressive spin to put on an incident where it is impossible to know for sure the racial or religious views of those who came to Rahman's rescue or applauded their actions. Nevertheless, the episode was rich in symbolic significance: a potent story of interfaith and interracial amity that was seized upon as a moment that reflected and might also help to perpetuate the region's cultures of welcome. Katrina Barber, who witnessed the ordeal of the two Muslim women was 'so moved by what happened, I gave the girls a hug as I got off the Metro,' in an impromptu gesture of friendship and solidarity. 'Tyneside has for many decades been seen as a friendly, welcoming place,' wrote Peter Sagar in a letter about the incident to the *Journal*, 'It is good to see that this tradition is continuing.'[31]

But this tradition, the precarious triumph of tolerance and inclusivity over intolerance and exclusion, is not something to be taken for granted. As has been emphasised throughout this book, there is nothing natural, inevitable, or permanent about the cultures of welcome that the region celebrates: they have always needed constant nurture and will continue to do so if they are to survive. And this is why Martin Luther King's example, with his blend of political realism, pragmatism, and prophetic vision continues to resonate and inspire.

Speaking to the press immediately after the Honorary Degree ceremony in Newcastle, King had earnestly explained that 'Progress never rolls in on the wheels of inevitability, but through the tireless and persistent work of dedicated individuals.'[32] This was an important addendum to one of King's favourite aphorisms, in which he insisted, borrowing from the 19ᵗʰ century Boston abolitionist Theodore Parker, that 'the moral arc of the universe is long, but it bends towards justice.'[33] For King, personal faith in God's divine plan for a world that would ultimately be defined by peace and justice was the driving force for his social activism. When J.H. Burnett, the University's Public Orator, presented him for his award as a 'Christian pastor and social revolutionary,' he yoked together two roles that King saw as virtually synonymous. King's faith demanded that he work towards a peaceful social revolution that would end racism, war and poverty.[34]

Yet, ever the pragmatist when it came to political and social realities, King also recognised that it was vital for people of goodwill, regardless of their religious beliefs, to take action to shorten the curvature of that historic arc. He called for people to identify and confront bigotry and discrimination wherever and whenever they encountered it; to join educational efforts to dispel the ignorance and fear that underpins intolerance; to protest against social inequalities and racial injustice; to use the ballot and the power of the media to compel legislators to ensure that laws are in place to restrain those who preach hatred and to punish those who practice discrimination; he also urged people to reject violence, to denounce the proliferation of nuclear weapons, and to protest against the use of war as an instrument of diplomacy.

Above all, King believed that bold, responsible, collective action directed towards a vision of social equality, economic justice and respect for difference would increase the likelihood—and hasten the day—when peace, freedom and justice would prevail in a world that he admitted was 'sometimes sick and often terribly schizophrenic.' Fifty years after his visit, as plans for Freedom City 2017 came to fruition, the need to rise to the challenges that Martin Luther King laid down in Newcastle had never been greater. Nor had his confidence that by dealing 'forthrightly and in depth with these great and grave problems that pervade our world,' it would be possible 'to transform the jangling discords of our nation, and of all the nations of the world, into a beautiful symphony of brotherhood,' ever been more sorely tested by global events—or more valuable in inspiring a new generation to meet the trials of an uncertain future.

Guide to abbreviations used in Notes

AST   Anti-Slavery Tracts, Local Studies Centre, City Library, Newcastle upon Tyne

Chronicle   *Newcastle Chronicle* (1793-April, 1858); *Newcastle Daily Chronicle* (May 1, 1858-July 29, 1922)

Courant   *Newcastle Courant*

Courier   *The Courier: The Newspaper of the Students of Newcastle*

DM   *Daily Mail*

DT   *Daily Telegraph*

E-Chronicle   *Evening Chronicle* (Newcastle: November 2, 1885-present)

Guardian   *The Manchester Guardian* (to 1959); *The Guardian* (1959-present)

HCWF   Honorary Congregations Working File, April and November 1967, Special Collections, Robinson Library, Newcastle University

HDC   Honorary Degrees Correspondence, 1961-1974, Special Collections, Robinson Library, Newcastle University

Journal   *Newcastle Journal* (i. April 7, 1739-April 1788; ii. January 12, 1832-present, with name change to *The Journal*)

JtJOHP   Journey to Justice Oral History Project, journeytojustice.org.uk/projects/oral-history-project-sharing-heritage/

KCA   The King Center Archives, Atlanta, Georgia, thekingcenter.org/archive

L&P   Literary and Philosophical Society, Newcastle upon Tyne

LODAL   Letters on the Death of Abraham Lincoln, Abraham Lincoln: Citizen of the World Collection, Abraham Lincoln Presidential Library and Museum, Springfield, Illinois, citizenlincoln.org

LSC-SS   Local Studies Collection, Central Library, South Shields

LSC-N   Local Studies Centre, City Library, Newcastle upon Tyne

LT   Local Tracts, Local Studies Centre, City Library, Newcastle upon Tyne

MLK-Dup   Dr. Martin Luther King, Jnr, Honorary Degree, 13.11.67, Duplicate File, Special Collections, Robinson Library, Newcastle University

MLK-FBI Martin Luther King Jr., FBI File, Part II: The King-Levison
File, Alderman Library, University of Virginia,
Charlottesville, Virginia

MLK-Lect Martin Luther King Lecture File (at the time of writing held
in The Registry, King's Gate, Newcastle University, though
likely to be deposited in Special Collections, Robinson
Library, Newcastle University

MLK-Mem Martin Luther King Jr Memorial Conference – October
1993, May 1998, Special Collections, Robinson Library,
Newcastle University

MLK-Reg Registrar's File: Martin Luther King, Special Collections,
Robinson Library, Newcastle University

MLK-VC Vice-Chancellor's File: Martin Luther King, Special
Collections, Robinson Library, Newcastle University

MS *Morning Star*

NFHD Nominations for Honorary Degrees, 1966-67, Special
Collections, Robinson Library, Newcastle University

NG *Newcastle Guardian*

NSG *North & South Shields Gazette*

NYT *New York Times*

Reg The Registry, King's Gate, Newcastle University

SDN *Shields Daily News* (South Shields)

Times *The Times* (London)

TWA Tyne and Wear Archives, Discovery Museum, Newcastle
upon Tyne

W-Chronicle *Newcastle Chronicle, or General Weekly Advertiser* (March 24,
1764 – 1793); *Newcastle Weekly Chronicle* (1864-April 5,
1953)

Notes

Introduction: 'An Inextricable Network of Mutuality'

1. The North East is defined here as the old counties of Northumberland and Durham, extending roughly from Berwick on the River Tweed in the north to Middlesbrough on the River Tees in the south, with the city of Newcastle and the Tyneside conurbation it dominates as the main focus of this book. The concept of 'the North East' as a distinct, somewhat unified region within the British Isles is a relatively recent development, dating back to the 1930s. The term was in widespread, if not always precise, usage by the 1950s and 1960s. Robert Colls, *Identity of England* (Oxford: Oxford University Press, 2002), p.322. See also, Adrian Green and A.J. Pollard (eds), *Regional Identities in North-East England, 1300-2000* (Martlesham, UK: Boydell & Brewer, 2007); Rob Colls and Bill Lancaster (eds), *Geordies: Roots of Regionalism* (1992; Newcastle upon Tyne: Northumbria University Press, 2005).

2. Literary scholar J. Michelle Coughlin notes that 'scholars of memory in US literature and history have primarily focused on the domestic contours of events' while arguing, as do I, for 'the necessity of approaching cultural memory as a phenomenon within and beyond the nation.' J. Michelle Coughlin, *Sensational Internationalism: The Paris Commune and the Remapping of American Memory in the Long Nineteenth Century* (Edinburgh: Edinburgh University Press, 2016), p.4. One scholar who has insightfully explored transatlantic memorials to the slave trade and African American history is Alan Rice, *Creating Memorials, Building Identities: The Politics of Memory in the Black Atlantic* (Liverpool: Liverpool University Press, 2010). Classic texts on social memory and race in the US include, David Blight, *Race and Reunion: The Civil War in American Memory* (Cambridge, Mass.: Harvard University Press, 2001) and W. Fitzhugh Brundage, *The Southern Past: A Clash of Race and Memory* (Cambridge, Mass.: Harvard University Press, 2005).

3. For an introduction to the global coordinates of the US civil rights movement during the Cold War, see Mary L. Dudziak, *Cold War Civil Rights: Race and the Image of American Democracy* (Princeton: Princeton University Press, 2000); James H. Meriwether, *Proudly We Can Be African: Black Americans and Africa, 1935-1961* (Chapel Hill: University of North Carolina Press, 2002); Penny Von Eschen, *Satchmo Blows up the World: Jazz Ambassadors Play the Cold War* (Cambridge, MA: Harvard University Press, 2006). For the need to internationalise the study of African American history, see also Gerald Horne, 'Towards a Transnational Research Agenda for African American History in the 21st Century,' *Journal of African American History*, 91, 3 (2006), pp.288-303.

4. F.M. Leventhal, *Arthur Henderson* (Manchester: Manchester University Press, 1989), p.215.

5. David Olusoga, *Black and British: A Forgotten History* (London: Macmillan, 2016), pp.25, 28. There were important efforts to incorporate non-whites into British history and to examine the role of the African slave trade in British domestic and imperial developments long before the 1980s. See, for example, Roger Anstey, *The Atlantic Slave Trade and British Abolitionism, 1760-1810* (London: Macmillan, 1975); Michael Banton, *White and Coloured: The Behaviour of British People Towards Coloured Immigrants* (London: Jonathan

Cape, 1959; Dilip Hiro, *Black British, White British: A History of Race Relations in Britain* (c.1971; London: Grafton, 1991); K.L. Little, *Negroes in Britain: A. Study of Racial Relations in English Society* (London: Kegan, 1947); Douglas A. Lorimer, *Colour, Class and the Victorians: English Attitudes to the Negro in the Mid-Nineteenth Century* (Leicester: Leicester University Press, 1978); Clare Taylor, *British and American Abolitionists: An Episode in Transatlantic Understanding* (Edinburgh: Edinburgh University Press, 1974); Howard Temperley, *British Antislavery* (London: Longman, 1972); James Walvin, *Black and White: The Negro and English Society* (London: Penguin, 1973). However, scholarly attention to these themes has grown exponentially since the 1980s with R.J.M. Blackett, *Building an Antislavery Wall: Black Americans in the Atlantic Abolitionist Movement, 1830-1860* (Ithaca: Cornell University Press, 1983) and Peter Fryer, *Staying Power: The History of Black People in Britain* (London: Pluto, 1984) among the seminal texts near the start of this new wave.

6. Olusoga, *Black and British*, p.xv. See also, Arifa Akbar, 'David Olusoga: 'There's a dark side to British history, and we saw a flash of it this summer',' *GuardianOnline*, November 4, 2016, theguardian.com/books/2016/nov/04/david-olusoga-interview-black-history. Accessed November 23, 2016; Sarfraz Mansoor, 'David Olusoga Is The New Face of BBC History – But As a Boy he was Driven Out of His Home by Racists,' *Radio Times*, November 9, 2016, radiotimes.com/news/2016-11-09/david-olusoga-is-the-new-face-of-bbc-history--but-as-a-boy-he-was-driven-out-of-his-home-by-racists. Accessed November 28, 2016. 'Geordie' is a common colloquial term for the residents of Newcastle and greater Tyneside and for their dialect.

7. Olusoga, *Black and British*, pp.254-255.

8. Paul Gilroy, *Black Atlantic Modernity and Double Consciousness* (London: Verso, 1993). See also, Caryl Phillips, *The Atlantic Sound* (2000; London: Vintage, 2001).

9. For more on the relationships between the Black Atlantic and the broader Atlantic World, see Thomas Benjamin, *The Atlantic World: Europeans, Africans, Indians, and Their Shared History, 1400-1900* (Cambridge: Cambridge University Press, 2009); Toyin Falola and Kevin D. Roberts (eds), *The Atlantic World, 1450-2000* (Bloomington: Indiana University Press, 2000).

10. William Blake, 'Auguries of Innocence,' 1803, in *The Norton Anthology of Poetry*, rev. ed. (New York: Norton, 1975), p.555. On granular approaches to Atlantic World history, see Brian Ward, 'Caryl Phillips, David Armitage, and the Place of the American South in Atlantic and Other Worlds,' in Brian Ward, Martyn Bone and William A. Link (eds), *The American South and the Atlantic World* (Gainesville: University Press of Florida, 2013), pp.8-44 (especially, pp.28-34).

11. There is some confusion around terms such as migrant, immigrant, asylum-seeker and refugee. Here 'migrant' is used as a broad umbrella term to describe anyone who has moved into the North East from elsewhere for any reason, whether with a view to staying relatively briefly or permanently. Within this overarching migrant category, 'immigrant' describes people who have chosen to come to the region, sometimes via other parts of Britain, from another country, with a view to staying permanently or at least long-term. 'Refugee' is used to designate people who have come to the region to escape war, terror, political or religious persecution, natural disaster or extreme poverty (where the term sometimes overlaps with 'economic migrant'). Technically speaking 'refugee status' has to be granted by the British government. 'Asylum seeker' refers to a refugee who is awaiting the outcome of a request to the British government for official refugee status. For a guide

through this political and constantly evolving lexical minefield, see Camilla Ruz, 'The Battle over the Words Used to Describe Migrants,' *BBC News Magazine*, August 28, 2015, bbc.co.uk/news/magazine-34061097. Accessed January 18, 2017.

12. The phrase 'cultures of welcome' is adapted from Dave Renton, *Colour Blind?: Race and Migration in North East England Since 1945* (Sunderland: University of Sunderland Press, 2007), pp.60-1. Renton's book offers a judicious, cautiously positive assessment of the extent to which 'the region has indeed provided as uniquely warm a welcome as once was believed' to a succession of migrants (p.21). For more on Newcastle's status as a City of Sanctuary, see newcastle.cityofsanctuary.org/. Accessed January 18, 2017.

13. Martin Luther King, 'Acceptance Speech on Receipt of an Honorary Doctorate at the University of Newcastle upon Tyne,' November 13, 1967 (first quote), MLK-Reg. Martin Luther King, 'I Have a Dream,' August 28, 1963 (second quote), in James M. Washington (ed.), *I Have a Dream: Writings and Speeches that Changed the World* (San Francisco: HarperSanFrancisco, 1992), p.103.

Part One: The Visit

Chapter One: 'Happy and Honored to Accept': Bringing Martin Luther King to Newcastle

1. G. Ashley (Assistant Registrar), 'Press Release,' March 8, 1967, HCWF.

2. There are many fine biographies of King. Of particular use here were the trilogy by Taylor Branch, *Parting the Waters: America in the King Years, 1954-1963* (New York: Simon & Schuster, 1988); *Pillar of Fire: America in the King Years, 1963-1965* (New York: Simon & Schuster, 1998) and *At Canaan's Edge: America in the King Years, 1965-68* (New York: Simon & Schuster, 2006); Adam Fairclough, *To Redeem the Soul of America: The Southern Christian Leadership Conference and Martin Luther King, Jr.* (Athens, Ga.: University of Georgia Press, 1987); David Garrow, *Bearing the Cross: Martin Luther King, Jr., and the Southern Christian Leadership Conference* (New York: William Morrow and Company, 1986); Thomas F. Jackson, *From Civil Rights to Human Rights: Martin Luther King, Jr., and the Struggle for Economic Justice* (Philadelphia: University of Pennsylvania Press, 2007); John A. Kirk, *Martin Luther King Jr* (Harlow: Pearson, 2005); Peter J. Ling, *Martin Luther King* (2nd ed. Abingdon: Routledge, 2015).

3. [Lord] Wynne-Jones, letter to E.M. Bettenson, October 22, 1966, NFHD; 'Document B of the Agenda of the Honorary Degrees Committee Meeting,' November 3, 1966, MLK-Reg.

4. For Lord Wynne-Jones, see the obituary in *Times*, November 17, 1982, p.12; T. Dan Smith, *An Autobiography* (Newcastle: Oriel Press, 1970), pp.130-133.

5. 'Report of the Honorary Degrees Committee,' November 28, 1966, MLK-Reg.

6. C.I.C. Bosanquet (Vice-Chancellor) letter to Prof E.S. Page; Prof. J.H. Burnett; Prof. J. Baddiley; Prof. A.F. Burstall; Prof. R.L. Russell; Prof. K. Rowntree; P. Brenikov; The Bursar; Dr. W.S. Mitchell; Dr. D.J. Smith; Dr. W. Muckle; Mr. N. Shott; Wardens of Embleton; Garnett and Gurney Houses; Prof. S.K. Runcorn, November 29, 1965, HDC.

7. Nick Nicholson, telephone interview with Francis W. Glover, April 2014, quoted in Francis W. Glover, 'Newcastle's Forgotten King: Dr. Martin Luther King, Jr., in Newcastle-upon-Tyne, 13th November, 1967,' BA dissertation, Northumbria University, 2013, pp.36-37.

8. Sylvia Ellis, 'A Demonstration of British Good Sense?: British Student Protest During the Vietnam War,' in Gerard DeGroot, ed., *Student Protest: The Sixties and After* (London: Longman, 1998), pp.58-99.

9. Nick Nicholson, quoted in Glover, 'Newcastle's Forgotten King,' p.17.

10. Bosanquet, letter to Page et al.

11. C.I.C. Bosanquet, 'Address at the Memorial Service for Dr. Martin Luther King,' April 26, 1968, MLK-VC.

12. 'Dr. Miller, Next V.C.. New Man Faces a Huge Task,' *Courier*, January 24, 1968, p.1.

13. Kathleen Potter, interview with Murphy Cobbing, for *Martin Luther King: A King's Speech*, BBC Radio Newcastle, broadcast, January 1, 2013.

14. E.M. Bettenson, letter to M.L. King, December 14, 1966, MLK-Reg.

15. Dora McDonald, letter to E.M. Bettenson, December 23, 1966, MLK-Reg.; Martin Luther King, Jr., *Where Do We Go From Here: Chaos or Community?* (Boston: Beacon Press, 1967). On the circumstances surrounding the writing of King's book, see David J. Garrow, 'Where Martin Luther King, Jr. Was Going: *Where Do We Go From Here* and the Traumas of the Post-Selma Movement,' *Georgia Historical Quarterly*, 75 (Winter 1991), pp.719-736.

16. E.M. Bettenson, letter to Dora McDonald, January 7, 1967, MLK-Reg.

17. E.M. Bettenson, telegram to Dora McDonald, January 17, 1967, MLK-Reg.

18. E.M. Bettenson, letter to Dr. King., February 23, 1967, MLK-Reg.

19. Martin Luther King, telegram to E.M. Bettenson, February 23, 1967, MLK-Reg.

20. E.M. Bettenson, letter to Dr. King, March 1, 1967, MLK-Reg.

21. E.M. Bettenson, letter to Dr. King, March 23, 1967, MLK-Reg.

22. Ashley, 'Press Release.'

23. E.M. Bettenson, letter to Dr. King, March 23, 1967, MLK-Reg.

24. Dora McDonald, telegram to E.M. Bettenson, September 2, 1967; E.M. Bettenson, telegram to Dora McDonald, September 13, 1967; E.M. Bettenson, letter to Dora McDonald, September 19, 1967, all MLK-Reg.

25. C.I.C Bosanquet, letter to Martin Luther King, Jr, October 2, 1967, MLK-Dup.

26. Martin Luther King, letter to Professor Hugh Watt, November 5, 1950, in Clayborne Carson, Ralph Luker, and Penny A. Russell (eds), *The Papers of Martin Luther King, Jr., Volume 1: Called to Serve, January 1929-June 1951* (Berkeley: University of California Press, 1992), pp.333-334.

27. James Douglas-Hamilton, letter to Martin Luther King, Jr., May 20, 1965, thekingcenter.org/archive/document/letter-edinburgh-university-debate-club-mlk. Accessed October 16, 2016. For Douglas-Hamilton's role in the Oxford Union debate series that featured Malcolm X, see Stephen Tuck, *The Night Malcolm X Spoke at the Oxford Union: A Transatlantic Story of Antiracist Protest* (Berkeley: University of California Press, 2014), pp.123-4, 126-7.

28. For King's arrest, trial and eventual imprisonment, see Garrow, *Bearing the Cross*, pp. 240-47, 579-80; Fairclough, *To Redeem the Soul of America*, pp.121-24; Branch, *At Canaan's Edge*, pp.649-650. See also, Martin Luther King, 'Letter from a Birmingham Jail,' April 12, 1963, in James M. Washington (ed.), *I Have a Dream: Writings and Speeches that Changed the World* (San Francisco: HarperSanFrancisco, 1992), pp.83-100.

29. C.I.C. Bosanquet, letter to Dora McDonald, November 1, 1967, MLK-VC.

30. Dora McDonald, letter to C.I.C. Bosanquet, November 1, 1967, MLK-VC. The original schedule for King's visit was outlined in C.I.C. Bosanquet, letter to Dr. M.L. King, October 2, 1967, MLK-VC.

31. E.M. Bettenson, letter to Mr. Wardle (Lord Mayor's secretary), November 3, 1967, MLK-Reg.

32. E.M. Bettenson, letter to Duke of Northumberland, November 4, 1967; Duke of Northumberland, letter to E.M. Bettenson, November 7, 1967, MLK-Reg.

33. Dora McDonald, letter to E.M.Bettenson, September 27, 1967, MLK-VC. The travel arrangements can be traced through C.I.C. Bosanquet to the Station Master, British Rail, November 2, 1967; R.W. Collier (British Rail Passenger Agent, Newcastle), letter to C.I.C. Bosanquet, November 4, 1967; Bosanquet's secretary, letter to Collier, November 6, 1967; C.I.C Bosanquet, letter to cashier, November 9, 1967; C.I.C. Bosanquet, letter to Dr. King, November 9, 1967, all MLK-VC.

34. Miss M. Sanderson, letter to G.R. Howe, esq., September 22, 1967, HCWF.

35. E.M Bettenson (Registrar) 'Special Honorary Degree Congregation on Monday, 13th November 1967, at 2.30pm, November 3, 1967. Distributed to All Members of Staff (including external members of Court, Council and Senate); Emeritus Professors; President of the Union Society,' November 3, 1967, HCWF. Originally the invitation was destined for President of the SRC, but handwritten note indicates that a 'Mrs McQ' (Mrs McQuillan) would invite the SRC President as Mace Bearer.

36. E.M. Bettenson, Invitation to Members of Senate, and Reply Slip, November 3, 1967, HCWF.

37. C.I.C Bosanquet, letter to C.B. Nicholson and Paul Brooks, November 2, 1967, MLK-VC; See also E.M. Bettenson, letter to C.B. Nicholson, November 3, 1967, MLK-Reg.

38. Paul Barry, interview with Space 2, April 2015, JtJOHP. C.B. Nicholson, letter to C.I.C Bosanquet, November 9, 1967, MLK-Dup.

39. E.M. Bettenson, memo to Mr. C.B. Nicholson, November 10, 1967, HCWF.

40. George R. Howe, memo: Special Honorary Degree Congregation, Monday 13th November, 1967, to Mr. Rickerby (c/o Messr Gray and Son [Robemakers] Ltd, Durham), November 3, 1967, HCWF.

41. George R. Howe, memo: Special Honorary Degree Congregation, Monday 13th November, 1967 at 2.30pm, to Miss Sanderson (bursar's office), November 3, 1967, HCWF.

42. George R. Howe, memo: Honorary Degree Congregation, Monday, 13th November, 1967, to Mr. J. Stapylton (Bedel), November 6, 1967, HCWF.

43. George R. Howe, memo: Honorary Degree Congregation, Monday, 13th November, 1967, to Professor Petch (Dept of Metallurgy), November 6, 1967, HCWF.

44. George R. Howe, memo: Special Honorary Degree Congregation, Monday 13th November, 1967, to Mr. Harris (estates), November 3, 1967, HCWF.

45. George R. Howe, memo: Special Honorary Degree Congregation, Monday 13th November, 1967, to Clerk of Works, November 3, 1967; George R. Howe memo: Congregation – 13th November 1967, to Clerk of Works, November 10, 1967, both HCWF.

46. George R. Howe, memo: Special Honorary Degree Congregation, Monday 13th November, 1967 at 2.30p.m., to Mr. McLaren, November 3, 1967, HFCW.

47. George R. Howe, memo: Special Honorary Degree Congregation, Monday 13th November, 1967, to Mr. Blair (heating engineer), November 3, 1967, HCWF.

48. "Today's Weather,' Journal, November 13, 1967, p.1; 'Notes for Mr. Saunders at Marshals Briefing at 1.45p.m. on Monday 13th November, 1967, n.d., HCWF.

49. Ibid. The seating arrangements are noted in 'Congregation, King's Hall – Seating Plan – Ground Floor,' n.d., HCWF. Keith Gregson, a student attendee at the November 13 ceremony, suggests that there was sufficient student demand that lots had to be drawn to get a place in the King's Hall. Although the University's documentation makes no reference to this process, and it did have provisional plans to deal with excess demand, it is possible that a late rush to attend the event necessitated an ad hoc balloting process. Keith Gregson, email to Lorna Fulton, December 7, 2016. Copy in possession of author.

50. 'Congregation, King's Hall – Seating Plan – Ground Floor.'

51. [George R. Howe], 'Special Congregation. 13 Nov 1967,' handwritten checklist, n.d., HCWF.

52. G.R. Howe, memo: Special Honorary Degree Congregation, Monday 13th November, 1967 at 2.30pm, November 3, 1967, to Mr McLaren (head porter), HCWF. Other documents detailing security and marshalling include, G(eorge).R. Howe (Chief Clerk), memo: Special Honorary Degree Congregation, Monday 13th November, 1967 to A.R. Peace (administration officer), HCWF; 'Notes for Mr. Saunders at Marshals Briefing at 1.45p.m'; J.K., 'University of Newcastle Congregation – 13th November, 1967, Information for Marshals, Draft,' November 7, HCWF.

53. 'Notes for Mr. Saunders at Marshals Briefing at 1.45p.m.'

54. Howe, memo to Peace.

55. Paul Barry and Meredyth Bell (née Patton), who attended both the coffee morning and the degree ceremony have spoken, respectively, of an 'entourage' and 'three bodyguards.' Paul Barry and Meredyth Bell, interviews with Space 2, April 2015, both JtJOHP. Laurence Kane, the Vice-Chancellor's steward, wrote in his diary that King was by 'two pte detectives (to whom I gave coffee…).' Laurence Kane Diary, November 13, 1967, copy in possession of author, kindly provided by Peter Kane.

56. C.I.C. Bosanquet, letter to Duke of Northumberland, October 3, 1967, MLK-VC. In the copy of this letter in the Vice-Chancellor's file, the words 'his son' have been crossed out and the 'King' after Andrew corrected to Young. However, in the copy sent to the Registrar for reference, the errors remain and were likely to have been in the version mailed to the Duke. See copy in MLK-Reg.

57. Dorothy Booth, letter to D.C. Foster, March 1992 (copy in possession of the author).

58. Jimmy Carter, 'Remarks at the Newcastle Civic Centre,' May 6, 1977, *Public Papers of Presidents of the United States: Jimmy Carter, 1977: Book One - January 20 – June 24, 1977* (Washington: US Government Printing Office, 1977) pp.811-813. 'The Day Wor Jimmy Won Geordie's Heart,' *Journal*, May 7, 1977, p1; 'Howay the Lads, Says President,' ibid., p.3

59. Kane, Diary, November 13, 1967. Peter Kane, email correspondence with Brian Ward, October 13, 2016 and November 6, 2016. Copies in possession of the author.

60. Mr. G.R. Howe, memo: Bookings for King's Hall, to Miss Sanderson, Bursar's Office, November 14, 1967, HCWF.

Chapter Two: 'Barbs and Arrows':
Explaining Martin Luther King's Decision to Come

1. David Bilk, letter to Martin Luther King, October 5, 1966, KCA, thekingcenter.org/archive/document/lecture-tour-request-david-bilk-mlk. Accessed December 5, 2016.

2. Martin Luther King, letter to David Bilk, February 7, 1967, KCA, thekingcenter.org/archive/document/letter-mlk-david-bilk.Accessed December 5, 2016.

3. Bilk, letter to King.

4. Dora McDonald, letter to E.M. Bettenson, September 27, 1967, MLK-Reg.

5. David Garrow, *Bearing the Cross: Martin Luther King, Jr., and the Southern Christian Leadership Conference* (New York: William Morrow and Company, 1986), pp.579-80.

6. Martin Luther King, quoted in *Courier*, November 15, 1967, p.1. The details of King's activities during this period are drawn from Taylor Branch, *At Canaan's Edge: America in the King Years, 1965-68* (New York: Simon & Schuster, 2006), pp.648-656; Garrow, *Bearing the Cross*, pp.579-81; Adam Fairclough, *To Redeem the Soul of America: The Southern Christian Leadership Conference and Martin Luther King, Jr.* (Athens, Ga.: University of Georgia Press, 1987), pp.352-53.

7. As was often the case, King's oration of his November 11, 1967 speech departed from the written text and the Chicago audience never heard the section on British Labour Party responses to Vietnam. For the written text see, Martin Luther King, 'The Domestic Impact of the War in America,' November 11, 1967, KCA, thekingcenter.org/archive/document/domestic-impact-war-america. For audio and transcript of King's actual speech, see Martin Luther King, 'Domestic Impact of the War,' aavw.org/special_features/speeches_speech_king03.html. Both accessed December 6, 2016. For Labour Party policy on Vietnam see Sylvia Ellis, *Britain, America and the Vietnam War* (Westport: Prager, 2004) and Jonathan Colman, *A 'Special Relationship'? Harold Wilson, Lyndon B. Johnson and Anglo-American Relations 'at the Summit', 1964-68* (Manchester: Manchester University Press, 2004).

8. Dorothy Booth, letter to D.C. Foster, March 1992 (copy in possession of author).

9. For the history and impact of the Watts riots, see Gerald Horne, *The Fire this Time: The Watts Uprising and the 1960s* (Charlottesville: University of Virginia Press, 1996).

10. For the rise of black power, see Peniel E. Joseph, *Waiting 'til the Midnight Hour: A Narrative History of Black Power in America*, (New York: Henry Holt and Co, 2006); Jeffrey Ogbar, *Black Power: Radical Politics and African American Identity* (Baltimore: Johns Hopkins University Press, 2004).

11. James R. Ralph, *Northern Protest: Martin Luther King, Jr., Chicago, and the Civil Rights Movement* (Cambridge, MA: Harvard University Press, 1993).

12. In 1962, King had insisted that 'no Christian can be a communist,' but urged his congregation to think of communist critiques of inequality as a source of inspiration for 'a Christianity that has been all too passive and a democracy that has been all too inert.' Martin Luther King, 'Sermon at Ebenezer Baptist Church,' September 30 1962, kingencyclopedia.stanford.edu/encyclopedia/documentsentry/can_a_christian_be_a_communist_30_sept_1962.1.html. Accessed March 4, 2017.

13. Martin Luther King, 'Address to 11th Annual SCLC Convention, August 16, 1967,' kinginstitute.stanford.edu/king-papers/documents/where-do-we-go-here-delivered-11th-annual-sclc-convention. Accessed January 9, 2017.

14. Martin Luther King, 'Message from the President,' Remarks to SCLC Annual Conference, October 11-13, 1960, Clayborne Carson, Tenisha Armstrong, Susan Carson, Adrienne Clay, and Kieran Taylor (eds), *The Papers of Martin Luther King, Volume V: Threshold of a New Decade, January 1959 - December 1960* (Berkeley: University of California Press, 2005), p.517.

15. Martin Luther King, 'Speech to SCLC Staff, November 14, 1966,' KCA, thekingcenter.org/archive/document/mlk-speech-sclc-staff-retreat#. Accessed January 8, 2017. Garrow, *Bearing the Cross*, pp.581-82. The sharpest analysis of King's relationship to Marxist theory and democratic socialism is in Fairclough, *To Redeem the Soul*, pp.357-383. See also Adam Fairclough, 'Was Martin Luther King a Marxist?' *History Workshop* 15 (Spring 1983), pp.117-125. For the Poor People's Campaign, see Gerald McKnight, *The Last Crusade: Martin Luther King, Jr., the FBI, and the Poor People's Campaign* (New York: Basic Books, 1998).

16. Martin Luther King, 'Notes on American Capitalism,' n.d., 1951, in Clayborne Carson, Ralph Luker, and Penny A. Russell (eds), *The Papers of Martin Luther King, Jr. Volume I: Called to Serve, January 1929-June 1951* (Berkeley: University of California Press, 1992), pp.435-436.

17. For the split with Johnson, see Sylvia Ellis, *Freedom's Pragmatist: Lyndon Johnson and Civil Rights* (Gainesville: University Press of Florida, 2013), pp.235-238, 254-256. For the FBI campaigns against King, see Kenneth O'Reilly, *Racial Matters: The FBI's Secret File on Black America* (New York: Free Press, 1989), pp. 121-155, 242-245, 286-291.

18. For King's increasingly isolated and embattled position, see Garrow, *Bearing the Cross*, pp. 474-525, 537-74; Richard Lentz, *Symbols, the Newsmagazines and Martin Luther King* (Baton Rouge: Louisiana State University Press, 1990), pp.308-337; Fairclough, *To Redeem the Soul*, pp.309-331, 333-45; Adam Fairclough, 'Martin Luther King and the War in Vietnam,' *Phylon*, 45 (1983-84), pp.19-39.

19. Martin Luther King, quoted in Garrow, *Bearing the Cross*, p.587. For a useful discussion of King's growing sense of guilt and insecurity, see ibid., pp. 587-588.

20. D.E. King, quoted in ibid., p.580.

21. Ibid., pp.577-78; Coretta Scott King, *My Life With Martin Luther King, Jr.* (New York: Holt, Rinehart and Winston, 1969), p.308.

22. Andrew Young, quoted in Howell Raines, *My Soul is Rested* (c.1977, London: Penguin, 1983), p.431.

23. Joan Baez, quoted in Garrow, *Bearing the Cross*, p.578.

24. Coretta Scott King, quoted in 'Why Dr. M.L. King Jr., Entered an Atlanta Hospital,' *Jet*, October 29, 1964, p.23. See also, Coretta Scott King, *My Life*, pp.14-18.

25. Garrow, *Bearing the Cross*, pp.354-55.

26. David Levering Lewis, *King: A Biography* (Chicago: University of Illinois Press, 1970), pp.262-63.

27. Martin Luther King, 'The Three Dimensions of a Complete Life,' speech at St. Paul's Cathedral, London, December 6, 1964, quoted in Thomas A. Mulhall, *A Lasting Prophetic Legacy: Martin Luther King, Jr., The World Council of Churches and the Global Crusade against Racism and War* (Eugene, OR: Wipf and Stock, 2014), p.50. It is sometimes erroneously claimed that King was the first non-Anglican to preach in St. Paul's since its foundation 300 years earlier. In 1950, George MacLeod, a Presbyterian minister in the Church of Scotland, may have had that honour. See, Ron Ferguson, *George MacLeod: Founder of the Iona Community* (Glasgow: Wild Goose Publications, 2001), p.253. For

King's growing sense of his international role and the impact of global forces on his thinking, see Thomas F. Jackson, *From Civil Rights to Human Rights: Martin Luther King, Jr., and the Struggle for Economic Justice* (Philadelphia: University of Pennsylvania Press, 2007); Thomas A. Mulhall, 'On Racism and War as Global Phenomena: Martin Luther King, Jr. and the World Council of Churches,' in Lewis V. Baldwin and Paul R. Dekar (eds), *'In an Inescapable Network of Mutuality: Martin Luther King, Jr. and the Globalization of an Ethical Ideal* (Eugene, OR: Cascade, 2013), pp.91-105.

28. Martin Luther King, 'Speech at City Temple Hall,' London, December 7, 1964, Pacifica Radio, 'Exclusive: Newly Discovered 1964 MLK Speech on Civil Rights, Segregation & Apartheid South Africa,' January 19. 2015, democracynow.org/2015/1/19/exclusive_newly_discovered_1964_mlk_speech. Accessed November 28, 2016.

29. King, 'Speech at City Temple Hall.'

30. *DM*, Dec 8, 1964, p.4.

31. 'Britain's Coloured Leaders Join Forces,' ibid., February 12, 1965, p.7.

32. Kalbir Shukra, *The Changing Pattern of Black Politics in Britain* (London: Pluto, 1998), p.19. For the history of CARD see, ibid., pp.19-26; Benjamin W. Heinemann, *The Politics of the Powerless: A Study of the Campaign Against Racial Discrimination* (Oxford: Oxford University Press, 1972).

33. Martin Luther King, 'A Christian Movement in a Revolutionary Age,' September 28, 1965, KCA, thekingcenter.org/archive/document/christian-movement-revolutionary-age. Accessed January 9, 2017.

34. Martin Luther King, 'Acceptance Speech on Receipt of an Honorary Doctorate in Civil Law from the University of Newcastle upon Tyne,' November 13, 1967, MLK-Reg. On arrival in Heathrow, King had told journalists that 'I am very honoured to receive a degree from an English University because of the great educational tradition of the United Kingdom and of all that it has done to enrich the cultural life of the world.' 'Luther King Warns Britain,' *MS*, November 13 1967, p.3.

35. Martin Luther King, 'Statement Regarding the Nobel Peace Prize,' October 14, 1964, KCA, thekingcenter.org/archive/document/statement-mlk-regarding-nobel-peace-prize. Accessed January 9, 2017.

36. King, 'Acceptance Speech.'

37. Andrew Young, quoted in *A King's Speech - Martin Luther King on Tyneside*, BBC North East, 2014. See also, 'Martin Luther King: Americans Shown 'lost' Newcastle Speech,' BBC News, June 1, 2014, bbc.co.uk/news/uk-england-tyne-27602173. Accessed November 29, 2016.

38. Martin Luther King, letter to C.I.C. Bosanquet, January 30, 1968, MLK-VC.

39. Arguments that King was rather limited as an original theological thinker were subsequently reinforced by the discovery that he had plagiarised sections of his Boston University PhD. The discovery and its implications are discussed in 'Becoming Martin Luther King, Jr.: Plagiarism and Originality, A Round Table,' *Journal of American History*, 78, 1 (1991), pp.11-119.

40. Ralph Holland, letter to Brian Ward, March 19, 1992. Copy in possession of author.

41. 'Speech delivered by the Public Orator (J.H. Burnett) when presenting a candidate (Martin Luther King) for an honorary degree at a Congregation in King's Hall on Monday, 13th November 1967' (Newcastle, June 1968), MLK-Reg. Walter Rauschenbusch was one of the leading figures in the social gospel movement dedicated to making Christianity a force for progressive social reform, a viewpoint with which King clearly

sympathised. While he had some disagreements with the opinions of late 18th and early 19th Century German philosopher Georg Wilhelm Friedrich Hegel, King was attracted to the notion that positive change could come through struggle in which opposites and extremes are reconciled to produce a new synthesis. As King wrote of his commitment to nonviolence, 'Like the synthesis in Hegelian philosophy, the principle of nonviolent resistance seeks to reconcile the truths of two opposites—acquiescence and violence—while avoiding the extremes and immoralities of both.' Martin Luther King, *Stride Towards Freedom* (New York: Harper & Brothers, 1958), p.213.

Chapter Three: 'What Your Movement is Doing is Right': Reactions to Martin Luther King and the Early Civil Rights Movement on Tyneside

1. C.L.R. James, letter on meeting Dr. Martin Luther King, Jr., March 25, 1957, reprinted in *Urgent Tasks*, 12 (Summer 1981), Sojourner Truth Organization Archives, sojournertruth.net/letters.html. Accessed January 22, 2017. James also wrote to King after the meeting sending him a copy of *Black Jacobins*, his book on the Haitian Revolution, and asking that he forward it to legendary jazz trumpeter Louis Armstrong once he had read it. C.L.R. James, letter to Martin Luther King, April 5, 1957, in Clayborne Carson, Susan Carson, Adrienne Clay, Virginia Shadron, and Kieran Taylor, (eds) *The Papers of Martin Luther King, Jr. Volume IV: Symbol of the Movement, January 1957-December 1958* (Berkeley: University of California Press. 2000), p.150.

2. *Times*, October 30, 1961, p.11; ibid., December 7, 1964, p.6. Martin Luther King, letter to Dr. Martin Fischer, September 28, 1964, KCA, thekingcenter.org/archive/document/letter-mlk-dr-martin-fischer-theological-seminary-berlin. Accessed November 28, 2016. Aside from the awards from Berlin and Newcastle, the only other overseas honorary doctorate accepted by King during his lifetime was from the Amsterdam Free University in 1965.

3. Alistair Cooke, 'The Ordeal of the South IV – The Boycott City,' *Guardian*, May 15, 1956, p.6; Harvey Lee Moon, 'The Negro and the South: Letter to the Editor,' ibid., July 3, 1956, p.6. Cooke replied, rather defensively, to Moon's accusations in 'A Reporter's Observations,' ibid., July 3, 1956, p.6. Officially the paper was still known as *The Manchester Guardian* until 1959 but it was a major national daily newspaper.

4. *Letter from America*, quoted in Nick Clarke, *Alistair Cooke: The Biography* (London: Weidenfeld & Nicolson, 1999), p.317.

5. 'Southern Revolt,' *The Crisis*, May 1956, p.280.

6. While we still await an authoritative account of British press, popular and governmental responses to the US civil rights and black power movements, that literature is slowly growing in quantity and quality. See, Anne-Marie Angelo, 'The Black Panthers in London, 1967-1972: A Diasporic Struggle Navigates the Black Atlantic,' *Radical History Review*, 103 (Winter 2009), pp.17-35; Brian Dooley, *Black and Green: The Fight For Civil Rights in Northern Ireland & Black America* (London: Pluto, 1998); Robin D.G. Kelley and Stephen Tuck (eds), *The Other Special Relationship: Race, Rights, and Riots in Britain and the United States* (New York: Palgrave Macmillan, 2015); Mike Sewell, 'British Responses to Martin Luther King, Jr and the Civil Rights Movement, 1954-1968,' in Brian Ward and Tony

Badger (eds), *The Making of Martin Luther King and the Civil Rights Movement* (Basingstoke: Macmillan, 1996), pp.194-212; Marika Sherwood, *Malcolm X Visits Abroad: April 1964 - February 1965* (Faversham: Savannah Press, 2010); Joe Street, 'Malcolm X, Smethwick and the Influence of the African American Freedom Struggle on British Race Relations,' *Journal of Black Studies*, 38, 6, (2008), pp.932-950; Stephen Tuck, *The Night Malcolm X Spoke at the Oxford Union: A Transatlantic Story of Antiracist Protest* (Berkeley: University of California Press, 2014); Robin D.G. Kelley and Stephen Tuck, (eds), *The Other Special Relationship: Race, Rights, and Riots in Britain and the United States* (London: Palgrave Macmillan, 2016); Stephen Tuck, 'The March on London: British-American Connections during the Civil Rights Movement,' *Bulletin of the German Historical Institute*, Supplement 11, (2015), pp.81-97; Clive Webb, 'Reluctant Partners: African Americans and the Origins of the Special Relationship,' *Journal of Transatlantic Studies*, 14, 14 (2016), pp.350-364.

7. Stanley Burch, 'The Bewildered Millions of Black America,' *DM*, February 23, 1965, p.8.

8. Alistair Cooke, 'No Unity on Negro Strategy in the Struggle over Civil Rights,' *Guardian*, August 23, 1966, p.9.

9. *E-Chronicle*, October 28, 1961, p.2.

10. 'Down in Dixie They Just Couldn't Believe it... ibid' May 18, 1954, p.13; 'Southern States Oppose Court Ruling,' *Sunderland Echo and Shipping Gazette*, May 18, 1954, p.4.

11. 'Two Buses Fired on as 'Jim Crow Law' is Ended,' *E-Chronicle*, December 27, 1956, p.18.

12. 'Pastor's Call to U.S. Negroes,' *Northern Daily Mail* (West Hartlepool), March 26, 1956, p.7.

13. 'Little Rock's Troops Stay On, Says Governor,' *E-Chronicle*, December 11, 1957, p.3.

14. 'Little Rock: Ike Acts,' *Journal*, August 25, 1958, p.1.

15. 'Race Riot Flares in Britain,' ibid., August 25, 1958, p.1; 'Britain 'Divided by Racial Tensions',' ibid., September 1, 1958, p.3. For more on transatlantic coverage of Little Rock, see, Kennetta Hammond Perry, ''Little Rock' in Britain: Jim Crow's Transatlantic Topographies,' *Journal of British Studies*, 51, 1 (January 2012), pp.155-177.

16. 'Whites, Negroes Reach an Agreement,' *Journal*, May 11, 1963, p.1.

17. Paul Barry, interview with Space 2, April 2015, JtJOHP.

18. 'Freedom Carnival,' *Journal*, August 29, 1963, p.1.

19. 'Negro Marchers Defy Court,' ibid., March 10, 1965, p.1.

20. 'Negroes Defy Marching Ban,' and 'Officer's Wore K.K.K. Costumes,' both ibid., March 11, 1965, p.5.

21. 'Beaten-Up Minister Dies-Four Charged,' *E-Chronicle*, March 12, 1965, p.1; 'Beaten-up Minister Dies,' *Journal*, March 12, 1965, p.1.

22. 'LBJ Brings in 'Voted for All' Bill,' *E-Chronicle*, March 16, 1965, pp.1/7.

23. 'Johnson Acts to Protect Marchers,' ibid., March 20, 1965, p.1.

24. 'Selma Marathon,' *Journal*, March 22, 1965, p.1. Also 'Selma Marchers are cut to 300,' ibid., March 23, 1965, p.1.

25. '15,000 Complete the Selma Freedom March,' ibid., March 26, 1965, p.1; 'War Against Klan,' ibid., March 27 1965, p.1; 'White Mother Shot Dead in Alabama,' *E-Chronicle*, March 26, 1965, p.1.

26. 'War against Klan'; 'Marchers Plan Murder Protest,' ibid., March 27, 1965, p.1; 'Washington to Probe Ku Klux Klan,' *Journal*, March 31, 1965, p.1.

27. Eric Burdon, quoted in Chris Phipps, John Tobler and Sid Smith (eds), *Northstars* (Newcastle upon Tyne: Zymurgy Publishing, 2005), p.16.

28. Eric Burdon, interview with Brian Ward, Philadelphia, February 15, 2006. Copy in possession of author.

29. Eric Burdon with J. Marshall Craig, *Don't Let Me Be Misunderstood* (New York: Thunder's Mouth Press, 2001), p.55; John Steel, quoted in Sean Egan, *Animal Tracks: The Story of the Animals: Newcastle's Rising Sons* (London: Helter Skelter, 2001), p.62.

30. Eric Burdon, quoted in, Phipps, Tobler and Smith, *Northstars*, p.16.

31. Ibid., p.14.

32. For more on attitudes towards race and US race relations among British blues revivalists, see Christian O'Connell, *Blues, How Do You Do?: Paul Oliver and the Transatlantic Story of the Blues* (Ann Arbor: University of Michigan Press, 2015).

33. Eric Burdon, 'An 'Animal' Views America,' *Ebony*, 22 (December 1966), pp.166-171 (first quote, p.166; second quote, p.168). For more on how Burdon's generation of musicians responded to the US South and its race relations, see Brian Ward, "By Elvis and All the Saints': Images of the American South in the World of 1950s British Popular Music,' in Joseph Patrick Ward (ed.), *Britain and the American South: From Colonialism to Rock and Roll* (Jackson: University of Mississippi Press, 2003), pp.187-214.

34. *Melody Maker*, July 4, 1964, p.8; Burdon, 'An 'Animal' Views America,' p.168; Egan, *Animal Tracks*, p.133; Burdon interview.

35. *New Musical Express*, July 24, 1964, p.14.

36. Burdon, 'An 'Animal' Views America,' p.168.

37. Burdon, *Misunderstood*, pp.57-58 (quote p.58); Eric Burdon, *I Used to be an Animal, But I'm Alright Now* (London: Faber and Faber, 1986), pp.95-96. See also, Brian Ward, 'That White Man, Burdon: The Animals, Race and the American South' in Jill Terry and Neil A. Wynn (eds), *Transatlantic Roots Music: Folk, Blues and National Identities* (Jackson: University of Mississippi Press, 2012), pp.153-178.

38. Margaret Blenkinsop, letter to Martin Luther King Jr., n.d. (received August 19, 1965), KCA, thekingcenter.org/archive/document/letter-british-high-school-student-mlk.

39. Dr. Brian Lishman, interview with Murphy Cobbing, for *Martin Luther King: A King's Speech*, BBC Radio Newcastle, broadcast, January 1, 2013. Lishman would go on to serve as President of the Newcastle University Union Society. See, 'Unpopular Presidents,' *Courier*, February 5, 1969, p.1.

40. Martin Luther King, quoted in ibid., November 15, 1967, p.1 (first quote); *E-Chronicle*, November 13, 1967, p.3 (second quote).

Chapter Four: 'We Do Not Have a Copy': Martin Luther King's Lost Newcastle Speech

1. Dora McDonald, letter to E.M. Bettenson, September 27, 1967, MLK-Reg; C.I.C. Bosanquet to Martin Luther King, October 3, 1967, MLK-VC.

2. Rev. B. Ingliss-Evans, letter to C.I.C. Bosanquet, November 7, 1967; Alan Booth, letter to C.I.C. Bosanquet, November 7, 1967; R.H. Pain, letter to C.I.C. Bosanquet, November 6, 1967; MLK-VC.

3. C.I.C. Bosanquet, letter to Rev. B. Ingliss-Evans, November 10, 1967, MLK-VC.

4. C.I.C. Bosanquet, letter to R.H. Pain, November 9, 1967, MLK-VC.

5. C.I.C. Bosanquet, letter to Martin Luther King, November 9, 1967, MLK-VC.

6. *Vice-Chancellor's Report, 1967-68* (Newcastle: University of Newcastle upon Tyne, 1968), p.9.

7. See Henry Miller, Vice-Chancellor, letter to Miss B. Mellor, September 1, 1975, MLK-VC.

8. The footage is now curated by the North East Film Archive. northeastfilmarchive.com/videos/19445/martin-luther-king-honorary-degree-ceremony-newcastle-university. Accessed January 9, 2017. Laurence Kane also noted in his diary that there was coverage of the degree ceremony on Tyne Tees that evening. Laurence Kane Diary, November 13, 1967, copy in possession of author, kindly provided by Peter Kane.

9. The newly recovered 1 minute 48 second fragment of King's interview with Clyde Alleyne, probably an un-broadcast portion of the interview, was revealed to the public on November 1, 2016. It can be viewed at, British Film Institute, player.bfi.org.uk/film/watch-13-november-1967-martin-luther-king-interview-1967/. See also, Kris Jepson, 'Rare Footage of Martin Luther King in the North East, itv.com/news/tyne-tees/2016-11-01/rare-footage-of-martin-luther-king-in-the-north-east/. All accessed November 23, 2016.

10. 'English TV Gets First Negro Announcer,' *Jet*, May 11, 1967, p.11. See also, Antony Brown, *Tyne-Tees Television: The First 20 Years* (Newcastle: Tyne-Tees Publishing, 1978), p.23.

11. Stephen Tuck outlines some of the US coverage of British race relations in the 1950s and 1960s, and makes a case for the reciprocal influence of overseas travel on key US civil rights figures in 'Malcolm X's Visit to Oxford University: U.S. Civil Rights, Black Britain and the Special Relationship on Race,' *American Historical Review*, 118, 1 (2013), pp.76-103 (especially pp. pp.91-98).

12. 'Great Day for Freedom Fighter,' *Courier*, November 15, 1967, p.1.

13. Martin Luther King, 'Acceptance Speech on Receipt of an Honorary Doctorate at the University of Newcastle upon Tyne,' November 13, 1967, MLK-Reg. Martin Luther King, 'Speech at City Temple Hall,' December 7, 1964, Pacifica Radio, 'Exclusive: Newly Discovered 1964 MLK Speech on Civil Rights, Segregation & Apartheid South Africa,' January 19, 2015, democracynow.org/2015/1/19/exclusive_newly_discovered_1964_mlk_speech. Accessed January 9, 2017.

14. Martin Luther King, 'Facing the Challenge of a New Age,' *Phylon*, XVIII, 1 (1957), reprinted in James W. Washington (ed.), *A Testament of Hope: The Essential Writings and Speeches of Martin Luther King, Jr.* (New York: HarperCollins, 1990), p.142. Martin Luther King, 'The American Dream,' Commencement Address, Lincoln University, June 6, 1961, KCA, thekingcenter.org/archive/document/american-dream; Martin Luther King, speech to Cornell College, October 15, 1962, news.cornellcollege.edu/dr-martin-luther-kings-visit-to-cornell-college/. Both accessed January 9, 2017. This is an illustrative, not exhaustive list of the many times King used variants on this phrase.

15. Martin Luther King, 'Speech to SCLC Staff, November 14, 1966,' KCA, thekingcenter.org/archive/document/mlk-speech-sclc-staff-retreat#. Accessed January 8, 2017.

16. Martin Luther King, quoted in 'Great Day for Freedom Fighter,' *Courier*, November 15, 1967, p.1.

17. Martin Luther King, 'Where Do We Go From Here?' Address to 11th Annual Convention, SCLC, Atlanta, August 16, 1967,

stanford.edu/group/King/publications/speeches/Where_do_we_go_from_here.html. Accessed November 29, 2016.

18. King, 'Speech to SCLC Staff, November 14, 1966'; Martin Luther King, 'Acceptance Speech.' Lewis Baldwin points out that King expressed similar sentiments and used much the same phrasing in an address to the Chicago staff of the SCLC's Operation Breadbasket in March 1967 and again in his 1968 'Testament of Hope' speech. See, Lewis V. Baldwin, *The Voice of Conscience: The Church in the Mind of Martin Luther King, Jr.* (New York: Oxford University Press, 2010), p.313, n.114.

19. King, 'Speech to SCLC Staff, November 14, 1966'; King, 'Acceptance Speech.'

20. Ibid.; 'Great Day for Freedom Fighter.'

21. King, 'Speech to SCLC Staff, November 14, 1966.'

22. King, 'Acceptance Speech.' Martin Luther King, 'America's Chief Moral Dilemma,' Address to the Hungry Club of Atlanta, May 10, 1967, KCA, thekingcenter.org/archive/document/americas-chief-moral-dilemma. Accessed January 9, 2017.

23. Martin Luther King, 'Advice for Living,' *Ebony*, December 1957, p.120.

24. Canon John L. Collins, letter to Martin Luther King, (n.d.; Received, January 20, 1964), KCA, thekingcenter.org/archive/document/letter-campaign-nuclear-disarmament-mlk. Accessed January 9, 2017.

25. Peggy Duff, letter to Martin Luther King, April 28, 1967, KCA, thekingcenter.org/archive/document/letter-peggy-duff-mlk-1. Accessed January 9, 2017.

26. Peggy Duff, letter to Martin Luther King, May 4, 1967, KCA, thekingcenter.org/archive/document/letter-peggy-duff-mlk-2. Accessed January 9, 2017. This letter bears a handwritten note, 'Answered by phone 5-26.'

27. Peggy Duff, letter to Martin Luther King, May 31, 1967, KCA, thekingcenter.org/archive/document/letter-peggy-duff-mlk-3. Accessed January 9, 2017.

28. Peggy Duff, letter to Martin Luther King, September 13, 1967, KCA, thekingcenter.org/archive/document/letter-peggy-duff-mlk-0. Duff wrote again to ask King if he would sign an 'Appeal to Stop the Bombing' to President Johnson. Peggy Duff, letter to Martin Luther King, September 21, 1967, thekingcenter.org/archive/document/letter-peggy-duff-mlk. Both accessed January 9, 2017.

29. 'Johnson Should Admit Mistake – Luther King,' *MS*, November 14, 1967, p.3.

30. 'Debate,' *Courier*, October 27, 1965, p.3; Chris Payne, 'Student Political Awareness,' ibid., November 11, 1965, p.6. See also, Sylvia Ellis, 'A Demonstration of British Good Sense?: British Student Protest During the Vietnam War,' in Gerard DeGroot (ed.), *Student Protest: The Sixties and After* (London: Longman, 1998), pp.54-69.

31. Fiona Clarke, quoted in, Anna Flowers and Vanessa Histon (eds), *It's My Life!: 1960s Newcastle* (Newcastle upon Tyne: Tyne Bridge Publishing, 2009), p.158.

32. King, 'Acceptance Speech'; King, 'America's Chief Moral Dilemma.'

33. Dorothy Booth, letter to D.C. Foster, March 1992 (copy in possession of the author). Charles Bosanquet, 'Address at the Memorial Service for Dr. Martin Luther King,' April 26, 1968, MLK-VC. Ken Jack, letter to Brian Ward, March 13, 1992 (copy in possession of the author).

34. Boris Kidel, 'Hoover Attacks a 'liar named Luther',' *DM*, November 20, 1964, p.2.

35. Mr. E(dwin) A.F. Fenwick, letter to Bosanquet, November 14, 1967; C.I.C. Bosanquet, letter to Mr. Fenwick, November 16, 1967, MLK-VC.

36. Peter H. Woodhead, 'A Retrospective of 13th November 1967,' n.d. (copy in possession of the author).

37. Meredyth Bell, interview with Space 2, April 2015, JtJOHP.

38. Paul Barry, interview with Space 2, April 2015, JtJOHP. For coverage of the Anti-Apartheid campaign against the South African rugby tour, see, 'Support for Rugby Tourists,' *Courier*, November 22, 1967, p.1; 'Rugby Tour – Protests Fail,' ibid. December 6, 1967, p.1; 'Tour Protest Today,' ibid., January 31, 1968; 'Durham Joins Varsity in Apartheid Protest,' ibid., February 7, 1968, p.12.

39. Kasim Reed and Raphael Warnock, both quoted in 'Martin Luther King: Americans Shown 'Lost' Newcastle Speech,' BBC News, June 1 2014, bbc.co.uk/news/uk-england-tyne-27602173. Accessed November 30, 2016.

Part Two: Local Contexts, Global Connections

Chapter Five: Deep Roots:
Slavery, Race and Radicalism in the North East to 1833

1. There is a vast literature on the sources and nature of British and international 'radicalism' from the 17th to 20th centuries. Much of it is concerned with parsing definitions and identifying doctrinal and tactical differences among a wide range of putatively 'radical', 'reformist' and 'revolutionary' groups who challenged an equally diverse set of social, economic and political norms. See, Eugenio F. Biagini (ed.), *Citizenship and Community: Liberals, Radicals and Collective Identities in the British Isles, 1865-1931* (Cambridge: Cambridge University Press, 1996); Michael T. Davis and Paul A. Pickering (eds), *Unrespectable Radicals: Popular Politics in the Age of Reform* (Aldershot: Ashgate, 2008); J.R. Dinwiddy, *Radicalism and Reform in Britain, 1780-1850* (London: Hambledon, 1992); Laurent Curelly and Nigel Smith (eds), *Radical Voices, Radical Ways: Articulating and Disseminating Radicalism in Seventeenth- and Eighteenth-Century Britain* (Manchester: Manchester University Press, 2016); D.G. Wright, *Popular Radicalism: The Working-Class Experience, 1780-1880* (1988; Abingdon: Routledge, 2013). For an introduction to Tyneside radicalism, see, Joan Allen, *Joseph Cowen and Popular Radicalism on Tyneside 1829–1900* (Monmouth: Merlin Press, 2007); W.L. Burn, 'Newcastle upon Tyne in the Early Nineteenth Century,' *Archaeologia Aeliana*, 4th Series, 34 (1956), pp.1-13; Peter Cadogan, *Early Radical Newcastle* (Consett: Sagittarius Press, 1975); H. T. Dickinson, *Radical Politics in the North East of England in the Later Eighteenth Century* (Durham: Durham County Local History Society, 1979); T.J. Nossiter, *Influence, Opinion and Political Idioms in Reformed England: Case Studies from the North East, 1832-1871* (Brighton: Harvester Press, 1978); and Kathleen Wilson, *The Sense of the People: Politics, Culture and Imperialism in Britain, 1715-1785* (Cambridge: Cambridge University Press, 1998), pp.287-311, 315-375.

2. John Charlton, *Hidden Chains: The Slavery Business and North East England, 1600-1865* (Newcastle: Tyne Bridge Publishing, 2008), p.140.

3. Ibid., pp.99-107, 119-146.

4. Ibid., pp.108-118; Graeme J. Milne, *North East England, 1850-1914: The Dynamics of a Maritime Industrial Region* (Woodbridge, UK: Boydell Press, 2006), p.161.

5. Charlton, *Hidden Chains*, pp.19-20, 140-146.

6. For Quakers, race, and slavery, see Brycchan Carey and Geoffrey Plank (eds), *Quakers and Slavery* (Urbana-Champaign: University of Illinois Press, 2014); Donna McDaniel and

Venessa Julye, *Fit for Freedom, Not for Friendship: Quakers, African Americans and the Myth of Racial Justice* (Philadelphia: Quaker Press, 2009).

7. Kirstin Olsen, *Daily Life in 18th Century England* (Westport, CT: Greenwood, 1999), pp.6-7.

8. Wilson, *Sense of the People*, p.340.

9. Derek Benjamin Heater, *Citizenship in Britain: A History* (Edinburgh: Edinburgh University Press, 2006), pp.33-34. See also, Pauline Gregg, *Free Born John – The Biography of John Lilburne* (1961; repr. London: Phoenix Press, 2000).

10. 'From Our Yearly-Meeting, Philadelphia and New Jersey, July 21-27, 1737, to the Quarterly and Monthly Meetings,' p.3, The Society of Friends, Minutes of Yearly Epistles and Advice from the London Meetings. 1714-1820, MF210, TWA.

11. 'The Epistle from the Yearly-Meeting, London, May 15-20, 1758,' p.3, The Society of Friends, Minutes of Yearly Epistles, MF210, TWA. See also, Geoffrey Plank, *John Woolman's Path to the Peaceable Kingdom* (Philadelphia: University of Pennsylvania Press, 2012), pp.103-120; Patricia Hix, 'American and North East England's Quaker Anti-Slavery Networks,' *North East History*, 39 (2008), pp.25-44.

12. Eneas Mackenzie, 'Protestant Dissent: Chapels and Meeting-Houses,' in *A Descriptive and Historical Account of Newcastle-Upon-Tyne Including the Borough of Gateshead* (Newcastle-upon-Tyne: Mackenzie and Dent, 1827), pp.370-414, *British History Online*, british-history.ac.uk/no-series/newcastle-historical-account/pp370-414. Accessed January 10, 2017.

13. Charlton, *Hidden Chains*, p.160. Sharp's pioneering work is noted in, *Declaration of the Objects of the Newcastle Upon Tyne Society for the Abolition of Slavery All Over the World*, (Newcastle upon Tyne: J. Blackwell & Co., 1836), p.5, Tracts 042/4, v.470, n.18, L&P.

14. Seymour Drescher, *Capitalism and Antislavery: British Mobilization in Comparative Perspective* (New York: Oxford University Press, 1987), pp.130-1. Here Drescher uses 'abolitionism' generically to include opposition to both the slave trade and support for emancipation – even though not all those opposed to the continuation of the slave trade were committed to immediate, or even gradual, emancipation of the enslaved. The class-profile of non-conformist and or dissenting traditions continues to be hotly debated by historians. See, Michael R. Watts, *The Dissenters: Volume Three: The Crisis and Conscience of Nonconformity* (Oxford: Oxford University Press, 2015). Watts argues that Wesleyans on Tyneside were largely working-class (p.121).

15. A.W. Purdue, *Newcastle: The Biography* (Stroud, UK: Amberley, 2011), pp.174-175. See also, C.M. Fraser and K. Emsley, *Tyneside* (Newton Abbot: David & Charles, 1973), pp.44-126; Joyce Ellis, "The 'Black Indies': The Economic Development of Newcastle, c.1700-1840,' in Robert Colls and Bill Lancaster, (eds), *Newcastle upon Tyne: A Modern History* (Chichester: Phillimore, 2001), pp.1-26.

16. P.M. Ashraf, *The Life and Times of Thomas Spence* (Newcastle upon Tyne: Frank Graham, 1983), especially pp.28-33 on the radicalising influence of the Town Moor quarrel.

17. Michael Scrivener, *Seditious Allegories: John Thelwell and Jacobin Writing* (University Park: Pennsylvania State University Press, 2001), p.131.

18. Justin Roberts notes that while Enlightenment ideals around natural rights and liberty fuelled abolitionist sentiment and action, paradoxically Enlightenment principles of rationality, science, pragmatism and efficiency sometimes encouraged the factory discipline associated with industrialisation and the regimented brutality of plantation slavery. Justin Roberts, *Slavery and the Enlightenment in the British Atlantic, 1750-1807* (Cambridge: Cambridge University Press, 2013), p.6.

19. J.R. Oldfield, *Popular Politics and British Anti-Slavery: The Mobilisation of Public Opinion against the Slave Trade, 1787-1807* (Manchester: Manchester University Press, 1995).

20. *A Representation of the Injustice and Dangerous Tendency of Admitting the Least Claim of Private Property in the Persons of Men, in England, In Four Parts* (London: Printed for Benjamin White in Fleet Street and Robert Horsfield in Ludgate Street, 1769), archive.org/details/representationof00shar. Accessed January 10, 2017.

21. Olaudah Equiano, *The Interesting Narrative of the Life of Olaudah Equiano or Gustavus Vassa, the African*, (1814; New York, Cosimo, 2009), p.179. Olaudah Equiano, *The Interesting Narrative of the Life of Olaudah Equiano or Gustavus Vassa, the African Written by Himself* (1789; New York: Penguin, 2003); Vincent Caretta, *Equiano The African: Biography of a Self-Made Man*, (Athens: University of Georgia Press, 2005). For the importance of these autobiographical testimonies to our understanding of the Black Atlantic, see also, Alan J. Rice, *Radical Narratives of the Black Atlantic* (New York: Continuum, 2003).

22. James Walvin. *The Zong: A Massacre, The Law and the End of Slavery* (New Haven and London: Yale University Press, 2011).

23. Caretta, *Equiano*, p.354. Newcastle's famous Bigg Market was initially spelled Bigge.

24. *Courant*, October 6, 1792, p.1. See also, Sean Creighton, 'Black People and the North East,' *North East History*, 39 (2008), pp.11-24 (especially, pp.12-14).

25. Charlton, *Hidden Chains*, p.25.

26 On Turner, see Stephen Harbottle, *The Reverend William Turner: Dissent and Reform in Georgian Newcastle upon Tyne* (Leeds: Northern Universities Press, 1997); Charlton, *Hidden Chains*, pp.26-27.

27. 'Preface,' *An Abstract of the Evidence Delivered Before a Select Committee of the House of Commons in the Years 1790 and 1791, on the Part of the Petitioners for the Abolition of the Slave Trade*, (Newcastle upon Tyne: The Society in Newcastle for Promoting the Abolition of the Slave-Trade,' 1791), p.6, LT.

28. Ibid.

29. 'Preface,' p.6.

30. Sean Creighton, 'Tyneside, the North East and Slavery and Abolition,' p.10, seancreighton.com/pdf/Overview%20of%20Slavery%20&%20Abolition%20at%20N%20East%20Sean%20Creighton.pdf. Accessed January 10, 2017.

31. Clare Midgley, *Women Against Slavery: The British Campaigns, 1780-1870* (London: Routledge, 1992), p.23.

32. Humanus, letter, *Courant*, January 7, 1792, p.2. For the Quaker-led boycott movement, see, Julia L. Holcomb, *Moral Commerce: Quakers and the Transatlantic Boycott of the Slave Labor Economy* (Ithaca: Cornell University Press, 2015); Charlton, *Hidden Chains*, pp.27-28.

33. Martin Luther King, 'Acceptance Speech on Receipt of an Honorary Doctorate at the University of Newcastle upon Tyne,' November 13, 1967, MLK-Reg.

34. Charles Grey held several titles during his life: he was the second Earl, but was called Baron Grey between 1801 and 1806, and between 1806-07 was Viscount Howick. For Grey's life, see, E.A. Smith, *Lord Grey 1764–1845* (Stroud: Alan Sutton, 1996).

35. Matthew Forster and John Fenwick, *Declaration of the Objects of the Newcastle upon Tyne Society for Promoting the Gradual Abolition of Slavery Throughout the British Dominions* (Newcastle upon Tyne: W.A. Mitchell, 1823), p.7, AST.

36. *Substance of the Debate in the House of Commons on the 15th May, 1823, on a Motion for the Mitigation and Gradual Abolition of Slavery Throughout the British Dominions*, (London: Ellerton & Henderson, 1823), pp.xxxvii-xxxix.

37. Forster and Fenwick, *Declaration*, pp.10-11.

38. Ibid., p.8. See also, *First Report of the Committee of the Newcastle upon Tyne Society for Promoting the Gradual Abolition of Slavery Throughout the British Dominions: Read at the General Meeting Held on the 16th June, 1824, with an Account of the Proceedings of the General Meeting, &c,* (Newcastle upon Tyne: n.p., 1825), AST.

39. *The Speech of James Losh, Esq. in the Guildhall, Newcastle upon Tyne, on the 31st March, 1924, at a Meeting of the Inhabitants Called By the Right Worshipful Mayor for the Purpose of Petitioning Parliament for the Improvement and Gradual Emancipation of The Slave Population of the British Colonies* (Newcastle upon Tyne: T. and J. Hodgson, 1824), p.12, Tracts 042/4, v.126, n.7, L&P.

40. A Free Born Briton, letter to Electors of the Counties of Northumberland and Newcastle upon Tyne, March 4, 1826, in *A Letter to the Electors of the Counties of Northumberland and Newcastle upon Tyne* (Newcastle upon Tyne: J. Clark, 1826), p.1, Northumberland Election Papers, 1826, Local N324/12, v.4. n.2, L&P. Neither Lambton nor Beaumont were elected in 1826, nor was Earl Grey's son, Lord Howick, who also contested the election. The two available seats were claimed by Tory candidates Matthew Bell and Henry Liddell. Beaumont subsequently returned to Parliament that year following a by-election in Stafford. See, J.G. Millingen, *The History of Duelling* (London: Richard Bentley, 1841), pp.284-286.

41. Bob Whitfield, *The Extension of the Franchise, 1832-1931* (Oxford: Heinemann, 2001), pp.58-81 (figures from p.72). John A. Phillips and Charles Wetherell, 'The Great Reform Act of 1832 and the Political Modernization of England,' *American Historical Review,* 100, 2 (1995), pp. 411–436, argue for a more modest increase in numbers from 450,000 to 600,000 (see pp.413-414).

42. Purdue, *Newcastle*, pp.168-9. The number of voters in Newcastle increased by 704 in 1835 compared with 1832, but this was at a time when the population was increasing by around 1,500 annually. See, Cadogan, *Early Radical Newcastle*, p.112.

43. Whitfield, *Extension of the Franchise*, p.73. On the conservatism of Whigs like Grey, see Norman Gash, *Aristocracy and People: Britain 1815-1865* (Cambridge, MA: Harvard University Press, 1979), pp.142-155.

44. Cadogan, *Early Radical Newcastle*, p.112.

45. Charlton, *Hidden Chains*, pp.66-67.

46. *Declaration of the Objects of the Newcastle Upon Tyne Society for the Abolition of Slavery All Over the World*, p.7.

47. Charlton, *Hidden Chains*, p.59.

48. Creighton, 'Tyneside, the North East and Slavery and Abolition,' p.13.

49. Charlton, *Hidden Chains*, pp.60-62 (Howick quote on p.61).

50. Creighton, 'Tyneside, The North East and Slavery and Abolition,' p.13.

51. *Ladies Petition for the Immediate Abolition of West India Slavery, May 13, 1833*, (Newcastle upon Tyne: J. Clark, 1833), DX17/1/122, TWA; Charlton, *Hidden Chains*, p.67; Midgely, *Women Against Slavery*, pp.62-63.

52. Rev. G.W.F. Mortimer, *The Immediate Abolition of Slavery Compatible with the Safety and Prosperity of the Colonies in a Letter to the Representatives of the Southern Division of Northumbria and the Town and County of Newcastle upon Tyne* (Newcastle upon Tyne: J. Blackwell & Co., 1833), pp.7, 11, 3, Tract 042/4, v.126, n.15, L&P.

53. William Burns, 'Abolition of Slavery Act (1833),' in Junius P. Rodriguez (ed.), *Encyclopedia of Emancipation and Abolition in the Transatlantic World*, (Abingdon: Routledge, 2015), pp.4-6.

54. 'Charity and Pulpit Notices,' *Journal,* November 2, 1833, p.4; Charlton, *Hidden Chains,* pp.68-69.

55. *An Account of Meetings held in the Counties of Durham, and Northumberland, Newcastle upon Tyne, and Berwick upon Tweed: in ... 1834, to address the Right Hon. Earl Grey, on his Retirement from Office, with Copies of the Addresses* (Newcastle: T. & J. Hodgson, 1834), p.5. Tracts 042/4 v. 470: n.6, L&P

56. Inscription, Grey's Monument, Newcastle upon Tyne, National Recording Project, Public Monuments and Sculpture Association, pmsa.org.uk/pmsa-database/9484/. Accessed January 10, 2017.

Chapter Six: 'Brethren in the Cause of Universal Freedom in America': Peace, Politics and Abolitionism in the North East before the US Civil War

1. *Speech of George Thompson, Esq., At The Great Anti-Slavery Meeting, Held in Hood Street Chapel, Newcastle on Thursday, January 20, 1838,* (Gateshead: Lowthin & Douglas, 1838), p.3, Tracts 042/4, v.470, n.1, L&P.

2. 'Negro Apprenticeship,' *Chronicle,* August 3, 1838, p.1. See also, John Charlton, *Hidden Chains: The Slavery Business and North East England, 1600-1865* (Newcastle: Tyne Bridge Publishing, 2008), pp.73-77.

3. Marc-William Palen, 'Free-Trade Ideology and Transatlantic Abolitionism: A Historiography,' *Journal of the History of Economic Thought,* 37, 2 (2015), pp.291-304 (quote, p.295). Palen's essay is a good introduction to a vast literature on free-trade and transatlantic abolitionism. See also, Kenneth Morgan, *Slavery, Atlantic Trade and the British Economy, 1660-1800* (Cambridge: Cambridge University Press, 2000).

4. See, Martin Lynn, 'British Policy, Trade, and Informal Empire in the Mid-Nineteenth Century,' in Andrew Porter (ed.) *The Oxford History of the British Empire: Volume III: The 19th Century* (New York: Oxford University Press, 1999), pp.101-121.

5. 'Report of the Newcastle-Upon-Tyne Auxiliary,' *The Herald of Peace, Jan, Feb and March 1832* (London: Hamilton, Adams & Co., 1832), p.284.

6. 'Fifth Report of the Newcastle Upon Tyne Auxiliary to the London Society for the Promotion of Permanent and Universal Peace,' 1837, p.4. See research.ncl.ac.uk/martinlutherking/activities/publicmeetings/twocenturies/. Accessed January 9, 2017.

7. David Saunders. 'Challenge, Decline and Revival: The Fortunes of Pacifism in Nineteenth- and Early Twentieth-Century Newcastle,' *Northern History,* April 2017, 1-16 (quote, p.15). (Online) DOI:10.1080/0078172X.2017.1309755. Accessed June 26, 2017.

8. 'Intelligence: Peace Societies, &c,' *American Advocate of Peace,* 1, 4 (March 1835), pp.192-198.

9. Clare Midgley, *Women Against Slavery: The British Campaigns, 1780-1870* (London: Routledge, 1992), p.136.

10. Ibid., pp.126-127; Charlton, *Hidden Chains,* p.72; *Chronicle,* April 9, 1836, p.2.

11. Charlton, *Hidden Chains,* p.82.

12. W. Caleb McDaniel, 'World Anti-Slavery Convention,' in Peter P. Hinks, John R. McKivigan and R. Owen Williams (eds), *Encyclopedia of Antislavery and Abolition* (Westport: Greenwood, 2007), pp. 760–762; Midgley, *Women Against Slavery,* p.51 (on Sturge)

and pp.158-165 (on the 1840 convention). See also, Bruce Dorsey, *Reforming Men and Women: Gender in the Antebellum City* (Ithaca, NY: Cornell University Press, 2002), p.179.

13. For connections to the Universal Abolition Society from earlier national anti-slavery organisations, see David Turley, *The Culture of English Antislavery, 1780-1860*, (London: Routledge, 1991), pp.52-57; Richard Huzzey, *Freedom Burning: Anti-Slavery and Empire in Victorian Britain* (Ithaca: Cornell University Press, 2012), p.9; Midgley, *Women Against Slavery*, p.126.

14. *Declaration of the Durham Society for the Universal Abolition of Slavery* (Durham: Fewster and James, 1836), p.2, Samuel J. May Anti-Slavery Collection, Cornell University, ebooks.library.cornell.edu/cgi/t/text/pageviewer-idx?c=mayantislavery;idno=06837511;view=image;seq=1;cc=mayantislavery;page=root;size =100. Accessed April 11, 2017. Charlton, *Hidden Chains*, pp.84-88.

15. *Declaration of the Objects of the Newcastle Upon Tyne Society for the Abolition of Slavery All Over the World* (Newcastle upon Tyne: J. Blackwell & Co., 1836), pp.9-10, Tracts 042/4, v.470, n.18, L&P; *Chronicle*, April 9, 1836, p.2.

16. *Declaration of the Objects*.

17. Huzzey, *Freedom Burning*, p.7.

18. Peter Cadogan, *Early Radical Newcastle* (Consett: Sagittarius Press, 1975), pp.113-131; A.W. Purdue, *Newcastle: The Biography* (Stroud: Amberley, 2011), pp.182-186. See also Richard Brown, *Chartism: Localities, Spaces and Places, The North, Scotland, Wales and Ireland* (n.p.: Authoring History: 2015), pp.1-4, 20-32, 117-143; John Flanagan, "A Gigantic Scheme of Co-operation': The Miners' and Seamen's United Association in the North-East, 1851–1854,' *Labour History Review*, 74, 2 (August 2009), pp.143–159.

19. Richard Bradbury, 'Frederick Douglass and the Chartists,' in Alan J. Rice and Martin Crawford (eds), *Liberating Sojourn: Frederick Douglass & Transatlantic Reform* (Athens: University of Georgia Press, 1999), pp.169-186 (first quote, p.169; second quote, p.175). See also, Betty Fladeland, 'Our Cause Being One and the Same: Abolitionists and Chartism,' in James Walvin (ed.), *Slavery and British Society, 1776-1846* (Baton Rouge: Louisiana State University Press, 1982), pp.69-99.

20. William Lloyd Garrison, October 20, 1888, letter to *The Liberator*, in *The Letters of William Lloyd Garrison: No Union with the Slaveholders, 1841-1849* (Cambridge, MA: Harvard University Press, 1973), pp.437-440 (quotes on p.439). The letter appeared in *The Liberator*, November 20, 1846, p.187.

21. Harriet Martineau, letter to Fanny Wedgewood, February 11, 1846, in Elisabeth Sanders Arbuckle (ed.), *Harriet Martineau's Letters to Fanny Wedgewood*, (Stanford, CA: Stanford University Press, 1983) pp.46-49 (quotes on p.47). The current Martineau Guest House stands at 57, Front Street, Tynemouth, but Martineau repeatedly gave her address as 12, Front Street. See, for example, Harriet Martineau, letter to Fanny Wedgewood, (Summer 1840), in Sanders, *Harriet Martineau's Letters*, p.35. Martineau suffered from poor health for much of her life, including partial deafness and, at the time of her recuperation in Tynemouth, probably had a uterine tumour. Her condition only really improved, somewhat, when she left for Ambleside in 1845 and found renewed strength in an odd mix of mesmerism and religious enthusiasm.

22. Harriet Martineau, *Society in America*, (London: Saunders and Otley, 1837).

23. Harriet Martineau, *The Martyr of the Age of the United States of America with and Appeal on Behalf of the Oberlin Institute in Aid of the Abolition of Slavery*, (Newcastle upon Tyne: Finley and Charlton, 1840). See also, Alexis Easley, 'Rewriting the Past and Present: Harriet Martineau, Contemporary Historian,' in Valerie Sanders and Gaby Weiner (eds),

Harriet Martineau and the Birth of Disciplines: Nineteenth-Century Powerhouse (Abingdon, UK: Routledge, 2017), p.106; Midgely, Women Against Slavery, p.129 (also pp.127-9 on Martineau generally).

24. 'Uncle Tom in England,' Chronicle, October 8, 1852, p.2; 'A Glance Across the Atlantic,' ibid., October 8, 1852, p.4; 'Will Be Ready in A Few Days,' ibid., October 15, 1852, p.2. See also, Sarah Meer, Uncle Tom Mania: Slavery, Minstrelsy, and Transatlantic Culture in the 1850s (Athens: University of Georgia Press, 2005).

25. Harriet Beecher Stowe, letter to Dear Husband [Calvin Stowe], October 10, 1856, in The Life of Harriet Beecher Stowe: Compiled from Her Letters and Journals by her Son, Charles Edward Stowe, (Boston: Houghton, Mifflin & Co.,1889), pp.278-9. After hostilities broke out, Stowe's views in support of the North were summarised for North East readers in 'Mrs. Beecher Stowe on English Public Opinion,' Journal, January 13, 1863, p.2.

26. Judie Newman, 'The Afterlife of Dred on the British Stage,' in Denise Kohn, Sara Meer and Emily B. Todd (eds), Transatlantic Stowe: Harriet Beecher Stowe and European Culture (Iowa City: Iowa University Press, 2006), pp.217-220.

27. Minutes of Meeting, June 10, 1850, Ladies Negro Friend and Emancipation Society for Newcastle Minute Book from 1838 to 1854, 3744/389, TWA.

28. Minutes of Meeting, September 12, 1850, Ladies Negro Friend and Emancipation Society for Newcastle Minute Book from 1838 to 1854, 3744/389, TWA. Elizabeth A. O'Donnell, "There's Death in the Pot!': The British Free Produce Movement and the Religious Society of Friends, With Particular Reference to the North-East of England,' Quaker Studies, 13, 2 (2009), pp.184-204; Midgley, Women Against Slavery, pp.37, 206.

29. David Brown, 'William Lloyd Garrison, Transatlantic Abolitionism and Colonisation in the Mid Nineteenth Century: The Revival of the Peculiar Solution,' Slavery & Abolition: A Journal of Slave and Post-Slave Studies, 33, 2 (2012), p.246. See also Julia L. Holcomb, Moral Commerce: Quakers and the Transatlantic Boycott of the Slave Labor Economy (Ithaca: Cornell University Press, 2015).

30. Meeting of Committee, February 27, 1850, Ladies Negro Friend and Emancipation Society for Newcastle Minute Book from 1838 to 1854, 3744/389, TWA.

31. Meeting of Committee, May 10, 1844, Ladies Negro Friend and Emancipation Society for Newcastle Minute Book from 1838 to 1854, 3744/389, TWA.

32. Bryan Prince, A Shadow on the Household: One Enslaved Family's Incredible Struggle for Freedom (Toronto: McClelland & Steward, 2009), pp.63-64.

33. Fergus M. Bordewich, America's Great Debate: Henry Clay, Stephen A. Douglas, and the Compromise that Preserved the Union (New York: Simon & Schuster, 2012).

34. James Watkins, Narrative of the Life of James Watkins, Formerly a 'Chattel' in Maryland, U. S.; Containing an Account of His Escape from Slavery, Together with an Appeal on Behalf of Three Millions of Such 'Pieces of Property,' Still Held Under the Standard of the Eagle (Bolton: Kenyon and Abbatt, 1852), pp.32-33.

35. Ibid., pp.35-6.

36. 'A Glance Across the Atlantic.'

37. James Watkins, Struggles for Freedom; or The Life of James Watkins, Formerly a Slave in Maryland, U. S.; in Which is Detailed a Graphic Account of His Extraordinary Escape from Slavery, Notices of the Fugitive Slave Law, the Sentiments of American Divines on the Subject of Slavery, etc., etc. (19th Edition, Manchester: A. Heywood, 1860), p.44, Documenting the American South, University of North Carolina at Chapel Hill, docsouth.unc.edu/neh/watkins/watkins.html. Accessed January 11, 2017.

38. Ibid., p.56.

39. Ibid.

40. William Wells Brown, *The American Fugitive in Europe: Sketches of Places and People Abroad* (Boston: John P. Jewett, 1854), reprinted in Paul Jefferson (ed.), *The Travels of William Wells Brown* (Edinburgh: Edinburgh University Press, 1991), pp.139-140. *Clotel* was also published in Britain: William Wells Brown, *Clotel, or the President's Daughter* (London: Partridge and Oakey, 1853). For an overview of African American visitors to Britain during this period, see R.J.M. Blackett, *Building an Antislavery Wall: Black Americans in the Atlantic Abolitionist Movement, 1830-1860* (Baton Rouge: Louisiana State University Press, 1983).

41. William Wells Brown, 'Note to the Present Edition,' *Narrative of William W. Brown, An American Slave* (London: Charles Gilpin, 1840), pp.iii-iv.

42. *The Anti-Slavery Harp: A Collection of Songs for Anti-Slavery Meetings, Compiled by William W. Brown, An American Fugitive Slave*, (Newcastle: J. Blackwell & Co., 1850), p.1.

43. See, Joan Hugman, 'Print and Preach: The Entrepreneurial Spirit of Nineteenth-Century Newcastle,' in Bill Colls and Bill Lancaster (eds), *Newcastle upon Tyne: A Modern City* (Chichester, UK: Phillimore, 2001), pp.113-132. It has been estimated that between 1626 and 1860, some 1,700 people across the counties of Northumberland and Durham were employed in some aspect of the book trade (p.117). See also, C.M. Fraser and K. Emsley, *Tyneside* (Newton Abbot: David & Charles, 1973), pp.71-72.

44. 'American Slavery: Public Meeting in Newcastle,' *NG*, December 15, 1849, p.3.

45. 'Soiree to William Wells Brown in Newcastle,' ibid., January 5, 1850, p.5; Ezra Greenspan, *William Wells Brown: An African American Life* (New York: W.W. Norton, 2014), p.230.

46. Ibid., pp.244-248; William Wells Brown, *A Description of William Wells Brown's Original Panoramic Views of the Scenes in the Life of an American Slave, from His Birth in Slavery to His Death or His Escape to His First Home of Freedom on British Soil* (London, 1850), reprinted in C. Peter Ripley (ed.), *The Black Abolitionist Papers, Volume I, The British Isles, 1830—1865* (Chapel Hill: University of North Carolina Press, 1985), p.191.

47. 'William Wells Brown Poster - South Shields Central Hall,' n.d., LSC-SS.

48. 'Anti-Slavery Meeting in Newcastle,' *NG*, March 15, 1851, p.4. The report rather missed the point of Craft's escape narrative by erroneously suggesting that Ellen Craft was a 'white slave.'

49. William Wells Brown, letter to Dear Mr. Garrison, *The Liberator*, January 24, 1851, p.3.

50. William Wells Brown, letter to Frederick Douglass, *North Star*, April 17 1851, p.3.

51. 'Exchange by William Craft and Dr. James Hunt,' *Anti-Slavery Standard*, September 26, 1863, Black Abolitionist Archives, Doc. No. 26947 research.udmercy.edu/digital_collections/baa/Craft_26947spe.pdf. Accessed March 12, 2017. The meeting was also reported in 'Anthropology at the British Association,' *Anthropological Review*, 1, 3 (November 1863), pp.408-410.

52. 'Exchange.'

53. A Free Born Briton, letter to Electors of the Counties of Northumberland and Newcastle upon Tyne, March 4, 1826, in *A Letter to the Electors of the Counties of Northumberland and Newcastle upon Tyne* (Newcastle upon Tyne: J. Clark, 1826), p.1, Northumberland Election Papers, 1826, Local N324/12, v.4. n.2, L&P. Martin Luther King, 'Acceptance Speech on Receipt of Honorary Doctorate at the University of Newcastle upon Tyne,' November 13, 1967, MLK-Reg.

54. 'Exchange.'

55. Vanessa R. Dickerson, *Dark Victorians* (Urbana: University of Illinois Press, 2008), pp.3-4. Dickerson offers a fine account of how African American visitors interacted with a Victorian Britain that was less white than often believed (especially pp.44-73).

56. Accurate figures on the numbers of non-white people in Britain before the mid-19th century are impossible to ascertain, with estimates in the 1770s and 1780s ranging between 3,000 and 40,000. For a discussion of the difficulties around numbers, see James Walvin, *Black and White: The Negro and English Society, 1555-1945* (London: Penguin, 1973), p.46. For the development of racial thought in Georgian and Victorian Britain, see Norma Myers, *Reconstructing the Black Past: Blacks in Britain, 1780-1830* (1996; London: Frank Cass, 2000); Damon Ieremia Salesa, *Racial Crossings: Race, and Intermarriage and the Victorian British Empire* (Oxford: Oxford University Press, 2011); Catherine Hall, *Civilising Subjects: Metropole and Colony in the English Imagination, 1830-67* (Chicago: University of Chicago Press, 2002) and Douglas A. Lorimer, *Colour, Class and the Victorians: English Attitudes to the Negro in the Mid-Nineteenth Century* (Leicester: Leicester University Press, 1978). For development of US racial thought, see, George M. Fredrickson, *Black Image in the White Mind: Debate on Afro-American Character and Destiny, 1817-1914* (New York: Harper & Row, 1971) and William Stanton, *The Leopard's Spots: Scientific Attitudes Towards Race in America, 1815-1859* (Chicago: University of Chicago Press, 1960). See also, Adrian Desmond and James Moore, *Darwin's Sacred Cause: Race, Slavery and the Quest for Human Origins* (London: Penguin, 2009).

57. Watkins, *Struggles for Freedom.*

58. Peter Wood, 'The Newcastle Song Chapbooks,' in David Atkinson and Steve Roud (eds), *Street Ballads in Nineteenth Century Britain, Ireland and North America: The Interface Between Print and Oral Traditions* (Abingdon: Routledge, 2016), pp.70-71. 'Miss Lucy Neal,' (Newcastle: W.R. Walker: c.1860), Broadside Ballads Online, ballads.bodleian.ox.ac.uk/static/images/sheets/05000/03471.gif. Accessed December 18, 2016. The best overview of minstrelsy in Britain is Michael Pickering, *Blackface Minstrelsy in Britain* (Aldershot: Ashgate, 2008). See also, Robert Nowatzki, *Representing African Americans in Transatlantic Abolitionism and Blackface Minstrelsy* (Baton Rouge: Louisiana State University Press, 2010) and Hazel Waters, *Racism on the Victorian Stage: Representations of Slavery and Black Character* (Cambridge: Cambridge University Press, 2007).

59. 'Messrs Cobb and Chapman Delineators of Negro Life,' *Journal*, September 28, 1861, p.1; 'Oxford Music Hall,' ibid., February 8, 1868, p.2; 'Negro Minstrels at the Seaside,' *Courant,* September 2, 1893, p.6; "Dixieland' at the Empire,' *Journal*, July 18, 1914, p.4; "The Sugar Babe at the Empire',' ibid., February 19, 1918, p.5. Theatre-going Tynesiders were exposed to very different images when the commanding New York-born black Shakespearean actor Ira Aldridge performed in Newcastle and Sunderland in March 1827, again in 1845 and 1857 (when he also appeared in South Shields), and for the last time in the North East in 1859. 'Playbill advertising Ira Aldridge's appearance as Othello, Richard III and Shylock in Newcastle, 1845,' A Collection of Playbills from Miscellaneous Newcastle-upon-Tyne Theatres, 1791-1855, Playbill 262, British Library, bl.uk/collection-items/playbill-advertising-ira-aldridges-appearance-as-othello-richard-iii-and-shylock-in-newcastle-1845. Accessed December 18, 2016. See also, Bernth Lindfors, *Ira Aldridge: The Early Years, 1807–1833* (Rochester, NY: University of Rochester Press, 2011), p.112; Bernth Lindfors, *Ira Aldridge: The Last Years, 1855 – 1867* (Rochester, NY: University of Rochester Press, 2015), pp.40-41; 139-142.

60. Playbill for Scott and Whaley, Sunderland, 1918, TH.EMP/1/94, TWA.

61. Michael Pickering, 'The BBC's Kentucky Minstrels, 1933–1950: Blackface Entertainment on British Radio,' *Historical Journal of Film, Radio and Television*, 16, 2 (1996), pp.161-195.

62. Moses Roper, *Narrative of the Adventures and Escape of Moses Roper, from American Slavery. With an Appendix, Containing a List of Places Visited by the Author in Great Britain and Ireland and the British Isles, and Other Matter* (Berwick upon Tweed: Warder Office, 1848), Documenting the American South, University of North Carolina at Chapel Hill, docsouth.unc.edu/neh/roper/roper.html. Accessed June 27, 2017.

63. C. Lenox Remond, letter to My Very Dear Friend, March 7, 1841, *The Liberator*, May 21, 1841, p.88. See also, Fionnaghuala Sweeney, 'Richardson, Anna and Ellen,' in Paul Finkelman (ed.) *Encyclopedia of African American History, 1619-1895: From the Colonial Period to the Age of Frederick Douglass. Volume 3* (New York: Oxford, 2006), p.43.

64. Elizabeth Pease, letter to Esteemed Friend, May 2, 1841, *The Liberator*, May 21, 1841, p.88.

65. 'American Slavery,' *NG*, October 2, 1852, p.4; 'Slavery! In All Its Horrors!' *NSG*, November 5, 1852, p. 5. See also, *Narrative of the Life of Henry Box Brown, Written by Himself*, (Manchester: Lee and Glynn, 1851). See Blackett, *Building an Antislavery Wall*, p.15.

66. Special thanks to Hannah-Rose Murray for information on the 1860 visit to Cullercoats, where Douglass had probably also spoken in 1846. See, 'Local and District News,' *NG*, March 3, 1860, p.5. It is difficult to locate every North East venue at which Douglass spoke, but he appears to have given his first talk in the region in Newcastle on August 2, 1846 followed by another on August 3, 1846 at Salem Methodist Chapel, Newcastle. See 'Lecture on American Slavery,' ibid., August 8, 1846, pp.2-3. Other talks on this visit included, Baptist Church, Howard Street, North Shields (August 4, 1846); Atheneum Hall, Sunderland (September 18, 1846); Brougham Street Tabernacle, Sunderland (December 30, 1846); the Nelson Street Music Hall, Newcastle, (December 31, 1846); Assembly Rooms, Darlington (January 11, 1847). See, 'A Map of Speaking Locations,' Frederick Douglass in Britain, frederickdouglassinbritain.com/frederick-douglass-s-mission-to-britain/map-of-speaking-locations; Mapping Radical Tyneside, radicaltyneside.org/events/frederick-douglass-speaks. Both accessed January 5, 2017. See also, Joan Allen, *Joseph Cowen and Popular Radicalism on Tyneside 1829–1900* (Monmouth: Merlin Press, 2007), p.23.

67. Frederick Douglass, quoted in "Anti-Slavery Soiree," *NG*, January 2, 1847, p.6.

68. Elizabeth Pease, letter to 'Esteemed Friend,' February 16, 1847, *The Liberator*, March 26, 1847, p.3.

69. Elizabeth Pease, *Society of Friends in the United States: Their Views of The Anti-slavery Question, and Treatment of the People of Colour*, (Darlington: J. Wilson, 1840), Samuel J. May Anti-Slavery Collection, Cornell University Library, Ithaca, NY, ebooks.library.cornell.edu/cgi/t/text/text-idx?c=mayantislavery;idno=08839407. Accessed, January 5, 2017. See also, Donna McDaniel and Venessa Julye, *Fit for Freedom, Not for Friendship: Quakers, African Americans and the Myth of Racial Justice* (Philadelphia: Quaker Press, 2009), especially, pp.194-197.

70. 'Departure of Frederick Douglass: Disgraceful Proceedings,' *NG*, April 10, 1847, p.3. See also, 'The Douglass Testimonial,' ibid. October 2, 1847, p.3; 'The Douglass Testimonial,' ibid, December 4, 1847, p.3.

71. It is often claimed in biographies of Douglass that one of the most important figures in his life, Julia Griffiths, was also from Newcastle upon Tyne. Griffiths, who travelled to the US to administer, fundraise and set the literary tone for Douglass's influential abolitionist paper *The North Star*, was acquainted with Anna Richardson and this appears to be the basis for this oft-repeated misassumption. However, there is no concrete evidence that Griffiths ever visited, let alone lived in Newcastle and she first met Douglass in London. The error seems to have started with Douglass's first two academic biographers, Benjamin Quarles, *Frederick Douglass* (Ann Arbor: University of Michigan Press, 1948), p.87, and Philip S. Foner, *The Life and Writings of Frederick Douglass*, I, (New York: International Publishers, 1950), pp.87-90, and has been perpetuated by successive generations. For a discussion of this historiographical glitch see, Leigh Fought, 'More Source Creep,' January 23, 2012, at Frederick Douglass's Women: In Progress. leighfought.blogspot.co.uk/2012_01_01_archive.html. Accessed January 5, 2017.

Chapter Seven: 'God Bless the Policy of Emancipation!': The North East and the African American Freedom Struggle from the Civil War to the rise of Jim Crow

1. 'Mr. Frederick Douglass in Newcastle,' *Chronicle*, February 20, 1860, p.2; 'Frederick Douglass at North Shields,' *NSG*, February 23, 1860, p.4; 'Frederick Douglass at Morpeth,' ibid., March 1, 1860, p.5. See also, David W. Blight, *Frederick Douglass's Civil War: Keeping Faith in Jubilee* (Baton Rouge: Louisiana University State Press), pp.96-97.
2. James M. Gregory, *Frederick Douglass The Orator: Containing An Account of His Life; His Eminent Public Services; His Brilliant Career as Orator; Selections from his Speeches and Writings*, (Springfield, MA: Willey & Co. 1893), pp.82-83.
3. R.J.M. Blackett, *Divided Hearts: Britain and the American Civil War* (Baton Rouge: Louisiana State Press, 2001); Duncan Andrew Campbell, *English Public Opinion and the American Civil War* (Rochester: Boydell Press, 2003); Peter O'Connor, *American Sectionalism in the British Mind, 1832-1863*, (Baton Rouge: Louisiana State University Press, 2017); Tom Sebrell, *Persuading John Bull: Union and Confederate Propaganda in Britain, 1860-1865* (Lanham, MD: Lexington Books, 2014).
4. William Gladstone, 'Speech at Newcastle, October 7, 1862,' in Belle Becker Sideman and Lillian Friedman (eds), *Europe Looks At the Civil War*, (New York: Collier Books, 1962), p.157.
5. Kenneth Warren, *Armstrong: The Life and Mind of an Armaments Maker* (Seaton Burn: Northern Heritage, 2014), pp.116-117.
6. O'Connor, *American Sectionalism*, pp.126-127.
7. For Joseph Cowen and race, see Nigel Todd, *The Militant Democracy: Joseph Cowen and Victorian Radicalism* (Whitley Bay: Bewick Press, 1991), pp. 69-76; For Cowen's life and politics more generally, see Allen, *Joseph Cowen*. The *Newcastle Chronicle* began life in 1764, with a name change to the *Newcastle Daily Chronicle* in May 1858.
8. John Charlton, *Hidden Chains: The Slavery Business and North East England, 1600-1865* (Newcastle: Tyne Bridge Publishing, 2008), pp.148-150; Nigel Todd, 'Black-on-Tyne: The Black Presence on Tyneside in the 1860s,' *North East Labour History Journal*, 21 (1987), pp.17-27.
9. W.E. Adams, *The Slaveholders' War: An Argument for the North and the Negro* (Manchester: Union and Emancipation Society, 1863), pp.4, 14.

10. 'The Rev W.H. Channing on the American Question,' *Courant*, October 16, 1863, p.2.

11. Adams, *The Slaveholders' War*, pp.15, 19.

12. 'An Approving Voice,' *The Liberator*, September 16, 1864, p.1.

13. 'Visit of Mr. Wm. Lloyd Garrison to Newcastle,' *Chronicle*, July 13, 1867, p.3. William Lloyd Garrison, letter to Henry C. Wright, January 11, 1867, in Walter M. Merrill and Louis Ruchames (eds), *Letters of William Lloyd Garrison, Vol. 6* (Cambridge, Mass.: Harvard University Press, 1981) pp.31-32 (quote p.31).

14. Francis Jackson Garrison, *William Lloyd Garrison, 1805-1879: The Story of his Life told by his Children, Vol. 4* (New York: Century Company, 1889) pp.219-220.

15. For British responses to Lincoln's death, which actually occurred on April 15, the day after he was shot, see Nimrod Tal, *The American Civil War in British Culture* (New York: Palgrave Macmillan, 2015), pp.67-9. See also Don H. Doyle, 'Abraham Lincoln 'Was Not Yours Only': After the Assassination, Common Citizens Around the World Mourned the Loss,' Salon.com, April 14, 2015, salon.com/2015/04/14/abraham_lincoln_%E2%80%9Cwas_not_yours_only%E2%80%9D_after_the_assassination_common_citizens_around_the_world_mourned_the_loss/. Accessed April 19, 2017.

16. Anthony Nicol, Esq. (Deputy Mayor), 'Resolution,' Quarterly Meeting of the Council of the Borough of Newcastle upon Tyne, May 3, 1865; William Lockey Harle (Sheriff), 'Resolution,' May 4, 1865, both LODAL. See also 'Meetings of Sympathy with America,' *Chronicle*, May 5, 1865, pp.2-3.

17. J. Martin, letter to Hon. Charles Adams, May 4, 1865, LODAL.

18. (Rev) Henry Kendall, 'Resolution,' May 2, 1865, LODAL.

19. Blackett, *Divided Hearts*, 237-42; Philip Foner, *British Labor and the American Civil War*, (New York: Holmes and Meier, 1981), pp.90-95.

20. For an introduction to Reconstruction, the origins and encrustation of Jim Crow in the South, and black resistance to those developments, including migration, see Edward L. Ayers, *The Promise of the New South: Life after Reconstruction* (New York: Oxford University Press, 1992); David Brown and Clive Webb, *Race in the American South* (Edinburgh: Edinburgh University Press, 2007), pp.169-232; Eric Foner, *Reconstruction: America's Unfinished Revolution* (New York: Harper Row, 1988); James R. Grossman, *Land of Hope: Chicago, Black Southerners and the Great Migration* (Chicago: University of Chicago Press, 1989); Stephen Hahn, *A Nation Under Our Feet: Black Political Struggles in the Rural South from Slavery to the Great Migration* (Cambridge, MA: Harvard University Press, 2005); Leon Littwack, *Trouble in Mind: Black Southerners in the Age of Jim Crow* (New York: Knopf, 1998); Joel Williamson, *The Crucible of Race: Black-White Relations in the American South since Emancipation* (New York: Oxford University Press, 1984); C. Vann Woodward, *The Strange Career of Jim Crow* (1955; New York: Oxford University Press, 1974). For the links between immigration, imperialism and racist attitudes, see John Higham, *Strangers in the Land: Patterns of American Nativism, 1860-1925* (New Brunswick, NJ: Rutgers University Press, 1955); Michael H. Hunt, *Ideology and U.S. Foreign Policy* (New Haven: Yale University Press, 1987); Paul A. Kramer, 'Race-Making and Colonial Violence in the U.S. Empire: The Philippine-American War as Race War,' *Diplomatic History*, 30, 2 (April 2006), pp.169–210.

21. Martin Luther King, 'I Have a Dream,' August 28, 1963, in James M. Washington (ed.), *I Have a Dream: Writings and Speeches that Changed the World* (San Francisco: HarperSanFrancisco, 1992), pp.102-106.

22. David W. Stowe, "An Inestimable Blessing': The American Gospel Invasion of 1873,' *American Transcendental Quarterly*, 16, 3 (2002), pp.189-212.

23. J.B.T. Marsh and F. Loudin, *The Story of the Jubilee Singers, Including Their Songs* (London: Hodder & Stoughton, 1903), pp.63 (first quote), 67 (second, Robjohns quote). See also, Andrew Ward, *Dark Midnight When I Rise: The Story of the Jubilee Singers Who Introduced the World to the Music of Black America* (New York: Farrar, Straus and Giroux, 2000), p.243.

24. 'Thirty Negroes Killed in a Riot,' *Journal*, September 23, 1868, p.3; 'More Negro Riots,' ibid., October 10, 1868, p.3.

25. 'Anarchy in the Southern States,' ibid., March 28, 1871, p.3.

26. 'The Massacre in Louisiana,' ibid., May 5, 1873, p.3. Foner, *Reconstruction*, p.437.

27. 'Illiterate Negroes,' *Courant*, November 10, 1900, p.2.

28. 'Shocking Lynching Scene,' ibid., February 27, 1892, p.4; 'A Negro Burned Alive.' *NYT*, February 21, 1892, p. 6; Charles Frank Robinson II, *Dangerous Liaisons: Sex and Love in the Segregated South* (Fayetteville: University of Arkansas Press, 2003), p.77. Accurate statistics on lynching numbers are impossible to ascertain, but a 2015 report by the Equal Justice Initiative suggested that 4,075 black men, women, and children were lynched in twelve former Confederate states between 1877 and 1950. See, Equal Justice Initiative, *Lynching in America: Confronting the Legacy of Racial Terror* (2nd edition. Montgomery, AL: Equal Justice Initiative, 2015) eji.org/sites/default/files/lynching-in-america-second-edition-summary.pdf. Accessed February 5, 2017. For more on how rape accusations fitted into broader patterns of accusations against African Americans that could lead to lynching, see Lisa Lindquist Dorr, *White Women, Rape, and the Power of Race in Virginia, 1900-1960* (Chapel Hill: University of North Carolina Press, 2004).

29. 'Lynching in the United States: Horrible Barbarities by the White Population: Interview with a Coloured Lady in Newcastle,' *Newcastle Daily Leader,* April 20, 1894, p.5. For Wells's international mission, see Sarah Silkey, *Black Woman Reformer: Ida B. Wells, Lynching, and Transatlantic Activism* (Athens: University of Georgia Press, 2014).

30. 'Lynching in Georgia,' *Journal*, January 22, 1914, p.12; 'Negroes Burned at the Stake,' ibid., August 31, 1915, p.6.

31. G.J. Harney, 'American Notes and Boston Notions,' *W-Chronicle*, December 31, 1864, p.2. For more on Harney's American journalism, see Owen R. Ashton and Joan Hugman, 'George Julian Harney, Boston, U.S.A., and Newcastle upon Tyne, England, 1863-1888,' *Proceedings of the Massachusetts Historical Society*, 3rd Series, 107, (1995), pp.165-184.

32. W. Lockley Harle and Joseph Cowen, quoted in 'Meetings of Sympathy with America,' *Chronicle*, May 5, 1865, pp.2-3. See also, Adam I.P. Smith, 'The 'Cult' of Abraham Lincoln and the Strange Survival of Liberal England in the Era of the World Wars,' *Twentieth Century British History*, 21, 4 (2010), pp.486-509 (especially, pp.489-494).

33. G. Julian Harney, 'American Matters,' *W-Chronicle*, August 5, 1865, p.4.

34. G. Julian Harney, 'America,' ibid., March 23, 1867, p.8. Also, G. Julian Harney, 'State of Parties and Progress of Republicanism in America,' ibid., March 30, 1867, p.4.

35. Harney, 'America,' ibid., March 23, 1867, p.8. For the 1867 Reform Act see, Catherine Hall, Keith McLelland and Jane Rendell, *Defining the Victorian Nation: Class, Race, Gender and the British Reform Act of 1867* (Cambridge: Cambridge University Press, 2000).

Chapter Eight: The Challenges of Diversity:
Cultures of Welcome, Cultures of Hate

1. 'North Country Notes,' *Journal*, May 15, 1917, p.4.

2. John Charlton, *Hidden Chains: The Slavery Business and North East England, 1600-1865* (Newcastle: Tyne Bridge Publishing, 2008), p.161.

3. For a history of contested notions of Englishness, see Peter Mandler, *The English National Character: The History of an Idea from Edmund Burke to Tony Blair* (New Haven, CT: Yale University Press, 2006).

4. David Feldman, 'Migration,' in Martin Daunton, *The Cambridge Urban History of Britain: Volume III, 1840-1950* (Cambridge: Cambridge University Press, 2000), pp.185-186; David Byrne, 'Immigrants and the Formation of the North East Industrial Working Class,' *North East Labour History Bulletin*, 30 (1996), pp.29-36; Mike Barke, 'The People of Newcastle: A Demographic History,' in Robert Colls and Bill Lancaster, *Newcastle upon Tyne: A Modern History* (Chichester: Phillimore, 2001), p.155.

5. Richmond served briefly as an apprentice cabinet maker before becoming a bare-knuckle boxer and coach. Smart, witty, and with a range of sporting talents that included being an excellent cricketer, Richmond became something of an exotic celebrity in London society. Sean Creighton, 'Black People and the North East,' *North East History*, 39 (2008), pp.15-16.

6. Elizabeth Montagu, letter to Mrs Scott (her sister), n.d. 1758, in Emily J. Climenson, *Elizabeth Montagu: The Queen of the Blue Stockings. Her Correspondence From 1720 to 1761*, II, (London: William Clowes and Sons, 1906), p.138. Creighton, 'Black People and the North East,' p.17.

7. Mary Ann Mackham's Baptism Record, RS2007/TWA/1, TWA. Creighton, 'Black People in the North East,' pp.20-21.

8. Frank Neal, 'The Foundations of the Irish Settlement in Newcastle upon Tyne: The Evidence in the 1851 Census,' in Donald MacRaild (ed.), *The Great Famine and Beyond: Irish Migrants in Britain in the Nineteenth and Twentieth Centuries* (Dublin: Irish Academic Press, 2000), p.74.

9. Sydney Middlebrook, *Newcastle upon Tyne: Its Growth and Achievement* (Newcastle: S.R. Publishing, 1968), p.273.

10. Joan Hugman, 'Print and Preach: The Entrepreneurial Spirit of Nineteenth-Century Newcastle,' in Colls and Lancaster (eds), *Newcastle upon Tyne*, pp.128-130. See also, Franca Puddu, *The Irish on Tyneside: Migration and Identity* (PhD: Durham University, 1997), pp.94-95, 105. etheses.dur.ac.uk/1710/. Accessed September 19, 2016.

11. 'Mr. Charles Johnstone - Obituary,' *The Shipyard*, 150, 18 (January-February 1936), p.10; Charles Johnson, Burial Record 37385, Burial Register, Byker and Heaton Cemetery, 1932-9, p.118, MF2145, TWA; 1911 Census of England and Wales, Northumberland ukcensusonline.com/search/index.php?sn=Johnson&fn=Charles&kw=&phonetic_mode=1&event=1911&source_title=Northumberland+1911+Census&year=0&range=0&token=DwI6ioNTbZ7OUH3ESUm6DMCnapysk3W0PRJpEd6PUHI&search=Search. Accessed March 24, 2017.

12. Sidney Collins, *Coloured Minorities in Britain: Studies in British Race Relations Based on African, West Indian and Asian Immigrants* (London: Ludworth Press, 1957).

13. Tyneside Campaign Against Racial Discrimination, *Colour Discrimination in Newcastle upon Tyne* (Newcastle: CARD, 1967), LSC-N.

14. David Bean, 'Islam-on-Tyne,' *Guardian*, March 17, 1961, p.9. See also, Dave Renton, *Colour Blind?: Race and Migration in North East England Since 1945* (Sunderland: University of Sunderland Press, 2007), pp.2, 105, although Renton mistakenly dates Bean's report as March 1, 1962.

15. Bean, 'Islam-on-Tyne.'

16. Maureen Knight, 'The Town Where Colour Doesn't Count,' *Journal*, April 11, 1968, p.6. See also Maureen Knight, 'The Further North You Go the Better it is,' ibid., April 9, 1968, p.6; Maureen Knight, 'When You Got to School in a Strange Land,' ibid., April 10, 1968, p.6.

17. 'The Slave Trade,' ibid., June 9, 1832, p.3.

18. *Trial at Newcastle Assizes, February 1832, of Geo. Mallet & Wm. Craggs, Seamen*, (Newcastle: Douglas and Kent, 1832), DX17/1/15, TWA.

19. 'An Arab Melee,' *SDN*, March 25, 1927, p.1.

20. 'Outside the Pale,' ibid., August 16, 1912, p.3. See also, Richard Lawless, *From Ta'izz to Tyneside: An Arab Community in the North East of England* (Exeter: University of Exeter Press, 1995), p.10. Lawless, whose book is the best history of the Arab community in South Shields, notes that in 1913 Ali Hassan was still able to open his own boarding house in East Holborn.

21. 'Two Arabs and a Woman,' *SDN*, August 16, 1912, p.3.

22. 'Arab and Girl,' ibid., July 21, 1923, p.1.

23. 'Arab's Crime,' ibid., March 21, 1923, p.1; 'Arab to Pay Penalty,' ibid., August 7, 1923, p.4. Deputy Coroner of South Shields, quoted in Lawless, *From Ta'izz to Tyneside*, p.179. Lawless gives extensive coverage of the tensions around 'mixed marriages' in South Shields before World War Two, pp.174-206. See also, 'Two Arabs and a Woman'; Arab and Girl'; 'An Arab's Death,' *SDN*, September 17, 1920, p.4 (this story about the murder of Gannem Ahmed by his fellow seaman, Ali Hassan, aboard the Newcastle steamer Tosto, still took care to note that 'the deceased man...was married to an Englishwoman'); 'Arab v Soldier,' ibid., March 11, 1919, p.3 (this story involved a razor attack on a white soldier).

24. Lawless, *From Ta'izz to Tyneside*, pp.174-187. See also, Lucy Bland, 'White Women and Men of Colour: Miscegenation Fears in Britain after the Great War,' *Gender and History*, 17, 1 (April 2005), pp.29–61. For the popularity of eugenic ideas in Britain between the wars, see, Richard Overy, *The Morbid Age: Britain Between the Wars*, (London: Allen Lane, 2009), pp. 101-102, 105-108, 128-129. See also, Robert A. Nye, 'The Rise and Fall of the Eugenics Empire: Recent Perspectives on the Impact of Biomedical Thought in Modern Society,' *Historical Journal*, 36, 3 (1993), pp.687-700; Paul B. Rich, *Race and Empire in British Politics* (Cambridge: Cambridge University Press, 1986); Catherine Hall and Keith McClelland, *Race, Nation and Empire: Making Histories, 1750 to the Present* (Manchester: Manchester University Press, 2010).

25. Kenneth J. Gergen, 'The Significance of Skin Color in Human Relations,' in John Hope Franklin (ed.), *Color and Race* (Boston: Houghton Mifflin, 1968), pp.112-128; Gary D. Sherman and Gerald L. Clore, 'The Color of Sin: White and Black Are Perceptual Symbols of Moral Purity and Pollution,' *Psychological Science*, 20, 8 (August 2009), pp.1019–1025.

26. 'A South Shields Riot,' *SDN*, August 17, 1918, p.3.

27. Lawless, *From Ta'izz to Tyneside*, pp.79-98. For the national context of racial disturbances in 1919, see Jacqueline Jenkinson, *Black 1919: Riots, Racism and Resistance in Imperial Britain* (Liverpool: Liverpool University Press, 2009).

28. Barry Carr, 'Black Geordies,' in Robert Colls and Bill Lancaster (eds), *Geordies: Roots of Regionalism* (1992; Newcastle: Northumbria University Press, 2005), p.137. See also, Lawless, *From Ta'izz to Tyneside*, p.271, n.20.

29. J.B. Fye, quoted in ibid., pp.80-81. In 1914, Fye had been attacked by Mahomed Abdulla following abusive remarks during another dockside labour dispute. Abdulla was fined 10s for the assault. 'Scene at Mill Dam,' *SDN*, September 2, 1914, p.1.

30. 'Newcastle as Fascist Storm-Centre,' *Journal*, May 9, 1934, p.12. Nigel Copsey, 'Anti-Semitism and the Jewish Community of Newcastle Upon Tyne,' *Immigrants and Minorities*, 21, 3 (2002), pp.52-69; Gordon Stridiron, *Blackshirts in Geordieland* (London: Black House, 2013); Nigel Todd, *In Excited Times: The People Against the Blackshirts* (Whitley Bay: Bewick Press/Tyne & Wear Anti-Fascist Association, 1995), pp.88-91; Renton, *Colour Blind?*, pp.45-47, 60-62.

31. 'Mosley Arrested in Fascist Round Up,' *Journal*, May 24, 1940, pp.1/5. Todd, *In Excited Times*, pp.14-15, 20-27.

32. 'Big South Shields Demonstration against Fascism and War,' *Journal*, September 9, 1935, p.14; Matt Perry, *'Red Ellen' Wilkinson: Her Ideas, Movements and World* (Manchester: Manchester University Press, 2014), pp.251-298; Todd, *In Excited Times*, pp.42-49, 93-4.

33. 'Basque Refugee Children,' *E-Chronicle*, June 29, 1937, pp.7, 9. Don Watson and John Corcoran, *An Inspiring Example: The North East of England and the Spanish Civil War, 1936-1939* (London: McGuffin Press, 1996).

34. For the role of the North East branches of the NUWM in confronting fascism see, Don Watson, *No Justice Without Struggle: The National Unemployed Workers' Movement in the North East of England, 1920-1940* (London: Merlin, 2014), pp.181-185. Tom Callaghan, quoted in Todd, *In Excited Times*, p.82.

35. Renton, *Colour Blind?*, pp.88-90.

36. David Byrne, 'The 1930 'Arab Riot' in South Shields: A Race Riot That Never Was,' *Race and Class* 18, 3 (1977), pp.262-277; Carr, 'Black Geordies,' pp.139-143; Lawless, *From Ta'izz to Tyneside*, pp.113-152.

37. Justice Roche, quoted in, 'Danger of Idle Arabs in England,' *E-Chronicle*, November 30, 1930, p.1. See also, 'Sequel to Arab Riots at South Shields,' *SDN*, December 24, 1931, p.3.

38. 'The Ramadan Fast,' ibid., January 20, 1931, p.3.

39. Cone Street School Admissions Register, October 2, 1933 – September 30, 1935, E.SS10/2, TWA.

40. Carr, 'Black Geordies,' p.143.

41. Mary Winters and J. Hatch, 'Colour Persecution on Tyneside,' *Pan-Africa*, 1 (February 1947), pp.24-30.

42. Roi Ottley, *No Green Pastures* (London: John Murray, 1952), pp.25, 27.

43. Lord Pakenham, 'Colour Prejudice and Violence,' House of Lords Debate, November 19, 1958, *Hansard*, 212, p.634. hansard.millbanksystems.com/lords/1958/nov/19/colour-prejudice-and-violence. Accessed December 28, 2016.

44. 'Audience Research Report,' September 3-4, 1958, cited in Darrell M. Newton, *Paving the Empire Road: BBC Television and Black Britons* (Manchester: Manchester University Press, 2011), p.95.

45. Collins, *Coloured Minorities in Britain*, p.14.

46. Councillor Mrs Gaunt, quoted in Richard I. Lawless, *Teesside Muslims: Their Migration Histories, Settlement Patterns and Community Developments* (Cleveland: Cleveland County Council, 1995), p.32.

47. 'Girl Says She Loves Pakistani,' *E-Chronicle*, February 21, 1958, p.24; 'Discrimination Gets a Setback,' ibid., p.5.

48. Kenneth Dodd, 'Protest over Indian Busmen,' ibid., February 24, 1958, pp.1/9; John W. Ramsey, 'Coloured Busmen 'Get no Special Treatment',' ibid., February 25, 1958, p.5.

49. Sidney Hills, quoted in, Dodd, 'Protest over Indian Busmen,' ibid., February 24, 1958, p.9.

50. Renton, *Colour Blind?*, p.106.

51. Tony Stride, 'From the Burning Sun of Asia to the Smog of Tyneside,' *E- Chronicle*, February 18, 1958, p.8; Tony Stride, 'Buy Something–Their Golden Words to Wealth,' ibid., February 19, 1958, p.11; Tony Stride, 'False Ages so that Children can go to School,' ibid., February 20, 1958, p.8; Tony Stride, 'Children Laugh at the Turban,' ibid., February 21, 1958, p.11.

52. All quotes from Stride, 'From the Burning Sun of Asia,' p.8.

53. Stride, 'From the Burning Sun of Asia'; Stride, 'False Ages.'

54. Ibid.

55. J. H. Taylor, 'Newcastle upon Tyne: Asian Pupils do Better than Whites,' *British Journal of Sociology*, 24, 4 (1973), pp.431-447 (quote p.445). The data Taylor used was drawn from 1962-1967.

56. Stride, 'False Ages,' p.8.

57. Callum G. Brown, *The Death of Christian Britain* (Abingdon: Routledge, 2001), pp.170-192.

58. Stride, 'Children Laugh,' p.11.

59. Ibid.

60. Ibid.

61. Ibid.

62. Miss Patricia A.M. Geraghty, letter, *E-Chronicle*, February 25, 1958, p.22.

63. 'No 'Bar', But a Big Problem,' *Journal*, September 3, 1958, p.1.

64. Ibid.

65. 'Coloured Police May Track Vice to Smash Race Riots,' *E-Chronicle*, September 3, 1958, p.1.

66. Panikos Panayi, 'Middlesbrough 1961: A British Race Riot of the 1960s,' *Social History* 16, 2 (1991), pp.139-153. See also, Renton, *Colour Blind?*, pp.134-137; David Taylor, 'The Middlesbrough Race Riot of 1961: A Comment,' *Social History*, 18, 1 (1993), pp.73-79.

67. Renton, *Colour Blind?*, pp.136-137.

Part Three: Take A Look At America

Chapter Nine: 'The Developing Darkness': Martin Luther King and the Intersection of North East, British and US Race Relations in the 1960s

1. Harold MacMillan, 'Wind of Change' Speech, February 3, 1960, Cape Town, South Africa. Available at BBC Archive, bbc.co.uk/archive/apartheid/7203.shtml. Accessed January 31, 2016. See, Richard Ovendale, 'Macmillan and the Wind of Change in Africa, 1957–1960,' *Historical Journal*, 38, 2 (June 2005), pp.455–477.

2. There are many fine books on British race relations in the post-World War Two period. This account of national developments in the 1950s and 1960s is especially indebted to Nicholas Deakin, *Colour, Citizenship and British Society* (London: Panther, 1970); Peter Freyer, *Staying Power: The History of Black People in Britain* (London: Pluto, 1984), pp.372-399; Paul Gilroy, *There Ain't No Black In The Union Jack: The Cultural Politics of Race and Nation* (London: Unwin Hyman, 1987); Randall Hansen, *Citizenship and Immigration in Post-War Britain: The Institutional Origins of a Multicultural Nation* (Oxford: Oxford University Press, 2000); Dilip Hiro, *Black British, White British: A History of Race Relations in Britain* (c.1971. Revd. ed London: Grafton, 1991); Colin Holmes, *John Bull's Island: Immigration and British Society, 1871-1971* (Basingstoke: Palgrave Macmillan, 1988), pp.209-274; Charles Husband (ed.), *Race in Britain: Change and Continuity* (London: Hutchinson, 1982); Kathleen Paul, *Whitewashing Britain: Race and Citizenship in the Postwar Era* (Ithaca: Cornell University Press, 1997); Kennetta Hammond Perry, *London is the Place for Me: Black Britons, Citizenship and the Politics of Race* (New York: Oxford University Press, 2015), pp.48-248; Mike Phillips and Trevor Phillips, *Windrush: The Irresistible Rise of Multi-Racial Britain* (London: HarperCollins, 1998), pp.120-263.

3. J.E.T. Aldridge, 'Workers with Different Coloured Skins,' *Voice of North East Industry*, December 1964, cited in Dave Renton, *Colour Blind?: Race and Migration in North East England Since 1945* (Sunderland: University of Sunderland Press, 2007), p.70.

4. Anthony Messina, *Race and Party Competition in Britain* (Oxford: Oxford University Press, 1989); Paul, *Whitewashing Britain*, pp.156-157. See also, Jodi Burkett, *Constructing Post-Imperial Britain: Britishness, 'Race' and the Radical Left in the 1960s* (Basingstoke: Palgrave Macmillan, 2013).

5. Hiro, *Black British, White British*, 215, 323, n.13.

6. Paul, *Whitewashing Britain*, p.157.

7. Keith Hindell, 'The Genesis of the Race Relations Bill,' *Political Quarterly*, 36, 4 (1965), pp.390-405.

8. 'The New Voice of the Racialists,' *DM*, February 21, 1966, pp.1, 4. See also, Mark Pitchford, *The Conservative Party and the Extreme Right* (Manchester: Manchester University Press, 2011), pp.137-138.

9. Robin Beauclair, quoted in 'The New Voice of the Racialists,' p.4. George Lewis, "'Scientific Certainty': Wesley Critz George, Racial Science and Organised White Resistance in North Carolina, 1954-1962,' *Journal of American Studies*, 38, 2 (2004), pp. 227-247.

10. David Olusoga, *Black and British: A Forgotten History* (London: Macmillan, 2016), p.12.

11. 'The New Voice of the Racialists,' pp.1, 4.

12. On the birth of the National Front, see Richard Thurlow, *Fascism in Britain: From Mosley's Blackshirts to the National Front* (London: I.B. Tauris, 2006), pp.247-255. On the National Front in the North East, see David Renton, *Colour Blind?*, pp.162-169.

13. Political and Economic Planning Ltd., *Racial Discrimination* (London: PEP, 1967); *Report of the Race Relations Board For 1966-67* (London: Her Majesty's Stationary Office, 1967), p.16.

14. 'Race Wars Flare Across America,' *Journal*, July 24, 1967, p.1; 'Crush Rioters, Paratroopers Told,' ibid., July 26, 1967, p.1; 'Negro Rioters Blitz a City,' ibid., July 28, 1967, p.1; 'Mobs Riot Near White House,' ibid., August 2, 1967, p.1.

15. For the transnational significance of Malcolm X's visits to Britain, particularly his December 3, 1964 appearance at the Oxford Union, see, Stephen Tuck, *The Night Malcolm X Spoke at the Oxford Union: A Transatlantic Story of Antiracist Protest* (Berkeley: University of California Press, 2014).

16. For the impact of King on the campaign for Catholic rights in Northern Ireland, see Brian Dooley, *Black and Green: The Fight For Civil Rights in Northern Ireland & Black America* (London: Pluto, 1998); Bob Purdie, *Politics in the Streets: The Origins of the Civil Rights Movement in Northern Ireland* (Belfast; Blackstaff Press, 1990), pp.2-3, 91-93, 134, 156-57, 216-217, 231, 244-245.

17. Tuck, *The Night Malcolm X Spoke*, p.184. Robert G. Weisbord, 'Black Power with a British Accent,' *Negro Digest*, May 1969, pp.29-33. See also, R.E.R. Bunce and Paul Field, 'Obi B. Egbuna, C. L. R. James and the Birth of Black Power in Britain: Black Radicalism in Britain 1967–72,' *Twentieth Century History*, 22, 3 (2011), pp.391-414; Benjamin W. Heineman, *Politics of the Powerless: A Study of the Campaign Against Racial Discrimination* (London: Oxford University Press for the Institute of Race Relations, 1972), p.181.

18. Tuck, *The Night Malcolm X Spoke*, pp.184-185.

19. Ibid., p.186.

20. Hiro, *Black British, White British*, pp.47-48; Heineman, *Politics of the Powerless*, pp.180-184.

21. Roy Jenkins, House of Commons Debate, July 27 1967, *Hansard*, v. 751, p.214, hansard.millbanksystems.com/written_answers/1967/jul/27/mr-stokely-carmichael#S5CV0751P0_19670727_CWA_158. Accessed December 1, 2016.

22. King's personal stock also rose among certain sections of the American press when he was compared favourably with firebrands like H. Rap Brown and Carmichael. In the States, however, this admiration was often tempered by reservations about King's anti-Vietnam stance, which in Britain carried no stigma. Richard Lentz, *Symbols, Newsmagazines and Martin Luther King* (Baton Rouge: Louisiana State University Press, 1990), pp.308-337.

23. Sir Cyril Osborne, House of Commons Debate, November 15, 1967, *Hansard*, v. 754, p.519. hansard.millbanksystems.com/commons/1967/nov/15/acts-continued-till-end-of-december-1968#S5CV0754P0_19671115_HOC_362.
Accessed December 1, 2016. As he was speaking on November 15, Osborne was mistaken to say that King had received his award in Newcastle 'yesterday.'

24. David Winnick and Sir Cyril Osborne, House of Commons Debate, November 15, 1967, *Hansard*, v. 754, pp.519-520, hansard.millbanksystems.com/commons/1967/nov/15/acts-continued-till-end-of-december-1968#S5CV0754P0_19671115_HOC_362.
Accessed December 1, 2016.

25. Sir Cyril Osborne, House of Commons Debate, July 26, 1967, v. 751, p.167, hansard.millbanksystems.com/written_answers/1967/jul/26/commonwealth-immigration-act#S5CV0751P0_19670726_CWA_190.
Accessed December 1, 2016.

26. Roy Jenkins, 'This is the Goal,' May 23, 1966, in Brian McArthur (ed), *The Penguin Book of Great British Speeches* (London: Penguin 1999), pp.362-363.

27. Ibid., p.364.

28. For more on the circumstances in which Jenkins's speech was composed, see John Campbell, *Roy Jenkins: A Well Rounded Life* (London: Jonathan Cape, 2014), pp.270-272. Jenkins repeated key passages of his May speech almost verbatim in another House of Commons debate on immigration on November 8, 1966. See, Roy Jenkins, House of Commons Debate, November 8, 1966, *Hansard*, v. 754, p.1235, hansard.millbanksystems.com/commons/1966/nov/08/schedule-acts-continued-till-end-of#S5CV0735P0_19661108_HOC_392.
Accessed December 1, 2016.

29. Jenkins, 'Goal,' p.365.

30. 'Report on Anti-Discrimination Legislation (Street Report),' November 1967, BT 64/5354, Board of Trade: Industries and Manufactures Department: Correspondence and Papers, National Archives, Kew. See also, B.A. Hepple, 'Reports of Committees: The Street Report on Anti-Immigration Legislation and Report of the Committee on Immigration Appeal,' *Modern Law Review*, 31, 3 (May 1968), pp.810-821.

31. 'Racial Integration British Style,' *Guardian*, November 13, 1967, p. 8.

32. 'Luther King Warns Britain,' *MS*, November 13, 1967, p.3.

33. 'Speech delivered by the Public Orator (J.H. Burnett) when presenting a candidate (Martin Luther King) for an honorary degree at a Congregation in King's Hall on Monday, 13th November 1967,' MLK-Reg.

34. Minutes, November 9, 1966, Commonwealth Immigrants Working Group of Newcastle Planning Committee, Minutes, 1966-1968, MD.NC/149, TWA.

35. Sudha D. Telang, *The Coloured Immigrant in Newcastle upon Tyne: Research Report* (Newcastle: Newcastle City Planning Department, September/October 1967), pp.6-7, 14, LSC-N. The higher figure for Newcastle's 'New Commonwealth Migrants' comes from Sheila Patterson, *Immigration and Race Relations in Britain, 1960-1967* (London: Oxford University Press for the Institute of Race Relations, 1969), p.12.

36. 'Report by City Planning Officer,' incorporated in Telang, *Coloured Immigrant*, p.28.

37. Renton, *Colour Blind?*, p.20.

38. Council Minutes, October 19, 1960; January 4, 1961; April 5, 1961; April 19, 1961, *Proceedings of the Council of the City and County of Newcastle upon Tyne for 1960-1961* (Newcastle: Cooperative Printing Company, 1961) pp.402-403; 746-747; 1075; 1148-1153, LSC-N.

39. Minutes, September 19, 1966, Commonwealth Immigrants Working Group of Newcastle Planning Committee, Minutes, 1966-1968, MD.NC/149, TWA.

40. Renton, *Colour Blind?*, pp.106-123. For Jamiat al-Muslimeen, see, Antoine Sfeir (ed.), *The Columbia World Dictionary of Islamism* (New York: Columbia University Press, 2007), p.96.

41. Council Minutes, September 5, 1967, *Proceedings of the Council of the City and County of Newcastle upon Tyne for 1967-1968* (Newcastle: Cooperative Printing Company, 1968), p.463, LSC-N.

42. Ibid., p.464.

43. Ibid., pp.464-465. See also, Commonwealth Immigrants Working Group of Newcastle Planning Committee, Minutes, 1966-1968, MD.NC/149, TWA.

44. Council Minutes, December 6, 1967, *Proceedings of the Council of the City and County of Newcastle upon Tyne for 1967-1968* (Newcastle: Cooperative Printing Company, 1968), pp.1022-1026, LSC-N.

45. Connie Lewcock, in ibid., p.1024. For Lewcock's earlier engagement in progressive politics, see Nigel Todd, *In Excited Times: The People Against the Blackshirts* (Whitley Bay:

Bewick Press/Tyne & Wear Anti-Fascist Association, 1995), p.48. Martin Luther King, 'Acceptance Speech on Receipt of an Honorary Doctorate at the University of Newcastle upon Tyne,' November 13, 1967, MLK-Reg. The Council's new home in the purpose-built Civic Centre at the Haymarket was completed in 1967, but not formally opened until November 1968.

46. Dominic Sandbrook, *White Heat: A History of Britain in the Swinging Sixties* (London: Little, Brown, 2006), p.56.

47. Ibid., pp.400-408.

48. A.W. Purdue, *Newcastle: The Biography* (Stroud: Amberley, 2011), p.295.

49. John W. House, *Industrial Britain: The North East* (Newton Abbot: David & Charles, 1969), pp.163-164; Renton, *Colour Blind?*, p.92.

50. 'Tyne Jobs Lobby Gets London Backing,' *MS*, November 13, 1967, p.3.

51. Figures drawn from House, *Industrial Britain*, pp.106-111; Purdue, *Newcastle*, pp.293-294; Renton, *Colour Blind?*, p.92.

52. House, *Industrial Britain*, p.23.

53. In 1973, Smith was sentenced to six years in jail for corruption as it emerged that his companies and those of his friends and associates had financially benefitted from the urban renewal through kick-backs and the preferential awarding of contacts.

54. Board of Trade, *The North East: A Programme for Regional Development and Growth*, (London: Her Majesty's Stationery Office, 1963).

55. *Shipbuilding Inquiry Committee, 1965-1966: Report* (London: Her Majesty's Stationery Office, 1966).

56. Purdue, *Newcastle*, pp.297-303; House, *Industrial Britain*, p.111; N. Vall, 'The Emergence of the Post-Industrial Economy in Newcastle, 1914-2000,' in Robert Colls and Bill Lancaster (eds), *Newcastle upon Tyne: A Modern History* (Chichester: Phillimore, 2001), pp.64-66.

57. It was not only the redevelopment schemes of the 1960s and 1970s that struggle to deal effectively with some of the West End's economic and social problems. See, Fred Robinson, 'Regenerating the West End of Newcastle: What Went Wrong?' *Northern Economic Review*, 36 (Summer 2005), pp.15-41.

58. Tyneside Campaign Against Racial Discrimination, *Colour Discrimination in Newcastle upon Tyne* (CARD: Newcastle, 1967), LSC-N.

59. 'Report by City Planning Officer,' pp.28-29.

60. D.C.H. Fulton, letter to the Editor, *Journal*, November 7, 1967, p.6.

61. King, 'Acceptance Speech'; C.I.C. Bosanquet, 'Vice-Chancellor's Address at the Memorial Service for Martin Luther King,' April 26, 1968,' MLK-Dup.

62. This portion of King's speech is not in the surviving film, but was reported in 'Luther King Warns of 'Black Ghetto',' *E-Chronicle*, November 14, 1967, p.4; 'A Degree of Admiration,' *Journal*, November 14, 1967, p.3.

63. Bosanquet, 'Vice-Chancellor's Address.'

64. 'Johnson Should Admit Mistake – Luther King,' *MS*, November 14, 1967, p.3.

65. Martin Luther King-Clyde Alleyne Interview, November 13, 1967, British Film Institute, player.bfi.org.uk/film/watch-13-november-1967-martin-luther-king-interview-1967/. Accessed January 15, 2017.

66. 'Dr. King's Warning on Racialism,' *Guardian*, November 15, 1967, p.5.

67. 'Britain Could Be Next Says King,' *DM*, November 14, 1967, p.5.

68. 'Integration,' *E-Chronicle*, November 14, 1967, p.6.

69. Ibid.

70. Kevin Myers, *Struggles for a Past: Irish and Afro-Caribbean Histories in England, 1951-2000* (Manchester: Manchester University Press, 2015), p.128.

71. 'Editorial.'

72. Ibid.

73. Paul, *Whitewashing Britain*, p.26.

74. Alistair Moffat, *The British: A Genetic Journey* (Edinburgh: Berlinn, 2013), pp.234-239 (on the Indian and Armenian bloodlines in the Spencer family), p.255 (on fish and chips). See also, Eric Hobsbawm and Terence Ranger, *The Invention of Tradition* (Cambridge: Cambridge University Press, 1983).

75. Myers, *Struggles for a Past*, p.4. This trend played out in a succession of increasingly restrictive Immigration Acts, including one in 1971 that redefined British citizenship by stipulating Commonwealth citizens had the right of abode only if they, their husband (if female), their parents, or their grandparents were directly connected to the United Kingdom. The provision meant some British nationals could be denied entry into their country of nationality if they were deemed 'undesirable'—the criteria for which was sometimes, if not always and rarely simply, determined along racial lines. See, Evan Smith and Marinella Marmo, 'The Myth of Sovereignty: British Immigration Control in Policy and Practice in the Nineteen-Seventies,' *Historical Research*, 87, 236 (May 2014), pp.344-369.

76. Rev. John Muir, letter, *E-Chronicle*, November 22, 1967, p.8.

77. Renton, *Colour Blind?*, pp.125-126.

78. C. Arthur, letter, *E-Chronicle*, November 27, 1967, p.6.

79. J. K. Moffat, letter, *E-Chronicle*, December 1, 1967, p.14.

80. Stanley Levison, Martin Luther King and Andrew Young, telephone conversation, November 19, 1967, MLK-FBI.

Chapter Ten: From Righteous Streams to Rivers of Blood: Martin Luther King, Enoch Powell and Race Relations on Tyneside, 1968

1. E.M. Bettenson, quoted in, 'City Students Pay Tribute to Dr. King,' *E-Chronicle*, April 5, 1968, p.1.

2. Coretta Scott King, postcard to Peter O'Donnell, n.d. Copy in possession of author, kindly provided by Peter O'Donnell. Not everyone on Tyneside was so sympathetic. One of Peter O'Donnell's co-workers was unable to understand his distress at news of King's murder, commenting to the effect that King was 'only a darkie.' Peter O'Donnell, conversation with Brian Ward, July 12, 2017.

3. 'America on Brink of Race War,' *Journal*, April 6, 1968, p.1; 'The Shame of Memphis,' ibid., April 6, 1968, p.8.

4. Ibid., April 9, 1968, p.6.

5. Enoch Powell, 'Speech to the Annual General Meeting of the West Midland Area Conservative Political Centre,' April 20, 1968, reprinted in Enoch Powell, *Reflections of a Statesman: The Writings and Speeches of Enoch Powell* (London: Bellew, 1991), pp.373-379.

6. This exchange and details of Powell's visit to America appear in Andrew Roth, *Enoch Powell: Tory Tribune* (London: MacDonald, 1970), pp.340-341. See also, Camilla Schofield, *Enoch Powell and the Making of Post-Colonial Britain* (Cambridge: Cambridge University Press, 2013), pp.208-263, especially pp.21-24, 219 and 220 on Powell's responses to the Detroit riots.

7. Powell, *Reflections of a Statesman*, p.379. See also, Nicholas Deakin, *Colour, Citizenship and British Society* (London: Panther Books, 1970), pp.57-59; 'Keep Britain Civilised,' *New Statesman*, April 26, 1968, p. 533.

8. Chris Waters, "'Dark Strangers' In Our Midst: Discourses of Race and Nation in Britain, 1947-1963,' *Journal of British Studies*, 36 (1997), p.234.

9. For reaction to Powell's speech, see Roth, *Tory Tribune* , pp.339, 340-361; Roy Lewis, *Enoch Powell: Principle in Politics* (London: Cassell, 1979), pp.105-127; T. E Uttley, *Enoch Powell: the Man and his Thinking* (London: William Kimber, 1968), pp.9-44; Dilip Hiro, *Black British, White British: A History of Race Relations in Britain* (c.1971. Revd. ed London: Grafton, 1991), pp.213-214, 246-250; Bill Schwartz, *The White Man's World: Memories of Empire, Vol. 1* (Oxford: Oxford University Press, 2011), pp.33-52; Diana Spearman, 'Enoch Powell's Postbag,' *New Society* 11 (May 9, 1968), pp.667-669; Diana Spearman, 'The Anti-Enoch Letters,' ibid., 11 (June 27, 1968), p.945; Alan Watkins, 'Enoch and After,' *New Statesman* (April 26, 1968), p.533.

10. Maureen Knight, 'The Further North You Go the Better it is,' *Journal*, April 9, 1968, p.6.

11. 'Powell: 500 in Walk-out at Gateshead,' *E-Chronicle*, April 25, 1968, p.1.

12. Alan Nicholson, letter, ibid., April 26, 1968, p.14.

13. Mrs Phillip Layne, letter, *Journal*, April 24, 1968, p.6.

14. J. Crews, P. Robinson, M. Gould, R. White, N.W.H. Wood, N. Clark and J. West, letter, *Journal*, April 25, 1968, p.6.

15. J. Short, letter, *E-Chronicle*, April 26, 1968, p.14.

16. R.T. Oxford, letter, ibid., April 26, 1968, p.14.

17. Mrs. B. Hunter, letter, ibid., April 24, 1968, p.10.

18. Mrs. R.A. Boyes, letter, ibid., April 26, 1968, p.14.

19. Schwartz, *The White Man's World*, p.52.

20. Joan Hoggard, letter, *Journal*, April 24, 1968, p.6.

21. 'Blind Prejudice,' ibid., April 26, 1968, p.8.

22. Ted Fletcher, quoted in 'The Seeds of Hate,' ibid., May 6, 1968, p.5.

23. Will George, letter, *E-Chronicle*, May 10, 1968, p.14.

24. Peter E. Oliver, letter, ibid., May 10, 1968, p.14.

25. Jessie Scott-Batey, John Rafferty and Austin Mallet, letter, ibid., May 10, 1968, p.14.

26. J.F. Clarke and T.P. McDermott, *The Newcastle and District Trades Council, 1873-1973: A Centenary History* (Newcastle upon Tyne: Frank Graham, 1973), p.43. Minutes of Meetings, October 15, 1959 and January 21, 1960, Minute Book, Newcastle and District Trades Council, TU/TC/1/1/2, TWA. *Proceedings of the Council of the City and County of Newcastle upon Tyne for 1959-60* (Newcastle upon Tyne: Cooperative Printing Society, 1960), pp.768-775, LSC-N. Tunde Oloko, letter, *Courier*, December 11, 1959, p.2.

27. Motion, May 17, 1968, Newcastle Trades Council Minutes, 1965-9, TU/TC/1/3, TWA.

28. *E-Chronicle*, May 7, 1968.

29. 'As Powell Speaks, Protests Flare,' and 'The Neet Afore,' both *Courier*, January 22, 1969, p.1.

30. 'Labour Counts the Cost of Disaster,' *E-Chronicle*, May 10, 1968, p.11.

31. 'Day of Decision,' ibid., May 9, 1968, p.8.

32. 'Labour Counts the Cost of Disaster,' and Hilton Cozens, 'City Victory in Tribute to Young Tories,' ibid., May 10, 1968, p.11.

33. Council Minutes, July 3, 1968, *Proceedings of the Council of the City and County of Newcastle upon Tyne for 1968-1969* (Newcastle: Cooperative Printing Company, 1969), pp.204-219, (Morpeth quote, p.211; Grey quote, p. 212) LSC-N.

34. Chris Mullard, *Black Britain* (London: Allen and Unwin, 1973), p.32.

35. Mullard, quoted in Dave Renton, *Colour Blind?: Race and Migration in North East England Since 1945* (Sunderland: University of Sunderland Press, 2007), p.121.

36. 'Lord Mayor Not to Lead Race March,' *E-Chronicle*, May 8, 1968, p.1.

37. 'Day of Decision,' ibid., May 9, 1968, p.8.

38. Martin Luther King, 'Letter from a Birmingham Jail,' 1963, in James M. Washington (ed.), *I Have a Dream: Writings and Speeches that Changed the World* (San Francisco: HarperSanFrancisco, 1992), p.86.

39. 'Day of Decision.'

40. 'Boycott City Race March - Chairman,' *E-Chronicle*, May 9, 1968, p.3.

41. 'Appeal to Reason,' ibid., May 7, p.8; 'Boycott Race March'; 'Day of Decision.'

42. 'Boycott City Race March.'

43. 'Lord Mayor Not to Lead Race March.'

44. Ibid.

45. 'Little Support for Race March,' *Journal*, May 13, 1968, p.9.

46. '100 Meet to Stand up to Racialism,' ibid., May 27, 1968, p.5.

47. Maureen Knight, 'The Further North You Go the Better it is,' ibid., April 9, 1968, p.6.

48. Maureen Knight, 'When You Go to School in a Strange Land,' ibid., April 10, 1968, p.6.

49. Arthur Aughey, *The Politics of Englishness* (Manchester: Manchester University Press, 2007), p.127.

50. Barry Carr, 'Black Geordies,' in Robert Colls and Bill Lancaster (eds), *Geordies: Roots of Regionalism* (1992; Newcastle: Northumbria University Press, 2005), pp.142-143.

51. Rev. E. Harriott, 'Unholy Things,' *E-Chronicle*, April 8, 1968, p.6.

52. Martin Luther King, Jr., Speech to SCLC Annual Convention, Atlanta, August 16, 1967, KCA, kingencyclopedia.stanford.edu/encyclopedia/documentsentry/where_do_we_go_from_here _delivered_at_the_11th_annual_sclc_convention/. Accessed January 2, 2017.

53. Ibid.

54. Ibid.

55. Martin Luther King, Jr., 'Acceptance Speech on Receipt of an Honorary Doctorate at the University of Newcastle upon Tyne,' November 13, 1967, MLK-Reg.

Part Four: Legacies And Lessons

Chapter Eleven: Tending the Cords of Memory: The Road to Freedom City 2017

1. Chi Onwurah, 'Speech,' Westminster Hall, *Hansard*, 616, 54 (November 1, 2016), p.308WH.

2. Ibid., pp. 309-310WH.

3. Freedom City 2017, freedomcity2017.com/about-freedom-city-2017/. Accessed January 6, 2017.

4. For the Mining Institute launch, see David Whetstone, 'Freedom City 2017 Launched to Commemorate the Visit to Newcastle by Martin Luther King,' *ChronicleLive*, November 13, 2015, chroniclelive.co.uk/whats-on/arts-culture-news/freedom-city-2017-launched-commemorate-10443214. Accessed January 6, 2017.

5. Mark Landler, "All Talk,' 'No Action,' Says Trump in Twitter Attack on Civil Rights Icon,' *NYT*, January 14, 2017, nytimes.com/2017/01/14/us/politics/john-lewis-donald-trump.html; Jamiles Lartey, "In Horrible Shape'?: Visit to John Lewis's District Undermines Trump's Claims,' *GuardianOnline*, January 19, 2017, theguardian.com/us-news/2017/jan/19/john-lewis-donald-trump-georgia-atlanta. Both accessed January 22, 2017.

6. Keiran Southern, 'Donald Trump Protest Sees Hundreds Gather at Grey's Monument in Newcastle,' *ChronicleLive*, January 20, 2017, chroniclelive.co.uk/news/north-east-news/donald-trump-protest-sees-hundreds-12486182; 'President Trump: Newcastle Protests in Pictures,' January 20, 2017, ITV News, itv.com/news/tyne-tees/2017-01-20/newcastle-anti-trump-protest-in-pictures/. Both accessed January 21, 2017.

7. Uri Friedman, 'Where America's Terrorists Actually Come From,' *The Atlantic*, January 30, 2017, theatlantic.com/international/archive/2017/01/trump-immigration-ban-terrorism/514361/. See also, Alan Yuhas and Mazin Sidahmed, 'Is this a Muslim Ban?: Trump's Executive Order Explained,' *GuardianOnline*, January 31, 2017, theguardian.com/us-news/2017/jan/28/trump-immigration-ban-syria-muslims-reaction-lawsuits; Garrett Epps, 'Will the Courts Find Trump's Ban Unconstitutional?' *The Atlantic*, February 6, 2017, theatlantic.com/politics/archive/2017/02/will-the-courts-find-trumps-ban-unconstitutional/515751/. All accessed February 26, 2017.

8. Mike Kelly, 'Were Donald Trump Protests in Newcastle a Waste of Time? Our Readers Have Their Say,' *ChronicleLive*, January 31, 2017, chroniclelive.co.uk/news/north-east-news/were-donald-trump-protests-newcastle-12532345. At the time of writing, a second travel ban, in which Trump removed Iran from the list of predominantly Muslim nations under its purview, was also stymied by several federal judges who believed that it may be discriminatory and therefore unconstitutional. Oliver Laughland, 'Trump's Second Travel Ban was Blocked. How Did it Happen, and What's Next?' *GuardianOnline*, March 16, 2017, theguardian.com/us-news/2017/mar/16/trump-new-travel-ban-blocked-explainer-what-next. On June 26, the US Supreme Court announced that it would hold hearings on the ban in October 2017. In the interim, it allowed the ban to function only for those people from the designated countries who could not demonstrate a 'bona fide' reason to enter the US, such as family connections, a university place or a job. Michael D. Shears and Adam Liptak, 'Supreme Court Takes Up Travel Ban Case, and Allows Parts to Go Ahead,' *NYT*, June 26, 2017, www.nytimes.com/2017/06/26/us/politics/supreme-court-trump-travel-ban-case.html. All accessed, June 28, 2017.

9. Kathryn Riddell, Jonathan Walker-Nec and Hannah Graham, 'Stop Trump Protest in Newcastle RECAP: Protesters Take to Street as MPs Debate President's State Visit,' *ChronicleLive*, February 20, 2017, chroniclelive.co.uk/news/north-east-news/donald-trump-protest-mp-debate-12631227?service=responsive. Accessed February 26, 2017. For Theresa Easton's anti-Trump posters see, Anti-Trump Poster Zines, theresaeaston.wordpress.com/2017/02/21/anti-trump-poster-zines/. Accessed April 19, 2017.

10. Rev. Jeffrey L. Brown, 'The Courage to Listen,' Insights Lecture, Newcastle University, February 21, 2017, campus.recap.ncl.ac.uk/Panopto/Pages/Embed.aspx?id=e0f56730-aaf3-

4eca-b4f5-5d777ac6dd94&v=1. The King quotation came from Martin Luther King, 'Letter from a Birmingham Jail,' in James M. Washington (ed.), *I Have a Dream: Writings and Speeches that Changed the World* (San Francisco: HarperSanFrancisco, 1992), p.85. For more on The Boston Miracle, see Nik DeCosta-Klipa, 'How Preachers Cut Violence – But Not by Preaching,' *boston.com*, May 31, 2015, archive.boston.com/news/local/massachusetts/2015/05/31/how-local-preachers-propelled-the-boston-miracle/IdLBbKjsCVk0GOSXkoKECK/story.html Both accessed, February 26, 2017. See also, Rev. George W. Williams, *History of the Twelfth Baptist Church, Boston, Mass., From 1840-1874* (Boston: James H. Earl, 1874); Lewis V. Baldwin, *The Voice of Conscience: The Church in the Mind of Martin Luther King, Jr.,* (New York: Oxford University Press, 2010), pp.42-43, 49, 273-274(n.131).

11. For the post-Brexit rise in hate crimes, see, Matthew Weaver, "Horrible Spike' in Hate Crimes Linked to Brexit Vote, Met Police Say,' *GuardianOnline*, September 28, 2016, theguardian.com/society/2016/sep/28/hate-crime-horrible-spike-brexit-vote-metropolitan-police. Accessed January 22, 2017.

12. Sajid Javid, 'Topical Questions,' January 16, 2017, House of Commons, *Hansard*, available at hansard.parliament.uk/Commons/2017-01-16/debates/6A4D929C-C2A5-4EF2-B8AB-20D8740EA658/TopicalQuestions#contribution-B59B901E-2080-42D9-A6B7-266AC128F6B4. Accessed January 22, 2017.

13. Marcus Jones, 'Comments,' Westminster Hall, *Hansard*, 616, 54 (November 1, 2016), p. 311WH.

14. Onwurah, 'Speech,' pp. 308-309WH.

15. 'Memorial Service for Dr. Martin Luther King,' Programme, April 26, 1968, copy in possession of author, kindly provided by Peter Kane. Charles Bosanquet, 'Address at the Memorial Service For Dr. Martin Luther King,' April 26, 1968, MLK-VC. Brooks read from Isaiah, 58, vv.6-12; Ceres from John, 15, vv.12-18. Ceres's debating skills are celebrated in 'Exhilarating Speakers in Saturday Debate,' *Courier*, November 15, 1967, p.7.

16. C.I.C. Bosanquet, letter to Andrew Young, April 30, 1968, MLK-Dup. Arrangements for the service can be tracked in E.M. Bettenson, 'Dr. Martin Luther King,' Announcement, April 22, 1968; (Anon) C.I.C Bosanquet, Letter to Rudyard Ceres, April 23, 1968; Rudyard Ceres, Letter to Vice Chancellor, April 24, 1968; Anon (C.I.C. Bosanquet), Letter to Paul J. Brooks, April 25, 1968, all MLK-Dup.

17. Bosanquet, 'Address at the Memorial Service For Dr. Martin Luther King.'

18. Barbara M.H. Strang, Memorandum to The Vice-Chancellor, April 26, 1968, MLK-Dup.

19. *Our Friends in the North*, BBC TV Series, 1996. Davies was not the only member of the Newcastle University community to spend time with the civil rights movement in Mississippi; at least one other student went in the summer of 1967. David Wise, Stuart Wise and Ann Ryder, 'A Picture of Campus Life: Student Revolt!' *Courier*, February 14, 1968, p.9.

20. J.G. Davies, letter to Vice-Chancellor, April 10, 1968, MLK-Dup.

21. Vice Chancellor, letter to Mr. J.G. Davies, April 22, 1968, MLK-Dup.

22. 'Fund for Dr. King,' *Courier*, October 9, 1968, p.2; C.I.C. Bosanquet, 'Memorial to the Late Dr. Martin Luther King,' June (n.d.) 1968, MLK-Dup.

23. 'Minute 610: XXIX: Memorial to the Late Dr. Martin Luther King,' June 10, 1968, *The University of Newcastle upon Tyne, Minutes of Council, 1967-1968*; 'Minute 761: XXII: Memorial to Dr. Martin Luther King,' July 7, 1969, *The University of Newcastle upon Tyne, Minutes of Senate, 1968-1969*; 'Minute 590: XVIV: Memorial to Dr. Martin

Luther King,' July 7, 1969, *The University of Newcastle upon Tyne, Minutes of Council, 1968-1969*, p.350, both Reg. The £200 'Original Book Value' of the Lecture Fund was confirmed by the University's Finance Department, Umbereen Rafiq, email to Brian Ward, March 17, 2017. Copy in possession of author.

24. Flyer for 'Race Relations and the Hungry World,' MLK-Lect.

25. Flyer for 'Whatever Happened to Non-Violence,' MLK-Lect.

26. 'Minute 590: XVIV: Memorial to Dr. Martin Luther King.'

27. Ian McBride, 'Future Hopeful in Rhodesia,' *Courier*, March 12, 1980, p.6; see also, ibid., March 5, 1980, p.4.

28. John Hume, letter to Margaret Lewis, June 17, 1985, MLK-Lect.

29. John Hume, 'Nobel Lecture,' Oslo, December 10, 1998, nobelprize.org/nobel_prizes/peace/laureates/1998/hume-lecture.html. Accessed January 26, 2017.

30. Margaret B. Lewis, letter to Bishop Tutu, June 14, 1986; Right Reverend Desmond M. Tutu, letter to Dr. (Margaret) Lewis, July 1, 1986; Dr. M (Margaret) B. Lewis, letter to Archbishop Tutu,' November 14, 1986; Most Reverend Desmond M. Tutu, letter to Dr. (Margaret) Lewis, January 8, 1987; Vice-Chancellor Professor Laurence Martin, letter to Mr. President (Jimmy Carter), November 24, 1987; Nancy R. Konigsmark (Director of Scheduling, The Carter Center), Atlanta, letter to Professor (Laurence) Martin, December 13, 1988, all MLK-Lect.

31. Mike Kelly, 'Race Activist Chris Mullard Talks of His Time in North East,' *ChronicleLive*, June 12, 2016, chroniclelive.co.uk/news/north-east-news/race-activist-chris-mullard-talks-9443844. Accessed January 6, 2017. Although there is no reason to doubt Mullard's memory, it is not entirely clear when he would have had the opportunity to meet with King. As he was not at the coffee morning or the lunch, the most likely moment would have been during the very brief post-ceremony meeting with the press.

32. 'The Day Wor Jimmy Won Geordie's Heart,' *Journal*, May 7, 1977, p.1; 'Howay the Lad, Says President,' ibid., p.3; 'Carter Meets 5 of 6 Leaders in A Prelude to Economic Parley,' *NYT*, May 7, 1977, p.1; 'Canny Jimmy is a Geordie,' *Newcastle City News*, 29 (May 1977), p.1; Jimmy Carter, letter to Hugh White, May 10, 1977, LSC-N. See also, Antony Brown, *Tyne Tees Television: The First 20 Years* (Newcastle: Tyne Tees Television, 1978), pp.50-51; 'Memories of ...*President Carter's Visit to the Old Hall*,' raggyspelk.co.uk/washington_pages/selections5/pres_carter_visit_2.html. Accessed January 26, 2017; *President Jimmy Carter Live From BBC Radio Newcastle* (RCA of Washington and Newcastle City Council: 206/OBBI, 1977).

33. Jimmy Carter, letter to Counsellors David Faulkner, Nick Forbes, and the Lord Mayor of Newcastle, May 6, 2017 (thanks to David Faulkner for sharing this letter).

34. Kate Proctor, 'Former US President Jimmy Carter Reignites his Friendship with the North East,' *ChronicleLive*, August 25, 2013, chroniclelive.co.uk/news/north-east-news/former-president-jimmy-carter-reignites-5783197. Accessed January 26, 2017. Carter, letter to Faulkner, et al.

35. '...And the formal Mr. and Mrs. Ali,' *Journal*, July 15, 1977, p.1; Peter Mortimer, 'A Man of Few Words, This Muhammad Ali,' ibid., p.9; 'Ali and Bride are Blessed in Style,' ibid., July 18, 1977, pp.1/2. For the background and details of Ali's visit, see Russell Routledge, *Muhammad Ali: Tyneside 1977* (Stroud: Amberley, 2014).

36. Muhammad Ali, *World of Sport*, ITV, July 16, 1977, youtube.com/watch?v=JoHZZVYS0qc. Accessed February 24, 2017.

37. Ibid.

38. BBC North East and Cumbria, *Inside Out: The Greatest in South Shields*, February 2, 2004, bbc.co.uk/insideout/northeast/series5/muhammad_ali_boxing.shtml; Tina Gharavi (dir), *King of South Shields* (Bridge + Tunnel, 2008); Hannah Graham, 'Newcastle Man to be Reunited with Rare Muhammad Ali Coin - 39 years after losing it,' *ChronicleLive*, June 14, 2016, chroniclelive.co.uk/news/north-east-news/newcastle-man-reunited-rare-muhammad-11469523. All accessed January 26, 2017.

39. J.G. Davies, letter to Vice-Chancellor, April 30, 1968, MLK-Hon Deg file.

40. Adam Sharp, 'We Don't Need Another (White) Hero: Black-White Anti-Slavery Allies in Local Commemoration and Hollywood Film,' BA Dissertation, Northumbria University, 2017, p.3. David Morton, 'How Jimi Hendrix Rocked Newcastle and South Shields,' *ChronicleLive*, September 18, 2015, chroniclelive.co.uk/news/history/how-jimi-hendrix-rocked-newcastle-10079033. Accessed May 3, 2017.

41. Robert Colls and Bill Lancaster (eds), *Geordies: The Roots of Regionalism*, (1992; Newcastle: Northumbria University Press, 2005), p.xvi.

42. Brian Ward, 'Proposal for a Martin Luther King, Jnr. Memorial Lecture Series and Conference, October 1993,' March 25, 1992; Jeremy Paterson, Letter to Margaret Lewis, April 11, 1992, MLK-Lect. Brian Ward and Tony Badger (eds), *The Making of Martin Luther King and the Civil Rights Movement*, (Basingstoke: Macmillan, 1996); Brian Ward and Stephen Walsh, 'Martin Luther King Jr. At the University of Newcastle upon Tyne: A Documentary Record,' Newcastle, October 1993. Copy in possession of author.

43. 'Martin Luther King Memorial Conference: Civil Rights and Race Relations, October 21-23, 1993,' *Courier*, October 14, 1993, p.2.

44. Jeremy D. Mayer, 'Reagan and Race: Prophet of Color Blindness, Baiter of the Backlash,' in Kyle Longley, Jeremy D. Mayer, Michael Schaller and John W. Sloan, *Deconstructing Reagan: Conservative Mythology and America's Fortieth President* (London: Routledge, 2007), pp.70-89; Maurice A. St. Pierre, 'Reaganomics and Its Implications for African-American Family Life.' *Journal of Black Studies*, 21, 3 (1991), pp.325–340.

45. For a pacy account of the riots and race relations in 1980s Britain, see Andy McSmith, *No Such thing as Society: A History of Britain in the 1980s*, (London: Constable, 2011), pp.86-110.

46. Chris Jones, 'The Smoke Lifts – on Ruined Lives and Hopes,' *Journal*, September 11, 1991, p.9.

47. Paul Robertson, 'Asian Shops Bore Brunt of Meadow Well Looting,' ibid., September 13, 1991, p.11.

48. Peter Hetherington, 'Racist Element' in Tyneside Riot,' *Guardian*, July 14, 1992, p.2.

49. Jon Bennett, 'Singer's Struggle Honoured at Last,' *Journal*, May 8, 1998, p.8; 'Memories of the Movement: Conference Re-unites Two Veterans of the American Civil Rights Struggle,' *Newsletter: University of Newcastle upon Tyne*, 59 (July 1998), pp.1-2 (both quotes p.2). The Conference Programme and other related ephemera can be found in MLK-Lect. Additional internal support for the 1998 Conference also came from the Catherine Cookson, Buxton Bequest and Dove Funds. Mr. J.R.G. Wright, memo to Mr. D. Reed, December 23, 1967 and Mr. J.R.G. Wright, memo to Mr. D. Reed, December 27, 1997, both MLK-Mem.

50. The idea of 'sites of memory' is associated with Pierre Nora, 'Between Memory and History: Les Lieux de Mémoire,' *Representations*, 26 (Spring 1989), pp.7-24. See also, Geoffrey Cubitt, *History and Memory* (Manchester: Manchester University Press, 2007); James Fentress and Chris Wickham, *Social Memory* (London: Blackwell, 1992); Jacques Le

Goff, *History and Memory* (New York: Columbia University Press, 1992); Kendall R. Phillips (ed.), *Framing Public Memory* (Tuscaloosa: University of Alabama Press, 2004).

51. Another partial exception was the naming of a room in the student's union in King's honour. The room contains no reference to the connection between the University and the civil rights leader and may even have been named out of general respect for King's legacy but in ignorance of his visit to Newcastle.

52. Garibaldi's visit to Newcastle, and its polarizing effect on Tyneside radicals in the 1850s, is discussed in Marcella Pellegrino Sutcliffe, 'Negotiating the 'Garibaldi moment' in Newcastle-upon-Tyne (1854–1861),' *Modern Italy*, 15, 2 (May 2010), pp.129-144.

53. Neil Cameron, 'Shaka Hislop Suffered Racism from Newcastle United Fans,' *ChronicleLive*, May 27, 2013, chroniclelive.co.uk/sport/football/football-news/shaka-hislop-suffered-racism-newcastle-4019379. For Show Racism the Red Card, see srtrc.org/home. Both accessed January 6, 2017.

54. Mark Scrimshaw, 'Foreword,' *Arches*, 9 (Summer 2007), p.3; 'Helping to Make Poverty History,' ibid., pp.9-11; Brian Ward, 'To Honour a King,' ibid., pp.12-13; Dan Howarth, 'The Voice of Freedom,' ibid., pp.16-17.

55. For the World War One Christmas Truce teaching resources pack, see research.ncl.ac.uk/martinlutherking/activities/worldwaronechristmastruces/. Accessed January 22, 2017.

56. Kerry Wood, 'Film Footage of Dr Martin Luther King's Tyneside Visit is Found,' *ChronicleLive*, October 6, 2012, chroniclelive.co.uk/news/local-news/film-footage-dr-martin-luther-1372409. Accessed January 6, 2017.

57. Nicola Weatherall, 'Newcastle University Honours Four at Winter Congregation Ceremony,' *Journal*, December 5, 2012, the Journal.co.uk/news/north-east-news/newcastle-university-honours-four-winter-4399105. Accessed January 6, 2017.

58. Andrew Young, quoted in 'Martin Luther King: Americans Shown 'Lost' Newcastle Speech,' June 1, 2014, BBC News, bbc.co.uk/news/uk-england-tyne-27602173. Accessed January 6, 2017. Cobbing's BBC Radio Newcastle features can be heard at 'Dr. Martin Luther King,' BBC Radio Package 1-7, nuvision.ncl.ac.uk/Play/3670. Accessed January 22, 2107.

59. 'Martin Luther King's Tyneside speech to feature in BBC documentary,' *Journal*, May 30, 2014, theJournal.co.uk/news/north-east-news/martin-luther-kings-tyneside-speech-7192365. Accessed January 6, 2017.

60. Royal Television Society, 'NETB AWARDS 2014 — Broadcast, Factual,' d6.rts.org.uk/netb-awards-2014-%E2%80%94-broadcast-factual. Accessed January 24, 2017.

61. See, Footsteps to Freedom in the North East, journeytojustice.org.uk/projects/footsteps-to-freedom/. Nicola Bell, 'Journey to Justice: Footsteps to Freedom in the North East – Evalution Report,' July 2015, p.70. journeytojustice.org.uk/wp/wp-content/uploads/2016/08/FootstepsToFreedom_Evaluation1.pdf. Both accessed January 6, 2017. In 2016, Journey to Justice also visited Sunderland.

62. Newcastle University, 'Mission Statement,' ncl.ac.uk/about/vision/mission/. See also, Newcastle University Institute for Social Renewal, ncl.ac.uk/socialrenewal/. Both accessed January 6, 2017.

63. Here I should declare another conflict of interest—or at least acknowledge my status as a participant-observer—in so far as I served on the Steering Committee for Freedom City 2017.

64. Carol Bell, quoted in 'Freedom City 2017 Awarded Arts Council Funding,' Newcastle University Press Release, October 25, 2016, ncl.ac.uk/press/news/2016/10/freedomcity/. Accessed January 5, 2017.

65. Details of some of the activities planned for Freedom City 2017 were still unconfirmed at the time this book went to press. A full itinerary can be found at freedomcity2017.com/events. Accessed May 30, 2017. There has been other official recognition for King's achievements in Britain, ranging from a statue in Westminster Abbey unveiled in 1998 to an annual Martin Luther King Memorial Lecture at Canterbury Christ Church University started in 2009.

66. Stevie Wonder, quoted in Adam Collerton, email to Brian Ward, May 2, 2017. For Wonder's work on the Martin Luther King Day Holiday, see, 'Birthday Celebration for M.L.K.: Stevie Wonder and More Than 100,000 Persons Rally for a National King Holiday,' *Ebony*, March 1981, pp.126-129; 'The Making of the King Holiday,' *Jet*, January 16, 1989, pp.16-18.

67. Bell, quoted in 'Freedom City 2017.'

Chapter Twelve: Echoes and Arcs: Martin Luther King, Race, Religion and Politics on Tyneside in the 21st Century

1. Tables KS201EW_Percentages and KS201EW_Numbers, 2011 Census: Ethnic Group, Local Authorities in England and Wales,' Office for National Statistics, webarchive.nationalarchives.gov.uk/20160105160709/ons.gov.uk/ons/rel/census/2011-census/key-statistics-for-local-authorities-in-england-and-wales/rft-table-ks201ew.xls. Accessed January 5, 2017. Within Newcastle's communities of South Asian descent, the largest proportion came from Pakistan, representing 2.3 percent of the total city population, followed by India (1.8 percent) and Bangladesh (1.7 percent). Racial and ethnic categories in censuses are notoriously problematic, but they are useful in indicating the broad trends at work in Newcastle and the North East.

2. The people classified by the 2011 Census as 'Mixed Race' included 'White and Black Caribbean', 'White and Black African', 'White and Asian' and 'Multiple Ethnic Groups,' yet probably still did scant justice to the complex interplay of racial and ethnic lineages within essentialist categories such as 'White' or 'Asian.' Tables KS201EW_Percentages and KS201EW_Numbers, 2011 Census. Hannah Flint, 'Where do Immigrants in your Area Really Come From?' *ChronicleLive*, November 30, 2014, chroniclelive.co.uk/news/north-east-news/immigrants-your-area-really-come-8197510. Accessed January 13, 2017.

3. Chi Onwurah, 'Speech,' Westminster Hall, *Hansard*, 616, 54 (November 1, 2016), pp.309-10WH.

4. Ged Grebby, quoted in Dave Renton, *Colour Blind?: Race and Migration in North East England Since 1945* (Sunderland: University of Sunderland Press, 2007), p.22.

5. Dominic Casciani, 'Analysis: The Prevent Strategy and its Problems,' BBC News, August 26, 2014, bbc.co.uk/news/uk-28939555; Homa Khaleeli, "You Worry They Could Take Your Kids: Is the Prevent Strategy Demonising Muslim Schoolchildren?,' *GuardianOnline*, September 23, 2015, theguardian.com/uk-news/2015/sep/23/prevent-counter-terrorism-strategy-schools-demonising-muslim-children. Both accessed January 6, 2017.

6. Keiran Southern, 'Newcastle Journalist Launching Anti-extremism Workshops After Family Member Joined Terrorist Group,' *ChronicleLive*, October 3, 2015,

chroniclelive.co.uk/news/north-east-news/newcastle-journalist-launching-anti-extremism-10167504. Accessed January 6, 2017.

7. David Bean, 'Islam-on-Tyne,' *Guardian*, March 17, 1961, p.9.

8. Sean Seddon, 'Newcastle EU Referendum Results: Did Your Area Vote Leave or Remain?' *ChronicleLive*, June 24, 2016, chroniclelive.co.uk/news/local-news/newcastle-eu-referendum-results-your-11504497. Accessed January 6, 2017; Will Metcalfe, 'EU Referendum Results: How the North East Voted in Full,' *ChronicleLive*, June 24, 2016, chroniclelive.co.uk/news/north-east-news/eu-referendum-results-how-north-11518256. Accessed January 6, 2017.

9. Alistair Moffat, *The British: A Genetic Journey* (Edinburgh: Birlinn, 2013), p.259.

10. Anoop Nayak, 'Young People's Geographies of Racism and Anti-Racism: The Case of North East England,' in Caroline Bressey and Claire Dwyer (eds), *New Geographies of Race and Racism* (Abingdon: Taylor & Francis, 2008), pp. 270-271; 'Immigration Statistics – April to June 2016: Asylum Seekers,' vol. 4, Table as16q (August 25 2016), gov.uk/government/publications/immigration-statistics-april-to-june-2016/asylum. Accessed January 5, 2017; Simon Meechan, 'Gateshead Has Taken the Second Highest Number of Syrian Refugees in the UK Since Crisis Began,' *ChronicleLive*, August 29, 2016, chroniclelive.co.uk/news/north-east-news/gateshead-taken-second-highest-number-11813692. Accessed January 21, 2017.

11. Christopher Ingraham, 'If You Thought Income Inequality Was Bad, Get a Load of Wealth Inequality,' *Washington Post*, May 21, 2015, washingtonpost.com/news/wonk/wp/2015/05/21/the-top-10-of-americans-own-76-of-the-stuff-and-its-dragging-our-economy-down/?utm_term=.812578b9318c; Eric Sherman, 'America is the Richest, and Most Unequal Country,' *Fortune*, September 20, 2015, fortune.com/2015/09/30/america-wealth-inequality/; Heather Stewart, 'Almost Half of Britain's Private Wealth Owned by Top 10% of Households,' *GuardianOnline*, December 18, 2015, theguardian.com/money/2015/dec/18/britain-private-wealth-owned-by-top-10-of-households; The Equality Trust, 'The Scale of Economic Inequality in the UK,' n.d. (2017) equalitytrust.org.uk/scale-economic-inequality-uk. All accessed January 21, 2017. For an overview of inequality in world history, see, Walter Scheidel, *The Great Leveler: Violence and the History of Inequality from the Stone Age to the 21st Century* (Princeton: Princeton University Press, 2017).

12. Joe Biden, in Melissa Chan, 'Read Joe Biden's Speech Warning of the Collapse of the 'World Order',' *Fortune*, January 18, 2017, fortune.com/2017/01/18/joe-biden-speech-world-economic-forum-davos-transcript/. Accessed January 22, 2017.

13. Newcastle City Council, 'Newcastle 2020: Investing for a Fairer Future – Newcastle City Councils Draft Budget Proposals for 2017-2020,' October 2016, newcastle.com/sites/default/files/wwwfileroot/your-council-and-democracy/budget-annual-report-and-spending/newcastle_2020_investing_in_a_fairer_future_-_main_report.pdf; William Jarrett, 'Newcastle Council Cuts: Opportunity for Trade Union fightback,' *Socialist Newspaper*, November 9, 2016, available at socialistparty.org.uk/articles/23909; Rod Ardehali, 'More than 1800 Newcastle Council Staff Could See Pay Slashed in Latest Cost-cutting Move,' November 1, 2016, *ChronicleLive*, chroniclelive.co.uk/news/north-east-news/more-1800-newcastle-council-staff-12111375. All accessed January 13, 2017.

14. Rachel Wearmouth, 'Northern Powerhouse: Average Disposable Income in North East £7,589 Lower than London's,' *ChronicleLive*, August 15, 2015, chroniclelive.co.uk/news/north-east-news/northern-powerhouse-average-disposable-income-9813371. Accessed January 6, 2017.

15. Mike Kelly, 'North East Unemployment Falls by 1% - But Region is Still the Worst in the UK,' *ChronicleLive*, March 16, 2016, chroniclelive.co.uk/news/north-east-news/north-east-unemployment-falls-1-11047939. Accessed January 6, 2017.

16. Joe Sharkey, *Akenside Syndrome: Scratching the Surface of Geordie Identity* (Petersfield: Jajosa Books, 2014), pp.145, 156.

17. Stephen J. Macdonald, Catherine Donovan, and John Clayton, 'Research Briefing No.9,' North East Race Equality Forum, (n.d.). ncl.ac.uk/media/wwwnclacuk/socialrenewal/files/NEREF%20ResearchBriefing%20No%2 09.docx. Accessed January 6, 2017. Nine percent of the attacks involved written threats or abuse, increasingly via social media.

18. Sharkey, *Akenside Syndrome*, p.145.

19. Helen Rae, 'Our Health is improving,' *E-Chronicle*, July 20, 2009, p.8.

20. Ged Grebby, quoted in Sharkey, *Akenside Syndrome*, p.144.

21. Ibid., p.144; Dave Renton, *Colour Blind?*, pp.4, 215.

22. For a sensible discussion of the limitations of Marxist and neo-Marxist class-based analyses of history and historical processes, see David Cannadine, *The Undivided Past: History Beyond our Differences* (London: Penguin, 2013), pp.93-132.

23. 'Newcastle City Council Sign in Favour of Becoming a City of Sanctuary,' July 8, 2013. cityofsanctuary.org/2013/07/08/newcastle-city-council-sign-in-favour-of-becoming-a-city-of-sanctuary/. Accessed January 5, 2017.

24. Amartya Sen, quoted in James Harkin, 'Identity Crisis,' *GuardianOnline*, February 18, 2006, theguardian.com/world/2006/feb/18/religion.uk1. Accessed January 5, 2017. See also, John Nagle, *Multiculturalism's Double Bind: Creating Inclusivity, Cosmopolitanism and Difference* (Farnham: Ashgate, 2009).

25. Moffat, *The British*, p.261. See also, Tony Kushner, *The Battle of Britishness: Migrant Journeys, 1685 to the Present* (Manchester: Manchester University Press, 2012).

26. Newcastle City Council, 'Newcastle's Response to the Refugee Crisis,' Updated January 9, 2017, newcastle.gov.uk/communities-and-neighbourhoods/asylum-and-immigration/newcastles-response-refugee-crisis. Accessed January 28, 2017.

27. ''Anti-Islamisation' Group Pegida UK Holds Newcastle March,' BBC News, February 28, 2015, bbc.co.uk/news/uk-england-tyne-31657167; Michael Brown, Adam Luke, 'Newcastle Unites: Thousands Turn Out as Counter-March Outnumbers Pegida Protest Five to One,' *ChronicleLive*, February 28, 2015, chroniclelive.co.uk/news/north-east-news/newcastle-unites-thousands-turn-out-8740851. Both accessed January 22, 2017.

28. 'Christ Church Church of England Primary School Report on Children with English as an Additional Language,' April 27, 2017 (copy in possession of the author). 82 of the pupils were born in the UK; the next largest cohorts came from Libya (11) and Iran (8). Thanks to Jenny Ward and Sandra Furno for making available this demographic information. It is important to note that 'country of birth' is not synonymous with 'citizenship' and that official statistics on English as an Additional Language collated in British schools do not reveal the levels of competency in either English or the 'other' languages in play. Rather they indicate that the children come from homes where languages other than English are spoken by their parents or guardians, though not necessarily more than English.

29. Thanks to Alison West (Ravenswood Primary School), Wendy Mar (West Jesmond Primary School) and Helen McKenna (Broadway East Primary School) for sharing demographic data on their schools for 2016-17.

30. Ruhi Rahman, quoted in Craig Thompson, 'Abused by a Racist Yob on the Metro – But Luckily it Turned Out She Had a Few Friends Along for the Ride,' *Journal*, November

24, 2015, p.7; Craig Thompson, 'Decency 1, Hatred 0,' *E-Chronicle*, November 24, 2015, pp.1/7.

31. Katrina Barber, quoted in Thompson, 'Abused by a Racist Yob'; Peter Sagar, letter to *Journal*, November 26, 2015, p.24.

32. 'Johnson Should Admit Mistake – Luther King,' *MS*, November 14, 1967, p.3.

33. Theodore Parker, 'Of Justice and the Conscience,' in *Ten Sermons of Religion* (Boston: Crosby, Nichols and Company, 1853), p.85. Martin Luther King, 'Acceptance Speech on Receipt of an Honorary Doctorate at the University of Newcastle upon Tyne,' November 13, 1967, MLK-Reg.

34. 'Speech delivered by the Public Orator (J.H. Burnett) when presenting a candidate (Martin Luther King) for an honorary degree at a Congregation in King's Hall on Monday, 13th November 1967,' MLK-Reg.

Index

6.05 (TV show) 65-6

Abernathy, Ralph 30
Abolition of Slavery Act (1833) 77, 90–2, 99
Abolition of the Slave Trade Act (1807) 87
abolitionism 15, 56, 89, 117, 128, 131; Civil War
   (USA) 118–23; petitions 86–8, 90–1; Quakers and
   non-conformists 79–82, 85–6, 115; societies 84–6, 88,
   98–100, 104; visits to North East by campaigners 16,
   17, 82–4, 97–8, 102–10, 113–17, 122, 124, 126–7
Action Foundation 242
Adams, Charles 122–3
Adams, W.E. 120–1
Advocate of Peace (journal) 97
African communities (North East) 18, 58, 137, 155,
   172, 183, 233
Agencies Against Racist Crime and Harassment 238
Ahmad, Mrs 173
Ahmed, Ashfak 221
Akenside Syndrome (Sharkey) 238–9
A King's Speech – Martin Luther King on Tyneside
   (documentary film) 227
Alavi, Hamza 47
Aldermaston March (1964) 70
Alderson, John 214
Aldridge, J.E.T. 162
Ali, Mahomed (Mohammad Kassen) 138
Ali, Muhammad (boxer) 58, 215, 216–18, 230
Ali, Nabilla 234–5
Ali, Said 138
Allason, Thomas 85
Alleyne, Clyde 65, 67, 180
Alnwick, Northumberland 86, 88, 90, 104, 113
American and Foreign Slavery Society 99
American Anti-Slavery Society (AASS) 97–9
American Peace Committee for a Congress of Nations
   108
American Peace Society 97
Anglicans 55, 81
Animals (band) 58–60
anti-apartheid movement 71, 73, 194
anti-corn-law movement 95, 101
anti-fascist movement 141–3, 165
Anti-Nazi League 165
Anti-Slavery Harp (songbook) 108
anti-slavery movement *See* abolitionism
anti-Vietnam War movement 15, 41, 44, 69, 70
Arab communities (North East) 135, 137–40, 144–7,
   233
Arches (magazine) 225
Armstrong, William George 119
Armstrong College, Newcastle 24, 119, 141
Armstrong-Whitworth Shipyards, Elswick 185

Arthur, C. 185
Ashley, G. 34

Asian communities (North East) 18, 149–55, 161–2,
   171–2, 178, 183, 188, 221, 233
asylum seekers 18, 235–6, 238, 242
At the River I Stand (documentary film) 221
Atkins, Colin 221
Atlanta Hungry Club 69, 71
Atlantic World 16–17, 77, 95, 209, 227
Aughey, Arthur 200
Auld, Thomas 115

Badger, Tony 219
Baez, Joan 45
Baily, Frederick *see* Douglass, Frederick
Baldwin, James 29
Baptists 26–7, 39, 40, 51, 73, 209–10
Barber, Katrina 245
Barry, Paul 32, 55, 72
Barzun, Matthew J. 208
Basu, Dr. 173
Batson, William 85
BBC North East Television 218, 227
BBC Radio Newcastle 216, 226
Bean, David 135, 156–7
Beauclair, Robin 164
Beaumont, Thomas Wentworth 88, 89, 90, 100
Beckett, John 141
Beecham, Jeremy 195
Belafonte, Harry 221–2, 225
Belford, Northumberland 86
Bell, Carol 229, 231
Bell, Meredyth (née Patton) 72
Bell, Robert 88
Bell Terrace School 152
Benezet, Anthony 80
Benfield School 153
Berry, Chuck 59
Berry, Sam 105
Berwick, Northumberland 90, 91, 92, 123
Bessemer, Alabama 29–30, 40
Bettenson, Ernest M. 26, 28, 30–1, 37, 63, 187, 212
Bewick, Thomas 85
Biden, Joe 237
Bilk, David 39–40
Bindra, O.P. 199
Birmingham, Alabama 29, 40, 55, 220
Birth of a Nation (film) 131
Bishop Auckland, County Durham 90
Black and White Minstrel Show (TV show) 185
Black Atlantic 16, 77, 83, 104–10, 132–3, 220, 224
Black Minority Ethnic Education Group Conference
   234

Black Panther Party 42
black power 42–3, 53, 61, 68, 165–6, 187, 197–8
Blackett, John Erasmus 84
Blackwell, J. (printer) 108
Blackwell, J. Kenneth 220
Blair, Mr 34
Blake, William 17
Blenkinsop, Margaret 60–1
Blyth, James 133
Blyth, Northumberland 88
Bolden Colliery Labour Women's Section 142
Bond, Julian 220, 221
Bonham Carter, Mark 169
Boonham, Nigel 229
Booth, Alan 63
Booth, Dorothy 36, 41, 71
Booth, Norleigh 36
Bosanquet, Barbara 25–6, 37
Bosanquet, Charles 71–2, 199, 212, 213; invitation to
    MLK 24–5, 49, 63–4, 228; organisation of MLK visit
    31–3, 36–7
Boston University 26, 28
Bowsher, Andii 225
Boyes, R.A. 190–1
Bradbury, Ray 102
Bravo 22 Company 230
Brexit 16, 210, 208, 235
Bright, John 95
British and Foreign Anti-Slavery Society 98
British and Foreign Society for the Universal Abolition
    of Negro Slavery and the Slave Trade (Universal
    Abolition Society) 99–100
British Association for the Advancement of Science 109–
    10
British identity 132, 183–4, 191, 200, 234
British Nationality Act (1948) 161
British National Party (BNP) 163, 165
British People's Party 141
British Union of Fascists (BUF) 141, 142, 143
Broadway East Primary School 243
Brooks, Paul 32, 212
Brown, David 104
Brown, H. Rap 61
Brown, Henry 'Box' 114
Brown, John 117
Brown, Rev. Jeffrey 209–10
Brown, William Wells 107–9, 128, 209–10
Brown and Green (printers) 108
Brown vs Topeka Board of Education 54
Burch, Stanley 52, 53
Burdon, Eric 58–60
Burleigh, Charles 128
Burnett, J.H. 49–50, 65, 171, 245
Burns, Wilfred 172, 177, 179
Butler, R.A. 156

Byker, Newcastle 91

Cadogan, Peter 90
Callaghan, James 188
Campaign Against Racial Discrimination (CARD) 47–8,
    51, 166, 170, 174, 195, 197–9; Tyneside branch 134,
    173, 178–9, 192
Campaign for Nuclear Disarmament (CND) 70, 71,
    225
Canadian Broadcasting Company 41
Caribbean communities (Tyneside) 18, 46, 52, 150,
    161–2, 164, 172, 200, 224
Carmichael, Stokely 53, 61, 166–7, 187
Carr, Barry 140, 146, 200
Carson, Clayborne 219
Carter, Jimmy 36, 215–16
Carter, Rosalynn 216
Cassim, Ali Hassan 147
Caulker, Doreen 58
Ceda, William 113
Central Negro Emancipation Committee 98
Ceres, Rudyard 212
Chakrabarti, Shami 226
Chandler, Chas 60, 218
Channing, Rev. William Henry 121
Charles, Ray 59
Charlton, John 77, 84, 131, 132
Chartism 98, 101–2, 127
Chester-le-Street, County Durham 88
Chicago, Illinois 41, 43
Chinese communities (North East) 185, 233
Christ Church Church of England Primary School 242-
    4
Christie, Miss 35
Christy Minstrels 112
Chronicle (Newcastle newspaper) 226; abolitionism 103,
    106, 122; British race relations 151, 155–6; Irish
    community 133; US race relations 57, 149
Circus Central (Newcastle) 242–3
City of Sanctuary (Newcastle) 18, 241–2
Civil Rights Acts (1957, 1960, 1964) 42, 163
Civil War (USA) 97, 109, 118–23
Clark, J. 108
Clarke, Fiona 71
Clarke, John Altham Graham 77–8
Clarkson, Thomas 82, 84
Claudia Jones Memorial Lecture 225
Cleveland, Ohio 40–1
Clotel, or the President's Daughter (Brown) 107
coal industry 81, 83–4, 176–7
Cobbing, Murphy 73, 226–7
Cobden, Richard 95
Cold War 14, 69–70
Collerton, Adam 228
Collerton, Patrick 228

Collins, Canon John 70
Collins, Sydney 134, 148
Colls, Robert 219
Colour Discrimination in Newcastle upon Tyne (CARD) 134–5, 178–9
Comfrey Project 242
Commonwealth Immigrants Act (1962) 48, 162, 169, 188
Commonwealth Immigrants Act (1968) 162
Commonwealth Immigrants Working Group (CIWG) 173, 174–5, 195, 197–8
communism 14, 43, 143, 144, 194
Community Relations Council (CRC) 173, 195, 196
Cone Street School, South Shields 146
Confederate States of America 42, 54, 67, 111, 124–7, 131; secession 97, 118 *See also* Civil War
Confederation of Shipbuilding and Engineering Unions 176
Connor, Eugene 'Bull' 55
Conservative Party 161, 188–9, 194, 220, 234
Cooke, Alistair 51–2, 53
Cooks' and Stewards' Union 140
Co-operative Women's Guild 142
Coordinating Committee against War and Fascism 142
Courier (Newcastle student newspaper) 32, 66, 71, 73, 214
Cowen, Joseph 108, 114, 120–3, 128, 133
Coy, Edward 126
Craft, Ellen 109
Craft, William 109–10, 112
Craggs, William 136–7
Creighton, Sean 90, 132
Crisis (magazine) 52
Crossings (band) 242
Crozer Theological Seminary, Chester, Pennsylvania 28
Cullercoats, Northumberland 114
cultures of welcome, North East 18, 134, 141, 143, 174, 240–2

Daily Mail (newspaper) 52, 53, 164, 181
Darlington, County Durham: abolitionism 86, 88, 90–1, 98, 102, 104, 107–8, 113–14; Basque refugees 142; Lincoln's assassination 123; Pease family 80, 96–7, 102, 108
Darnton, Robert 83
Davies, Jon Gower 213, 218
Davies, Richard 228–9
Davis, Jefferson 119
Davison, R. 157
de Freitas, Michael (Abdul Malik, Michael X) 166, 170
Dean, Maud 137
Democratic Party National Convention, Atlantic City (1964) 46
Derry, John 219
Detroit riots 68, 165–6

Dexter Avenue Baptist Church, Montgomery, Alabama 26, 39
Dickerson, Vanessa 111
Diddley, Bo 59
Discovery Museum, Newcastle 220, 227
discrimination 59–60, 115–16; anti-discrimination legislation 42, 129, 163, 165, 188, 211; Britain 65, 143, 188; Campaign Against Racial Discrimination (CARD) 47–8, 166, 173, 197–9; North East 17, 134–5, 147, 171, 173, 178–9; structural discrimination 180, 211; USA 100, 124 *See also* racism
Dodds, Ruth 142
Douglas-Hamilton, Lord James 29
Douglass, Frederick (Frederick Baily) 16, 102, 114–18, 124, 209–10
Dowell, John 145
Dowson, Gordon 152
Doyle, James 164
Dred: A Tale of the Dismal Swamp (Stowe) 103
Dred Scott case (1857) 105
Drescher, Seymour 81
Duff, Peggy 70
Durham 86, 88, 90–1, 92, 113, 114
Durham University 24
Durley, Rev. Gerald 226
Dylan, Bob 244

Easton, Theresa 209
Ebenezer Baptist Church, Atlanta, Georgia 26, 27, 40, 73
Ebony (magazine) 59
economy 14–15, 77–8, 186; economic regeneration 175–8; post-industrial 18, 147–8, 176, 220–1, 236–9
Edgar, Charles 139
Edinburgh University 28–9, 40
education: importance of 131, 152, 168, 181, 193, 234–6; initiatives 125, 135, 144, 146, 163, 211, 224, 227; Tyneside schools 152–3, 242–4
Egbuna, Obi 166
Ellis, Sylvia 25
English Defence League 242
Equiano, Olaudah (Gustavus Vassa) 82–4
eugenics 112, 164
European Volunteer Workers Scheme (EVWS) 162–3
Evening Chronicle (Newcastle newspaper): civil rights movement 53–4, 150; poverty 237; race relations 181–2, 184–5, 189, 193, 194, 197, 199, 244

Face to Face (TV show) 51, 53
Faubus, Orval 54–5
Faulkner, David 216
Fawdon, Newcastle 91
Federal Bureau of Investigation (FBI) 44–5, 72
Felling, Tyne & Wear 113
Fenwick, Edwin 72

Fenwick, John 88
Fischer, Dr. Geoffrey 55
Fischer, Dr. Martin 51
Fisk Jubilee Singers 124–5
Fletcher, Ted 192
Foner, Eric 125
Forbes, Nick 216, 235
Fordyce, W. & T. 112
Forster, Matthew 88
Fortune (magazine) 236
Foss, Andrew T. 128
Foster, Abby Kelly 128
Foster, Stephen S. 128
Fox, George 79
Franco, General Francisco 142
Frazer, Margaret Ann 138
Fredrickson, George 219
Free Speech (newspaper) 126
free trade movement 95–6, 101, 104
Freedom! (film) 229
Freedom City 2017 14, 207–8, 223–5, 228–31, 243–4, 246
Freeman, Jonathan 51
Friends of Summerhill 230
Friendship Force 216
Frye, Charles 220
Fugitive Slave Act (1850) 105, 109
fugitive slaves 16, 17, 104–10
Fulton, D.C.H. 179
Fun-da-Mental (band) 220
Fye, J.B. 140

Galloway, Alonze 57
Garibaldi, Giuseppe 223
Garnet, Henry Highland 104, 105, 114
Garrison, William Lloyd 97, 98–9, 102, 113, 122–3, 124, 223
Garrow, David 46
Gary, Indiana 41
Gateshead: abolitionism 88, 91, 104, 114; anti-fascist movements 143; Irish community 133; Jewish community 141; Lincoln's assassination 123; non-comformists 81; peace activism 97; race relations 189, 192–3; refugees 235–6; slave trade 78
George, Wesley Critz 164
George, Will 192, 195, 198
Georgetown University, Washington DC 230
Geraghty, Patricia 155
Geronimo, Joana 230
Gharavi, Tina 218
Gladstone, William 119, 133
Glean, Marion 46, 47
Glover, Francis 25
Goldsmith, Maurice 24
Goldwater, Barry 67

Gompertz, Albert 141
Good Morning Britain (TV show) 245
Gosforth, Newcastle 141
Gray and Sons (clothier), Durham 32
Great North Museum: Hancock, Newcastle 227, 229, 231
Great Reform Act (1832) 89–90, 98, 118, 121
Greater London Council 47
Grebby, Ged 224, 234, 239
Greenhow, Thomas Michael 102
Grenby, Matthew 230
Grey, Arthur 195
Grey, Charles, second Earl 87–9, 91–3; monument 93, 208–9
Griffith, Mike 230
Guardian (newspaper) 51, 52, 64, 135, 156, 170
Gutteridge, Reg 217

Hackett, Brian 23
Hackett, Eric 199
Hadrian's Wall 15
Hailsham, Lord 177
Harding, Eric 194–5
Hargreaves, Rev. James 97
Harle, W. Lockley 128
Harney, George Julian 127–9
Harper, F.W. 128
Harriott, Rev. E. 202
Harris, Rev. George 102
Harrison, William 145
Hartlepool, County Durham 104, 113
Hassan, Ali 137
Hatcher, Richard 41
Headlam, Thomas Emerson 102
Heath, Edward 188, 189
Henderson, Andrea 229
Henderson, Arthur 15
Hendrix, Jimi 218
Henry, Lenny 227
Herald of Peace (journal) 97
Hexham, Northumberland 88, 90, 114, 117, 142, 225
Hills, Sid 150
Hindu communities (Tyneside) 151, 153–4, 196, 199
Hislop, Shaka 224
Hodges, Luther 24
Hoggard, Joan 191–2
Holland, Ralph 49
Holmes, Hannah 136
Hooker, John Lee 59
Hoover, J. Edgar 72
Houghton le Spring, Tyne & Wear 91
Houston, Ben 229
Howarth, Dan 225
Howe, George R. 31, 32–3, 34–5, 37–8, 64
Howick, Lord 91

Huddleston, Trevor 214
Hugman, Joan 133–4
Humanus (pseudonym) 86–7
Hume, John 214–15
Humphrey, T.B. 147
Hungry Club, Atlanta 69, 71
Hunt, Dr. James 109–10, 112
Hunt, John 157
Hunt, Megan 229
Hunter, B. 190
Huzzey, Richard 100–1

Iddon, Don 52
immigrant communities 15, 17, 184, 189, 223, 242;
   African 18, 58, 137, 155, 172, 183, 233; Arab 135,
   137–40, 144–7, 233; Asian 18, 149–55, 161–2, 171–
   2, 178, 183, 188, 221, 233; Caribbean 18, 46, 52,
   150, 161–2, 164, 172, 200, 224; Hindu 151, 153–4,
   196, 199; Irish 133; Muslim 135, 146, 153–4, 196,
   244–5; population in the North East 171–2, 233–4,
   235–6; Sikh 151, 153–4, 196
immigration: assimilation 156; attitudes in the North
   East 151, 3, 154–5, 196, 199; Britain 17–18, 47–8,
   52; controls 162, 184, 188–9; non-white 144, 148,
   151; threat to job opportunities 149–50, 151–2
imperialism 43, 96, 111, 128
Independent Labour Party 143
Independent Television Network (ITN) 34
Indian Association of Newcastle 196
Indian Forum 173
Ingliss-Evans, Rev. B. 63
Inside Out (TV show) 218
The Interesting Narrative of the Life of Olaudah Equiano
   or Gustavus Vassa, the African (Equiano) 83
International Brigade 142
International Conference for Disarmament and Peace
   (ICDP) 70
Irish communities (Tyneside) 133
Islam 135, 144, 209, 234–5 See also Muslim
   communities
Islamophobia 18, 208–9, 234–5, 237, 242

Jack, Ken 71
Jackson, Michael 244
Jamaica slave uprising (1831) 91
James, C. L. R. 51
Jamiat al-Muslimeen 154, 173
Jarrow Crusade 141
Javid, Sajid 210
Jayaraman, Geetha 229
Jenkins, Roy 167, 169–70, 174, 187
Jesmond, Newcastle 141
Jet (magazine) 65
Jewell, Mrs Henry 126
Jewish communities (North East) 141, 143

Jewish Representative Council 143
Jim Crow's Song Book 112
Johnson, Andrew 123
Johnson, Charles 134
Johnson, George 84
Johnson, Lyndon B. 41, 42, 44, 57, 71
Jones, Claudia 225–6
Jones, Marcus 210–11
Journal (Newcastle newspaper) 53–4, 56, 150;
   abolitionism 125, 131, 136; assassination of MLK
   187–8; civil rights movement 55, 57; fascism 141; race
   relations 155–6, 189–90, 192, 199, 245
Journey to Justice 227

Kane family (Edna, Laurence and Peter) 37
Kaspar, John 54
Kassen, Mohammad (Mahomed Ali) 138
Kay, Robert 83
Kell, Mrs 35–6
Kennedy, John F. 44
Kenton, Newcastle 141
Kentucky Minstrels (radio show) 113
Khwaja, M. 173
King, B.B. 59
King, Coretta Scott 45, 46, 187
King, Rev. D.E. 45
King, Rodney 220
King, Martin Luther 42, 45, 49–51, 72; anti-war
   movement 41, 44, 69, 70–1; assassination 187–8, 212;
   Atlanta Hungry Club speech 69, 71; Boston
   University 26, 44, 210; civil rights activities 29–30,
   39–46, 53–8, 149; commemoration in Newcastle
   212–28; international recognition 46–9, 51, 211; ;
   Newcastle speech 14, 64–9, 71–4, 219, 225;
   Newcastle visit 13-14, 17, 23-38, 40–2, 48-50, 171,
   180–2, 222, 226, 245; Nobel Peace Prize (1964) 46,
   49, 51; nonviolent direct action 117, 166, 167; peace
   activism 69–71; poverty, views on 43, 68–9, 72, 201–
   3; profile in Britain 51–3, 55–61, 70–2; race relations
   in Britain 47–8, 181, 201; Knight, Maureen 135, 189,
   199–200
Kossuth, Lajos 223
Ku Klux Klan 54, 57, 124, 131

labour organisations 101, 143; unions 140, 142, 144–5,
   150, 176, 225 See also working class
Labour Party 41, 142–3, 162–3, 187–8, 194
Ladies' Anti-Slavery Society 98
Ladies' Association of New England 98
Ladies' Free-Labour Produce Societies 104–5
Ladies Negro Friend and Emancipation Society of
   Newcastle (LNFESN) 104–5, 113
Lambton, John George 89
Lamming, George 51
Lancaster, Bill 219

Larrow, Dennis 150
Lawless, Richard 132
Layne, Mrs 190
League of Empire Loyalists (LEL) 47, 163, 165
Letter from America (radio show) 51–2
Levellers 79
Lewcock, Connie 175
Lewis, David 46
Lewis, John 208
Liberator (newspaper) 97, 114, 115, 122
Lilburne, John 'Freeborn John' 79–80
Lincoln, Abraham 118–20, 122–4, 128
Lishman, Brian 61
Little Rock, Arkansas 54–5
London 47, 51, 55, 148, 220
London Abolition Committee 84
London and Westminster Review (magazine) 103
Lorin, Ellis Gray 115
Losh, James 88
Lowrie, Walter 115
Luizzo, Viola 57
lynchings 126–7

Mackenzie, Eneas 81
Mackham, Mary Ann 132–3
MacMillan, Harold 161
Malcolm X 14, 29, 53
Malik, Abdul (Michael de Freitas, Michael X) 166, 170
Malik, Manju 221
Mallet, George 136–7
Manning, Leah 142
Marlette, Doug 220
Marshall, Roy 199
Martin, J. 123
Martin, Jane 136
Martin Luther King Lectures 213–15, 222
Martin Luther King Memorial Conferences (1993, 1998) 219–20, 221–2, 224
Martin Luther King Peace Committee (MLKPC) 225
Martineau, Elizabeth Rankin 102
Martineau, Harriet 102–3, 109
Martyr Age of the United States (Martineau) 103
Marxism 43
Mawson, John 122–3
Maxwell, Africanus 136–7
McCarran-Walter Act (1952) 161
McCarty, Joyce 241
McDonald, Dora 26, 28, 30, 40, 63
McDonald, Ian 229
McLaren, Mr 34
McLeod, Basil 173–4, 197–8
Meadow Well riots, North Shields 220–1
Meah, Mrs 157
Media, Culture and the Modern African American Freedom Struggle (book) 221

Megoran, Nick 225, 229
Mellon, Paul 219
Melody Maker (magazine) 59
Menza, Claudia 220
Meredith, James 42
Methodists 81, 85, 92–3
Mexican War (1846-8) 105
Michael X (Michael de Freitas, Abdul Malik) 166, 170
Middlesbrough, Teesside 104, 149, 157
Mighty Stream (book) 230
Milbanke, Sir Ralph 86
militarism 68–9, 72 *See also* Vietnam War
Miller, Henry 213–14
Miller, Rev. M. 121
Miners' Association 101
minstrelsy 112–13, 185
Miskin, Paul 218
Mississippi Freedom Democratic Party 46
Mississippi Freedom Summer (1964) 53
Modood, Tariq 219
Moffat, Alistair 241
Moffat, J.K. 185
Mohammad, Hassan 138
Monkwearmouth, Tyne & Wear 91
Montagu, Elizabeth 132
Montgomery, Alabama: Bus Boycott 23, 51–2, 54, 149
Monthly Illustrations of American Slavery (journal) 97
Moody, Dwight M. 125
Moon, Harvey Lee 52
Morpeth, John 195
Morpeth, Northumberland 90–1, 113, 117, 123
Morpeth Anti-Slavery Society 91
Morrison, David 227
Mortimer, Rev. G.F.W. 91–2
Mosley, Sir Oswald 141, 143
Mott, Lucretia 98
Muhammad, Elijah 53
Muir, Rev. John 184
Mullard, Chris 48, 178, 195–8, 215
Mulreany, Mr 157
multiculturalism 169–70, 179, 183, 211, 233, 239, 241–4
Muslim communities (Tyneside) 135, 146, 153–4, 196, 244–5 *See also* Islam
Myers, Kevin 182, 184

Nagi, Janet 138
Narang, H.K. 196, 199
Narrative of William W. Brown, An American Slave (Brown) 108
National Association for the Advancement of Colored People (NAACP) 39, 44, 48, 51–2, 54
National Charter Association 101
National Committee for Commonwealth Immigrants 169

National Council for Civil Liberties 194
National Front (NF) 18, 165
National Joint Committee for Spanish Relief 142
National Labor Leadership Assembly for Peace 41
National Unemployed Workers' Movement (NUWM) 142–3
National Union of Journalists 225
National Union of Seamen (NUS) 140, 144–5
National Union of Students 39
National Union of Teachers 142
Neptune Steam Navigation Company 78
New Commonwealth 162, 172
New Musical Express (magazine) 60
Newbottle, Tyne & Wear 91
Newcastle and District Trades Council 194
Newcastle City Council 24, 171–9, 194–5, 216, 229, 237, 241–2
Newcastle Combat Group 143
Newcastle Common Council 84, 88
Newcastle Corporation Transport Undertaking 149–50
Newcastle Courant (newspaper) 86–7, 108, 113, 125–6
Newcastle Daily Chronicle (newspaper) 83–4, 120
Newcastle Daily Leader (newspaper) 126
Newcastle Gateshead Initiative (NGI) 229, 231
Newcastle Guardian (newspaper) 116
Newcastle Hindu Temple 199
Newcastle Ladies' Emancipation Society (NLES) 98, 104
Newcastle Literary and Philosophical Society 97
Newcastle Mining Institute 208
Newcastle Stop the War Coalition 225
Newcastle Unites 208, 242
Newcastle University *See* University of Newcastle upon Tyne
Newcastle upon Tyne Emancipation and Aborigines Society 103
Newcastle upon Tyne Grammar School 91-2
Newcastle upon Tyne Society for Abolishing Slavery All Over the World 100
Newcastle Weekly Chronicle (newspaper) 121, 127
Nicholson, Alan 190
Nicholson, C.B. 'Nick' 25, 32
Nixon, Richard 203
Nobel Peace Prize 15, 214; awarded to MLK (1964) 46, 49, 51
non-comformism 81–2, 96 nonviolent direct action 43, 54, 117, 166, 167
North East Economic Planning Council 24
North East Regional Planning Council 177
North of England Refugee Service 242
North Shields Reform League 122
North Shields, Tyne & Wear: abolitionism 86, 90–2, 104, 114, 117; seamen 136–7
Northern Daily Mail (newspaper) 54
Northern Political Union 101

Northern Roots 229
Northumberland, 2nd Duke (Hugh Percy) 86, 132
Northumberland, 10th Duke (Hugh Algernon Percy) 30, 36, 37
Northumbria Police 196, 238
Northumbria University (formerly Newcastle Polytechnic) 194, 225, 227, 229
Notting Hill race riot (1958) 55, 148
Nottingham race riot (1958) 55, 148

Oberlin Institute, Ohio 103
O'Brien, Conor Cruise 214
Observations on Inslaving, Importing and Purchasing Negroes (Benezet) 80
Observer (newspaper) 214
O'Connor, Fergus 101
O'Connor, Peter 120
O'Donnell, Peter (Royal Mail worker) 187
O'Donnell, Peter (seaman) 145
The Olive Leaf (magazine) 97
Oliver, Peter E. 192–3
Olusoga, David 15–16, 164
Onwurah, Chi 207–8, 211, 223, 226, 234
Ormston, Robert 85, 100
Osborne, Sir Cyril 168
Ottley, Roi 148
Ouseburn Learning Trust 244
Oxford, R.T. 190
Oxford University Union 29

Pain, R.H. 63–4
Pakistan League 173
Palen, Marc-William 95
Pan-Africanism 166–7
Parker, Theodore 245
Paterson, Jeremy 219
Patterson, Sheila 172
Paul, Kathleen 163, 183
peace activism 15, 43, 69-71, 95–8 *See also* anti-Vietnam war movement; Campaign for Nuclear Disarmament; Peace Society
Peace Convention, Paris (1849) 108
Peace Society (London Society for the Promotion of Permanent and Universal Peace) 97, 98, 225; Newcastle Auxiliary 96
Peart-Smith, Paul 230
Pease family 80, 96–7, 108, 115; Elizabeth 98, 99, 102, 113, 115–16; Joseph 98
Pegida 242
Pennington, Dr. James 104
Petch, Professor 33
Phillips, Wendell 99, 128
Phylon (journal) 67
Pick, Hella 52
Pierre, Neville 173

Pinkney family 78
Pitt, David (Baron Pitt of Hampstead) 47–8, 51
Pleasant, Ian 218
Plessy vs Ferguson case 54, 124
Polish communities (North East) 233
Political and Economic Planning Ltd (PEP) 165, 170
Poor People's Campaign 41, 43–4, 45, 69, 193, 202
Potter, Kathleen 25
poverty 178, 236–8; link with racism 43, 68–9, 72,
    140–1, 181, 201–2, 207, 220–1, 224
Powell, Enoch 188–9, 191–2, 195, 196, 198
Presbyterians 81, 85
Press, Thomas 139
Prevent programme 234
Price, Alan 58, 60
Prowitt, Edward 85
Purdue, A.W. 81

Quakers 46, 85, 225; abolitionism 79–82, 98, 117;
    Newcastle 80, 96–7; USA 115

race relations: Britain 47–8, 52, 55, 66–7, 155, 161–71,
    220; Gateshead 189, 192–3; Middlesbrough 157;
    Newcastle 152–3, 171–6, 178–80, 189; North East
    129–36, 154–8, 161–2, 178–86, 200, 220–1, 233–46;
    North Shields 136; South Shields 135, 137–41, 144–
    7, 243; USA 128, 188–9, 201–3
Race Relations Act (1965) 163
Race Relations Act (1968), 168, 170, 179, 187, 189–90,
    195, 200
Race Relations Board 163, 165, 169
Racial Action Adjustment Society (RAAS) 166
Racial Equality Council 221
Racial Preservation Society (RPS) 163–5
racism 42, 245; anti-racist movement 56, 163, 196–8,
    238–9; British Empire 110–12; international nature
    46, 66, 202; latent racism 180, 182; link with poverty
    43, 68–9, 72, 140–1, 181, 201–2, 207, 220–1, 224;
    minstrelsy 112–13, 185; North East 16, 112–13, 136–
    50, 221, 224–5; racial stereotypes 88, 109–11, 113,
    137, 146, 154, 164, 241; scientific 109–10, 111–12;
    structural 137, 211; white supremacists 16, 47, 54, 61,
    124 *See also* discrimination
radicalism 89–90, 101; North East 15, 77–81, 90, 96,
    118–19, 121–2
Rafiq, Umbereen 215
Rahman, Ruhi 244–5
Ravenswood Primary School 243
Ray, James Earl 187
Read, Mr 35
Reconstruction era (USA) 123–30
Redding. Otis 60
Reeb, Rev. James 57
Reed, Kasim 73
Reed, Melanie 224, 226

Reed, Richard 120
refugees 18, 142, 235–6, 242
Regional Refugee Forum North East 242
Remond, Charles Lenox 104, 113–14
Renton, Dave 132, 157–8, 173, 196
*Representation of the Injustice and Dangerous Tendency of
    Admitting the Least Claim of Private Property in the
    Persons of Men in England* (Sharp) 82
Representation of the People Act (1832) *See* Great
    Reform Act (1832)
Rex, John 199
Rice, Thomas Dartmouth 'Daddy' 112
Richardson, George 85
Richardson family 80, 97, 115, 210, 230; Anna 80, 97,
    105, 108-9, 114, 117; Ellen 80, 114, 117; Henry 80,
    97, 105, 108-9, 114, 116
Richmond, Bill 132
Richmond, Thomas 136
Rickerby, Mr 32
riots 42, 55, 68, 89, 148, 157, 165–6, 220
Robertson, W.J. 137
Robjohns, Henry Thomas 125
Robson, Dale 221
Roche, Mr Justice 145–6
Roman Catholics 133
Roper, Moses 113
Routledge, Russell 218
Rowan, Carl T. 44
Russell, Sandi 220
Rustin, Bayard 44, 46

Sagar, Peter 245
Said, Ali 145–6
Said, Hassan 157
Said, Mary Ellen 137
Sample, Rev. G. 88
Sandbrook, Dominic 176
Sanderson, Miss 32
Sankey, Ira 125
Saunders, David 96
Schwartz, Bill 191
Science of Science Foundation 24
Scott, Harry 113
Scott, Richard 52
Scott-Batey, Jessie M. 193, 196, 198–9
Scrimshaw, Mark 225
Seaman's United Association 101
Seamen's Minority Movement 144–5
Second Reform Act (1867) 101, 118
segregation 52, 54, 115–16, 126–7, 149, 164, 166
Selma, Alabama 28, 53, 56–7
Sen, Amartya 241, 244
Seward, W.H. 123
Sewell, Mike 219
Shah, Sayed 135, 144

Sharkey, Joe 238–40
Sharp, Adam 218
Sharp, Dr. John 81
Sharp, Gordon 218
Sharp, Granville 82, 83
Shields Daily News (newspaper) 138, 146
shipbuilding industry 81, 134, 176
Short, J. 190
Show Racism the Red Card (SRRC) 224, 234, 239
Shukla, Hari 221
Shukra, Kalbir 48
Sikh communities (Tyneside) 151, 153–4, 196
Simone, Nina 59
Singh, Indar 154
Slave (journal) 97
Slaveholders' War (Adams) 121
slaves 80, 88, 95, 97-9, 103-4, 111, 121; commercial links of the North East 77–8, 131; emancipation 118–21, 136; fugitive 16, 17, 104–10; massacres 83; rebellions 91, 117; slave plantations 77–8, 90; slave trade 15, 77–8, 87 *See also* abolitionism
Smith, T. Dan 24, 177, 199
social memory 14, 36–7, 64, 215–16, 222–5
Socialist League 143
Society for Effecting the Abolition of the Slave Trade in London 82
Society for Promoting the Abolition of Slavery throughout the British Dominions 88, 90
Society in America (Martineau) 103
Society in Newcastle for Promoting the Abolition of the Slave-Trade 84, 86
Society of Friends *See* Quakers
Some Considerations on the Keeping of Negroes (Woolman) 80
Sorenson, Tony 41
South Africa 46, 73, 194
South Shields, Tyne & Wear 58; abolitionism 86, 88, 90–3, 98, 104, 109, 114; anti-fascist movements 142–3; Arab community 135, 137–40, 144–7; Lincoln's assassination 123; Muhammad Ali 230; race relations 135, 137–41, 144–7, 243
Southern Christian Leadership Conference (SCLC) 23, 30, 39, 41, 43, 44, 48, 67-9, 202, 226
Soviet Union 14
Spanish Civil War 142
Special Committee as to Commonwealth Immigrants (SCCI) 173
Spence, T. (calligrapher) 33
Spence, Thomas 81–2
Srivener, Michael 82
Stanton, Elizabeth Cady 98
Stanton, Henry B. 99
Stapylton, J. 33
Steel, John 58, 59
Stockton, County Durham 88, 97, 104

Stokes, Carl 40–1
Stowe, Harriet Beecher 103
Strang, Barbara 213
Street, Harry 170
Stride, Tony 151–4
Stuart, Charles 98
Student Non-violent Coordinating Committee (SNCC) 48, 53, 208
students 39, 222; black students 54–5; Newcastle meeting with MLK 37, 55, 61, 72; Newcastle University 25, 33, 41, 71, 172, 194, 212, 215; Newcastle Polytechnic 194
Sturge, Joseph 98
suffrage 89–90, 101, 118, 127, 129
Sunderland: abolitionism 88, 90–1, 98, 104, 113, 114, 125; Lincoln's assassination 123; race relations 238
Sunderland Echo (newspaper) 54
Supple, Carrie 227
Supple, Tim 230
Supporting Migrants, Asylum-Seekers and Refugees Together (SMART) 242
Swalwell and Winlaton ironworks, Gateshead 78
Swan Hunter shipbuilders, Wallsend, Tyne & Wear 134
Swinburne, Sir John Edward 88, 100
Swing riots 89
Syrian Vulnerable Person Resettlement Scheme 242

Tappan, Lewis 98-9
Taylor, Frank 150
Taylor, Henry 85
Taylor, J.H. 153
Telang, Sudha 171–2, 175, 176, 179
Thatcher, Margaret 220
theatre 103, 114, 125, 220, 230; minstrelsy 112–13, 185
Theological School of the Protestant Church, Berlin 51
Thompson, George 98, 100, 102
Times (newspaper) 121
Tinker, Hugh 214
Todd, Nigel 132, 143
Tognoli, N. 141
Toxteth riots, Liverpool 220
Trades Union Congress 142
Transglobal Underground (band) 220
Transport and General Workers Union 150
Trevelyan family 78
Trimble, David 214
Trump, Donald 208–10, 237
Tuck, Stephen 166–7
Turner, Rev. William 84-5, 88, 100
Tutu, Desmond 215
Tynemouth, Tyne & Wear 88, 102–3, 142
Tyneside Inter-Racial League 147
Tyneside Radicals (comic book) 230
Tyne Tees Television 34, 64, 65, 67

Uncle Tom's Cabin (Stowe) 103
Union and Emancipation Society of the North of England 121
Unitarians 57, 81, 84–5, 88, 102
Universal Abolition Society (UAS) 99–100
Universal Coloured People's Association (UCPA) 166–7
University of Newcastle upon Tyne 207, 223, 225, 243; honorary degrees 24–5, 49–50; legacy of MLK visit 211–15, 218–27, 228; visit of MLK 17, 23–38, 171

Vassa, Gustavus *see* Olaudah Equiano
Vickers shipbuilders, High Walker, Tyne & Wear 176
Vietnam War 216–17; anti-Vietnam War movement 15, 41, 44, 69, 70–1
Vietnamese communities (North East) 233
Voice of North East Industry (journal) 162
Voting Rights Act (1965) 42, 44, 57

Walker, W.R. 112
Walker, Wyatt 30
Wallace, George 56
Walters, Rev. W. 123
Ward Thomas (band) 244
Warnock, Rev. Raphael 73
Watkins, James 105, 106–7, 112
Watson, Robert Spence 97
Watson and Burton Solicitors, Newcastle 36
Watt, Hugh 28
Watts Riots, Los Angeles 42
Wedgewood, Fanny 102
Wells, Ida B. 126–7
West Boldon, South Tyneside 91
West End Refugee Service 242
West Hartlepool, County Durham 123
West Indian communities (North East) 18, 46, 52, 150, 161–2, 164, 172, 200, 224
West Indian Gazette (newspaper) 226
West Jesmond Primary School 243
Whaley, Eddie 113
Where Do We Go From Here: Chaos or Community? (King) 26, 39

Whitburn, South Tyneside 91
White, Hugh 216
Wilberforce, William 82, 86
Wilkins, Roy 44
Wilkinson, Ellen 'Red' 141
Williams, Roy 230
Williamson, Sonny Boy 59
Wilson, Harold 176
Wilson, Kathleen 79
Winlaton, Tyne & Wear 104
Winnick, David 168–9
Winterburn, Dr. Thomas 92–3
Wolsingham, County Durham 91
women: abolitionism 86–7, 91, 98–9, 104–5; anti-fascist movements 141–3; interracial relationships 126–7, 137–9, 146, 147–9; sexual crimes against 126–7, 131; suffrage 89, 97
Wonder, Stevie 230–1
Woodhead, Peter H. 72
Woodman, William 91
Wooler, Northumberland 86
Woolman, John 80
working class 101, 133–4, 140, 201–2, 238–40 *See also* labour organisations
World Anti-Slavery Convention, London (1840) 98, 113
World Economic Forum, Davos (2017) 237
World of Sport (ITV show) 217
Wright, James 219, 222
Wynne-Jones, Lord William 23–4, 37, 169–70
Wysocki, Lydia 230

Young, Rev. Andrew 36, 45, 49, 56, 185–6, 212, 226; visit to Newcastle 23, 30, 37, 40, 41
Young Socialists 71

Zar, Mohamad 152
Zong massacre (1781) 83